# THE DORLING KINDERSLEY

# MILLENNIUM
# FAMILY
# ENCYCLOPEDIA

## VOLUME 5

Reference
and
Index

DORLING KINDERSLEY

London • New York • Moscow • Sydney

Indonesian bank note
see MONEY

Colt Peacemaker
see WEAPONS

Straw boater see SAILING AND
OTHER WATER SPORTS

Shipping signal
see FLAGS

1970s platform shoes
see CLOTHES AND FASHION

Postage stamps see
STAMPS AND
POSTAL
SERVICES

Yu'pik family, Alaska
see ARCTIC OCEAN

King and Queen
see CHESS

Picture book
see CHILDREN'S
LITERATURE

Tenor horn
see MUSICAL
INSTRUMENTS

Gecko see LIZARDS

Honey fungus
see MUSHROOMS

Monarch butterfly
see EVOLUTION

Clown fish see
ECOLOGY

Hoverfly
see INSECTS

Paradise riflebird egg
see EGGS

Kiwanos
see FRUITS AND SEEDS

Duckling
see DUCKS, GEESE, AND SWANS

Bloodhound see DOGS

Chemical reactions
see CHEMISTRY

Light bulb
see INVENTIONS

Ethane molecule
see ATOMS AND MOLECULES

Personal stereo
see RADIO

Hubble space telescope
see SPACE
EXPLORATION

Jaguar XK120
see CARS AND TRUCKS

Mobile phone
see TELEPHONES

SLR camera
see CAMERAS

DNA double helix
see GENETICS

Amulet
see EGYPT, ANCIENT

Board Game
see VIKINGS

Throwing dice
see ROMAN EMPIRE

Dagger
see WEAPONS

Thumbscrew
see WITCHES AND WITCHCRAFT

Portable sextant see EXPLORATION

Flint arrowhead
see STONE AGE

Clasp see CHINA, HISTORY OF

Ceremonial dress
see NORTH AMERICA,
HISTORY OF

Ancient coins
see SUMERIANS

Sabaton see ARMS AND ARMOUR

## A DORLING KINDERSLEY BOOK
www.dk.com

**Senior Editor** Jayne Parsons      **Senior Art Editor** Gill Shaw

### Project Editors
Marian Broderick, Gill Cooling, Maggie Crowley, Hazel Egerton, Cynthia O'Neill,
Veronica Pennycook, Louise Pritchard, Steve Setford, Jackie Wilson

### Project Art Editors
Jane Felstead, Martyn Foote, Neville Graham, Jamie Hanson, Christopher Howson,
Jill Plank, Floyd Sayers, Jane Tetzlaff, Ann Thompson

### Editors
Rachel Beaugié, Nic Kynaston, Sarah Levete, Karen O'Brien, Linda Sonntag

### Art Editors
Tina Borg, Diane Clouting, Tory Gordon-Harris

### DTP Designers
Andrew O'Brien, Cordelia Springer

**Managing Editor** Ann Kramer      **Managing Art Editor** Peter Bailey

**Senior DTP Designer** Mathew Birch

**Picture Research** Jo Walton, Kate Duncan, Liz Moore

**DK Picture Library** Ola Rudowska, Melanie Simmonds

**Country pages** by PAGE*One*: Bob Gordon, Helen Parker,
Thomas Keenes, Sarah Watson, Chris Clark

**Cartographers** Peter Winfield, James Anderson

**Research** Robert Graham, Angela Koo

**Editorial Assistants** Sarah-Louise Reed, Nichola Roberts

**Production** Louise Barratt, Charlotte Traill

First published in Great Britain in 1997
by Dorling Kindersley Limited,
9 Henrietta Street, London WC2E 8PS
Reprinted 1998
Updated 1999

4 6 8 10 9 7 5

A CIP catalogue record for this book is available from the British Library

ISBN 0-7513 5614-X

Colour reproduction by Colourscan, Singapore
Printed and bound in Hong Kong

# CONTENTS

**REFERENCE PAGES**

REFERENCE SECTION — 913

**LIVING WORLD**

CLASSIFYING LIVING THINGS — 914-915
HOW LIVING THINGS WORK — 916-917
PLANT AND ANIMAL RECORDS — 918-919
WILDLIFE IN DANGER — 920

**SCIENCE**

UNIVERSE — 921
EARTH — 922-923
PERIODIC TABLE — 924-924

MATHEMATICS — 926
WEIGHTS AND MEASURES — 927

**INTERNATIONAL WORLD**

POLITICAL WORLD — 928-929
WORLD POPULATION — 930
LIVING STANDARDS — 931
WORLD RESOURCES — 932
WORLD ECONOMY — 933
TRANSPORT AND ENGINEERING — 934

**PEOPLE, ARTS, AND MEDIA**

MYTHOLOGY — 935
SPORT — 936-937

ART AND ARCHITECTURE — 938
THEATRE, MUSIC, AND DANCE — 939
FILM AND THE MEDIA — 940
GREAT WRITERS AND THINKERS — 941

**HISTORY**

TIMELINE OF HISTORY — 942-948

**INDEX**

INDEX — 949
INDEX ENTRIES — 950-1002
CREDITS — 1003-1006
ACKNOWLEDGEMENTS — 1007-1008

# THE WRITTEN WORD

Cave art
*see* PREHISTORIC PEOPLE

Hieroglyphics
*see* EGYPT, ANCIENT

Cuneiform script
*see* SUMERIANS

Ancient writing implements
*see* ROMAN EMPIRE

**Ancient Roman ink pots**

Roman stoneworking tools and ancient tablet *see* WRITING

| | | | | | | | | | | | | | | | | | | | | | | | | | | |
|---|---|---|---|---|---|---|---|---|---|---|---|---|---|---|---|---|---|---|---|---|---|---|---|---|---|---|
| PHOENICIAN | 𐤀 | 𐤂 | 𐤆 | 𐤄 | 𐤅 | 𐤁 | | 𐤇 | 𐤈 | 𐤇 | | 𐤉 | 𐤋 | 𐤌 | 𐤍 | 𐤎 | 𐤏 | 𐤐 | 𐤑 | 𐤒 | 𐤓 | 𐤔 | 𐤕 | | | |
| HEBREW | א | ב | ג | ד | ה | ו | | ז | ח | ט | | י | כ | ל | מ | נ | ס | ע | פ | צ | ק | ר | ש | ת | | |
| EARLY GREEK | Α | Β | Γ | Δ | Ε | | | Ι | Η | | | Κ | Λ | Μ | Ν | | Ο | Π | | Ρ | Σ | Τ | Υ | Φ | Χ | Ψ |
| CLASSICAL GREEK | Α | Β | Γ | Δ | Ε | | | Ζ | Η | Θ | Ι | Κ | Λ | Μ | Ν | Ξ | Ο | Π | | Ρ | Σ | Τ | Υ | Φ | Χ | Ψ Ω |
| ETRUSCAN | Α | Β | | | Ε | | | Ι | | | | Κ | Λ | Μ | | | Ο | Π | | Ρ | Σ | Τ | | | Χ | |
| ROMAN | A | B | C | D | E | F | G | | H | | I | | K | L | M | N | | O | P | | Q | R | S | T | V | X Y Z |
| | | | | | | | | | | | | | | | | | | | | | | | | | | |

Stylus

**Evolving alphabets**

Fountain pen

**Typewriter**

Uses of paper
*see* PLANT USES

Compact discs
*see* COMPUTERS

Laptop computer
*see* INFORMATION TECHNOLOGY

# REFERENCE SECTION

# CLASSIFYING LIVING THINGS

BIOLOGISTS CLASSIFY LIVING things into large groups, called kingdoms. Each kingdom is then subdivided into several smaller groups. The classification chart on these pages shows the five kingdoms, together with most of the smaller groups that make up the living world.

### Scientific names
Every species has a two-part scientific name that is the same worldwide. The first part of the name gives the genus; the second part the species. All numbers of species are approximate, as many more species still await discovery.

### Classifying a species
Living things are classified according to the features they have in common. Kingdoms are the largest groups in the classification system, and species are the smallest groups. Each species contains a group of living things that can breed together. The chart below shows how biologists would classify one species – the tiger – in the animal kingdom.

**Kingdom** Animals (Animalia)
A kingdom is the largest grouping in the classification of living things.

**Phylum** Chordates (Chordata)
A phylum is a major group within a kingdom. It is sometimes called a division in the classification of plants.

**Class** Mammals (Mammalia)
A class is a major part of a phylum or sub-phylum. A sub-class is a large group within a class.

**Order** Carnivores (Carnivora)
An order is part of a class or sub-class.

**Family** Cats (Felidae)
A family is a large collection of species that have several features in common.

**Genus** Big cats (*Panthera*)
A genus is a small collection of similar species.

**Species** Tiger (*Panthera tigris*)

### Protists
This kingdom contains simple organisms that mostly have a single cell. There are at least 65,000 species.

## PROTISTS (PROTISTA)

**Ciliate**

AMOEBAS (Sarcodina) 20,000 species

FLAGELLATES (Zoomastigina) 15,000 species

CILIATES (Ciliophora) 8,000 species

SPOROZOANS (Sporozoa) 5,000 species

ALGAE (Several phyla) 20,000 species

## MONERANS (MONERA)

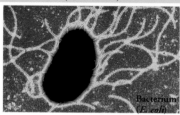
**Bacterium (E. coli)**

### Monerans
This kingdom includes the single-celled organisms, such as bacteria. Monerans were the first life forms, and there are now over 5,000 species. It also covers blue-green algae.

PRIMITIVE BACTERIA (Archaebacteria) 500 species

TYPICAL BACTERIA (Eubacteria) 5,000 species

### Plants
Plants cannot move; they reproduce by making spores or seeds. The kingdom contains more than 400,000 species.

## PLANTS (PLANTAE)

**Cushion moss**

**Fern**

FLOWERING PLANTS (Angiospermophyta)

**Yellow yarrow**

**Delphiniums**

MONOCOTYLEDONS 80,000 species

DICOTYLEDONS 170,000 species

CONIFERS (Coniferopsida) 500 species

CYCADS (Cycadopsida) 100 species

JOINT PINES (Gnetopsida) 70 species

MOSSES AND LIVERWORTS (Bryophyta) 15,000 species

CLUB MOSSES (Lycopodophyta) 1,000 species

HORSETAILS (Sphenophyta) 15 species

FERNS (Pteridophyta) 12,000 species

GYMNOSPERMS (Gymnospermophyta) about 1,000 species

## FUNGI (FUNGI)

**Saffron milk caps**

### Fungi
Fungi absorb food made by plants and animals. There are many thousands of species, classified into several phyla.

FUNGI IMPERFECTI (Deuteromycota) 25,000 species

CLUB FUNGI (Basidiomycota) 25,000 species

MOULDS (Zygomycota) 750 species

WATER MOULDS (Oomycota) 600 species

SAC FUNGI (Ascomycota) 30,000 species

# ANIMALS (ANIMALIA)

ROTIFERS (Rotifera)
2,000 species

MOLLUSCS (Mollusca)
110,000 species

## Animals
The animal kingdom contains organisms that cannot make their own food. Most animals can move around, but some spend their adult lives in one place.

ECHINODERMS
(Echinodermata)
6,000 species

SEA SPIDERS
(Pycnogonida)
1,000 species

CENTIPEDES
(Chilopoda)
2,500 species

ARTHROPODS
(Arthropoda) at least
1,000,000 species

MOSS ANIMALS
(Bryozoa)
4,000 species

OCTOPUSES, SQUIDS
(Cephalopoda) 600 species

**Octopus**

MILLIPEDES (Diplopoda)
10,000 species

HORSESHOE CRABS
(Merostomata) 4 species

c.13 OTHER SMALL
PHYLA c.2,000 species

SEA URCHINS
(Echinoidea)
950 species

ARACHNIDS (Arachnida) 73,000 species

VELVETWORMS
(Onychophora)
100 species

DEEP-SEA LIMPETS
(Monoplacophora)
10 species

STARFISH
(Asteroidea)
1,500 species

Camel spiders
Harvestmen
Micro-whip scorpions
Mites and ticks
Pseudoscorpions

**Scorpion**

Scorpions
Spiders
Tail-less whip scorpions
Tick spiders
Whip scorpions

SOLENOGASTERS
(Aplacophora) 250 species

SPONGES (Porifera)
9,000 species

TUSK SHELLS
(Scaphopoda)
350 species

BRITTLE STARS
(Ophiuroidea)
2,000 species

INSECTS (Insecta) at least 1,000,000 species

MUSSELS, CLAMS
(Bivalvia) 15,000 species

COMB JELLIES
(Ctenophora)
90 species

SNAILS (Gastropoda)
35,000 species

CHITONS
(Polyplacophora)
500 species

SEA CUCUMBERS
(Holothuroidea)
900 species

Ants, bees, wasps
Beetles
Booklice
Bristletails
Bugs
Butterflies and moths
Caddis flies
Cockroaches
Diplurans
Dragonflies
Earwigs

Fleas
Flies
Grasshoppers, crickets
Grylloblattids
Lacewings and antlions
Lice
Mayflies
Praying mantids
Scorpion flies
Silverfish

Springtails
Stick and leaf insects
Stoneflies
Stylopids
Termites
Thrips
Webspinners
Zorapterans

WORMS, LEECHES
(Annelida)
18,600 species

ROUNDWORMS
(Nematoda)
20,000 species

HORSEHAIR WORMS
(Nematomorpha)
250 species

WATERBEARS
(Tardigrada)
600 species

LAMPSHELLS
(Brachiopoda)
300 species

**Morpho butterfly**

FLATWORMS, FLUKES, TAPEWORMS
(Platyhelminthes)
15,000 species

SEA ANEMONES, HYDRAS, CORALS,
JELLYFISH (Cnidaria)
9,500 species

SPINY-HEADED WORMS
(Acanthocephala)
1,500 species

BIRDS
(Aves) 9,000 species

CHORDATES (Chordata) 45,000 species

CRUSTACEANS (Crustacea)
40,000 species

AMPHIBIANS
(Amphibia)
4,200 species

Caecilians
Frogs and toads
Newts and salamanders

MAMMALS
(Mammalia) 4,600 species

Albatrosses, petrels, shearwaters, fulmars
Cassowaries, emus
Cranes, rails, coots, bustards
Cuckoos, roadrunners
Divers or loons
Ducks, geese, swans
Eagles, hawks, vultures, falcons, kites, buzzards
Grebes
Herons, storks, ibises, flamingos
Kingfishers, bee-eaters, rollers
Kiwis
Mousebirds
Nightjars, frogmouths
Ostriches
Owls
Parrots
Passerines
Pelicans, gannets, cormorants, frigate birds, darters
Penguins
Pheasants, partridges, grouse, turkeys
Pigeons, doves
Rheas
Sandgrouse
Swifts, hummingbirds
Tinamous
Trogons
Turacos
Wading birds, gulls, terns, auks
Woodpeckers, toucans, barbets, honeyguides, puffbirds, jacamars

**Orange weaver**

BRANCHIOPODS (Branchiopoda)
1,000 species

REPTILES
(Reptilia)
6,000 species

**Red-tailed racer**

Crocodilians
Lizards and snakes
Tuatara
Turtles, tortoises, and terrapins

Aardvarks
Bats
Carnivores
Edentates (anteaters, armadillos, sloths)
Elephants
Elephant shrews
Even-toed hoofed mammals
Flying lemurs
Hares, rabbits, pikas
Hyraxes
Insectivores
Marsupials (pouched mammals)
Monotremes (egg-laying mammals)
Odd-toed hoofed mammals
Pangolins
Primates
Rodents
Seals, sea lions, walruses
Sea cows
Tree shrews
Whales and dolphins

**Silverback gorilla**

BARNACLES (Cirripedia)
1,220 species

SPINY SAND SHRIMPS
(Branchiura)
125 species

More than 20 orders including:
Carp
Catfish
Eels
Flying fish
Herrings, anchovies
Perch, marlins, swordfish, tunas
Salmon, trout

**Clown fish**

SAND SHRIMPS (Cephalocarida)
9 species

MYSTACOCARIDEANS
(Mystacocarida)
10 species

BONY FISH
(Osteichthyes)
20,000 species

JAWLESS FISH
(Agnatha)
75 species

CRABS, LOBSTERS, AND SHRIMPS
(Malacostraca) 20,000 species

SEA SQUIRTS
(Ascidiacea)
2,500 species

**Crab**

SHARKS AND RAYS
(Chondrichthyes)
800 species

Sharks, dolphins
Skates, rays

MUSSEL SHRIMPS (Ostracoda)
2,000 species

COPEPODS (Copepoda)
7,500 species

# HOW LIVING THINGS WORK

ALL LIVING THINGS have characteristics in common: they grow, feed, reproduce, use energy, and respond to the outside world. Most living things have developed senses and patterns of behaviour that ensure the survival of their species.

## REPRODUCTION RATES

Some animals can reproduce extremely rapidly, but only a few of their offspring survive to become adults.

| SPECIES | BREEDING AGE | OFFSPRING PER YEAR |
|---|---|---|
| Fruit fly | 10–14 days | Up to 900 |
| Mouse | 6 weeks | 50–70 |
| Rabbit | 8 months | 10–30 |
| Northern gannet | 5–6 years | 1 |
| Nile crocodile | 15 years | 50 |

Fourteen-day-old mice

## ANIMAL SPEEDS

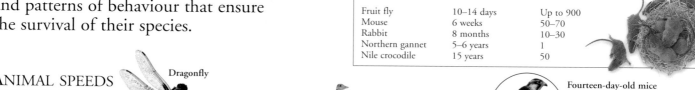

Dragonfly

**AIR**
Dragonfly
58 kmh (36 mph)
Fastest-flying insect

Frigate bird
153 kmh
(95 mph)

Spine-tailed swift
170 kmh (106 mph)
Fastest-flying bird

Peregrine falcon

Peregrine falcon
200 kmh (124 mph)
Fastest bird in a dive

**LAND**
American cockroach
5 kmh (3 mph)
Fastest-running insect

Ostrich
72 kmh (45 mph)
Fastest-running bird

Male ostrich

Pronghorn antelope
86 kmh (53 mph)
Fastest mammal over
long distances

Cheetah
96.5 kmh (60 mph) Fastest
mammal over short distances

Cheetah

**SEA**
Gentoo penguin
35 kmh (22 mph)
Fastest-swimming bird

Killer whale
55 kmh (34.5 mph)
Fastest-swimming
mammal

Marlin
80 kmh
(50 mph)

Sailfish
109 kmh (68 mph)

Gentoo penguin

Black marlin

## PLANT AND ANIMAL LIFESPANS

The chart below shows how long different animals and plants live. The ages given are the maximum average lifespans.

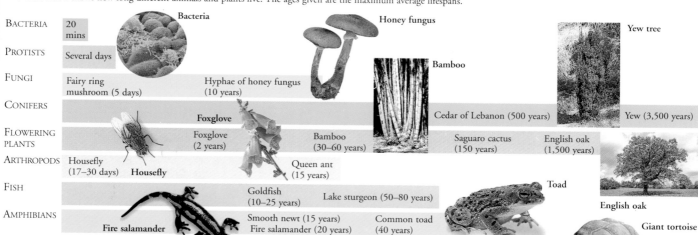

**BACTERIA** — 20 mins — Bacteria

Honey fungus

Yew tree

**PROTISTS** — Several days

**FUNGI** — Fairy ring mushroom (5 days) — Hyphae of honey fungus (10 years)

Bamboo

**CONIFERS** — Cedar of Lebanon (500 years) — Yew (3,500 years)

**FLOWERING PLANTS** — Foxglove — Foxglove (2 years) — Bamboo (30–60 years) — Saguaro cactus (150 years) — English oak (1,500 years)

**ARTHROPODS** — Housefly (17–30 days) — Housefly — Queen ant (15 years)

**FISH** — Goldfish (10–25 years) — Lake sturgeon (50–80 years)

Toad

English oak

**AMPHIBIANS** — Smooth newt (15 years) — Fire salamander (20 years) — Common toad (40 years)

Fire salamander

Giant tortoise

**REPTILES** — Boa constrictor (40 years) — American alligator (60 years) — Tuatara (101 years) — Giant tortoise (150 years)

**BIRDS** — Starling (1 year) — Wandering albatross (60 years) — Andean condor (70 years)

**MAMMALS** — Red fox — Red fox (8 years) — Giraffe (20 years) — African elephant (70 years) — Killer whale (90 years)

African elephant

Andean condor

### LIFESPAN FACTS

• The shrew has the shortest lifespan of all mammals. Shrews normally live for only 12–18 months in the wild.

• Humans are the longest-living mammals. The oldest elephant on record lived to the age of 78.

Shrew

• Giant tortoises are the longest-living reptiles. The oldest tortoise ever recorded came from the Seychelles. It lived to the age of 152.

• The giant marine clam (*Tridacna*) is the longest-living animal in the world. It can live to be more than 200 years old.

Giant clam

# BODY TEMPERATURES

The chart below shows the average body temperatures of exothermic ("cold-blooded") and endothermic ("warm-blooded") animals.

EXOTHERMIC ("COLD-BLOODED") ANIMALS

-2°C (28.4°F)　0°C (32°F)　5°C (41°F)　10°C (50°F)　15°C (59°F)　20°C (68°F)　25°C (77°F)　30°C (86°F)　35°C (95°F)　40°C (104°F)　45°C (130°F)

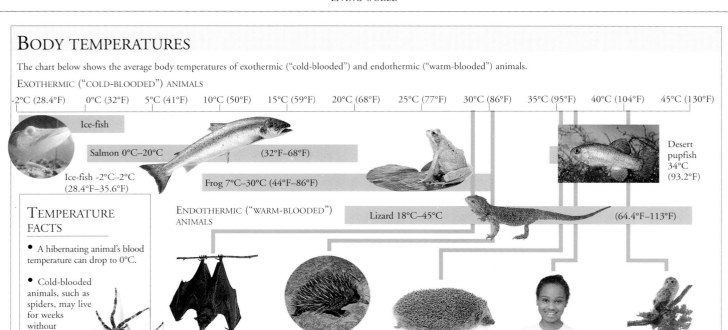

Ice-fish

Salmon 0°C–20°C　(32°F–68°F)

Ice-fish -2°C–2°C
(28.4°F–35.6°F)

Frog 7°C–30°C (44°F–86°F)

Desert pupfish 34°C (93.2°F)

ENDOTHERMIC ("WARM-BLOODED") ANIMALS

Lizard 18°C–45°C　(64.4°F–113°F)

## TEMPERATURE FACTS

• A hibernating animal's blood temperature can drop to 0°C.

• Cold-blooded animals, such as spiders, may live for weeks without food.

Bat 28°C (82.4°F)　Spiny anteater 30°C (86°F)　Hedgehog 35°C (95°F)　Human 37°C (98.6°F)　Bird 40°C (104°F)

# GESTATION PERIODS

The gestation period is the amount of time young take to develop inside the mother. Large mammals usually have long gestation periods, although kangaroos have gestation periods of only 33 days.

## Longest gestation periods

| MAMMAL | AVERAGE GESTATION (DAYS) |
| --- | --- |
| African elephant | 660 |
| Asian elephant | 660 |
| Baird's beaked whale | 520 |
| White rhinoceros | 490 |
| Walrus | 480 |
| Giraffe | 460 |
| Tapir | 400 |

Giraffes

## Shortest gestation periods

| MAMMAL | AVERAGE GESTATION (DAYS) |
| --- | --- |
| Short-nosed bandicoot | 12 |
| Opossum | 13 |
| Shrew | 14 |
| Golden hamster | 15 |
| Lemming | 16 |
| Mouse | 20 |

Opossum

## GESTATION FACT

• The 480-day gestation of the walrus includes a delay of up to five months so that the young can be delivered at the most favourable time of the year.

Walruses

# ANIMAL ENERGY NEEDS

The chart below shows how many kilojoules (kJ) different animal species need per day for a moderate amount of activity.

| ANIMAL | kJ REQUIRED |
| --- | --- |
| House mouse | 45.4 |
| European robin | 89.9 |
| Grey squirrel | 386 |
| Domestic cat | 1,554 |
| Female human | 10,080 |
| Male human | 13,713 |
| Llama | 16,128 |
| Tiger | 33,600 |
| Giraffe | 152,754 |
| Walrus | 159,852 |
| Asian elephant | 256,872 |

## ENERGY FACT

• A flea can jump more than 100 times its own height using energy stored in pads in its leg joints.

Flea jumping

# HEARING RANGES OF SELECTED ANIMALS

Sound is measured by its pitch in units called Hertz (Hz). A higher number means a higher pitch – a lower number, a lower pitch.

| SPECIES | HEARING RANGES IN HZ |
| --- | --- |
| Elephant | 1–20,000 |
| Dog | 10–35,000 |
| Human | 20–20,000 |
| Bat | 100–100,000 |
| Frog | 100–2,500 |

## HEARING FACTS

• Crickets have "ears" on their knees made from a taut membrane that is sensitive to sound vibrations.

• Owls' left and right ears are often at different levels in the skull. This helps them to track their prey more effectively.

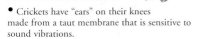

Cricket

# ANIMAL HEART RATES

Animals with small bodies have much faster heartbeats than animals with larger bodies.

| ANIMAL | BEATS PER MINUTE |
| --- | --- |
| Grey whale | 9 |
| Harbour seal (diving) | 10 |
| Elephant | 25 |
| Human | 70 |
| Sparrow | 500 |
| Shrew | 600 |
| Hummingbird (hovering) | 1,200 |

Hummingbird

# SLEEP REQUIREMENTS

This list excludes periods of hibernation, which can last up to several months.

| ANIMAL | AVERAGE HOURS OF SLEEP PER DAY |
| --- | --- |
| Koala | 22 |
| Sloth | 20 |
| Opossum | 19 |
| Cat | 15 |
| Squirrel | 14 |

Domestic cat

## SLEEPING FACTS

• Big cats, such as leopards, sleep for about 12–14 hours a day. Since they have no natural enemies, they can sleep unprotected in the open air.

• Sloths are among the world's sleepiest animals. They hang upside down and sleep for up to 20 hours per day. Some species of sloth leave their trees only once a week.

# PLANT AND ANIMAL RECORDS

THE PLANT AND ANIMAL kingdoms are the two largest groups of living things. These pages list the world's record breakers from the smallest and most poisonous frogs to the tallest and heaviest trees. Living things of the same species vary in size, so all measurements are approximate.

## TREES

Coast redwood

TALLEST SPECIES: Eucalyptus. These trees can grow to more than 130 m (427 ft) in height.

HEAVIEST SPECIES: Giant sequoia. Also known as wellingtonias, these conifers weigh up to 2000 tonnes (tons).

OLDEST SPECIES: Ginkgo. This ancient species first appeared about 160 million years ago in China.

OLDEST LIVING TREE: Bristlecone pine. Native to Arizona and Nevada, USA, this species can live for more than 5,000 years.

MOST DROUGHT-RESISTANT TREE: Baobab. This African tree can store up to 136,000 litres (29,920 UK gallons) of water in its trunk.

WORLD'S TALLEST LIVING TREE: A coast redwood in Humbolt Redwood State Park, California, USA. It stands 110.6 m (363 ft) tall.

WORLD'S BIGGEST LIVING TREE: The General Sherman giant sequoia in Sequoia National Park, California, USA. It is 84 m (276 ft) tall and its base is approximately 10 m (33 ft) wide.

Bristlecone pine

## FLOWERING PLANTS

Bamboo

LARGEST FLOWER: Giant rafflesia. This foul-smelling flower can grow up to 1.05 m (3.5 ft) across and weigh as much as 7 kg (15.4 lb).

SMALLEST FLOWER: Australian duckweed. The flowers of this floating plant measure only 0.61 mm (0.024 in) across.

SMALLEST LAND PLANT: Dwarf snow willow. This miniscule plant grows only a few centimetres long.

LONGEST SEAWEED: Pacific giant kelp seaweed. The fronds of this seaweed can grow as long as 60 m (197 ft).

FASTEST-GROWING PLANT: Bamboo. This is the tallest and fastest-growing grass. Some species can grow to 30 m (98.4 ft) at a rate of 1 m (3.2 ft) a day.

SLOWEST-GROWING PLANT: *Dioon edule.* This evergreen shrub grows at a rate of only 0.76 mm (0.29 in) per year.

Snow willow

## LEAVES

LARGEST LEAF: Raffia palm. Its leaves grow up to 20 m (66 ft) long.

SMALLEST LEAF: Floating duckweed. The leaves of this tiny plant are only 0.6 mm (0.02 in) long and 0.3 mm (0.01 in) wide.

Duckweed

## FUNGI

Fungi used to be classified as plants, but, since 1969, botanists have classified them as a separate kingdom.

BIGGEST FUNGUS: Bracket fungus. This huge species measures several metres across.

MOST POISONOUS FUNGUS: Death cap. If eaten, this deadly mushroom can cause death within 15 hours.

Death cap mushrooms

## SEEDS

LARGEST SEED: Coco-de-mer palm. Each seed can weigh up to 20 kg (44 lb) and take ten years to develop.

SMALLEST SEED: A species of orchid. A billion seeds weigh as little as 1 g (0.035 oz).

Coco-de-mer seed

Orchids

## MOST POISONOUS ANIMALS

REPTILE: *Hydrophis belcheri.* This sea snake is far more poisonous than any land snake. The Australian taipan is the deadliest land snake. Its bite is fatal without an antitoxin that counteracts the venom.

FISH: Death puffer. This harmless looking fish keeps poison in its blood and organs. If eaten, it can kill a person.

ARACHNID: Brazilian wandering spider. This aggressive spider bites if disturbed.

MOLLUSC: Blue-ringed octopus. The painful bite of this Australian octopus can kill in minutes.

AMPHIBIAN: Golden-yellow poison-dart frog. The colourful poison-dart frogs from South and Central America and the Madagascan mantellas have highly poisonous chemicals in their skins.

Golden mantella

# MAMMALS

LARGEST MAMMAL: Blue whale. The world's heaviest and longest animal, it can grow up to 34 m (111.5 ft) long and weigh up to 190 tonnes (tons).

LARGEST LAND MAMMAL: African elephant. The average male elephant is 3 m (9.8 ft) tall and weighs about 5 tonnes (tons).

TALLEST MAMMAL: Giraffe. The adult male giraffe can grow up to 5.9 m (19.4 ft) tall.

SMALLEST MAMMAL: Kitti's hog-nosed bat. Sometimes known as bumblebee bats, these tiny creatures have an average length of 3.3 cm (1.3 in) and weigh no more than 2 g (0.07 oz).

SMALLEST LAND MAMMAL: African pygmy shrew. From head to tail, it is only 70 mm (2.7 in) long and weighs between 1.5–2.5 g (0.05–0.08 oz).

HEAVIEST PRIMATE: Gorilla. The male gorilla can weigh as much as 220 kg (485 lb).

LARGEST FLYING MAMMAL: A flying fox (fruit bat of tropical Africa and Asia) can grow to the size of a small dog and have a wingspan of 2 m (6 ft).

Blue whale

# REPTILES AND AMPHIBIANS

LARGEST LIZARD: Komodo dragon lizard. This Indonesian reptile grows up to 3 m (10 ft) long and weighs up to 166 kg (365 lb).

SMALLEST LIZARD: British Virgin Island gecko. This tiny lizard is only 18 mm (0.7 in) long.

LONGEST REPTILE: Saltwater crocodile. This is the longest animal on land, growing up to 6 m (20 ft) long.

LARGEST AMPHIBIAN: Giant salamander. The average length of the Chinese giant salamander is 1.5 m (5 ft).

SMALLEST AMPHIBIAN: *Sminthillus limbatus*. This tiny frog from Cuba is only 1 cm (0.5 in) long.

LARGEST TURTLE: Leatherback turtle. This turtle can grow more than 2 m (6.6 ft) long and weigh up to 450 kg (1,000 lb).

Saltwater crocodile

# SNAKES

LONGEST SNAKE: Anaconda. The average length of the South American anaconda is 5.5 m (18 ft).

SHORTEST SNAKE: Thread snake. This tiny snake from the West Indies is less than 11 cm (4.4 in) long.

LONGEST FANGS: Gaboon viper. Its fangs can be as long as 5 cm (2 in).

FASTEST SNAKE: Black mamba. This African snake can travel at speeds of up to 19 kmh (12 mph).

Anaconda

# SPIDERS AND INSECTS

LARGEST SPIDER: Goliath bird-eating spider. The largest specimen on record had a legspan of 28 cm (11 in).

LARGEST WEB: Orb-web spider. Tropical orb-web spiders can spin webs of up to 1.5 m (5 ft) in circumference.

LARGEST BUTTERFLY: Queen Alexandra's birdwing. It is the largest and heaviest butterfly with a wingspan of up to 28 cm (11 in).

LARGEST PREHISTORIC INSECT: Dragonfly. This huge insect had a wingspan of 75 cm (29.5 in).

Goliath beetle

LONGEST INSECT: Giant stick insect. This insect from New Guinea has an average length of 45 cm (17.7 in).

LARGEST WINGSPAN: Owlet moth. Its wingspan can measure up to 30 cm (12 in).

HEAVIEST INSECT: Goliath beetle. This huge African beetle weighs up to 100 g (3.5 oz).

SMALLEST INSECT: Fairyfly wasp. These tiny wasps grow only 0.2 mm (0.007 in) long.

Fairyfly wasp

# MARINE ANIMALS

LARGEST FISH: Whale shark. Found in the Atlantic, Pacific, and Indian oceans, these huge fish can grow up to 12.65 m (41.5 ft) long.

SMALLEST FISH: Dwarf goby. The average length of a male fish is only 6 mm (0.3 in).

LARGEST MOLLUSC: Giant Atlantic squid. The largest specimens grow up to 17 m (55.7 ft) long.

LARGEST BIVALVE MOLLUSC: Giant clam. It can weigh as much as 300 kg (661 lb) and grow to 1.15 m (3.7 ft).

LARGEST CRUSTACEAN: Japanese spider crab. This huge crab has a legspan of 4 m (13 ft) and can weigh as much as 18.6 kg (41 lb).

SMALLEST CRUSTACEAN: *Alonella* water flea. This tiny crustacean grows only 0.25 mm (0.1 in) long.

Whale shark

# BIRDS

LARGEST FLYING BIRD: Great bustard. A male bird can weigh up to 19 kg (42 lb).

LARGEST FLIGHTLESS BIRD: Ostrich. The African ostrich weighs 130 kg (280 lb) and grows to a height of 2.7 m (8.9 ft).

LARGEST PREHISTORIC BIRD: Elephant bird. This massive flightless bird from Madagascar weighed around 438 kg (966 lb) and stood 3 m (10 ft) tall.

SMALLEST BIRD: Bee hummingbird. This Cuban bird measures only 5.7 cm (2.2 in) and weighs just 1.6 g (0.05 oz).

FARTHEST MIGRATION: Arctic tern. Every year, this bird flies from the Arctic to the Antarctic and back again – a round trip of about 40,000 km (25,000 miles).

LARGEST WINGSPAN: Wandering albatross. The wingspan of this huge seabird can stretch up to 3.6 m (12 ft) across.

Albatross

LARGEST EGG: Ostrich egg. The largest specimens can weigh up to 1.65 kg (3.64 lb) and measure up to 20 cm (8 in) long.

SMALLEST EGG: Bee hummingbird egg. These eggs weigh only 0.25 g (0.009 oz).

Ostrich egg

# WILDLIFE IN DANGER

SINCE LIFE BEGAN on Earth, many species of plants and animals have died out – mostly because of human interference. The main threats to wildlife today are habitat destruction, hunting and collecting, and pollution. Many plants and animals are now protected by law.

*Atlantic Empress disaster, 1979*

## ENVIRONMENTAL DISASTERS

In 1989, the *Exxon Valdez* oil tanker ran aground in Alaska. It spilled more than 35,000 tonnes of oil into the Pacific, causing the deaths of thousands of seabirds. The table below lists the world's worst oil spills.

| TANKER (LOCATION OF DISASTER) | DATE | OIL SPILLAGE IN TONNES |
|---|---|---|
| *Atlantic Empress* and *Aegean Captain* (Trinidad) | July 1979 | 300,000 |
| *Castillo de Bellver* (Cape Town, South Africa) | August 1983 | 255,000 |
| *Olympic Bravery* (Ushant, France) | January 1976 | 250,000 |
| *Showa-Maru* (Malacca, Malaysia) | June 1975 | 237,000 |
| *Amoco Cadiz* (Finistère, France) | March 1978 | 223,000 |
| *Odyssey* (Atlantic Ocean, Canada) | November 1988 | 140,000 |
| *Torrey Canyon* (Scilly Isles, UK) | March 1967 | 120,000 |
| *Sea Star* (Gulf of Oman) | December 1972 | 115,000 |
| *Irenes Serenada* (Pílos, Greece) | February 1980 | 102,000 |
| *Urquiola* (Corunna, Spain) | May 1976 | 101,000 |

## ENVIRONMENT FACTS

- It is estimated that over the next 20 years almost half a million species of plants and animals will become extinct.

- The ivory-billed woodpecker used to live in forest swamps. It is one of the world's rarest birds and may even be extinct.

- All species of rhinoceros are now protected by law. Many rhinoceroses were killed for their horns, which are reputed to have medicinal qualities.

- The population of the Komodo dragon, the largest-living lizard, is at a dangerously low level because of over-hunting by collectors.

**Green turtle**

- Turtles are often hunted for their shell, eggs, and meat. Seven species of marine turtles are now under threat.

## ENDANGERED PLANTS

Habitat destruction, wetland drainage, urban growth, and modern farming methods threaten many plant species. Those most at risk are listed below.

| COMMON NAME (LOCATION) | SCIENTIFIC NAME |
|---|---|
| Wild sago (USA) | *Zania floridans* |
| Chiapas slipper orchid (Mexico) | *Phragmipedium exstaminodium* |
| Sea bindweed (Europe) | *Calystegia soldanella* |
| Green pitcher plant (USA) | *Sarracenia oreophila* |
| Big-leaf palm (Madagascar) | *Marojejya darianii* |
| Socotran pomegranate (Yemen) | *Punica protopunica* |
| African violet (East Africa) | *Saintpaulia ionantha* |
| Green daffodil (Mediterranean) | *Narcissus viridiflorus* |
| Blue vanda (India/Thailand) | *Vanda coerulea* |
| Drago, or Canadian dragon, tree (Canary Islands/Madeira) | *Dracaena draco* |
| Caoba (Ecuador) | *Persea theobromifolia* |

**Sea bindweed**

## ENDANGERED ANIMALS

Endangered species all around the world are monitored by animal welfare organizations. The animals below are at risk of becoming extinct in the near future.

| COMMON NAME (LOCATION) | SCIENTIFIC NAME |
|---|---|
| Blue whale (Antarctic Ocean) | *Balaenoptera musculus* |
| Black-footed ferret (North America) | *Mustela nigripes* |
| Giant panda (China) | *Ailuropoda melanoleuca* |
| Kemp's Ridley sea turtle (Mexico) | *Lepidochelys kempii* |
| Javan rhinoceros (Southeast Asia) | *Rhinoceros sondaicus* |
| Southern sea otter (USA) | *Enhydra lutris nereis* |
| Woolly spider monkey (Brazil) | *Bracyteles arachnoides* |
| Queen Alexandra's birdwing butterfly (Papua New Guinea) | *Ornithoptera alexandrae* |
| Mediterranean monk seal (Mediterranean coasts) | *Monachus monachus* |
| Yangtze river dolphin (China) | *Lipotes vexillifer* |
| Magpie robin (Seychelles) | *Copsychus sechellarun* |
| Californian condor (California, USA) | *Gymnogyps californianus* |
| Florida manatee (Atlantic Ocean) | *Trichechus manatus* |

**Blue whale**

## DWINDLING FORESTS

Humans have destroyed almost half of the world's tropical rainforests. This table shows how many forests are being cut down annually for timber or building projects.

**South American rainforest**

| COUNTRY | ANNUAL LOSS IN KM² (MILES²) |
|---|---|
| Brazil | 36,500 (14,093) |
| India | 15,000 (5,791) |
| Indonesia | 9,200 (3,552) |
| Colombia | 8,900 (3,471) |
| Mexico | 6,150 (2,375) |
| Zaïre | 5,800 (2,239) |
| Congo | 5,260 (2,030) |
| Ivory Coast | 5,100 (1,969) |
| Sudan | 5,040 (1,946) |
| Nigeria | 4,000 (1,544) |

## ENVIRONMENTAL ORGANIZATIONS

These environmental organizations are dedicated to helping plants and animals in danger and finding solutions to worldwide ecological problems.

**GREENPEACE**
Greenpeace
Canonbury Villas
London N1 2PN

FRIENDS *of the* **earth**
Friends of the Earth
26–28 Underwood Street
London N1 7JQ

**IFAW**
International Fund for
Animal Welfare
Tubwell House
New Road
Crowborough
East Sussex TN6 2QH

**WWF**
World Wide Fund for Nature
Panda House
Weyside Park
Godalming
Surrey GU7 1XR

# UNIVERSE

THE KNOWN UNIVERSE contains countless millions of galaxies and stars. From Earth, the stars seem to form patterns in the sky. These patterns are known as constellations. We see different star patterns from month to month as Earth orbits the Sun.

**Spiral galaxy**

## SUN DATA

- Age: About 5 billion years
- Diameter: 1,392,000 km (865,000 miles)
- Distance from the Earth: 149.6 million km (92.9 million miles)
- Time taken to orbit galaxy: 240 million years
- Surface temperature: 5,500°C (9,900°F)
- Life expectancy: 10 billion years
- Mass (Earth = 1): 332,946

## MOON DATA

- Age: 4.6 billion years
- Diameter: 3,476 km (2,160 miles)
- Distance from the Earth: 384,000 km (238,000 miles)
- Surface temperature: −173 to 105°C (−279 to 221°F)
- Mass (Earth = 1): 0.012
- Gravity (Earth = 1): 0.16
- Rotation period: 27.3 days
- The pull of the Moon's gravity is largely responsible for the rise and fall of tides on Earth.

## CONSTELLATIONS OF THE NORTHERN HEMISPHERE

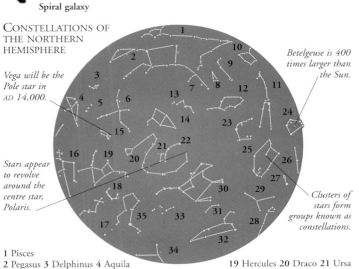

*Vega will be the Pole star in AD 14,000.*

*Stars appear to revolve around the centre star, Polaris.*

*Betelgeuse is 400 times larger than the Sun.*

*Clusters of stars form groups known as constellations.*

1 Pisces
2 Pegasus 3 Delphinus 4 Aquila
5 Sagitta 6 Cygnus 7 Andromeda
8 Triangulum 9 Aries 10 Cetus
11 Taurus 12 Perseus 13 Cassiopeia
14 Cepheus 15 Lyra 16 Ophiuchus
17 Serpens Caput 18 Corona Borealis
19 Hercules 20 Draco 21 Ursa
Minor 22 Polaris (North Star) 23 Auriga
24 Orion 25 Gemini 26 Monoceros
27 Canis Minor 28 Hydra 29 Cancer
30 Ursa Major 31 Leo Minor 32 Leo
33 Canes Venatici 34 Virgo 35 Boötes

## CONSTELLATIONS OF THE SOUTHERN HEMISPHERE

*Stars near the edge become visible month by month throughout the year.*

*Sirius is the brightest star in the night sky.*

*The edge of the map marks the celestial equator.*

1 Cetus
2 Eridanus
3 Orion
4 Monoceros
5 Canis Major
6 Lepus 7 Columba
8 Caelum 9 Horologium
10 Fornax 11 Phoenix 12 Sculptor 13 Aquarius
14 Piscis Austrinus 15 Capricornus
16 Microscorpium 17 Grus 18 Indus 19 Tucana
20 Pavo 21 Apus 22 Hydrus 23 Reticulum
24 Mensa 25 Chameleon 26 Dorado 27 Pictor
28 Volans
29 Carinar
30 Puppis
31 Vela 32 Musca
33 Crux 34 Antlia
35 Hydra 36 Sextans
37 Crater 38 Corvus 39 Virgo
40 Libra 41 Centaurus 42 Lupus
43 Norma 44 Triangulum Australe
45 Ara 46 Sagittarius 47 Aquila
48 Corona Australis
49 Ophiuchus 50 Scorpius

# INNER PLANETS / OUTER PLANETS

| PLANETS The nine planets in our solar system divide into two groups: the dense, rocky inner planets and the gaseous, icy outer planets. | MERCURY | VENUS | EARTH | MARS | JUPITER | SATURN | URANUS | NEPTUNE | PLUTO |
|---|---|---|---|---|---|---|---|---|---|
| DISTANCE FROM THE SUN IN MILLIONS OF KM (MILES) | 57.9 (36) | 108.2 (67.2) | 149.6 (93) | 227.9 (141.6) | 778.3 (483.6) | 1,427 (886.7) | 2,871 (1,784) | 4,497 (2,794) | 5,914 (3,675) |
| DIAMETER IN KM (MILES) | 4,878 (3,031) | 12,103 (7,520) | 12,756 (7,926) | 6,786 (4,217) | 142,984 (88,850) | 120,536 (74,901) | 51,118 (31,764) | 49,528 (30,775) | 2,284 (1,419) |
| TIME TAKEN TO ORBIT THE SUN | 87.97 days | 224.7 days | 365.26 days | 686.98 days | 11.86 years | 29.46 years | 84.01 years | 164.79 years | 248.54 years |
| TIME TAKEN TO TURN ON AXIS | 58 days, 16 hours | 243 days, 14 hours | 23 hours, 56 mins | 24 hours, 37 mins | 9 hours, 55 mins | 10 hours, 40 mins | 17 hours, 14 mins | 16 hours, 7 mins | 6 days, 9 hours |
| SURFACE TEMPERATURE | −180 to 430°C (−292 to 806°F) | 500°C (900°F) | −70 to 55°C (−94 to 131°F) | −120 to 25°C (−184 to 77°F) | −150°C (−238°F) At cloud tops | −180°C (−292°F) At cloud tops | −210°C (−346°F) At cloud tops | −210°C (−346°F) At cloud tops | −220°C (−364°F) |
| NUMBER OF MOONS | 0 | 0 | 1 | 2 | 16 | 18 | 15 | 8 | 1 |
| MASS (EARTH = 1) | 0.055 | 0.81 | 1 | 0.107 | 318 | 95.18 | 14.5 | 17.14 | 0.0022 |
| DENSITY (WATER = 1) | 5.43 | 5.25 | 5.52 | 3.95 | 1.33 | 0.69 | 1.29 | 2.1 | 2.03 |

# EARTH

MORE THAN SEVENTY per cent of the Earth's surface is covered by water. Above sea level, Earth's land surface is made up of seven vast land masses called continents. The Earth is in a constant state of change, both above and below the surface. Most volcanoes and earthquakes are caused by the movements of huge rocky plates in the Earth's crust.

## DESERTS

| LARGEST DESERTS | AREA IN KM² | AREA IN MILES² |
|---|---|---|
| Sahara (Africa) | 9,065,000 | 3,500,000 |
| Arabian (Asia) | 1,300,000 | 502,000 |
| Gobi (Asia) | 1,040,000 | 402,000 |
| Kalahari (Africa) | 580,000 | 224,000 |
| Great Sandy (Australia) | 414,000 | 160,000 |
| Chihuahua (USA) | 370,000 | 143,000 |
| Takla Makan (Asia) | 320,000 | 198,848 |
| Kara Kum (Asia) | 310,000 | 120,000 |
| Namib (Africa) | 310,000 | 120,000 |
| Thar (Asia) | 260,000 | 100,000 |

**Sahara Desert**

## HIGHEST AND LOWEST POINTS IN THE WORLD

| CONTINENT | HIGHEST POINT ABOVE SEA LEVEL | HEIGHT IN METRES (FEET) | LOWEST POINT BELOW SEA LEVEL | DEPTH IN METRES (FEET) |
|---|---|---|---|---|
| Asia | Mt. Everest | 8,848 (29,030) | Dead Sea | −400 (−1,312) |
| Africa | Kilimanjaro | 5,895 (19,341) | Qattâra Depression | −133 (−436) |
| North America | Denali (Mt. McKinley) | 6,194 (20,323) | Death Valley | −86 (−282) |
| South America | Aconcagua | 6,960 (22,834) | Peninsular Valdez | −40 (−131) |
| Antarctica | Vinson Massif | 5,140 (16,864) | Bentley Subglacial Trench | −2,538 (−8,327) |
| Europe | Elbrus | 5,633 (18,481) | Caspian Sea | −28 (−92) |
| Australia | Mt. Kosciusko | 2,228 (7,310) | Lake Eyre | −16 (−52) |

*Everest: 8,848 m (29,028 ft)*

*Makalu I: 8,481 m (27,824 ft)*

*K2: 8,611 m (28,250 ft)*

*Kanchenjunga: 8,598 m (28,208 ft)*

*Lhotse: 8,511 m (27,923 ft)*

**Highest mountains**
The ten highest mountains in the world are all in the Himalayas, which lie between Tibet, China, and the Indian subcontinent.

## OCEANS AND SEAS

The table below lists the world's largest oceans and seas.

| NAME | AREA IN KM² | AREA IN MILES² |
|---|---|---|
| Pacific Ocean | 165,241,000 | 63,800,000 |
| Atlantic Ocean | 81,500,000 | 31,500,000 |
| Indian Ocean | 73,452,000 | 28,360,000 |
| Arctic Ocean | 14,089,600 | 5,440,000 |
| Arabian Sea | 3,864,000 | 1,492,000 |
| South China Sea | 3,447,000 | 1,331,000 |
| Caribbean Sea | 2,753,000 | 1,063,000 |
| Mediterranean Sea | 2,505,000 | 967,000 |
| Bering Sea | 2,269,000 | 876,000 |

## LARGEST LAKES AND INLAND SEAS

| LAKE | LOCATION | AREA IN KM² | AREA IN MILES² |
|---|---|---|---|
| Caspian Sea | Asia | 370,980 | 143,236 |
| Lake Superior | Canada/USA | 82,098 | 31,698 |
| Lake Victoria | Africa | 68,880 | 26,595 |
| Lake Huron | Canada/USA | 59,566 | 22,999 |
| Lake Michigan | USA | 57,754 | 22,999 |
| Aral Sea | Asia | 37,056 | 14,307 |
| Lake Tanganyika | Africa | 32,891 | 12,699 |
| Lake Baikal | Siberia | 31,498 | 12,161 |

**Caspian Sea**

## LONGEST RIVERS

| NAME (LOCATION) | LENGTH IN KM (MILES) |
|---|---|
| Nile (Africa) | 6,738 (4,187) |
| Amazon (USA) | 6,500 (4,040) |
| Yangtze (Asia) | 6,300 (3,915) |
| Mississippi–Missouri–Red Rock (USA) | 6,020 (3,741) |
| Yenisey–Angara–Selenga (Asia) | 5,540 (3,442) |

**Greatest waterfalls**
The world's highest waterfalls are the Angel Falls in Venezuela. They were discovered by US pilot James Angel in 1935.

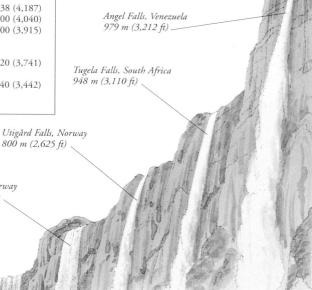

*Angel Falls, Venezuela 979 m (3,212 ft)*

*Tugela Falls, South Africa 948 m (3,110 ft)*

*Utigård Falls, Norway 800 m (2,625 ft)*

*Mongefossen, Norway 774 m (2,540 ft)*

*Yosemite Falls, USA 739 m (2,425 ft)*

## EARTH FACTS

- Diameter: 12,756 km (7,926 miles) at equator; 12,713 km (7,899 miles) at poles
- Age: 4.6 billion years old
- Distance from Sun: 150 million km (93 million miles)
- Mass: 5,854 billion billion tonnes
- Area: 29.2% land, 70.8% water
- Orbiting time: 365.26 days
- Orbiting speed: 29.8 km/sec (18.5 miles/sec)

# International time zones

The world is divided into 24 time zones, one for each hour of the day. Clocks in each zone are set to a different time. For instance, when it is noon in Greenwich, England, it is 10 p.m. in Sydney, Australia.

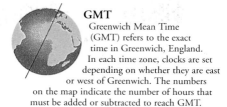

### GMT
Greenwich Mean Time (GMT) refers to the exact time in Greenwich, England. In each time zone, clocks are set depending on whether they are east or west of Greenwich. The numbers on the map indicate the number of hours that must be added or subtracted to reach GMT.

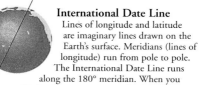

### International Date Line
Lines of longitude and latitude are imaginary lines drawn on the Earth's surface. Meridians (lines of longitude) run from pole to pole. The International Date Line runs along the 180° meridian. When you cross this line from east to west, the date changes. The western side is a day ahead of the eastern side.

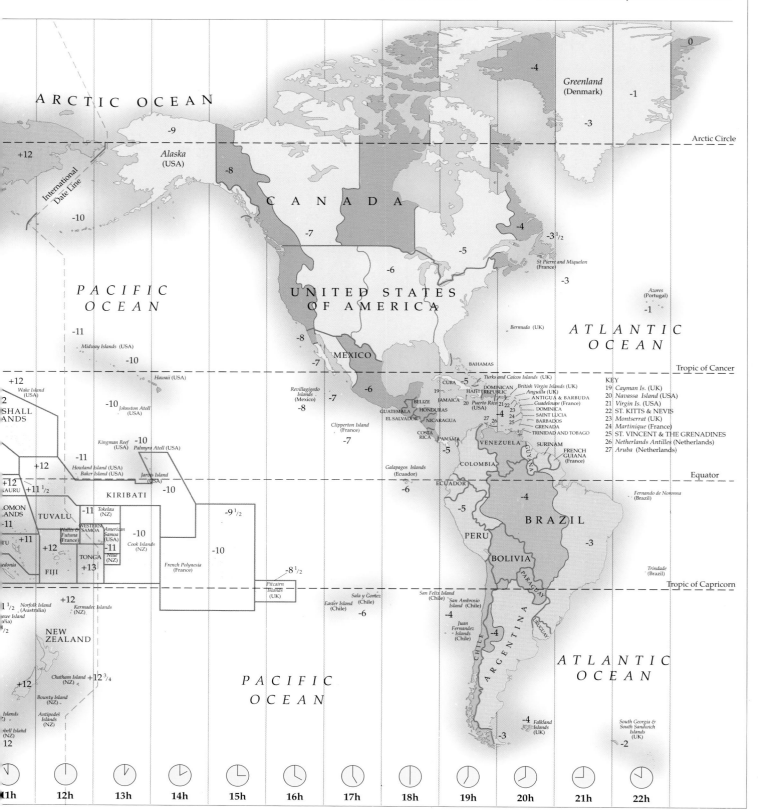

KEY
19  *Cayman Is.* (UK)
20  *Navassa Island* (USA)
21  *Virgin Is.* (USA)
22  ST. KITTS & NEVIS
23  *Montserrat* (UK)
24  *Martinique* (France)
25  ST. VINCENT & THE GRENADINES
26  *Netherlands Antilles* (Netherlands)
27  *Aruba* (Netherlands)

# WORLD POPULATION

IN 1500, THE WORLD'S POPULATION was about 435 million. Today, it stands at 5.5 billion, with more than a million children being born every day. The rapid growth in population since 1800 is largely due to improvements in food production and medical knowledge. In many parts of the world, rapid population growth causes serious problems, such as food shortages and overcrowding in cities.

## URBAN POPULATION

1n 1900, only 10 percent of the world's population lived in cities. Today, that figure is about 50 percent. The table below lists the world's most populated cities.

| CITY | POPULATION |
| --- | --- |
| Toyko | 27,245,000 |
| São Paulo | 19,235,000 |
| New York | 16,158,000 |
| Mexico City | 15,276,000 |
| Bombay | 13,322,000 |
| Shanghai | 12,670,000 |
| Los Angeles | 11,853,000 |
| Buenos Aires | 11,753,000 |

Tokyo, Japan

**World population**
The map below shows population figures for the world's main land areas. Between them, China and India account for about 40 percent of the world's population.

**Europe:**
747,042,000
13.8 percent of world population

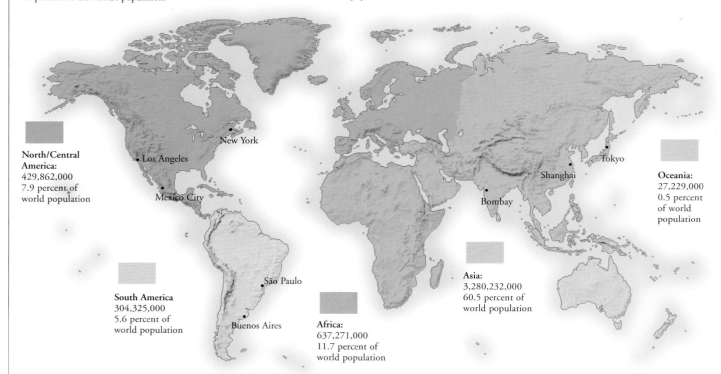

**North/Central America:**
429,862,000
7.9 percent of world population

New York

Los Angeles

Mexico City

Tokyo

Shanghai

Bombay

**Oceania:**
27,229,000
0.5 percent of world population

**South America**
304,325,000
5.6 percent of world population

São Paulo

Buenos Aires

**Africa:**
637,271,000
11.7 percent of world population

**Asia:**
3,280,232,000
60.5 percent of world population

## REFUGEES

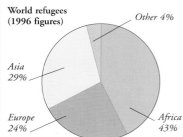

Hutu refugees in Rwanda

Throughout history, many millions of people have become refugees. Wars, drought, famine, and poverty are some of the reasons why people leave their homes and families. Today, more than 40 percent of the world's refugees come from Africa.

**World refugees (1996 figures)**

Other 4%

Asia 29%

Europe 24%

Africa 43%

## HIGHEST POPULATION

| COUNTRY | POPULATION |
| --- | --- |
| China | 1,252,188,000 |
| India | 953,000,000 |
| US | 265,800,000 |
| Indonesia | 200,600,000 |
| Brazil | 164,400,000 |

## LOWEST POPULATION

| COUNTRY | POPULATION |
| --- | --- |
| Vatican | 1,000 |
| Nauru | 11,000 |
| Tuvalu | 13,000 |
| Palau | 17,000 |
| San Marino | 23,000 |

## FERTILITY RATES

**Africa: 6**

**Middle East: 5.9**

**Asia: 3.2**

**Europe: 2**

**USA: 1.9**

*Figures shown are the average number of children per woman.*

Fertility rates measure the average number of children born to each woman. Fertility rates are declining rapidly in the industrialized world, and are highest in Africa.

# LIVING STANDARDS

Slovakian children

IN THE PAST 100 YEARS, living standards have improved greatly across the world. Better health care, even in poorer countries, means that fewer people now die of hunger and disease. Advances in medicine and improved diet and education have helped people to live longer and healthier lives. However, many problems remain, especially in the poorer countries of Africa and Asia.

## ADULT LITERACY

Adult literacy rates show how many adults over the age of 15 can read and write. The table below lists the average literacy rates for a variety of countries.

| COUNTRY | PERCENT OF POPULATION |
|---|---|
| US | 99 |
| UK | 99 |
| Brazil | 82 |
| China | 80 |
| Kuwait | 74 |
| India | 52 |
| Afghanistan | 32 |
| Somalia | 24 |
| Niger | 14 |

Shanty school in São Paulo, Brazil

## LIFE EXPECTANCY

Life expectancy is the average length of time a person is likely to live. Wealthier countries generally have higher life expectancies than poorer countries.

### Highest life expectancy (male)

| COUNTRY | AGE |
|---|---|
| Japan | 76.8 |
| Iceland | 76.3 |
| Sweden | 76.1 |
| Cyprus | 75.6 |
| Greece | 75.5 |

### Highest life expectancy (female)

| COUNTRY | AGE |
|---|---|
| Japan | 82.9 |
| Sweden | 81.9 |
| Switzerland | 81.7 |
| Italy | 81.4 |
| Iceland | 81.3 |

Japanese family

### Lowest life expectancy (male)

| COUNTRY | AGE |
|---|---|
| Sierra Leone | 39.4 |
| Uganda | 42.2 |
| Guinea-Bissau | 43.9 |
| Malawi | 44.3 |
| Afghanistan | 45.0 |

### Lowest life expectancy (female)

| COUNTRY | AGE |
|---|---|
| Sierra Leone | 42.6 |
| Uganda | 44.3 |
| Malawi | 45.4 |
| Afghanistan | 46.0 |
| Zambia | 46.8 |

## PEOPLE PER DOCTOR

The table below compares the average number of people per doctor in some developed and developing countries.

| COUNTRY | PEOPLE PER DOCTOR |
|---|---|
| Nigeria | 66,650 |
| Burkina-Faso | 57,300 |
| Malawi | 50,360 |
| Eritrea | 48,000 |
| Mali | 21,180 |
| Bangladesh | 12,500 |
| Zimbabwe | 7,692 |
| US | 420 |
| Austria | 230 |
| Russian Federation | 220 |
| Georgia | 180 |

Country hospital, Burkina-Faso

## SAFE WATER

Almost 2 billion people worldwide do not have access to the minimum level of safe water (6 gallons/20 litres per person per day). The table shows the average number of people with access to safe water in some developed and developing countries.

| COUNTRY | PERCENT OF POPULATION |
|---|---|
| Tunisia | 99 |
| Saudi Arabia | 93 |
| Mexico | 77 |
| Iran | 61 |
| Pakistan | 56 |
| Mali | 41 |
| Zimbabwe | 36 |
| Ethiopia | 28 |
| Vietnam | 27 |
| Afghanistan | 21 |
| Uganda | 15 |

## MAJOR CAUSES OF DEATH

The table below shows the major cause of death in various countries.

| DISEASE | HIGHEST INCIDENCE |
|---|---|
| Cancer | Netherlands |
| Heart attacks | Armenia |
| Infectious diseases | Guatemala |
| Motor accidents | Kuwait |
| Strokes | Ukraine |
| Injury/poisoning | Russia |
| AIDS | Bahamas |

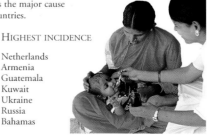
Nurse administering polio vaccine.

## FOOD SUPPLY

The "Dietary Energy Supply" (DES) is the amount of calories available per person per day. The mimimum amount of calories needed per day is 2,300. This table compares the DES of various countries.

| COUNTRY | CALORIES PER DAY |
|---|---|
| Ireland | 3,837 |
| Spain | 3,708 |
| Japan | 2,903 |
| Uruguay | 2,750 |
| Chad | 1,989 |
| Mozambique | 1,680 |

Village well, Vietnam

# WORLD RESOURCES

RAW MATERIALS ARE natural substances that are extracted from water, air, or from the ground. Some energy sources, such as solar or wind power, are renewable. Others, such as oil or coal, are non-renewable and will eventually run out. As world population grows, people are drawing more heavily on the Earth's natural resources.

## FOSSIL FUELS

### Electricity

This table shows annual production in kilowatt hours.

| COUNTRY | KW/HR |
|---|---|
| USA | 3,074,504,000,000 |
| Russia | 904,959,000 |
| Japan | 458,102,000 |
| China | 313,960,000 |
| Germany | 254,600,000 |

**Light bulb**

### Coal

This table shows coal production in tonnes per annum.

| COUNTRY | TONNES |
|---|---|
| China | 1,116,369,000 |
| USA | 904,959,000 |
| Germany | 458,102,000 |
| Russia | 313,960,000 |
| India | 254,600,000 |

**Coal**

### Crude oil

This table shows oil production in barrels per annum.

| COUNTRY | BARRELS |
|---|---|
| Saudi Arabia | 2,979,000,000 |
| Russia | 65,374,000 |
| USA | 56,762,000 |
| Iran | 42,480,000 |
| China | 29,324,000 |

**Oil plant, Libya**

### Energy consumption

This table lists the major consumers of coal, oil, electricity, and gas.

| COUNTRY | % OF WORLD TOTAL |
|---|---|
| USA | 24.6% |
| Russian Federation | 16.8% |
| China | 8.4% |
| Japan | 5.4% |
| Germany | 4.35% |
| UK | 2.9% |
| India | 2.8% |

## LEADING AGRICULTURAL PRODUCERS

Today, farming is a major international business, with many countries competing in the export market. This table shows the top producers of a wide range of agricultural products.

| PRODUCT | TOP PRODUCERS | PRODUCT | TOP PRODUCERS |
|---|---|---|---|
| Cattle | Australia | Potatoes | Russian Federation |
| Cocoa | USA | Rubber | Malaysia |
| Coffee | Brazil | Sheep | Australia |
| Cotton | China | Soya beans | USA |
| Cows' milk | USA | Tea | India |
| Hens' eggs | China | Tobacco | China |
| Oats | Russian Federation | Wood | USA |
| Pigs | China | Wool | Australia |

**Tea**          **Coffee**          **Cotton**

## CROP PRODUCERS

### Wheat

| COUNTRY | TONNES PER ANNUM |
|---|---|
| China | 105,005,000 |
| USA | 65,374,000 |
| India | 56,762,000 |
| Russia | 42,480,000 |
| Canada | 29,870,000 |
| France | 29,324,000 |

**Emmer**

### Rice

| COUNTRY | TONNES PER ANNUM |
|---|---|
| China | 187,211,000 |
| India | 111,011,000 |
| Indonesia | 47,883,000 |
| Bangladesh | 28,000,000 |
| Vietnam | 22,300,000 |
| Thailand | 19,090,000 |

**Basmati rice**

### Maize (Corn)

| COUNTRY | TONNES PER ANNUM |
|---|---|
| USA | 161,145,000 |
| China | 103,380,000 |
| Brazil | 29,967,000 |
| Mexico | 18,600,000 |
| France | 14,966,000 |
| Argentina | 10,897,000 |

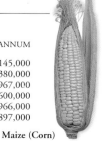

**Maize (Corn)**

## MINERAL PRODUCERS

This table shows the world's major mineral producers.

| MINERAL | TOP PRODUCERS | % OF WORLD TOTAL |
|---|---|---|
| Bauxite | Australia | 4.45% |
| Copper | Chile | 17.39% |
| Iron ore | Russian Federation | 24.49% |
| Salt | USA | 18.78% |
| Sulphur | USA | 19.23% |

## WORLD CONSUMPTION

This table lists the top consumers for a variety of commodities. The figures show the amount of tonnes consumed per annum.

| COMMODITY | TOP CONSUMERS | TONNES |
|---|---|---|
| Cereals | USA | 208,000,000 |
| Cocoa | Côte d'Ivoire | 884,000 |
| Coffee | USA | 1,053,000 |
| Copper | USA | 2,678,000 |
| Cotton | China | 431,000,000 |
| Lead | USA | 1,495,000 |
| Nickel | Japan | 181,100 |
| Rice | China | 129,000,000 |
| Rubber | USA | 3,119,000 |
| Tea | India | 580,000 |
| Wheat | China | 115,000,000 |
| Wool | China | 439,000 |

## FISH CATCHES

This table gives fish catches per year in million metric tonnes.

| AREA | TONNES |
|---|---|
| Pacific Ocean | 48.32 |
| Atlantic Ocean | 20.17 |
| Indian Ocean | 5.93 |
| Mediterranean and Black Sea | 1.29 |
| Antarctic | 0.40 |
| World total | 76.11 |

**Icelandic fishing**

# WORLD ECONOMY

THE WEALTH OF A COUNTRY depends on its industrial strength, natural resources, population size, and political stability. Trade creates wealth and jobs by encouraging countries to produce goods that can be sold abroad. However, many poor countries have to borrow money from richer countries to finance their industries.

## NATIONAL WEALTH

A country's wealth is measured in two ways. The Gross Domestic Product (GDP) measures the total value of goods and services produced by a national economy. The Gross National Product (GNP) measures GDP and a country's income from abroad. National wealth is measured by dividing either the GDP or the GNP by the country's population.

## FOREIGN DEBT

Some organizations, such as the World Bank and the International Monetary Fund (IMF), lend developing countries money to finance industry and welfare programmes. The interest charged on these loans is often very high. The countries listed below have the highest foreign debt.

| COUNTRY | DEBT (IN MILLIONS OF US$) |
|---|---|
| Brazil | 151,104 |
| Mexico | 128,302 |
| China | 100,536 |
| India | 98,500 |
| Indonesia | 96,500 |
| Russia | 94,232 |
| Argentina | 77,388 |
| Turkey | 66,332 |

International Monetary Fund

World Bank

## FOREIGN AID

Some countries depend on foreign aid (in the form of grants or loans) for most of their income. Many countries offer food, tents, medical supplies, and clothing following natural disasters or civil war.

### Main aid donors

| COUNTRY | AID GIVEN (IN MILLIONS OF US$) |
|---|---|
| Japan | 13,239 |
| USA | 9,927 |
| France | 8,466 |
| Germany | 6,818 |
| UK | 3,197 |
| Italy | 2,705 |

### Main recipients of aid

| COUNTRY | AID RECEIVED (IN MILLIONS OF US$) |
|---|---|
| China | 3,232 |
| Egypt | 2,695 |
| India | 2,324 |
| Bangladesh | 1,757 |
| Former Yugoslavia | 1,716 |
| Indonesia | 1,642 |

UN forces supplying food and medical equipment, Sarajevo, Bosnia and Herzegovina.

### Richest countries

The countries below have the highest GNP per head.

| COUNTRY | AMOUNT IN US$ |
|---|---|
| Luxembourg | 39,850 |
| Switzerland | 37,180 |
| Japan | 34,630 |
| Denmark | 28,110 |
| Norway | 26,480 |
| USA | 25,860 |
| Germany | 25,580 |
| Austria | 24,950 |
| Iceland | 24,590 |

Zürich, Switzerland

### Poorest countries

The countries below have the lowest GNP per head.

| COUNTRY | AMOUNT IN US$ |
|---|---|
| Mozambique | 80 |
| Ethiopia | 130 |
| Malawi | 140 |
| Burundi | 150 |
| Sierra Leone | 150 |
| Chad | 190 |
| Vietnam | 190 |
| Uganda | 200 |
| Nepal | 200 |

## INTERNATIONAL TRADE

### World trade

Five countries dominate world trade. These countries, known as the Big Five, account for almost half of all international trade.

| COUNTRY | PERCENTAGE OF WORLD TRADE |
|---|---|
| USA | 13.95% |
| Japan | 9.98% |
| Germany | 9.43% |
| France | 7.06% |
| UK | 6.43% |

### Export goods

The table below shows the kinds of goods that are traded worldwide. Manufactured goods, such as cars and computers, still dominate the export market, although service industries, such as tourism and banking, are growing rapidly.

| GOODS | PERCENTAGE OF WORLD TRADE |
|---|---|
| Manufacturing | 57.3% |
| Services | 21.9% |
| Agriculture | 9.4% |
| Mining | 9.3% |
| Other | 2.1% |

Car manufacturing plant, Germany

### World's largest stock markets

The activity of a stock market reflects a country's economic performance. The table below lists the world's most important financial centres.

New York, USA (Wall Street)
Tokyo, Japan
London, UK
Hong Kong, China
Frankfurt, Germany
Zürich, Switzerland
Kuala Lumpur, Malaysia
Paris, France
Toronto, Canada

Hong Kong stock market

Addis Ababa, Ethiopia

# TRANSPORTATION

PEOPLE HAVE ALWAYS moved around and over the centuries have searched for more efficient methods of transportation. In the past 100 years, advances in technology have led to a huge increase in global travel and trade. Today, vast road and rail networks link countries worldwide. Shipping transports most international goods, and each day airlines carry millions of passengers to every part of the globe.

## BUSIEST INTERNATIONAL AIRPORTS

| AIRPORT | INTERNATIONAL PASSENGERS PER YEAR |
|---|---|
| London Heathrow, UK | 40,844,000 |
| Frankfurt, Germany | 25,195,000 |
| Hong Kong, China | 24,421,000 |
| Charles de Gaulle, France | 22,336,000 |
| Schipol, Netherlands | 20,659,000 |
| Tokyo/Narita, Japan | 18,947,000 |
| Singapore International | 18,796,000 |
| London Gatwick, UK | 18,660,000 |
| JFK International, USA | 15,014,000 |
| Bangkok, Thailand | 12,755,000 |

Heathrow Airport, UK

## MAJOR PORTS

| PORT | TOTAL GOODS HANDLED (TONS) |
|---|---|
| Rotterdam, Netherlands | 294,000,000 |
| New Orleans, US | 190,000,000 |
| Singapore, Singapore | 188,000,000 |
| Kobe, Japan | 172,000,000 |
| Shanghai, China | 133,000,000 |
| Houston, US | 131,000,000 |

## LONGEST SUSPENSION BRIDGES

| BRIDGE | COUNTRY | DATE BUILT | LENGTH IN FEET (METERS) |
|---|---|---|---|
| Humber | UK | 1980 | 4,626 (1,410) |
| Verrazano Narrows | US | 1964 | 4,258 (1,298) |
| Golden Gate | US | 1937 | 4,199 (1,280) |
| Mackinac Straits | US | 1957 | 3,800 (1,158) |
| Bosphorus | Turkey | 1990 | 3,576 (1,090) |
| George Washington | US | 1931 | 3,500 (1,066) |

Golden Gate, San Francisco

## ROAD

### Countries with most roads

| COUNTRY | MILES (KM) OF ROAD |
|---|---|
| US | 3,905,190 (6,284,500) |
| India | 1,342,225 (2,160,000) |
| Brazil | 1,037,830 (1,670,150) |
| Japan | 938,780 (1,510,750) |
| China | 693,240 (1,115,610) |

### Top car-owning countries

| COUNTRY | NO. OF CARS |
|---|---|
| US | 144,213,429 |
| Japan | 38,963,793 |
| Germany | 39,086,000 |
| Italy | 29,497,000 |
| France | 24,020,000 |

Long Island Expressway, New York, USA

## RAIL

### Longest rail tunnels

| TUNNEL | COUNTRY | DATE OPENED | LENGTH IN MILES (KM) |
|---|---|---|---|
| Seikan | Japan | 1988 | 33.5 (53.9) |
| Channel Tunnel | France/UK | 1994 | 31 (49.9) |
| Moscow Metro (Medvedkovo/ Belyaevo section) | Russia | 1979 | 19.1 (30.7) |
| London Underground (Northern Line) | UK | 1939 | 17.3 (27.8) |

Bullet Train, Mt. Fuji, Japan

## TRANSPORTATION AND ENGINEERING

LONGEST ROAD: Pan American Highway. It runs from the USA to Brazil and is 15,000 miles (24,140 km) long.

TALLEST DAM: Rogunskaya, Tajikistan. Built in the 1990s, it is 1,066 ft (325 m) long.

LARGEST RAILROAD STATION: Grand Central Terminal, New York. It has 67 tracks and covers 19 hectares (48 acres).

MOST HIGHWAYS: US. There are 52,000 miles (84,900 km) of highway in the US.

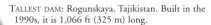

Grand Central Terminal, New York

### Longest subway systems

| CITY | STATIONS | MILES (KM) |
|---|---|---|
| Washington, D.C. | 86 | 380 (612) |
| London | 272 | 267 (430) |
| New York | 461 | 230 (370) |
| Paris | 430 | 187 (301) |
| Moscow | 115 | 140 (225) |
| Tokyo | 192 | 135 (218) |

### Countries with most rail track

| COUNTRY | TOTAL MILES (KM) OF TRACK |
|---|---|
| US | 167,970 (270,312) |
| Russia | 94,455 (152,000) |
| Canada | 44,120 (71,000) |
| China | 43,125 (69,400) |
| India | 38,435 (61,850) |

# THEATER, MUSIC, AND DANCE

THEATER HAS ITS roots in ancient Greece, when religious plays included singing and dancing as well as acting. Today, dramatic performances of many kinds continue to entertain audiences around the world.

Viola

## KEY CLASSICAL COMPOSERS

| NAME (NATIONALITY) | DATES | FAMOUS WORK |
|---|---|---|
| Antonio Vivaldi (Italian) | 1677–1741 | *The Four Seasons* (1725) |
| Johann Sebastian Bach (German) | 1685–1750 | *Brandenburg Concertos* (1721) |
| George Frederick Händel (German) | 1685–1759 | *Messiah* (1742) |
| Franz Joseph Haydn (Austrian) | 1732–1809 | *London Symphonies* (1791–1795) |
| Wolfgang Amadeus Mozart (Austrian) | 1756–1791 | *The Magic Flute* (1791) |
| Ludwig van Beethoven (German) | 1770–1827 | *Pastoral Symphony* (1807–1808) |
| Franz Schubert (Austrian) | 1797–1828 | *Die Winterreise* (1827) |
| Hector Berlioz (French) | 1803–1869 | *Symphonie Fantastique* (1830) |
| Felix Mendelssohn (German) | 1809–1847 | *A Midsummer Night's Dream* (1826) |
| Frédéric Chopin (Polish) | 1810–1849 | Piano works |
| Franz Liszt (Hungarian) | 1811–1886 | *Les Préludes* (1854) |
| Giuseppe Verdi (Italian) | 1813–1901 | *La Traviata* (1853) |
| Richard Wagner (German) | 1813–1883 | *The Flying Dutchman* (1843) |
| Johann Strauss (Austrian) | 1825–1899 | *Die Fledermaus* (1874) |
| Pyotr Ilyich Tchaikovsky (Russian) | 1840–1893 | *Swan Lake* (1877) |
| Antonin Dvorák (Czech) | 1841–1904 | *Slavonic Dances* (1878–1886) |
| Edward Elgar (English) | 1857–1934 | *Enigma Variations* (1898–1899) |
| Giacomo Puccini (Italian) | 1858–1924 | *La Bohème* (1896) |
| Ethel Smyth (English) | 1858–1944 | *The Wreckers* (1909) |
| Gustav Mahler (Austrian) | 1860–1911 | *Resurrection Symphony* (1884–1894) |
| Claude Debussy (French) | 1862–1918 | *La Mer* (1903–1905) |
| Richard Strauss (German) | 1864–1949 | *Der Rosenkavalier* (1911) |
| Sergei Rachmaninov (Russian) | 1873–1943 | Piano works |
| Gustav Holst (English) | 1874–1934 | *The Planets* (1914–1916) |
| Maurice Ravel (French) | 1875–1937 | *Boléro* (1928) |
| Igor Stravinsky (Russian) | 1882–1971 | *The Firebird* (1910) |
| Sergei Prokofiev (Russian) | 1891–1953 | *Peter and the Wolf* (1936) |
| Kurt Weill (German) | 1900–1950 | *The Threepenny Opera* (1928) |
| Benjamin Britten (English) | 1913–1976 | *Billy Budd* (1951) |
| Karlheinz Stockhausen (German) | b.1928 | *Gruppen* (1955–1957) |
| Philip Glass (American) | b.1937 | *Einstein on the Beach* (1976) |

Franz Schubert

Philip Glass

## KEY OPERAS

These "musical dramas" use spectacular singers, lavish stage sets, and a full orchestra to dramatic effect.

| TITLE | COMPOSER (NATIONALITY) | DATE |
|---|---|---|
| *The Marriage of Figaro* | Wolfgang Mozart (Austrian) | 1786 |
| *Così fan tutte* | Wolfgang Mozart (Austrian) | 1790 |
| *The Barber of Seville* | Gioacchino Rossini (Italian) | 1816 |
| *Tristan and Isolde* | Richard Wagner (German) | 1865 |
| *Aïda* | Giuseppe Verdi (Italian) | 1871 |
| *Carmen* | Georges Bizet (French) | 1875 |
| *The Ring of the Nibelung* | Richard Wagner (German) | 1876 |
| *La Bohème* | Giacomo Puccini (Italian) | 1896 |
| *Madame Butterfly* | Giacomo Puccini (Italian) | 1904 |
| *Peter Grimes* | Benjamin Britten (English) | 1945 |

*The Marriage of Figaro*

## KEY DRAMATISTS

| NAME (NATIONALITY) | DATES | FAMOUS PLAY |
|---|---|---|
| William Shakespeare (English) | 1564–1616 | *Hamlet* |
| Pierre Corneille (French) | 1607–1684 | *Le Cid* |
| Molière (French) | 1622–1673 | *Tartuffe* |
| Jean Racine (French) | 1639–1699 | *Phèdre* |
| Johann Goethe (German) | 1749–1832 | *Faust* |
| Richard Sheridan (Irish) | 1751–1816 | *The Rivals* |
| Henrik Ibsen (Norwegian) | 1828–1906 | *A Doll's House* |
| George Bernard Shaw (Irish) | 1856–1950 | *Pygmalion* |
| Anton Chekov (Russian) | 1860–1904 | *Uncle Vanya* |
| Luigi Pirandello (Italian) | 1867–1936 | *Six Characters in Search of an Author* |
| Susan Glaspell (American) | 1882–1948 | *Alison's House* |
| Eugene O'Neill (American) | 1888–1953 | *Strange Interlude* |
| Bertolt Brecht (German) | 1898–1956 | *The Threepenny Opera* |
| Samuel Beckett (Irish) | 1906–1989 | *Waiting for Godot* |
| Tennessee Williams (American) | 1911–1983 | *The Glass Menagerie* |
| Eugène Ionesco (French) | 1912–1994 | *The Bald Prima Donna* |
| Arthur Miller (American) | b.1915 | *Death of a Salesman* |
| John Osborne (English) | 1929–1994 | *Look Back in Anger* |
| Harold Pinter (English) | b.1930 | *The Caretaker* |

Quill pens

## FAMOUS BALLETS

Ballet uses dancing, mime, and music to tell a story.

| TITLE | CHOREOGRAPHER (NATIONALITY) | FIRST DANCED |
|---|---|---|
| *La Syphide* | Filippo Taglioni (Italian) | 1832 |
| *Giselle* | Jean Coralli/Jules Perot (French/French) | 1841 |
| *Sleeping Beauty* | Marius Petipa (French) | 1890 |
| *The Nutcracker* | Lev Ivanov (Russian) | 1892 |
| *The Rite of Spring* | Vaslav Nijinsky (Russian) | 1913 |
| *Manon* | Kenneth MacMillan (English) | 1974 |
| *Fait Accompli* | Twyla Tharp (American) | 1984 |
| *Still Life at the Penguin Cafe* | David Bintley (English) | 1988 |

## BEST-SELLING SINGLES WORLDWIDE

| SINGLE | ARTIST |
|---|---|
| *White Christmas* | Bing Crosby |
| *Rock Around The Clock* | Bill Haley and the Comets |
| *I Want to Hold Your Hand* | Beatles |
| *It's Now or Never* | Elvis Presley |
| *I Will Always Love You* | Whitney Houston |
| *Don't Be Cruel/Hound Dog* | Elvis Presley |
| *Diana* | Paul Anka |
| *Hey Jude* | Beatles |
| *I'm a Believer* | The Monkees |

Whitney Houston

## BEST-SELLING ALBUMS WORLDWIDE

| ALBUM | ARTIST |
|---|---|
| *Thriller* | Michael Jackson |
| *The Bodyguard* | Soundtrack |
| *Saturday Night Fever* | Soundtrack |
| *Sgt. Pepper's Lonely Hearts Club Band* | Beatles |
| *Bridge Over Troubled Water* | Simon and Garfunkel |
| *Born in the USA* | Bruce Springsteen |
| *The Sound of Music* | Soundtrack |
| *Rumours* | Fleetwood Mac |
| *Brothers in Arms* | Dire Straits |

*Saturday Night Fever*

# FILM AND THE MEDIA

DURING THE PAST 100 years, advances in modern technology have transformed the media and entertainment industries. Computers create feature-length films with special effects, satellites beam live broadcasts to television sets worldwide, and modern printing presses produce up to four million newspapers every day.

Technicolor camera

## KEY FILM DIRECTORS

| NAME (NATIONALITY) | DATES | KEY FILM |
|---|---|---|
| Cecil De Mille (American) | 1881–1959 | *The Ten Commandments* (1923) |
| Jean Cocteau (French) | 1889–1963 | *La Belle et la Bête* (1946) |
| Jean Renoir (French) | 1894–1979 | *La Règle du Jeu* (1939) |
| John Ford (American) | 1895–1973 | *Stagecoach* (1939) |
| Sergei Eisenstein (Russian) | 1898–1948 | *The Battleship Potemkin* (1925) |
| Alfred Hitchcock (British) | 1899–1980 | *Psycho* (1960) |
| Luis Buñuel (Spanish) | 1900–1983 | *Un Chien Andalou* (1928) |
| John Huston (American) | 1906–1987 | *The African Queen* (1951) |
| David Lean (British) | 1908–1991 | *Lawrence of Arabia* (1962) |
| Elia Kazan (Greek-born American) | b.1909 | *On the Waterfront* (1954) |
| Akira Kurosawa (Japanese) | 1910–1998 | *Seven Samurai* (1954) |
| Orson Welles (American) | 1915–1985 | *Citizen Kane* (1942) |
| Ingmar Bergman (Swedish) | b.1918– | *The Seventh Seal* (1957) |
| Federico Fellini (Italian) | 1920–1993 | *La Dolce Vita* (1960) |
| Satyajit Ray (Indian) | 1921–1992 | *Pather Panchali* (1955) |
| Stanley Kubrick (American) | b.1928 | *A Clockwork Orange* (1971) |
| Jean-Luc Godard (French) | b.1930 | *A Bout de Souffle* (1960) |
| Woody Allen (American) | b.1935 | *Annie Hall* (1977) |
| Francis Coppola (American) | b.1939 | *Apocalypse Now* (1979) |
| Bernardo Bertolucci (Italian) | b.1940 | *The Last Emperor* (1987) |
| Peter Weir (Australian) | b.1944 | *Picnic at Hanging Rock* (1975) |
| Steven Spielberg (American) | b.1947 | *E.T.* (1982) |
| Claude Berri (French) | b.1954 | *Jean de Florette* (1986) |
| Jane Campion (New Zealand) | b.1955 | *The Piano* (1993) |

**Ingmar Bergman**

**Scene from *The Piano* (1993)**

## RADIO

| COUNTRY | RADIO SETS PER 1,000 POPULATION |
|---|---|
| USA | 2,091 |
| Bermuda | 1,710 |
| UK | 1,240 |
| Australia | 1,144 |
| Finland | 984 |
| New Zealand | 902 |
| Virgin Islands (USA) | 884 |
| France | 866 |
| Sweden | 842 |
| Canada | 828 |

**Personal stereo**

## CINEMA FACTS

• The first feature film was *The Story of the Kelly Gang*, made in Australia in 1906.

• The first "talkie" was *The Jazz Singer*. Released in 1927, it starred Al Jolson (1886–1950).

• The most expensive film ever produced is *Waterworld* (USA, 1995). It cost an estimated $160 million (£104 million).

• The highest-grossing film at the box office is *Jurassic Park* (USA, 1993). By June 1996, it had earned $913 million (£568 million).

## MOST OSCARS WON

| NAME OF FILM | AWARDS |
|---|---|
| *Ben-Hur* (1959) | 11 |
| *Titanic* (1998) | 11 |
| *West Side Story* (1961) | 10 |
| *Gigi* (1958) | 9 |
| *The Last Emperor* (1987) | 9 |
| *The English Patient* (1997) | 9 |
| *Gone With the Wind* (1939) | 8 |
| *Gandhi* (1982) | 8 |
| *From Here to Eternity* (1953) | 8 |
| *On the Waterfront* (1954) | 8 |
| *Cabaret* (1972) | 8 |

## OSCAR® FACTS

• The first Oscars® (Academy Awards) were presented in 1929. *Wings* (1927) won the "Best Picture" award.

• The film nominated for the most Oscars was *All About Eve* (USA, 1950). It had 14 nominations and won six awards.

• Katharine Hepburn (b.1909) received more Oscar nominations than any other actor. She was nominated 12 times and won four awards.

Oscar®

## BEST-SELLING NEWSPAPERS

| NAME | COUNTRY | AVERAGE DAILY CIRCULATION |
|---|---|---|
| *Yomiuri Shimbun* | Japan | 8,700,000 |
| *Asahi Shimbun* | Japan | 7,400,000 |
| *People's Daily* | China | 6,000,000 |
| *Bild Zeitung* | Germany | 5,900,000 |
| *The Sun* | UK | 3,851,929 |
| *Daily Mirror* | UK | 2,523,944 |
| *Wall Street Journal* | USA | 1,857,131 |
| *Daily Mail* | UK | 1,716,070 |
| *USA Today* | USA | 1,632,345 |
| *Daily Express* | UK | 1397,852 |
| *New York Times* | USA | 1,230,461 |

*Asahi Shimbun* newspaper

## TELEVISION

### World television viewing

| COUNTRY | HOURS PER WEEK |
|---|---|
| USA | 49.35 |
| Italy | 28.93 |
| Hong Kong | 28.70 |
| Colombia | 23.80 |
| UK | 23.80 |
| Australia | 21.98 |
| Chile | 17.50 |
| China | 10.59 |
| Malaysia | 10.50 |
| World Average | 19.67 |

**1980s' television**

### First countries to have television

| COUNTRY | YEAR |
|---|---|
| UK | 1936 |
| USA | 1939 |
| USSR | 1939 |
| France | 1948 |
| Brazil | 1950 |
| Cuba | 1950 |
| Mexico | 1950 |
| Argentina | 1951 |
| Denmark | 1951 |
| Netherlands | 1951 |

**Watching TV in 1948.**

### TELEVISION FACTS

• By the early 1990s, there were 746,829,000 homes worldwide with a television set. By 2005, an estimated billion homes will have a television.

• Telstar was the world's first communications satellite. In 1962, it transmitted live television programmes across the globe for the first time.

# GREAT WRITERS AND THINKERS

EVERY SOCIETY HAS produced great writers and thinkers. The tables below list a selection of these influential men and women.

Ludwig Wittgenstein

## KEY PHILOSOPHERS

From the early Greek philosophers to modern thinkers, philosophers have offered opposing theories and beliefs. This table lists some of the world's most important thinkers with a summary of their philosophy.

| NAME (NATIONALITY) | DATES | PHILOSOPHY |
|---|---|---|
| Confucius (Chinese) | 551–479 bc | Emphasized moral order and ancient manners. |
| Socrates (Greek) | 470–399 bc | Taught that morality is based on knowledge. |
| Aristotle (Greek) | 384–322 bc | Believed that logic and reason are most important. |
| St. Augustine (Roman-born African) | ad 354–430 | Outlined his Christian beliefs in his work. |
| St. Thomas Aquinas (Italian) | 1225–1274 | Argued to prove the existence of God. |
| René Descartes (French) | 1596–1650 | Interpreted the world using mathematical laws. |
| John Locke (English) | 1632–1704 | Believed that all knowledge is based on experience. |
| David Hume (Scottish) | 1711–1776 | Believed that nothing can be known for certain. |
| Søren Kierkegaard (Danish) | 1813–1855 | The founder of existentialism (the belief that the individual must take responsibility for his or her own actions). |
| Friedrich Nietzsche (German) | 1844–1900 | Rejected Christianity and argued that people are driven by "the will to power". |
| Bertrand Russell (English) | 1872–1970 | Imprisoned for his outspoken pacifism. |
| Ludwig Wittgenstein (Austrian-born British) | 1889–1951 | Studied the relationship between language and the world. |
| Jean-Paul Sartre (French) | 1905–1980 | Philosopher, novelist, and leading existentialist. |
| Simone de Beauvoir (French) | 1908–1986 | Leading feminist philosopher. |

## KEY AUTHORS

Franz Kafka

Gabriel García Márquez

| NAME (NATIONALITY) | DATES | FAMOUS WORK |
|---|---|---|
| Madame de la Fayette (French) | 1634–1693 | La Princesse de Clèves |
| Jonathan Swift (Irish) | 1667–1745 | Gulliver's Travels |
| Johann Wolfgang von Goethe (German) | 1749–1832 | Faust |
| Jane Austen (English) | 1775–1817 | Pride and Prejudice |
| Mary Shelley (English) | 1797–1851 | Frankenstein |
| Victor Hugo (French) | 1802–1885 | Les Misérables |
| Hans Christian Andersen (Danish) | 1805–1875 | The Emperor's New Clothes |
| Charles Dickens (English) | 1812–1870 | Oliver Twist |
| George Eliot (English) | 1819–1880 | Middlemarch |
| Herman Melville (American) | 1819–1891 | Moby Dick |
| Fyodor Dostoyevsky (Russian) | 1821–1881 | Crime and Punishment |
| Leo Tolstoy (Russian) | 1828–1910 | War and Peace |
| Émile Zola (French) | 1840–1902 | Germinal |
| Robert Louis Stevenson (Scottish) | 1850–1894 | Treasure Island |
| James Joyce (Irish) | 1882–1941 | Ulysses |
| Virginia Woolf (English) | 1882–1941 | To the Lighthouse |
| Franz Kafka (Czech) | 1883–1924 | The Trial |
| F. Scott Fitzgerald (American) | 1896–1940 | The Great Gatsby |
| Ernest Hemingway (American) | 1899–1961 | For Whom the Bell Tolls |
| Vladimir Nabokov (Russian-born American) | 1899–1977 | Lolita |
| John Steinbeck (American) | 1902–1968 | Of Mice and Men |
| George Orwell (English) | 1903–1950 | Animal Farm |
| Graham Greene (English) | 1904–1991 | Brighton Rock |
| Albert Camus (French) | 1913–1960 | The Outsider |
| Italo Calvino (Italian) | 1923–1985 | The Path to the Nest of Spiders |
| Yukio Mishima (Japanese) | 1925–1970 | The Sound of Waves |
| Günter Grass (German) | b.1927 | The Tin Drum |
| Gabriel García Márquez (Colombian) | b.1928 | One Hundred Years of Solitude |
| Toni Morrison (American) | b.1931 | Beloved |
| Salman Rushdie (Indian-born British) | b.1947 | Midnight's Children |

## NOBEL PEACE PRIZES

Established in 1901, Nobel prizes are given annually for outstanding contributions to the fields of economics, physics, chemistry, physiology, literature, and peace. Recent winners of the Nobel Peace Prize are listed below.

Nobel Peace Prize

| NAME (NATIONALITY) | YEAR | WORK |
|---|---|---|
| United Nations Peacekeeping Forces | 1988 | Peacekeeping role. |
| Tenzin Gyatso (Tibetan) | 1989 | Leading Tibet as the Dalai Lama. |
| Mikhail Gorbachev (Russian) | 1990 | Assisting the end of the Cold War. |
| Aung San Suu Kyi (Burmese) | 1991 | Campaigning for democracy. |
| Rigoberta Menchú (Guatemalan) | 1992 | Campaigning for human rights. |
| Nelson Mandela and Frederik Willem de Klerk (South African) | 1993 | Assisting peace between the ANC and the Republic of South Africa. |
| Yasser Arafat (Palestinian), Shimon Peres, and Yitzhak Rabin (Israelis) | 1994 | Assisting peace between the PLO and Israel. |
| Joseph Rotblat (English) and the Pugwash Conferences | 1995 | Reducing the status of nuclear arms in international politics. |
| Carlos Filipe Ximenes Belo and José Ramos-Horta (Indonesian) | 1996 | Helping to bring peace to the conflict in East Timor. |
| International Campaign to Ban Land-mines and Jody Williams (American) | 1997 | Banning and clearing of anti-personnel mines. |
| John Hume (Irish) and David Trimble (Irish) | 1998 | Assisting peace process in Northern Ireland. |

## KEY POETS

| NAME (NATIONALITY) | DATES | FAMOUS WORK |
|---|---|---|
| Homer (Greek) | c.800 bc | The Iliad |
| Virgil (Roman) | 70–19 bc | The Aeneid |
| Dante Alighieri (Italian) | 1265–1321 | The Divine Comedy |
| Geoffrey Chaucer (English) | 1340–1400 | The Canterbury Tales |
| Luis de Camões (Portuguese) | 1524–1580 | The Lusiads |
| John Donne (English) | 1573–1631 | Divine Sonnets |
| John Milton (English) | 1608–1674 | Paradise Lost |
| Alexander Pope (English) | 1688–1744 | An Essay on Man |
| William Blake (English) | 1757–1827 | Songs of Innocence |
| Robert Burns (Scottish) | 1759–1796 | Tam o' Shanter |
| William Wordsworth (English) | 1770–1850 | The Prelude |
| George Byron (English) | 1788–1824 | Don Juan |
| Aleksander Pushkin (Russian) | 1799–1837 | Eugene Onegin |
| Emily Dickinson (American) | 1830–1886 | Bolts of Melody |
| Rabindranath Tagore (Indian) | 1861–1941 | Gitanjali |
| Hagiwara Sakutaro (Japanese) | 1886–1942 | Howling at the Moon |
| T. S. Eliot (American-born English) | 1888–1965 | The Waste Land |
| Jorge Luis Borges (Argentinian) | 1899–1986 | Labyrinths |
| John Betjeman (English) | 1906–1984 | Slough |
| Octavio Paz (Mexican) | 1914–1998 | Sunstone |
| Ted Hughes (English) | 1930–1998 | Birthday Letters |

Ted Hughes

Emily Dickinson

# HISTORY

THIS SECTION describes key events in world history from the earliest civilizations to the present day. Tables list the world's great leaders, and a comparative timeline shows what was happening in each continent at any one time.

## EGYPTIAN PERIODS AND DYNASTIES

Egyptian mummy case

| PERIOD | DATE | MAIN PHARAOH(S) |
|---|---|---|
| Early Dynastic | c.3000–c.2650 BC | Narmer (Menes) |
| Old Kingdom | c.2650–c.2160 BC | Zoser |
| | | Khufu |
| First Intermediate Period | c.2160–c.2100 BC | |
| Middle Kingdom | c.2100–c.1786 BC | Mentuhotep II |
| Second Intermediate Period | c.1786–c.1550 BC | Hyksos rule |
| New Kingdom | c.1550–c.1050 BC | Amenhotep I |
| | | Queen Hatshepsut |
| | | Thutmose III |
| | | Tutankhamun |
| | | Rameses II |
| Third Intermediate Period | c.1050–667 BC | Nubian rule |
| Late period | c.664–333 BC | Darius III |
| Foreign rulers | 332–30 BC | Alexander the Great |
| | | Ptolemy I Soter |
| | | Queen Cleopatra VII |

## CHINESE DYNASTIES AND REPUBLICS

| DATE (AD) | DYNASTY |
|---|---|
| 220–265 | Three Kingdoms |
| 265–316 | Western Chin |
| 316–420 | Eastern Chin |
| 420–589 | Southern |
| 589–618 | Sui |
| 618–690 | T'ang |
| 690–705 | Chou |
| 705–906 | T'ang |
| 906–960 | Northern Five, Southern Ten |
| 960–1279 | Song (Sung) |
| 1279–1368 | Yuan (Mongol) |
| 1368–1644 | Ming |
| 1644–1911 | Manchu (Qing) |
| 1911–1949 | Republic (Nationalist) |
| 1949– | People's Republic (Communist) |

## KEY POPES

| REIGN (AD) | POPE |
|---|---|
| c.42–67 | St. Peter |
| 88–97 | St. Clement I |
| 254–257 | St. Stephen I |
| 440–461 | St. Leo I, the Great |
| 590–604 | St. Gregory I, the Great |
| 1073–1085 | St. Gregory VII |
| 1088–1099 | Urban II |
| 1198–1216 | Innocent III |
| 1492–1503 | Alexander VI |
| 1534–1549 | Paul III |
| 1572–1585 | Gregory XIII |
| 1846–1878 | Pius IX |
| 1958–1963 | John XXIII |
| 1978– | John Paul II |

## JAPANESE PERIODS

Japanese periods began with the introduction of an emperor figure.

| DATE (AD) | PERIOD |
|---|---|
| 250–710 | Yamato |
| 710–794 | Nara |
| 794–1192 | Heian |
| 1192–1333 | Kamakura |
| 1333–1573 | Muromachi |
| 1573–1616 | Momoyama |
| 1616–1867 | Edo |
| 1868–1912 | Meiji |
| 1912–1926 | Taisho |
| 1926–1989 | Showa |
| 1989– | Heisei |

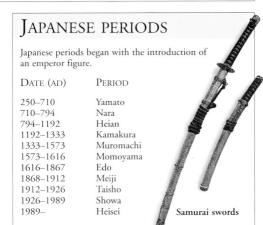
Samurai swords

| | 40,000 BC | 25,000 BC | 10,000 BC | 7000 BC | 3500 BC | 2500 BC |
|---|---|---|---|---|---|---|
| AFRICA | 30,000 BC Disappearance of the Neanderthals<br><br>Neanderthal skull | c.24,000 BC Cave walls painted at the Apollo site in Namibia, southwest Africa<br><br>18,000 BC Settlement of Zaïre, central Africa | 10,000 BC Hunting camps established in Sahara region after Ice Age ends<br><br>c.8000 BC Hunter-gatherers paint human figures on rock in North Africa | 6000 BC Cattle domesticated, Sahara<br><br>Egyptian hieroglyphs | 3000 BC Development of hieroglyphic writing<br><br>2590 BC Building of Great Pyramid of Khufu at Giza | 2500 BC Sahara region begins to dry out<br><br>c.2100 BC–c.1786 BC Middle Kingdom, Egypt<br><br>c.1550 BC–c.1050 BC New Kingdom, Egypt |
| ASIA | 40,000 BC Cro-Magnon humans living at Skhūl and Kafzel (Israel)<br><br>27,000 BC–19,000 BC Female statuettes made at various sites, including locations in Russia | 18,000 BC Coldest point of Ice Age<br><br>14,000 BC–11,000 BC El-Kabareh culture, Israel<br><br>12,500 BC Rise of Magdalenian toolmakers<br><br>10,500 BC Earliest pottery, Japan | 10,000 BC Ice cap retreats<br><br>9000 BC–8000 BC Cereals grown in Jordan and Syria<br><br>8000 BC Jericho, the world's first known city, is founded<br><br>7500 BC Domestication of pigs, Crimea | 5000 BC Rice first cultivated, China<br><br>5000 BC First cities founded in Mesopotamia and Sumer, western Asia<br><br>5000 BC Irrigation systems used, Mesopotamia<br><br>4500 BC Farming begins around River Ganges, India | 3500 BC Mesopotamians invent the wheel<br><br>3250 BC First pictographic writing, Mesopotamia<br><br>c.3000 BC Development of Sumerian cities | 2500 BC Beginning of Indus Valley civilization, Pakistan<br><br>1900 BC Iron Age begins, western Asia<br><br>c.1790 BC Hammurabi becomes King of Babylon<br><br>Terracotta pig, Indus Valley |
| EUROPE | 40,000 BC Cro-Magnons arrive in Europe from Africa<br><br>35,000 BC Earliest figurative art in the Dordogne, France<br><br>35,000 BC Start of Upper Paleolithic period | 15,000 BC Cave paintings, Lascaux, France<br><br>13,000 BC Magdalenian culture; high point of mural art<br><br>11,000 BC Cave paintings, Altamira, Spain | 10,000 BC Ice cap retreats<br><br>8300 BC Retreat of glaciers<br><br>Ice–Age snow knife | 6500 BC Britain separated from mainland Europe as ice melts<br><br>6500 BC First farming communities, southeast Europe<br><br>4500 BC First megalithic tombs, Brittany and Portugal | 2900 BC Danubian culture, central Europe<br><br>c.2800 BC Building of Stonehenge starts, England<br><br>2600 BC Bronze Age reaches Crete | 2500 BC–2200 BC Scandinavian Dolmen period<br><br>2000 BC Beginning of Minoan civilization, Crete<br><br>1600 BC Height of Mycenaean civilization, Greece |
| AMERICAS | 35,000 BC–20,000 BC First humans arrive in North America from Asia | 25,000 BC Cave-dwellers present in Brazil<br><br>15,000 BC Cave art begins in Brazil | 9000 BC First people reach tip of South America<br><br>8000 BC Semi-permanent settlements, North America | 6500 BC Cultivation of potatoes and grain crops, Peru, South America<br><br>5000 BC First settlements in Anáhuac, Mexico | c.3500 BC Maize first cultivated in South America<br><br>3000 BC First pottery in Americas | 2500 BC Earliest large settlements in Andes area<br><br>2000 BC Inuits reach northern Greenland |
| OCEANIA | c.40,000 BC Ancestors of Aboriginals arrive in Australia from Asia | 24,000 BC Earliest known cremation, Australia<br><br>16,000 BC Cave art, north coast of Australia | | 6000 BC New Guinea and Tasmania are separated from Australia as sea level rises | 3000 BC Probable introduction of dogs in Australia | 2000 BC Beginnings of settlement of Melanesia, South Pacific |

# BRITISH RULERS

The list below details the monarchs of England from 1042 until 1603, and subsequent joint British monarchs.

**King Henry VIII**    **Queen Victoria**

## MONARCHS OF ENGLAND

**SAXONS**
| | |
|---|---|
| 1042–1066 | Edward the Confessor |
| 1066 | Harold II |

**NORMANS**
| | |
|---|---|
| 1066–1087 | William the Conqueror |
| 1087–1100 | William II |
| 1100–1135 | Henry I |
| 1135–1154 | Stephen |

**PLANTAGENETS**
| | |
|---|---|
| 1154–1189 | Henry II |
| 1189–1199 | Richard I |
| 1199–1216 | John |
| 1216–1272 | Henry III |
| 1272–1307 | Edward I |
| 1307–1327 | Edward II |
| 1327–1377 | Edward III |
| 1377–1399 | Richard II |

**LANCASTERS**
| | |
|---|---|
| 1399–1413 | Henry IV |
| 1413–1422 | Henry V |
| 1422–1461 | Henry VI |

**YORKS**
| | |
|---|---|
| 1461–1483 | Edward IV |
| 1483 | Edward V |
| 1483–1485 | Richard III |

**TUDORS**
| | |
|---|---|
| 1485–1509 | Henry VII |
| 1509–1547 | Henry VIII |
| 1547–1553 | Edward VI |
| 1553–1558 | Mary I |
| 1558–1603 | Elizabeth I |

## MONARCHS OF BRITAIN

**STUARTS**
| | |
|---|---|
| 1603–1625 | James I (VI of Scotland) |
| 1625–1649 | Charles I |

### COMMONWEALTH

**STUARTS**
| | |
|---|---|
| 1660–1685 | Charles II |
| 1685–1688 | James II |
| 1689–1694 | Mary II |
| 1689–1702 | William III |
| 1702–1714 | Anne |

**HANOVERS**
| | |
|---|---|
| 1714–1727 | George I |
| 1727–1760 | George II |
| 1760–1820 | George III |
| 1820–1830 | George IV |
| 1830–1837 | William IV |

**SAXE-COBURG-GOTHAS**
| | |
|---|---|
| 1837–1901 | Victoria |
| 1901–1910 | Edward VII |

**WINDSORS**
| | |
|---|---|
| 1910–1936 | George V |
| 1936 | Edward VIII |
| 1936–1952 | George VI |
| 1952– | Elizabeth II |

# MONARCHS OF SCOTLAND

The monarchs of Scotland from 1306–1625.

| | |
|---|---|
| 1306–1329 | Robert I, the Bruce |
| 1329–1371 | David II |

**STUARTS**
| | |
|---|---|
| 1371–1390 | Robert II |
| 1390–1406 | Robert III |
| 1406–1437 | James I |
| 1437–1460 | James II |
| 1460–1488 | James III |
| 1488–1513 | James IV |
| 1513–1542 | James V |
| 1542–1567 | Mary, Queen of Scots |
| 1567–1625 | James VI |

# BRITISH PRIME MINISTERS

| | | | |
|---|---|---|---|
| 1828–1830 | Duke of Wellington | 1922–1923 | Andrew Bonar Law |
| 1830–1834 | Earl Grey | 1923–1924 | Stanley Baldwin |
| 1834 | Viscount Melbourne | 1924 | James Ramsay Macdonald |
| 1834–1835 | Robert Peel | 1924–1929 | Stanley Baldwin |
| 1835–1841 | Viscount Melbourne | 1929–1935 | James Ramsay Macdonald |
| 1841–1846 | Robert Peel | 1935–1937 | Stanley Baldwin |
| 1846–1852 | Lord John Russell | 1937–1940 | Neville Chamberlain |
| 1852 | Earl of Derby | 1940–1945 | Winston Churchill |
| 1852–1855 | Earl of Aberdeen | 1945–1951 | Clement Atlee |
| 1855–1858 | Viscount Palmeston | 1951–1955 | Winston Churchill |
| 1858–1859 | Earl of Derby | 1955–1957 | Anthony Eden |
| 1859–1865 | Viscount Palmeston | 1957–1963 | Harold Macmillan |
| 1865–1866 | Earl Russell | 1963–1964 | Alec Douglas-Home |
| 1866–1868 | Earl of Derby | 1964–1970 | Harold Wilson |
| 1868 | Benjamin Disraeli | 1970–1974 | Edward Heath |
| 1868–1874 | William Gladstone | 1974–1976 | Harold Wilson |
| 1874–1880 | Benjamin Disraeli | 1976–1979 | James Callaghan |
| 1880–1885 | William Gladstone | 1979–1990 | Margaret Thatcher |
| 1885–1886 | Marquess of Salisbury | 1990–1997 | John Major |
| 1886 | William Gladstone | 1997– | Tony Blair |
| 1886–1892 | Marquess of Salisbury | | |
| 1892–1894 | William Gladstone | | |
| 1894–1895 | Earl of Rosebery | | |
| 1895–1902 | Marquess of Salisbury | | |
| 1902–1905 | Arthur Balfour | | |
| 1905–1908 | Henry Campbell-Bannerman | | |
| 1908–1916 | Henry Asquith | | |
| 1916–1922 | David Lloyd-George | | |

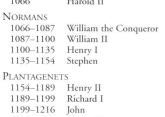

**William Gladstone**

| | 1500 BC | 1000 BC | 600 BC | 300 BC | AD 1 | AD 300 |
|---|---|---|---|---|---|---|
| **AFRICA** | **1300 BC** Temple of Abu Simbel, Nubia, built for Rameses II<br><br>**1218 BC** Sea peoples from the Aegean invade Egypt and the eastern Mediterranean | **900 BC** Foundation of kingdom of Kush in Nubia<br><br>**814 BC** Phoenicians found the city of Carthage, North Africa | **600 BC** Building of Temple of the Sun at Meroë, Sudan<br><br>**500 BC** Beginning of Nok culture in northern Nigeria<br><br>**332 BC** Alexander the Great conquers Egypt | **290 BC** Library founded at Alexandria, Egypt<br><br>**149–146 BC** Rome destroys Carthage in Third Punic War, founding province of Africa | **AD 50** Kingdom of Aksum (Ethiopia) begins to expand<br><br>**AD 150** Mandingos and Berbers dominate Sudan area<br><br>**AD 250** Aksum controls trade in Red Sea | **AD 325** Aksum destroys kingdom of Meroë<br><br>**AD 439** Vandals establish kingdom in northern Africa<br><br>**Gupta coin** |
| **ASIA** | **1400 BC** Chinese capital moved to Anyang<br><br>**1200 BC** Hittite Empire collapses<br><br>**1200 BC** Jews settle in Palestine<br><br>**1100 BC** Phoenicians spread out from eastern Mediterranean | **1000 BC** Kingdom of Israel under King David<br><br>**721–705 BC** Assyrian Empire at its greatest extent<br><br>**604 BC** Nebuchadnezzar II rules Babylonian Empire | **563–486 BC** Life of the Buddha<br><br>**550 BC** Cyrus II founds Persian Empire<br><br>**322 BC** Chandragupta Maurya founds Mauryan Empire<br><br>**Buddhist carving** | **221 BC** Qin Shih Huangdi, the first emperor, unites China<br><br>**185 BC** Bactrians conquer northwest India<br><br>**112 BC** Silk Road opens, giving West some access to China<br><br>**64 BC** Roman general Pompey conquers Syria | **AD 30** Jesus Christ is crucified in Jerusalem, Israel<br><br>**AD 60** Beginning of Kushan Empire, India<br><br>**AD 105** Paper invented, China<br><br>**AD 220** End of Han dynasty, China<br><br>**AD 224** Sassanian dynasty founded in Persia | **AD 320** Chandragupta I founds Gupta Empire in northern India<br><br>**AD 480** End of Gupta Empire<br><br>**AD 520** Decimal number system invented in India<br><br>**AD 550** Buddhism introduced into Japan |
| **EUROPE** | **1500 BC** Beginning of Bronze Age in Scandinavia<br><br>**1450 BC** End of Minoan civilization, Crete<br><br>**1200 BC** Decline of Mycenaean culture, Greece | **1000 BC** Etruscan people found city-states in Italy<br><br>**776 BC** First recorded Olympic Games, Greece<br><br>**753 BC** Rome founded | **509 BC** Roman Republic founded<br><br>**480 BC** Greeks defeat Persians at Battle of Marathon<br><br>**431–404 BC** Peloponnesian War, Greece: Sparta defeats Athens | **216 BC** Hannibal defeats Roman army at Cannae<br><br>**46 BC** Julius Caesar becomes Roman dictator<br><br>**27 BC** Augustus becomes first Roman Emperor | **AD 43** Romans invade Great Britain<br><br>**AD 235–284** Period of civil war in Roman Empire<br><br>**AD 285–305** Emperor Diocletian restores order to Rome | **AD 330** Emperor Constantine founds Constantinople<br><br>**AD 410** Visigoths sack Rome<br><br>**AD 486** Franks control France<br><br>**AD 527** Justinian I becomes Byzantine Emperor |
| **AMERICAS** | **1300 BC** Rise of Olmec civilization in Mexico | **800 BC** Zapotec civilization flourishes in central America | **400 BC** Decline of Olmec civilization, Mexico<br><br>**c.500 BC** Adena people build communal burial mounds, Ohio, USA | **300 BC** Beginning of Early Mayan Period, central America<br><br>**c.200 BC** Nazca civilization, Peru | **AD 1** Beginning of Moche civilization, northern Peru | **AD 500** Hopewell culture at its peak, North America<br><br>**AD 600** Height of Mayan civilization, central America |
| **OCEANIA** | **1300 BC** Settlers reach Fiji (then western Polynesia)<br><br>**Olmec mask** | **1000 BC** Most of Polynesian Islands settled | **500 BC** Trading contacts established in South Pacific islands | **Moche stirrup-spout vessel** | **AD 1–100** Hindu-Buddhists from Asia colonize Sumatra and Java | **AD 300** Settlement of eastern Polynesia |

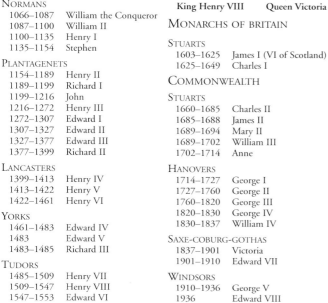

# PRESIDENTS OF THE USA

US presidents are elected to serve a four-year term of office. Since 1951, no president has been allowed to serve more than two terms.

| | |
|---|---|
| 1789–1797 | George Washington |
| 1797–1801 | John Adams |
| 1801–1809 | Thomas Jefferson |
| 1809–1817 | James Madison |
| 1817–1825 | James Monroe |
| 1825–1829 | John Quincy Adams |
| 1829–1837 | Andrew Jackson |
| 1837–1841 | Martin Van Buren |
| 1841 | William H. Harrison |
| 1841–1845 | John Tyler |
| 1845–1849 | James K. Polk |
| 1849–1850 | Zachary Taylor |
| 1850–1853 | Millard Fillmore |
| 1853–1857 | Franklin Pierce |
| 1857–1861 | James Buchanan |
| 1861–1865 | Abraham Lincoln |

| | |
|---|---|
| 1881 | James A. Garfield |
| 1881–1885 | Chester A. Arthur |
| 1885–1889 | S. Grover Cleveland |
| 1889–1893 | Benjamin Harrison |
| 1893–1897 | S. Grover Cleveland |
| 1897–1901 | William McKinley |
| 1901–1909 | Theodore Roosevelt |
| 1909–1913 | William H. Taft |
| 1913–1921 | Woodrow Wilson |
| 1921–1923 | Warren G. Harding |
| 1923–1929 | Calvin Coolidge |
| 1929–1933 | Herbert Hoover |
| 1933–1945 | Franklin D. Roosevelt |
| 1945–1953 | Harry S. Truman |
| 1953–1961 | Dwight D. Eisenhower |
| 1961–1963 | John F. Kennedy |

**John F. Kennedy**

| | |
|---|---|
| 1963–1969 | Lyndon B. Johnson |
| 1969–1974 | Richard Nixon |
| 1974–1977 | Gerald Ford |
| 1977–1981 | Jimmy Carter |
| 1981–1989 | Ronald Reagan |
| 1989–1993 | George Bush |
| 1993– | William Clinton |

**Abraham Lincoln**

| | |
|---|---|
| 1865–1869 | Andrew Johnson |
| 1869–1877 | Ulysses S. Grant |
| 1877–1881 | Rutherford B. Hayes |

# RUSSIAN MONARCHS

Until the Bolshevik Revolution in 1917, Russia was a monarchy in which the Tsar or Tsarina held absolute power. Today, supreme power lies with an elected president.

| | |
|---|---|
| 1462–1505 | Ivan III, the Great |
| 1505–1533 | Basil III |
| 1533–1584 | Ivan IV, the Terrible |
| 1584–1598 | Fyodor I |
| 1598–1605 | Boris Godunov |
| 1605 | Fyodor II |

**Kremlin Cathedral of the Annunciation**

| | |
|---|---|
| 1605–1606 | Demetrius |
| 1606–1610 | Basil IV (Shuiski) |
| 1610–1613 | Interregnum (interval in reigns) |
| 1613–1645 | Michael Romanov |
| 1645–1676 | Alexis |
| 1676–1682 | Fyodor III |
| 1682–1689 | Ivan V and Peter I, the Great |
| 1689–1725 | Peter I, the Great |
| 1725–1727 | Catherine I |
| 1727–1730 | Peter II |
| 1730–1740 | Anna |
| 1740–1741 | Ivan VI |
| 1741–1762 | Elizabeth |
| 1762 | Peter III |
| 1762–1796 | Catherine II, the Great |
| 1796–1801 | Paul I |
| 1801–1825 | Alexander I |
| 1825–1855 | Nicholas I |
| 1855–1881 | Alexander II |
| 1881–1894 | Alexander III |
| 1894–1917 | Nicholas II |
| 1917 | Bolshevik Revolution |

# RUSSIAN LEADERS

| | |
|---|---|
| 1917–1922 | Vladimir Lenin |
| 1922–1953 | Joseph Stalin |
| 1953–1964 | Nikita Khrushchev |
| 1964–1982 | Leonid Brezhnev |
| 1982–1984 | Yuri Andropov |
| 1984–1985 | Konstantin Chernenko |
| 1985–1992 | Mikhail Gorbachev |
| 1992– | Boris Yeltsin |

**Mikhail Gorbachev**

| | 600 | 850 | 1100 | 1175 | 1250 | 1350 |
|---|---|---|---|---|---|---|
| **AFRICA** | **622** Year One of Islamic calendar<br>**637** Muslims conquer Jerusalem<br>**c.700** Kingdom of Ghana prospers, West Africa | **900** Hausa kingdom of Daura founded in northern Nigeria<br>**1054** Ghana conquered by Muslim Almoravid dynasty | **c.1100** First stone settlements in Zimbabwe<br>**1169** Saladin becomes ruler of Egypt | **1187** Saladin recaptures Jerusalem from Crusaders<br>**1235** Sundiata Keita founds Mali Empire, West Africa | **1250** Mamelukes (rebel slave-soldiers) become rulers of Egypt<br>**1291** Saracens recapture the city of Acre, ending the Crusades | **1352** Moroccan scholar Ibn Battuta makes his great journey across Sahara to Mali<br>**1432** Portuguese explorers reach the Azores |
| **ASIA** | **647** Central Asian Hun tribes invade India, causing decline of Gupta Empire<br>**786–809** Harun al-Rashid is caliph of Baghdad<br>**794** Kyoto, ancient capital of Japan, is established | **888** Chola dynasty of Tamil kings replaces the Pallavas in southern India and Sri Lanka<br>**935–41** Civil war in Japan<br>**960** Song dynasty takes over China<br><br>**Chola statue** | **1104** Christian crusaders capture the city of Acre, Israel<br>**1156** Civil war between rival clans in Japan leads to domination by samurai warlords | **1175** Zen Buddhism introduced to Japan<br>**1206** Genghis Khan founds Mongol Empire<br>**1232** Explosive rockets used in war between Chinese and conquering Mongols<br>**1237** Mongol army begins to conquer Russia | **1290** Ottomans (Turkish Muslims) rise to power<br>**c.1294** Persians convert to Islam<br>**1340** Hindu Kushan Empire in India becomes centre of resistance to Islam<br><br>**Mongol quiver** | **1368** Hong Wu (Ming) drives Mongols from China<br>**1397** Mongol leader Tamerlane invades Delhi, India<br>**1404** Chinese admiral Zheng Ho sets off on his first voyage<br>**1405** Fall of Mongol Empire |
| **EUROPE** | **711** Moors invade Spain and Portugal<br>**732** Frankish leader Charles Martel defeats the Moors and halts Islam's spread to Europe<br>**800** Charlemagne is crowned first Holy Roman Emperor<br><br>**Peruvian tapestry** | **843** Kenneth MacAlpine unites Scotland<br>**997** Stephen I becomes first King of Hungary<br>**1000** Viking Leif Eriksson reaches North America<br>**1066** William of Normandy invades England to claim throne<br>**1096** First Crusade begins | **1119** Bologna University founded, Italy<br>**1143** Alfonso Henriques becomes first king of Portugal<br><br>**Toltec pyramid** | **1202–04** Fourth Crusaders sack Constantinople<br>**1209** St. Francis founds Franciscan Order<br>**1215** King John of England seals Magna Carta<br>**1215** St. Dominic founds Dominican Order | **1273** Rudolf Habsburg becomes ruler of Germany, founding the Habsburg dynasty<br>**1337** 100 Years' War begins between England and France<br>**1347** Plague (Black Death) reaches Europe | **1358** The *Jacquerie*: French peasants revolt against raised taxes<br>**1381** Peasants' Revolt in England<br>**1415** Battle of Agincourt: English defeat French<br>**1429** Siege of Orléans, lifted by Joan of Arc's forces |
| **AMERICAS** | **700** Peruvians weave wool tapestries | **980** Toltecs set up capital at Tula, Mexico<br>**1000** Chimu civilization founded, Peru | **1151** Fall of Toltec Empire in Mexico | **c.1200** Cuzco, Peru, becomes an Inca centre<br>**c.1200** First farmers settle along Mississippi banks | **c.1250** Mayans build new capital at Mayapán<br>**1325** Aztecs found their capital at Tenochtitlán | **1350** Acamapitzin becomes Aztec ruler<br>**1438** Inca overlord Pachacuti enlarges Inca Empire |
| **OCEANIA** | **c.700** Easter Islanders begin to build stone ceremonial platforms | **950** Polynesian navigator Kupe arrives in New Zealand<br>**c.1000** Maoris in New Zealand | **1100s** Giant carved stone statues first erected on Easter Island, South Pacific | | **c.1250** Religious assembly platforms built throughout Polynesian Islands | **1350** Maoris create rock art in New Zealand |

# FRENCH MONARCHS

## CAROLINGIAN
| | |
|---|---|
| 936–954 | Louis IV |
| 954–986 | Lothair |
| 986–987 | Louis V |

## CAPET
| | |
|---|---|
| 987–996 | Hugh Capet |
| 996–1031 | Robert II |
| 1031–1060 | Henry I |
| 1060–1108 | Philip I |
| 1108–1137 | Louis VI |
| 1137–1180 | Louis VII |
| 1180–1223 | Philip II |
| 1223–1226 | Louis VIII |
| 1226–1270 | Louis IX |
| 1270–1285 | Philip III |
| 1285–1314 | Philip IV |
| 1314–1316 | Louis X |
| 1316 | John I |
| 1316–1322 | Philip V |
| 1322–1328 | Charles IV |

## VALOIS
| | |
|---|---|
| 1328–1350 | Philip VI |
| 1350–1364 | John II |
| 1364–1380 | Charles V |
| 1380–1422 | Charles VI |
| 1422–1461 | Charles VII |
| 1461–1483 | Louis XI |
| 1483–1498 | Charles VIII |
| 1498–1515 | Louis XII |
| 1515–1547 | Francis I |
| 1547–1559 | Henry II |
| 1559–1560 | Francis II |
| 1560–1574 | Charles IX |
| 1574–1589 | Henry III |

## BOURBON
| | |
|---|---|
| 1589–1610 | Henry IV |
| 1610–1643 | Louis XIII |
| 1643–1715 | Louis XIV |
| 1715–1774 | Louis XV |
| 1774–1792 | Louis XVI |

## 1792–1804 FIRST REPUBLIC

## FIRST EMPIRE
| | |
|---|---|
| 1804–1814 | Napoleon I |

Henry IV

## BOURBON
| | |
|---|---|
| 1814–1824 | Louis XVIII |
| 1824–1830 | Charles X |
| 1830–1848 | Louis Philippe |

## 1848–1852 SECOND REPUBLIC

## SECOND EMPIRE
| | |
|---|---|
| 1852–1870 | Napoleon III |

Napoleon I

# FRENCH PRESIDENTS

## THIRD REPUBLIC
| | |
|---|---|
| 1871–1873 | Adolphe Thiers |
| 1873–1879 | Patrice de MacMahon |
| 1879–1887 | Jules Grévy |
| 1887–1894 | Marie François Sadi-Carnot |
| 1894–1895 | Jean Casimir-Périer |
| 1895–1899 | François Félix Faure |
| 1899–1906 | Emile Loubet |
| 1906–1913 | Armand Fallières |
| 1913–1920 | Raymond Poincaré |
| 1920 | Paul Deschanel |
| 1920–1924 | Alexandre Millerand |
| 1924–1931 | Gaston Doumergue |
| 1931–1932 | Paul Doumer |
| 1932–1940 | Albert Lebrun |

## VICHY GOVERNMENT
| | |
|---|---|
| 1940–1944 | Henri Philippe Pétain |

## PROVISIONAL GOVERNMENT
| | |
|---|---|
| 1944–1946 | Charles de Gaulle |
| 1946 | Félix Gouin |
| 1946 | Georges Bidault |

## FOURTH REPUBLIC
| | |
|---|---|
| 1947–1954 | Vincent Auriol |
| 1954–1959 | René Coty |

## FIFTH REPUBLIC
| | |
|---|---|
| 1959–1969 | Charles de Gaulle |
| 1969–1974 | Georges Pompidou |
| 1974–1981 | Valéry Giscard d'Estaing |
| 1981–1995 | François Mitterand |
| 1995– | Jacques Chirac |

Jacques Chirac

# SPANISH MONARCHS

| | |
|---|---|
| 1479–1516 | Ferdinand II of Aragon |
| 1474–1504 | Isabella of Castile |

## HABSBURG
| | |
|---|---|
| 1516–1556 | Charles I |
| 1556–1598 | Philip II |
| 1598–1621 | Philip III |
| 1621–1665 | Philip IV |
| 1665–1700 | Charles II |

## BOURBON
| | |
|---|---|
| 1700–1724 | Philip V (abdicated) |
| 1724 | Louis I |
| 1724–1746 | Philip V (restored) |
| 1746–1759 | Ferdinand VI |
| 1759–1788 | Charles III |
| 1788–1808 | Charles IV |
| 1808 | Ferdinand VII |
| 1808–1813 | Joseph Bonaparte |
| 1814–1833 | Ferdinand VII |
| 1833–1868 | Isabella II |
| 1870–1873 | Amadeus of Savoy |

## 1873–1874 FIRST REPUBLIC

## BOURBON
| | |
|---|---|
| 1874–1885 | Alfonso XII |
| 1885–1886 | Maria Cristina (Regent) |
| 1886–1931 | Alfonso XIII |

## 1931–1939 SECOND REPUBLIC
| | |
|---|---|
| 1939–1975 | Francisco Franco (Dictator) |

## BOURBON
| | |
|---|---|
| 1975– | Juan Carlos |

Ferdinand of Aragon and Isabella of Castile

| | 1450 | 1500 | 1550 | 1600 | 1640 | 1700 |
|---|---|---|---|---|---|---|
| **AFRICA** | **1464** Sonni Ali becomes ruler of Songhai, West Africa / **1488** Portuguese navigator Bartholomeu Diaz rounds Cape of Good Hope, South Africa | **1500s** Bantus in southern Africa trade with Europeans / **1500s** Hausa states develop in West Africa / **1517** Egypt and Syria conquered by Ottomans | **1591** Moroccans and European mercenaries destroy Songhai Empire / **Ottoman plate** | **1600s** All major European powers establish trading posts on African coast | **1651** Dutch found Cape colony in southern Africa / **1690s** Ashanti kingdom established on Gold Coast, Africa / **Ashanti golden eagles** | **1712** Rise of Futa Jalon kingdom in West Africa |
| **ASIA** | **1453** Constantinople falls, ending Byzantine Empire / **1467** Onin War, lasting over 100 years, begins in Japan | **1502** Safavid dynasty begins in Persia / **1520–21** Portuguese traders reach China / **1526** Babur becomes first Mughal Emperor of India / **1546** Burma united under King Tabin Shweti | **1566** Height of Ottoman Empire / **1577** Akbar the Great completes unification of northern India / **1592** Japan invades Korea under commander Hideyoshi | **1603** Tokugawa brings peace to Japan / **1602** Dutch East India company founded / **1632** Building of Taj Mahal begins, India / **1639** Japan closed to foreigners | **1644** Manchu (Qing) dynasty founded, China / **1658** Reign of Aurangzeb, last great Mughal emperor, begins in India / **1688** Genroku period begins, Japan / **Louis XIV of France** | **1707** Fall of Mughal Empire / **1727** Coffee first grown, Brazil / **1727** Border fixed between Russia and China / **1746** War between British and French colonists, India |
| **EUROPE** | **Gutenberg Bible** / **1450s** Johannes Gutenberg produces first printed books in Europe | **c.1503** Leonardo da Vinci paints *Mona Lisa* / **1512** Michelangelo completes ceiling of Sistine Chapel / **1517** Protestant Reformation / **1520** Suleiman I begins reign over Ottoman Empire / **1533** Ivan IV, the Terrible begins reign, Russia | **1572** St. Bartholomew's Day massacre of Protestants, France / **1579** Seven provinces unite in Union of Utrecht, Netherlands / **1588** English fleet defeats Spanish Armada / **1598** Edict of Nantes, France, gives Catholics and Huguenots equal rights | **1603** James VI unites Scotland and England / **1604** Russians settle in Siberia / **1610** Assassination of King Henry IV of France / **1618** Beginning of Thirty Years War, Europe | **1642–49** English Civil War, ending in the execution of King Charles I / **1643** Louis XIV begins reign, France / **1677** Ottoman Empire at war with Russia / **1682** Peter the Great begins reign, Russia | **1700** Great Northern War, Scandinavia / **1700s** Enlightenment begins / **1701–13** War of Spanish Succession / **1740** Frederick the Great becomes King of Prussia / **1741** Vitus Bering explores strait between Russia and Alaska |
| **AMERICAS** | **1492** Christopher Columbus arrives in the Caribbean / **1499** Amerigo Vespucci explores the Amazon | **1519** Ferdinand Magellan sails across Pacific Ocean / **1534** Jacques Cartier sails St. Lawrence River, Canada | **1579** Francis Drake establishes British claim to west coast of North America | **1609** Henry Hudson sails up Hudson River / **1620** *Mayflower* sails to America from England | **1675** War between colonists and Native Americans devastates New England | **1709** Mass emigration of Germans to America begins / **1739** Slave uprising in South Carolina |
| **OCEANIA** | **c.1450** Tongo people their ceremonial centre, South Pacific | **1526** Portuguese landings in Polynesia | **1567** Spanish explorer Mendaña is first European to reach Soloman Islands | **1606** Luis Vaez de Torres sails between Australia and New Guinea | **1642** Explorer Abel Tasman reaches Tasmania and New Zealand | **1722** Dutch navigator Jacob Roggeveen reaches Samoa and Easter Island |

# AUSTRALIAN PRIME MINISTERS

| | | | |
|---|---|---|---|
| 1901–1903 | Edmund Barton | 1941–1945 | John J. Curtin |
| 1903–1904 | Alfred Deakin | 1945 | Francis M. Forde |
| 1904 | John C. Watson | 1945–1949 | Joseph B. Chifley |
| 1904–1905 | George Houston Reid | 1949–1966 | Robert G. Menzies |
| 1905–1908 | Alfred Deakin | 1966–1967 | Harold E. Holt |
| 1908–1909 | Andrew Fisher | 1967–1968 | John McEwen |
| 1909–1910 | Alfred Deakin | 1968–1971 | John Grey Gorton |
| 1910–1913 | Andrew Fisher | 1971–1972 | William McMahon |
| 1913–1914 | Joseph Cook | 1972–1975 | E. Gough Whitlam |
| 1914–1915 | Andrew Fisher | 1975–1983 | J. Malcolm Fraser |
| 1915–1923 | William M. Hughes | 1983–1991 | Robert Hawke |
| 1923–1929 | Stanley M. Bruce | 1991–1996 | Paul J. Keating |
| 1929–1932 | James H. Scullin | 1996– | John Howard |
| 1932–1939 | Joseph A. Lyons | | |
| 1939 | Earle Page | | |
| 1939–1941 | Robert G. Menzies | | |
| 1941 | Arthur W. Fadden | | |

**Robert Menzies**

# NEW ZEALAND PRIME MINISTERS

| | | | | | |
|---|---|---|---|---|---|
| 1856 | Henry Sewell | 1879–82 | John Hall | 1935–40 | Michael J. Savage |
| 1856 | William Fox | 1882–83 | Frederick Whitaker | 1940–49 | Peter Fraser |
| 1856–61 | Edward W. Stafford | 1883–84 | Harry A. Atkinson | 1949–57 | Sidney G. Holland |
| 1861–62 | William Fox | 1884 | Robert Stout | 1957 | Keith J. Holyoake |
| 1862–63 | Alfred Domett | 1884 | Harry A. Atkinson | 1957–60 | Walter Nash |
| 1863–64 | Frederick Whitaker | 1884–87 | Robert Stout | 1960–72 | Keith J. Holyoake |
| 1864–65 | Frederick A. Weld | 1887–91 | Harry A. Atkinson | 1972 | John Marshall |
| 1865–69 | Edward W. Stafford | 1891–93 | John Ballance | 1972–74 | Norman Kirk |
| 1869–72 | Willliam Fox | 1893–06 | Richard J. Seddon | 1974–75 | Wallace E. Rowling |
| 1872 | Edward W. Stafford | 1906 | William Hall-Jones | 1975–84 | Robert D. Muldoon |
| 1872–73 | George M. Waterhouse | 1906–12 | Joseph G. Ward | 1984–89 | David Lange |
| 1873 | William Fox | 1912 | Thomas Mackenzie | 1989–90 | Geoffrey Palmer |
| 1873–75 | Julius Vogel | 1912–25 | William F. Massey | 1990 | Michael Moore |
| 1875–76 | Daniel Pollen | 1925 | Francis H. Bell | 1990– | James Bolger |
| 1876 | Julius Vogel | 1925–28 | Joseph G. Coates | | |
| 1876–77 | Harry A. Atkinson | 1928–30 | Joseph G. Ward | | |
| 1877–79 | George Grey | 1930–35 | George W. Forbes | | |

# CANADIAN PRIME MINISTERS

| | |
|---|---|
| 1867–1873 | John A. Macdonald |
| 1873–1878 | Alexander Mackenzie |
| 1878–1891 | John A. Macdonald |
| 1891–1892 | John J.C. Abbott |
| 1892–1894 | John S. Thompson |
| 1894–1896 | Mackenzie Bowell |
| 1896 | Charles Tupper |
| 1896–1911 | Wilfred Laurier |
| 1911–1920 | Robert Laird Borden |
| 1920–1921 | Arthur Meighen |
| 1921–1926 | W. L. Mackenzie King |
| 1926 | Arthur Meighen |
| 1926–1930 | W. L. Mackenzie King |
| 1930–1935 | Richard B. Bennett |
| 1935–1948 | W. L. Mackenzie King |
| 1948–1957 | Louis St. Laurent |
| 1957–1963 | John G. Diefenbaker |
| 1963–1968 | Lester B. Pearson |
| 1968–1979 | Pierre E. Trudeau |
| 1979–1980 | C. Joseph Clark |
| 1980–1984 | Pierre E. Trudeau |
| 1984 | John N. Turner |
| 1984–1993 | M. Brian Mulroney |
| 1993 | Kim Campbell |
| 1993– | Jean Chrétien |

**Pierre Trudeau**

| | 1750 | 1790 | 1830 | 1845 | 1860 | 1880 |
|---|---|---|---|---|---|---|
| **AFRICA** | **1768** Ali Bey becomes ruler of independent Egypt<br><br>**Tibetan mask** | **1822** Liberia founded as a home for freed slaves<br><br>**1824–27** First Ashanti War between British and Ashanti of Gold Coast, Ghana | **1830** British and Boers clash in South Africa<br><br>**1830** French invade Algeria<br><br>**1836** Great Trek of Boer farmers, South Africa | **1847** British defeat Bantus in southern Africa<br><br>**1855** David Livingstone arrives in Victoria Falls; this sparks off European exploration of African interior | **1869** Suez Canal opens<br><br>**1879** Zulu War: British defeat Zulus, South Africa<br><br>**Zulu shield** | **1880–81** First Boer War<br><br>**1895–96** Italy and Ethiopia at war: Ethiopia wins<br><br>**1899–1902** Second Boer War: Britain wins control of South Africa |
| **ASIA** | **1751** China conquers Tibet<br><br>**1757** Battle of Plassey: British conquer Bengal | **1819** Singapore founded by Stamford Raffles<br><br>**1824** Britain and Burma at war | **1839** Treaty of Nanking opens Chinese ports to British trade and gives Hong Kong to Britain | **1853** USA forces Japan to open up to foreign trade<br><br>**1857–58** Indian Mutiny: Indian soldiers in British army rebel against the British | **1861** Empress Tze Hsi begins 47-year rule of China<br><br>**1872** Samurai's feudal control in Japan ends | **1885** Indian National Congress Party founded<br><br>**1899–1900** Boxer Rebellion of Chinese peasants |
| **EUROPE** | **1756–63** Seven Years' War<br><br>**1762** Catherine the Great begins reign in Russia<br><br>**1771** Russia conquers Crimea<br><br>**1789** Storming of the Bastille; French Revolution underway | **1800** Union of Britain and Ireland<br><br>**1804** Napoleon Bonaparte becomes Emperor of France<br><br>**1792–1815** Napoleonic wars<br><br>**1815** Battle of Waterloo ends Napoleon's reign | **1830** July Revolution overthrows Charles X of France<br><br>**1832** First Reform Act extends voting rights in Britain<br><br>**1837** Queen Victoria begins reign, Britain<br><br>**French soldier's hat** | **1845** Potato famine begins in Ireland<br><br>**1848** Year of Revolution in Europe<br><br>**1853–56** Crimean War: Britain and France defeat Russia<br><br>**1859–61** War of Italian unification | **1864** International Red Cross founded<br><br>**1866** Austro–Prussian War<br><br>**1870–71** Franco–Prussian War: France defeated<br><br>**1871** Britain legalizes trade unions<br><br>**1871** Otto von Bismarck unites German Empire | **1884** Berlin conference decides colonial divisions in Africa<br><br>**1896** Modern Olympic Games begin in Greece<br><br>**1897** Greece and Turkey at war<br><br>**Native American warrior's weapons** |
| **AMERICAS** | **1759** Battle of Quebec<br><br>**1763** Native American uprising against British, North America<br><br>**1775–83** American Revolution<br><br>**1776** Declaration of Independence signed, USA | **1791** Revolution in Haiti led by Pierre Toussaint L'Ouverture<br><br>**1810–22** Many South American countries gain independence<br><br>**1812–14** Anglo–American war | **1832** Samuel Morse invents electric telegraph<br><br>**1836** Texas wins independence from Mexico<br><br>**1842** General anaesthetic first used by US surgeon Crawford Long | **1846–48** Mexican–American War: USA victorious<br><br>**1848** Californian Gold Rush<br><br>**1848** First US women's rights convention, New York State | **1861–65** American Civil War<br><br>**1867** Dominion of Canada created<br><br>**1876** Battle of Little Bighorn: Native Americans defeat US Army | **1890** Battle of Wounded Knee: last massacre of Native Americans in USA<br><br>**1896** Gold struck in Klondike, Canada<br><br>**1898** Spanish–American War |
| **OCEANIA** | **1769** James Cook claims New Zealand & Australia for Britain<br><br>**1788** British colony of New South Wales founded, Australia | **1817** First European free emigrants arrive to settle Australian grasslands | **1840** British and Maoris in New Zealand sign Treaty of Waitangi | **1850** Australian Colonies Act<br><br>**1851** Australian Gold Rush | **1860–70** Maoris fight white settlers in New Zealand | **1893** New Zealand becomes first country to give women the right to vote |

# MAJOR WARS

| DATE | CONFLICT | VICTOR(S) | LOSER(S) |
|---|---|---|---|
| c.1096–1291 | Crusades | Muslims | European Christians |
| c.1337–1453 | Hundred Years' War | France | England |
| 1455–1485 | Wars of the Roses | House of Lancaster | House of York |
| 1618–1648 | Thirty Years' War | European Protestants | European Catholics |
| 1642–1649 | English Civil War | Parlimentarians | Royalists |
| 1700–1721 | Great Northern War | Russia | Sweden |
| 1701–1713 | War of the Spanish Succession | Austria | France |
| 1756–1763 | Seven Years War | Britain, Prussia, Hanover | Austria, France Russia, Sweden |
| 1792–1815 | Napoleonic Wars | Austria, Britain, Russia, Prussia, Sweden | France |
| 1812–1814 | War of 1812 | USA | Britain |
| 1846–1848 | Mexican–American War | USA | Mexico |
| 1853–1856 | Crimean War | Britain, France, Sardinia, Turkey | Russia |
| 1861–1865 | American Civil War | Unionists | Confederates |
| 1870–1871 | Franco–Prussian War | Prussia | France |
| 1880–1902 | Boer Wars | British Commonwealth | Boers |
| 1894–1895 | Chinese–Japanese War | Japan | China |
| 1904–1905 | Russo–Japanese War | Japan | Russia |
| 1914–1918 | World War I | British Commonwealth, Belgium, Italy, France, Russia, USA | Germany, Austria, Hungary, Turkey |
| 1931–1933 | Chinese–Japanese War | Japan | China |
| 1936–1939 | Spanish Civil War | Nationalists | Republicans |
| 1939–1945 | World War II | British Commonwealth, USSR, USA | Germany, Italy, Japan |
| 1950–1953 | Korean War | South Korea, UN | North Korea |
| 1954–1975 | Vietnam War | North Vietnam | South Vietnam, USA |
| 1967 | Six-Day War | Israel | Egypt |
| 1967–1970 | Nigerian Civil War | Federalists | Biafrans |
| 1973 | October War | Israel | Arab Nations |
| 1980–1988 | Iran–Iraq War | Negotiated ceasefire | |
| 1990–1991 | Gulf War | UN forces | Iraq |
| 1992–1995 | Bosnian Civil War | Negotiated ceasefire | |

# MAJOR REVOLUTIONS

| DATE | REVOLUTION | VICTOR(S) | LOSER(S) |
|---|---|---|---|
| 1775–1783 | American | American colonies | Britain |
| 1789 | French | Jacobins | Royalists |
| 1917 | Russian | Bolsheviks | Royalists |
| 1945–1949 | Chinese | Communists | Nationalists |

# MAJOR BATTLES

| DATE | NAME (COUNTRY) | VICTOR(S) | LOSER(S) |
|---|---|---|---|
| 1066 | Hastings (England) | Normans | Saxons |
| 1415 | Agincourt (France) | England | France |
| 1429 | Siege of Orléans (France) | France | England |
| 1571 | Lepanto | Christians | Turks |
| 1588 | Spanish Armada (England) | England | Spain |
| 1757 | Plassey (India) | Britain | India |
| 1777 | Saratoga (USA) | USA | Britain |
| 1805 | Trafalgar | Britain | France, Spain |
| 1805 | Austerlitz (Czech Republic) | France | Austria, Russia |
| 1815 | Waterloo (Belgium) | Britain, Holland, Belgium, Prussia | France |
| 1854 | Balaclava (Crimea) | Britain | Russia |
| 1863 | Gettysburg (USA) | Unionists | Confederates |
| 1940 | Britain | Britain | Germany |
| 1942 | Midway (Pacific) | USA | Japan |
| 1943 | Stalingrad (Russia) | USSR | Germany |
| 1944 | Normandy (France) | USA, British Commonwealth | Germany |
| 1954 | Dien Bien Phu (Vietnam) | Vietnam | France |
| 1991 | Operation Desert Storm (Iraq) | UN forces | Iraq |

| | 1900 | 1911 | 1918 | 1930 | 1939 | 1942 |
|---|---|---|---|---|---|---|
| **AFRICA** | **1902** Ovimbundu people of Angola revolt against Portuguese rule<br><br>**1910** Union of South Africa formed from former Boer republics | **1912** African National Congress formed<br><br>**1917** Revolt against French rule; Chad forces three-year French withdrawal | **1922** Discovery of tomb of Tutankhamun, Egypt<br><br>**1922** Egypt wins independence from Britain<br><br>**1923** Ethiopia joins League of Nations | **1930** Ras Tafari is crowned Haile Selassie in Ethiopia<br><br>**1935** Italy invades Ethiopia<br><br>**Haile Selassie** | **1941** Allied troops overrun Italy's African colonies<br><br>**1941** German troops led by Erwin Rommel arrive in Libya to help Italy | **1942** Allied troops arrive in El Alamein, Egypt, and force Rommel's troops to retreat across North Africa<br><br>**1945** League of Arab States founded |
| **ASIA** | **1901** Peace of Peking ends Boxer Rebellion in China<br><br>**1904–1905** Japan wins Russo–Japanese War | **1911** Chinese Revolution overthrows Manchu dynasty<br><br>**1915** Mohandas Gandhi becomes leader of the Indian National Congress Party | **1919** Amritsar Massacre: British fire on peaceful Indian protest<br><br>**1923** Ottoman Empire ends | **1931–33** Chinese–Japanese War: Japan victorious<br><br>**1934–35** Long March in China | **1941–42** Japan takes over US, British, and Dutch colonies in Indian and Pacific Oceans | **1944** Japan attacks India but is defeated at Kohima<br><br>**1945** USA drops first atomic bombs on Japanese cities of Hiroshima and Nagasaki |
| **EUROPE** | **1903** Militant women's suffrage, UK<br><br>**1904** "Entente Cordiale" (friendly understanding) between Britain and France<br><br>**1905** Imperial troops crush workers' uprising, Russia<br><br>**1905** Norway becomes independent | **1912–13** Balkan Wars<br><br>**1914–18** World War I<br><br>**1916** Irish rising against British rule<br><br>**1917** Russian Revolution: Russia becomes first communist state<br><br>**Russian flag** | **1918–21** Russian Civil War<br><br>**1923** Ireland wins partial independence from Britain<br><br>**1924** Stalin becomes leader of USSR<br><br>**1926** General strike in Britain | **1933** Adolf Hitler becomes German Chancellor<br><br>**1936** Germany hosts Olympic Games in Berlin<br><br>**1936** Italy signs alliance with Germany<br><br>**1936–39** Spanish Civil War<br><br>**1938** Germany takes over Czechoslovakia | **1939–45** World War II<br><br>**1940** Germany occupies Denmark, Norway, France, Belgium, and the Netherlands<br><br>**1940** British air force prevents German invasion of Britain<br><br>**1941** Germans move into Eastern Europe | **1943** Allies invade Italy<br><br>**1943–44** Germans driven out of Russia<br><br>**1944** Allies invade France and drive back Germans<br><br>**1945** German forces surrender<br><br>**Nazi flag bearer** |
| **AMERICAS** | **1902** British and German fleets seize Venezuelan navy<br><br>**1906** Earthquake hits San Francisco, USA<br><br>**1909** US explorer Robert Peary claims to have reached North Pole | **1912–33** US troops occupy Nicaragua<br><br>**1914** Panama Canal opens<br><br>**1915–16** US troops put down uprising in Haiti<br><br>**1917** USA joins Britain and France in World War I | **1920** Women gain vote in USA<br><br>**1920** Sale of alcohol prohibited in USA<br><br>**1924** US military planes make first airborne trip around the world<br><br>**1929** Wall Street Crash | **1931** Canada gains full independence from Britain<br><br>**1931** Empire State Building built, New York<br><br>**1933** Alcohol ban lifted, USA<br><br>**1933** Fulgencio Batista becomes ruler of Cuba | **1940** Xerox machine invented<br><br>**1941** US navy attacked by Japanese planes at Pearl Harbor, Hawaii<br><br>**1941** USA joins Allies in war against Germany and Japan | **1942** Enrico Fermi builds first nuclear reactor, USA<br><br>**1943** Argentine Revolution brings Juan Perón to power<br><br>**1945** USA tests first atomic bomb in New Mexico |
| **OCEANIA** | **1901** Commonwealth of Australia proclaimed<br><br>**Australian coins, 1910** | **1914** Australia and New Zealand join Allies in World War I | **1919** Australia acquires former German colonies in the Pacific<br><br>**1927** Canberra becomes the capital of Australia | **1937** Royal New Zealand Air Force formed | **1939** Australia and New Zealand join Allied forces | **1942** Japanese bomb Darwin Australia, and invade New Guinea and part of Papua |

# BLACK CIVIL RIGHTS

**1600–1810** Ten million Africans are taken to the Americas as slaves

**1823–1833** Anti-slavery society set up in Britain to end slavery in the colonies

**1909** W. E. B. Du Bois (1868–1963) helps found National Association for the Advancement of Coloured People to end racial inequality in the USA

**1912** African National Congress (ANC) founded in South Africa to secure racial equality and black representation in parliament

**1914** Marcus Garvey (1887–1940) founds Universal Negro Improvement Association in Harlem, New York

**1925** A. Philip Randolph (1889–1979) organizes and leads the first successful black trade union

**1950–1959** Apartheid laws set up in South Africa. These discriminate against blacks and "coloureds"

**1954** US Supreme Court rules that segregated education (by colour) is "inherently unequal"

**1955** Martin Luther King (1929–68) organizes campaign to desegregate bus service in Montgomery, Alabama

**1960** 69 people die in the Sharpeville Massacre during a protest against South Africa's racist "Pass Laws"

**1964** Nelson Mandela (b. 1918), leader of military wing of ANC, jailed for life in South Africa

**1965–1968** US Congress outlaws discrimination. Martin Luther King is assassinated in 1968

**1989** F. W. De Klerk, president of South Africa, lifts ban on ANC and releases Nelson Mandela (1990)

**1994** First all-party elections take place in South Africa. Nelson Mandela becomes president

Nelson Mandela, voting in 1994 election in South Africa

# WOMEN'S VOTING RIGHTS

Although not a country, the Isle of Man was the first place to give women the vote in 1880. Certain states of the USA gave women the vote at earlier dates (Wyoming in 1869, Colorado in 1894, Utah in 1895, and Idaho in 1896), but it was not given nationally until 1920.

| COUNTRY | FIRST VOTE |
| --- | --- |
| New Zealand | 1893 |
| Australia | 1902 |
| Finland | 1906 |
| Norway | 1913 |
| Denmark | 1915 |
| Iceland | 1915 |
| Netherlands | 1917 |
| USSR | 1917 |
| Great Britain | 1918 |
| Austria | 1918 |
| Canada | 1918 |
| Germany | 1918 |
| Poland | 1918 |
| Czechoslovakia | 1920 |

British suffragette, Emmeline Pankhurst

# FIRST WOMEN PRIME MINISTERS AND PRESIDENTS

Indira Gandhi

| NAME | COUNTRY | DATES |
| --- | --- | --- |
| Sirimavo Bandaranaike (PM) | Ceylon (Sri Lanka) | 1960–1965/1970–1977 |
| Indira Gandhi (PM) | India | 1966–1977/1980–1984 |
| Golda Meir (PM) | Israel | 1969–1974 |
| María Estella Perón (President) | Argentina | 1974–1976 |
| Elisabeth Domitien (PM) | Central African Republic | 1975 |
| Margaret Thatcher (PM) | UK | 1979–1990 |
| Dr. Maria de Lurdes Pintassilgo (PM) | Portugal | 1979 |
| Vigdís Finnbogadóttir (President) | Iceland | 1980–1996 |
| Mary Eugenia Charles (PM) | Dominica | 1980–1993 |
| Gro Harlem Brundtland (PM) | Norway | 1981/1986–1989 |
| Corazon Aquino (PM) | Philippines | 1986–1992 |

| | 1947 | 1953 | 1960 | 1967 | 1976 | 1986–Present day |
| --- | --- | --- | --- | --- | --- | --- |
| **AFRICA** | **1950** Group Areas Act legalizes apartheid, South Africa<br>**1951** Libyan independence from Italy sanctioned by UN | **1956** Suez Crisis: Egyptian troops force French and British to withdraw<br>**1957** Pass Laws in South Africa state that all non-whites must carry passes | **1960** 17 African colonies gain independence<br>**1962** UN imposes sanctions on South Africa<br>**1964** ANC leader Nelson Mandela is jailed for life | **1967–70** Civil war in Nigeria<br>**1967** Dr. Christiaan Barnard completes first heart transplant in South Africa | **1976** Riots in black townships across South Africa<br>**1979** Ugandan leader Idi Amin ousted by Tanzanian-backed rebels<br>**1983** Famine in Ethiopia | **1990** Namibia becomes independent from South Africa<br>**1990** Nelson Mandela is released from prison<br>**1994** ANC wins South Africa's first free elections |
| **ASIA** | **1947** India and Pakistan win independence from Britain<br>**1948** State of Israel founded<br>**1949** Mao proclaims new Communist Republic of China | **1953** Edmund Hillary and Tenzing Norgay climb Everest<br>**1954** Vietnam divided into communist North and US-backed South | **1954–75** Vietnam War<br>**1966** Cultural Revolution begins in China<br><br>**Model of *Vostok I*** | **1967** Six-Day War between Israelis and Arabs<br>**1971** Independent state of Bangladesh founded<br>**1973** Arab–Israeli War | **1976** North and South Vietnam reunited<br>**1979** Iranian Revolution<br>**1980–88** Iran–Iraq War | **1989** Pro-democracy movement in Beijing's Tiananmen Square<br>**1990–91** Gulf War<br>**1995** Israel's prime minister Yitzhak Rabin is assassinated |
| **EUROPE** | **1948** Communist coup in Czechoslovakia<br>**1949** Germany split into East and West<br>**1949** NATO formed<br><br>**Nato flag** | **1955** Warsaw Pact signed by Communist nations<br>**1956** Soviet troops put down anti-communist uprising in Hungary<br>**1957** European Economic Community formed | **1961** Berlin Wall built<br>**1961** Russian cosmonaut Yuri Gagarin is first person in space in *Vostok I* | **1968** Anti-communist uprising in Prague crushed<br>**1968** Student riots in Paris<br>**1969** Britain sends troops to Northern Ireland<br>**1971** Women gain the right to vote, Switzerland | **1979** Margaret Thatcher becomes Britain's first woman prime minister<br><br>**Margaret Thatcher** | **1989** Berlin wall demolished<br>**1989** Communist governments overthrown in eastern Europe<br>**1991** Break-up of Soviet Union<br>**1992–96** Civil war in former Yugoslavia |
| **AMERICAS** | **1950** US senator Joseph McCarthy begins anti-communist "witch-hunts" | **1955** Black people in Alabama, USA boycott segregated buses<br>**1955** Military coup in Argentina overthrows President Juan Perón<br>**1959** Revolution in Cuba brings Fidel Castro to power | **1962** Cuban Missile Crisis<br>**1962** Jamaica wins independence from Britain<br>**1963** President John F. Kennedy is assassinated<br>**1965** Civil rights leader Malcolm X is assassinated | **1968** Civil rights leader Martin Luther King is assassinated<br>**1969** Neil Armstrong is the first person to walk on the moon<br>**1974** US president Richard Nixon resigns over Watergate scandal | **1979** Marxist Sandinistas take power in Nicaragua<br>**1982** Falklands War: Britain defeats Argentine forces<br>**1982** Canada creates constitution independent of UK | **1989** USA invades Panama<br>**1993** Canada creates Nunavut, its largest Native territory<br>**1996** US president Bill Clinton is re-elected |
| **OCEANIA** | **1947** South Pacific Commission formed<br>**1951** Australia, New Zealand, and USA sign ANZUS Pact | **1956** British nuclear testing in Maralinga, Australia<br>**1959** Antarctic Treaty preserves area for research | **1960** Aborigines granted the same social security benefits as the rest of Australian society and gain full voting rights two years later | **1967** New Zealand vote extends to 20-year-olds<br>**1975** Papua New Guinea becomes independent | **1985** *Rainbow Warrior*, a Greenpeace ship, is sunk by pro-nuclear protesters in New Zealand | *Rainbow Warrior* |

# INDEX
## AND
## CREDITS

# INDEX

Page numbers in **bold** refer to main entries

## A

Aa (block lava) 881
Aachen, Germany 197
Aardvarks 38
Abbas I, Shah 735
Abbasid dynasty 470
Abdul Hamid II, Sultan 631
Abernathy, Rev. Ralph 491
Abidjan, Ivory Coast 35
Abolitionists, slave trade 768
Aboriginal Australians 11, 94, 96
  ancestors 97
    corroboree 253
    religion 705
Abraham 427, 469, 486
Absolute magnitude, stars 808
Absolute zero 416
Abstract art 72, 73
  sculptures 745
Abu Bakr 469
Abu Dhabi, United Arab
  Emirates 408
Abuja, Nigeria 37
Abu Simbel, Egypt 59
Abu Talib 581
Abyssal plain 620
Abyssinian cat 185
Acacia trees 397, 667
Academy Awards 331
Academy of Science and
  Fine Art 744
*Acantherpestes* 687
Acceleration 352
Accidents, first aid 335
Accra, Ghana 36
Accretion disc, black holes 139
Achaemenid dynasty 648-9
Achebe, Chinua 516
Achondrite meteorites 279
Acicular crystals 248
Acid rain 12, 677
Acids 12-13
Aconcagua, Argentina 577, 787
Acorns 367, 847
Acrobatics 411
Acrylics 670
  paints 277
Actinides, periodic table 924-5
Actinium 924
Action photography 653
Act of Union (1707) 861
Act of Union (1801) 466
Actors
  drama 273
  films and film-making 330, 331
  theatre 836
Acupuncture 542, 543
Adam's Bridge, Sri Lanka 446
Adaptation
  ecology 284
  evolution 318
Addax 39
Adder, puff 397
Addiction, drugs 275
Addis Ababa, Ethiopia 26
Aden, Gulf of 26
Aden, Yemen 407
Adena people 613

Adenine 376
Adobe houses 435
Adolescence 405
Adonis blue butterfly 460
Adrenal gland 429
Adrenaline 429
Adrian IV, Pope 466
Adriatic coast, Croatia 106
Adriatic Sea 105
Adult education 288
"Advection" fog 221
Adventitious buds 668
Adventure stories 204
*Adventures of Huckleberry Finn, The*
  (Twain) 204, 856
*Adventures of Tom Sawyer, The*
  (Twain) 856
Advertising 14
  agencies 14
  newspapers and magazines 604
Aerial photography, archaeology 59
Aero engines 42
Aerobic respiration 519
Aerofoils 42
Aeroplanes *see* Aircraft
Aerosols 558
Aeschylus 402
Aesop 203
Aestivation 420
Aethelbald, King of Mercia 51
Afar people 26
Afforestation 353
Afghan hound 271
Afghanistan 81
Africa 15-39, 236
  art 73
  banknotes 564
  castles 183
  Central Africa 20-3
  climatic zones 16
  crafts 243
  dance 253
  East Africa 24-7
  exploration 321
  film posters 332
  Great Zimbabwe 400
  history of 17-19
  Mali Empire 526
  music 587
  Northwest Africa 28-9
  people 16
  physical features 15
  praise poetry 671
  religions 705
  resources 16
  slavery 768
  South Africa 784-6
  Southern Central 30-2
  West Africa 33-7
  wildlife 38-9
African Diaspora 18
African hunting dog 899, 900
African National Congress
  (ANC) 530, 786
Afrikaners 785, 786
Agama, armoured pricklenape 83
Agaristine moth 460
Agassiz, Louis 386
Ageing 405
Age roles, social stratification 775
Aggregates, crystals 248
Aggression, animal behaviour 53
Agincourt, Battle of (1415) 439
Agra 580
Agricultural Revolution 326
Agriculture *see* Farming
Agrippa moth, giant 159
Agrippina 724

Ahmad al-Mansur, Sultan of
  Morocco 781
Ahmad Baba 781
Ahmed I, Sultan 631
Ahura-Mazda 649
AIDS (Acquired Immune
  Deficiency Syndrome) 441
  human immunodeficiency virus
    (HIV) 268
  symbols 763
Aid, world economy 933
Ailerons, aircraft 42
Ainu people 478, 480
Air 40
  Earth sciences 282
  pollution 40, 678
  temperature 890
  winds 896
  *see also* Atmosphere
Aircraft 41-3
  history of flight 344
  Johnson, Amy 485
  Leonardo da Vinci 707
  navigation 598
  radar 695
  warplanes 882, 884
  weather planes 891
  *see also* Airports
Aircraft carriers 759, 885
Airedale terrier 271
Air forces 884
Airliners 41, 43, 844
Air masses, weather 890
Airports 44, 156
  facts 934
  Japan 479
Air pressure 40, 690
  and hearing 278
  weather 890
Air-raids, World War II 908
Air resistance 363
Air traffic control 44, 695
Air transport, history 844
Airships 45-6, 344
  history of 844
Airway, first aid 335
Ajanta hills, India 410
Ajman, United Arab Emirates 408
Akashi Kaikyo Bridge, Japan 148
Akbar, Emperor 447, 580
Akhal-Teke horses 81
Akhenaten, Pharaoh 292
Aksum 17
Alamein, Battle of El (1942)
  18, 907, 908
Alaric 477
Alarm clocks 839
Alaska, USA 169, 867
  earthquake 281
Albania 105, 107
Albatrosses 289, 343, 747
Alberta, Canada 171
Albright, Madeleine 391
Albums, best-selling 939
Alcatraz prison 244
Alchemy 743
Alcohol 275
  Prohibition 869
Alcott, Louisa May 204
Aldabra islands 450
Alder 347
Alexander, Bill 836
Alexander II, Tsar 730
Alexander VI, Pope 521, 684
Alexander the Great 47, 78,
  402, 539
  conquers Phoenicians 652
  invades Punjab 448

and Persia 648
Alexandria, Egypt 752
Alfonso I, King of Portugal 684
Alfred the Great, King of Wessex 51
Algae
  blue-green 687
  freshwater 500, 751
  kelp 554
  lichens 585
  seashore life 749
  seaweeds 751
  single-celled 554
  spores 663
  symbiosis 555, 585
Algarve, Portugal 682
Algebra 470, 537
Algeria 29
Algerian war 359
Algiers, Algeria 29
Ali (Muhammad's son-in-law) 469
Ali, Muhammad 229
*Alice in Wonderland* (Carroll) 204
Aliphatics 200
Alkali metals 298
  periodic table 924
Alkaline-earth metals 298
  periodic table 924
Alkalis 12-13
Allah 468, 581
Alleles, genetics 376
Allende, Salvador 790, 805
Allergies 441
Alligators 245
  American 615, 712
Allotropes 298
Alloys 550
Almaty, Kazakhstan 733
Almeida, Francisco de 521
Almodovar, Pedro 332
Alpaca 162
Alphabet 461, 910
  ancient Greek 402
  International Code of Signals
    341
  Morse code 224
  Phoenician 652
Alpha rays 697
*Alpha* space station 797
Alpine skiing 897
Alps
  alpine meadows 317
  Italy 475
  Switzerland 819
Altai Mountains 566, 733
Alternative medicine 542
Altiplano 141, 787
Altitude
  and pressure 690
Altocumulus clouds 221
Altrostratus clouds 221
Aluminium
  bauxite 173
  in Earth 279
  periodic table 925
Alveoli 519
*Alvin* submersible 812
Ama Dablam 114
Amazon Basin 787
  Brazil 146
  Ecuador and Peru 285
  rainforests 788
  wildlife 793
Amazon parrot, yellow-shouldered
  644
Amazon River 146, 787
Amazonstone 249
Amber 113, 249, 354, 355
Amaterasu 593

America *see* Central America;
  North America; South America;
  United States of America
American Civil War 48, 868,
  869, 883
  balloon reconnaissance 45
  Truth, Sojourner 849
American Federation of Labor
  (AFL) 857
American football 111, 351
American Revolution 49
  Franklin, Benjamin 360
  Washington, George 886
American Samoa 680
American shorthair cat 185
American wirehair cat 185
America's Cup 736
Americium 924
Amethyst 249
Amethyst deceiver 586
Amish 214
Amman, Jordan 822
Ammonites 354
Ammunition 409
Amnesty International 438
Amoebas
  190, 554, 555
Amor asteroids 230
Amorites 813
Amphibians 50
  desert wildlife 261
  frogs and toads 364
  lake and river wildlife 499
  marsh and swamp wildlife 533
  rainforest wildlife 700
  records 919
  salamanders and newts 737
  woodland wildlife 903
Amplitute modulation (AM) 825
Amsterdam, Netherlands 601, 602
Amu Darya River 80, 733
Amulets, ancient Egypt 293
Amun-re 291
Amundsen, Roald 673
Anabatic winds 896
Anaconda 499
  green 773
Anaesthetics 542, 544
Analects, Confucius 233
Analgesics 274
Analogue circuits 297
Analogue recordings 783
Analysis, chemical 559
Anasazi people 613
Anatolia 852
  Hittites 425
Anatomy 131
  human body 436, 707
  plants 665
  Vesalius, Andreas 874
Ancestor worship 705
  Africa 17
  China 233
  Great Zimbabwe 400
*Anchisaurus* 267
Andalucian horse 432
Andaman Sea 833
Andersen, Hans Christian 203, 204
Andesite 723, 880
Andes Mountains 787
  Argentina and Chile 65
  Ecuador and Peru 285
  wildlife 794
Andorra 799
Andorra la Vella, Andorra 799
Andromeda Galaxy 870, 871
Anemometers 891
Anemone (plant) 397

Anemone (sea), beadlet 750
*Anemone pavonina* 347
Aneroid barometers 890
Angel Falls 791
Angelfish, blue-ringed 338
Angevin Empire 358
Angiosperms 663, 687
Angkor Wat 490
Angler fish 337, 623
Angles (European people) 51, 116
Angles, geometry 536, 926
Angling 339
Anglo-Burmese wars 78
*Anglo-Saxon Chronicle* 51, 424
Anglo-Saxons 51, 860
Angola 31
Angola War 19
Angora goats 853
Angostura Congress (1819) 140
Animals 54-5
  African 38
  amphibians **50**
  animal stories 204
  anteaters, sloths, and armadillos 57
  Asian wildlife **82-3**
  Australian wildlife 99-100
  badgers, otters, and skunks 104
  bats **117-19**
  bears **120**
  behaviour **52-3**
  biology 131
  body temperatures 917
  buffalo and other wild cattle 154
  camels **162**
  camouflage and colour **165-6**
  cats **184-5**
  cave wildlife 189
  cells **190**
  classification 54 , **914-15**
  conservation **234-5**
  deer and antelopes **256-7**
  desert wildlife 260
  dinosaurs **265-6**
  dogs **270-1**
  eggs **289**
  elephants **299-300**
  endangered 920
  energy needs 917
  European wildlife **316-17**
  evolution **318-19**
  extinction 688
  farming 323, 325, 326
  flight 343
  food webs and chains **350**
  fossils 354, 355
  genetics **376-7**
  gestation periods 917
  giraffes **384**
  grassland wildlife **396-7**
  hearing ranges 917
  heart rates 917
  hedgehogs and other insectivores **418**
  hibernation **420**
  hippopotamuses **423**
  horses **431-2**
  island wildlife 472
  kangaroos and other marsupials **488-9**
  lake and river wildlife 499-500
  legends 593
  lifespans 916
  lions and other wild cats **511-13**
  mammals **527-9**
  marsh and swamp wildlife **533-4**
  migration **556**
  mongooses and civets **567**

  monkeys and other primates **568-70**
  nests and burrows **599-600**
  nocturnal animals **609**
  North American wildlife 615-16
  ocean wildlife **622-3**
  oxygen cycle 91
  pandas and raccoons **640**
  parasites **643**
  pigs and peccaries **657**
  poisonous animals **672**
  polar wildlife **674**
  pollution **677-8**
  prehistoric **687-8**
  rabbits and hares **694**
  rainforest wildlife **699-700**
  rats and rodents **701-2**
  records **918-19**
  rhinoceroses and tapirs **713**
  seals **748**
  seashore life **749-50**
  seed dispersal 366
  sheep and goats **756**
  signs and symbols 764
  sleep requirements 917
  social displays 166
  South American wildlife **793-4**
  space travel 86
  speeds **916**
  tortoises and turtles **854-5**
  tundra 850
  urban wildlife **872**
  warning signals 166
  weasels and martens **889**
  whales and dolphins **893-5**
  wolves and wild dogs **899**
  woodland wildlife **902**
  zoos **912**
  *see also* Amphibians; Birds; Insects; Reptiles
Animation **181**
  Disney, Walt **269**
Animism 705
Ankara, Turkey 852
*Anna Karenina* (film) 373
Annales school 424
Annan, Kofi 863
Annelids 54
Annual plants 663
Anole lizard 903
  green 518
Anselm, St 610
Ant lion 396
Antananarivo, Madagascar 32
Antarctic Treaty (1959) 56
Antarctica **56**, 236
  ice cap 386
  ozone hole 678
  polar exploration **673**
  polar wildlife **674-5**
Antares 808
Anteaters **57**
  giant 57, 794
Antelopes **256-7**
  four-horned 256, 257
  roan 256
  saiga 82
  sitatunga 533
Antennae
  butterflies and moths 158
  insects 53, 458
Anthony, Susan B 901
Anthracite 222
Anthropology 774
Antibiotics 274
Antibodies 413, 441
Anticyclones, weather 896
Antigua and Barbuda 174

Antimony 925
Antipater 752
Anti-personnel (AP) mines 887
Anti-Semitism 426, 487
Anti-venoms 672
Antique furniture 368
Antler hammers 809
Antlers, deer 256
Antony, Mark 161
Ants **58**, 460, 667
  army 58
  driver 460
  leafcutter 58, 600
  nests 600
  wood 58, 903
Anubis 291, 389
Anus 264
ANZACs (Australia and New Zealand Army Corps) 98
Aorta 415
Apache tribe 383
Apartheid 19, 530, 784, 786
Apartments 434
Apennines 475
Aperture, cameras 163
Apes
  human evolution 437
  monkeys and other primates **568-70**
Aphids 155
Aphrodite 389
Apia, Samoa 680
Apollo 388, 389, 401
Apollo asteroids 230
*Apollo* rockets 721, 797
Apostles 484
Appalachian Mountains 611, 864, 866
Appaloosa horse 432
Apparent magnitude, stars 808
Apple Macintosh computers 232, 457
Apples 366, 367
  farming 324
Appolonius 402
Appomattox, Virginia 48
Apprentices 242
Appropriate technology 823
Apricots 367
Aqa Mirak 735
Aqaba, Gulf of 822
Aquamarine 249
Aquariums 912
Aqueducts 148, 681, 725
Aquitaine, France 439
Arab horse 432
Arabian Peninsula 406
Arabic numbers 470
Arabic writing 910
Arabs
  Islamic Empire 470
  wars with Israel 79
Aracari, chestnut-eared 134, 904
Arachnids 74, 801
Aral Sea **733**
Ararat Plains 186
Aras, River 186
Araucanians 67
Arawak people 172, 176, 228
*Archaeogeryon* 355
Archaeology **59-60**
  bones 765
*Archaeopteryx* 267
Arch bridges 148
Arch dams 252
Archer fish 338, 534
Archery
  crossbows 183, 439, 887

longbows 439, 888
Mongol Empire 565
Arches
  churches and cathedrals 215
  Islamic 572
  in architecture 61
Archimedes 352, 742
Archimedes' screw 461
Archipelagos 471
Architects 62
Architecture **61-3**
  Anglo-Saxon 51
  facts **938**
  Greek 402
  houses and homes **434-5**
  Mali Empire 526
  medieval 547
  mosques 572
  Norman 610
  Roman 725
  *see also* Building and construction
Arctic
  Canada 169
  North America 612
  polar exploration **673**
  polar wildlife **674-5**
  tundra **850**
Arctic Ocean **64**, 621
Ardennais horse 432
Ardennes mountains 126
Area
  conversion tables 927
  measuring 892, 927
Ares 389
Argali 756
Argentina **65-6**
  history of 790
Argon 40, 91, 925
*Ariane-5* rocket 720
Aristotle
  and Alexander the Great 47
  and gravity 398
  medieval science 743
  and physics 655
Arithmetic 619
Ark of the covenant 486
Arkose 723
Arkwright, Richard 454
Armada, Spanish 301
Armadillos **57**, 319
Armani, Giorgio 476
Armchairs 495
Armenia 186, **187**
Armies **68**
  Assyrian Empire 84
  Napoleonic Wars 595
  Roman 724
  *see also* Soldiers; Warfare
Armonica 360
Arms and armour **69-70**
  knights 495
  samurai 70, 738
  Viking 879
Armstrong, Neil 571
Arnold, Eve 653
Aromatics 200
Arras, Council of (1435) 439
Arrhenius, Svante 12, 13
Arrowheads, flint 809
Arrowroot 175
Arrows 888
  as signs 763
  *see also* Archery
Arsenic 925
Art
  ancient Greek 402
  Assyrian 84
  Celtic 192

Chavín culture 198
Chinese **211**
Etruscan 307
facts **938**
Gupta Empire 410
history of **71-3**
Hittite 425
Inca 443
Islamic 572
Japanese 480
Leonardo da Vinci **507**
medieval 547
Monet, Claude **562**
museums 583
Olmec 627
painting and drawing **638**
paints 277
Persian 649
Picasso, Pablo **656**
Renaissance 707
Safavid Empire 735
sculpture **745-6**
Stone Age 809
Sumerian 813
symbolism 763
World War I 906
Art Deco architecture 63
Artemis 389
Arteries 415, 874
Art galleries 583
Arthropods 54 , 74, 458
Arthur, King 192, 593
Articulated lorries 179
Artificial elements 298
Artificial intelligence (AI) 457, 717
Artificial selection, breeding 319
Artillery 409
Artistic gymnastics 411, 412
Art nouveau 262
Arts and Crafts Movement 368
Arusha National Park, Tanzania 24
Aryan culture 447
Asarabacca 666
Ascension Island 89, 90
Asclepius 543
Asexual reproduction, plants 668
Ash, volcanoes 881
Ashanti people 36
Ashgabat, Turkmenistan 81
Ashikaga shoguns 480, 481, 738
Ashikaga Takauji 738
Ashikaga Yoshimąsa 738
Ashkenazi Jews 474, 486
Ashton, Frederick 108
Ashur 84
Ashurbanipal, King of Assyria 84
Ashurnasirpal II, King of Assyria 84
Asia **75-83**, 236
  architecture 62
  art 73
  Bangladesh and Nepal **114-15**
  banknotes 564
  Buddhism 153
  castles 183
  Caucasus Republics **186-7**
  China and Taiwan **206-8**
  climate 76
  dance 253
  drama 273
  film posters 332
  Hinduism 421
  history of **77-9**
  India and Sri Lanka **444-8**
  Indonesia **451-2**
  Japan **478-81**
  Khmer Empire **490**
  Malaysia and Singapore **523-5**
  Mongolia **566**

music 587
Pakistan **639**
Philippines **650**
physical features 75
Russian Federation and Kazakhstan **731-33**
South and North Korea **497**
Thailand and Burma **833-4**
Turkey **852-3**
Vietnam, Cambodia and Laos **876-7**
wildlife **82-3**
see also Central Asia; Southeast Asia
Asimov, Isaac 717
Askia Muhammad 781
Asmara, Eritrea 26
Asoka, Emperor 539
Asphodel, hollow-stemmed 347
Assassin bug 155, 165, 460
Asses, wild 431
Assler, Federico 745
Association football see Soccer
Association neurons 144
Assyrian Empire **84**
Astaire, Fred 254
Astarine 925
Asteroids **230**
asteroid belt 815
extinction of dinosaurs 688
Astrolabes 547
Astrology **85**
Astronauts **86**
Moon landings 571, 797
rockets 720
space stations 797
space suits 690
Astronomical units (au) 871
Astronomy **87**
and astrology 85
Big Bang **130**
black holes **139**
comets and asteroids **230**
galaxies **370**
Galilei Galilei **371**
history of 743
Hubble Space Telescope 321
Islamic Empire 470
Moon **571**
planets **660-2**
Renaissance 707
satellites 739
stars **807-8**
Sun and Solar System **814-15**
symbols 764
telescopes **828**
Universe **870-1**
Astrophysics 655
Astrophytum cactus 666
Asuncihytum cactus 666
Aswan Dam 25, 501
Asymmetric bars, gymnastics 411
Atacama Desert 65, 787, 788, 794
Atakora Mountains 37
Atanasoff, John 232
Atatürk 852
Aten asteroids 230
Athena 389, 401
Athens, Greece 401, 404
Athletics **88**, 803
Owens, Jesse **632**
Atlantic Ocean **89-90**, 621
Columbus crosses 228
hurricanes 810
plate tectonics 237
Atlantis 593
Atlas Mountains 16, 28
Atmosphere **91**, 279
air 40

meteorology 282
Northern lights 64
pollution 678
weather 890
Atolls 239, 471, 635, 679
Atomic bombs, World War II 481, 908
Atomic clocks 838
Atomic mass 924
Atomic number 924
Atoms **92**, 743
crystals 248
elements **298**
liquids 514
matter 538
nuclear power **618**
radioactivity **697**
solids 778
splitting 538
Attila the Hun 116
Attis 389
Audion valves 462
Auditorium, theatre 835
Augustine, St 51, 860
Augustus, Emperor (Octavian) 161, 724, 725
Auk, little 675
Aurangzeb, Emperor 447, 580
Aurora 64, 91, 522
Auschwitz 426, 908
Austen, Jane 516
Austin Mini Cooper 180
Australasia **93-4**
Australia 93, **95-100**, 236
Aboriginal Australians **11**
Amy Johnson's flight to 485
banknotes 564
deserts 259
exploration 320, 321
food 349
history of **97-8**
kangaroos and other marsupials **488-9**
prime ministers 946
wildlife **99-100**
Australian Alps 93, 94
Australian cattle dog 271
Australian pony 432
Australian rules football 96, 351
Australian stock horse 432
Australian terrier 271
Australopithecines 437, 506
Australopithecus afarensis 688
Austria **819-20**
Habsburg dynasty 428
Austro-Hungarian Empire 311, 820
World War I 905, 906
Autobahns, Germany 380
Autocues, television 830
Autocumulus clouds 221
Autonomic nervous system 144
Avalanches 386
Avars 116
Aveiro, Afonso d' 127
Aviation see Aircraft
Avicenna (Ibn Sina) 247, 470
Avocados 367
Avocet 761
Avogadro, Amedeo 375
Axes 69
Axles 520
Axolotls 50
Mexican 737
Ayers Rock (Uluru), Australia 11, 94, 95
Aymara Indians 67, 141
Ayurvedic medicine 446
Azerbaijan 186, **187**

Azimuthal projection 532
Azores 90, 682
Aztecs **101-2**, 551
architecture 62
calendar 837
creation myths 593
gods and goddesses 388, 389

# B

Ba'ath Party 822
Babbage, Charles 231, 232
Babies
growth and development 405
milk teeth 824
pregnancy 710
Babington, Anthony 301
Babirusa 657
Baboons 569
hamadryas 570
Babur, Emperor 580
Babylon 103
Hanging Gardens 752
Babylonian Empire 84, **103**, 871
Bach, JS 588
Bacillus subtilis 554
Backbone 527, 765
Backgammon 201
Backpacking 168, 845
Backstroke, swimming 818
Bacon, Francis 655, 742, 743
Bacteria 554
antibiotics 274
Black Death 138
diseases 268, 555
Pasteur, Louis 645
Bactrian camel 162, 260
Baden-Baden, Germany 379
Badgers **104**, 528
Eurasian 104
European 420, 902
honey 104
Badges 763
Badminton 831
Baekeland, Leo 200, 670
Baez, Joan 718
Baghdad, Iraq 464, 470
Bahamas 172, **173**, 228
Bahrain 406, **408**
Bahram I, King of Persia 649
Baikal, Lake 75, 501
Baikonur Cosmodrome, Kazakhstan **733**
Baird, John Logie 462, 830
Bairiki, Kiribati 680
Bajada 259
Bakelite 670
Bakewell, Robert 326
Baku, Azerbaijan 187
Bakunin, Mikhail 535
Balance, sense of 278
cats 184
Balance of payments 841
Balances, measuring weight 892
Balanchine, George 108
Balearic Islands 798
Baleen whales 893, 895
Balinese cat 185
Balkan Mountains 105
Balkan States **105-7**
Ball and socket joints 766
Ball bearings 363
Ball games **109-11**, 803
football **351**
Mesoamerican 549
tennis and other racket sports **831**
Ballet **108**, 939
Russian 732

Ballets Russes 108, 656, 811
Balloons 41, **45-6**
history of 844
weather 891
Ballpoint pens 462, 910
Ballroom dancing 254
Balm 666
Balsam, Himalayan 666
Baltic Sea 621
Baltic States **112-13**
Baluchistan 639
Bamako, Mali 36
Bambara people 36
Bamboo 393
Bananas 194
Banana spiders 802
Bandar Seri Bandarwan, Brunei 525
Bandaranaike, Sirimavo 446
Bandicoot, long-nosed 489
Bands, musical 630
Bangkok, Thailand 834
Bangladesh **114-15**, 639
Bangui, Central African Republic 21
Banjul, Gambia 34
Banknotes 562, **564**
Banks 563
Switzerland 820
United Kingdom 859
Banks, Joseph 97, 238
Banteng 154
Banting, Frederick 275
Bantu people 21, 786
Banyan tree 82
Baobab tree 20
Baptism 214
Barada, River 822
Barb horse 432
Barbados 172, **175**
Barbarians **116**
Barbarossa, Operation 907
Barbera, Joe 181
Barbets
bearded 134
fire-tufted 134
Barbuda 174
Barcelona, Spain 799
Barchan dunes 259
Bar charts 537
Bar codes 760
Barents, Willem 673
Barges 681
Barium 548, 924
Bark, trees 846
Barley 669
Barnacles 240
goose barnacle 240
Barnard, Dr Christiaan 541
Barometers 40, 890, 891
Barons, feudalism 329
Baroque architecture 62, 63
Baroque art 72
Baroque music 588
Barosaurus 267
Barred spiral galaxies 370
Barrie, JM 204
Barton, Otis 621
Baryonyx 267
Basalt 723, 881
Baseball 109, 111
champions 937
Bases, acids and alkalis 13
Basil II, Emperor 160
Basilisk, common 517, 518
Basketball 110, 111
champions 936
Basketwork 242, 243
Stone Age 809

Basques 357, 799, 800
Basset hound 271
Basseterre, St Kitts and Nevis 174
Bassoons 590, 592
Bast 291
Bastard balm 347
Bastille, Paris 361
Bataleur 137
Batéké people 22
Bates, Henry Walter 158, 166
Batesian mimicry 158
Bath, England 860
Bath-houses, Roman 725
Bathsheba 427
Bathyscaphes 321, 621
Batik 452
Batista, Fulgencio 176
Batman 604
Bats **117-19**
cave wildlife 189
echolocation 609
flight 343
hibernation 420
prehistoric 688
temperature control 528
Batteries
electric circuits 295
electrochemistry 200
electrolytes 13
Battersea shield 192
Battles 882
major battles 947
see also Warfare and individual battles
Bauhaus 262
Bauhaus Building, Dessau 63
Baum, L Frank 204
Bauxite 173
Bavarian Alps 379
Bayeux Tapestry 424, 860
Bay-head beaches 223
Bayonets 888
Bazaars 760
BBC see British Broadcasting Company
Beaches 223
Beaching, whales 894
Beadwork 242, 243
Beagle 270
Beagle, HMS 255
Beaks 132
birds of prey 135
hornbills 492
hummingbirds 817
parrots 644
shorebirds 761
songbirds 779
toucans 904
Beam, gymnastics 411
Beam bridges 148
Beans 349
Bears **120**
American black 120
Asian black 120
brown 120, 317, 420, 528
grizzly 120, 234
Kermodes 120
Kodiak 120
polar 120, 528, 529, 674
sloth 120
spectacled 120, 794
sun 120
Beatles, The **121**, 718
Beaufort scale 896, 923
Beaumont, William 264
Beauregard, General 48
Beauvoir, Simone de 901
Beavers 499, 615, 702

Becket, St Thomas 546
Beckett, Samuel 272
Becquerel, Antoine 697
Becquerel, Henri 250, 548
Bede 51
Bedford, 5th Duke of 326
Bedouin 407, 774, 821
Bedrock 777
Bee Gees, The 719
Beech, common 848
Beech jelly-discs 586
Beech nuts 367
Beecham, Sir Thomas 630
Beef, cattle ranching 867
Beefsteak fungus 586
Beer 313
Bees 122, 460
    colonies 53
    honey bee 122
    parasitic 122
    stings 13
Beethoven, Ludwig van **123**, 360, 589
Beetles **124-5**, 460
Begin, Menachem 646
Behaviour, animal **54-5**
Beijing, China 207, 498
    Forbidden City 216
    Tiananmen Square massacre (1989) 210
Beirut, Lebanon 822
Bekaa Valley, Lebanon 821
Belgian Congo *see* Zaire
Belgian draught horse 432
Belgium **126**
    banknotes 564
Belgrade, Yugoslavia 107
Belize 193, **194**
Belize City, Belize 194
Bell, Alexander Graham
    microphones 783
    telephones 825, 826, 827
Bellini, Giovanni 708
Bells 590
Belmopan, Belize 194, 196
Beluga 893
Benelux alliance 126
Benesh notation, ballet 108
Benetton 476
Bengal *see* Bangladesh
Bengal, Bay of 114, 833
Benin **37**
Benin City 127
Benin Empire **127**
    armour 69
    sculpture 746
    slave trade 17
Benz, Karl 179
Benzene 200
*Beowulf* 515
Berbers 25, 28
Berg, Alban 629
Bering Sea 75
Bering Strait 613
Berkelium 925
Berlin, Germany 311, 379
Berliner, Emile 783
Berlin Olympics (1936) 632
Berlin Wall 225, 382
Bermuda 90
Bermuda grass 394
Bern, Switzerland 820
Bernini, Gianlorenzo 72
Berries 366, 367
Berry, Chuck 718
Beryl 722
Beryllium 924

Bessemer, Henry 467
Best, Pete 121
Betamaribé people 37
Beta rays 697
Betelgeuse 808
Bethe, Hans 618
*Bhagavad Gita* 421
Bharal 756
Bhumibol Adulyadej, King of Thailand 834
Bhutan 114, **115**
Bhutan glory 578
Bialowieza National Park 312
Bible 214, 427, 484
Bichat, Marie François 190
Bicycles **128-9**, 251
    history of 843, 844
    sport 803
Biennial plants 663
Big Bang **130**, 870, 871
Big Crunch 130
Bighorn sheep 53 , 756
Biko, Steve 786
Bile 264
Billiards 110, 111
Bill of Rights 438
Bimbisara, King 151
Binary system, mathematics 619, 926
Bindusara, Emperor 539
Bindweed, black 666
Bingham, Hiram 286
Binocular microscopes 553
Binoculars 828
Biochemistry 200
Bioko Island 22
Biological weapons 887
Biology **131**
    evolution 255
Bioluminescence 508
Biomass fuels 304
Biomes 283
Biophysics 655
Biosphere 280
Biplanes 41, 344
Birch, silver 848
Birds **132-4**
    Asian wildlife 82-3
    Australian wildlife 99-100
    birds of prey **135-7**
    camouflage and colour 165
    cave wildlife 189
    classification 915
    courtship 53
    crows **246**
    desert wildlife 260
    ducks, geese and swans **276**
    eggs **289-90**
    European wildlife 316-17
    flight 53, 343
    flightless birds **345**
    grassland wildlife 397
    herons, storks and flamingos **419**
    hibernation 420
    island wildlife 472
    kingfishers and hornbills **492**
    lake and river wildlife 499
    marsh and swamp wildlife 533
    migration 556
    mountain wildlife 578
    nests 599
    North American wildlife 615-16
    owls and nightjars **633**
    Pacific islands 635
    parrots **644**
    penguins **647**
    poisonous 672
    polar wildlife 675

    pollination of flowers 346, 347
    prehistoric 687, 688
    rainforest wildlife 699
    records 919
    seabirds 747
    seed dispersal 366
    shorebirds **761**
    songbirds **779-80**
    South American wildlife 793-4
    swifts and hummingbirds **817**
    warning signals 166
    woodland wildlife 902
    woodpeckers and toucans **904**
Birds-of-paradise 53 , 165
Birman cat 185
Birth 710
    ceremonies 775
    medicine 544
Biscay, Bay of 308
Bishkek, Kyrgyzstan 81
Bishops, medieval Europe 546
Bismarck, Otto von 359, 382
Bismarck Archipelago 636
Bismuth 925
Bison 154
    American 396
Bissau, Guinea-Bissau 34
Bitterling 338
Bittern 419
    European 533
Bittersweet (plant) 664
Bituminous coal 222
Bivalves 770, 771
Black-banded snake 773
Blackbeard (Edward Teach) 659
Blackberries 367
Blackbuck 396
Black Consciousness 786
Black Death **138**, 546
Black-footed cat 511
Black Forest 379
Black holes **139**
Black Muslims 491
Black people
    apartheid 19, 784, 786
    civil rights 438, 948
    King, Martin Luther **491**
    Truth, Sojourner **849**
Black Sea 308
    Caucasus Republics 186
    Crimea 727
    Turkey and 852
"Black smokers" 620
Blackwell, Elizabeth 544
Black widow spider 801
Bladder 873
Bladderworts 177
Bladed crystals 248
Blake, William 671
Blazonry 495
Bleda 116
Blenny 338
Blights 584
Blitzkrieg 907
Blizzards 698
Block and tackle 520
Bloemfontein, South Africa 784
Blood
    blood groups 415
    blood vessels 874
    clots 415
    heart and circulatory system **414-15**
    transfusions 415
    urinary system 873
Bloodhound 270
Blood-letting rituals, Maya Empire 540

Bloodsuckers 342
Bloodworms 909
Blowholes, whales 893
Blubber 893
Blucher, Marshal 595
Bluebird, mountain 616
Blue bottle 342
Blue butterfly 159
Blue-green bacteria 554
Blue Lagoon, Iceland 90
Blue morpho butterfly 159, 700
Blue Nile 25
Blue Nile Falls 24
Blues music 482
Blume, Judy 205
BMW motorcycles 129
BMX (Bicycle Motocross) 129
BOAC 844
Boa constrictor 712, 772
    tree 700
Board games **201-2**
Boars, wild 657
Boat people 877
Boats *see* Ships and boats
Bobcat 512, 513
Bobsleighs 897
Boccaccio 707
Bodhisattvas 762
Bodiam Castle, England 183
Bodichon, Madame 901
Body *see* Human body
Body building 582
Body decoration 219
Body language 502
Body temperatures 917
*Boeing 747-400* 41
Boer Wars 98, 786
Boers 786
Bogbean 664
Bogong moth 556
Bogotá, Colombia 792
Bohemia, Czech Republic 313
Bohemian glass 313
Bohol Island, Philippines 650
Bohr, Neils 548
Bohrium 924
Boiling point 416, 417, 514, 924
Bokmakierie 290
Boleyn, Anne 301
Bolívar, Simon 30, **140**, 142, 790
Bolivia 140, **141-2**
Bolsheviks 734
Bolshoi Ballet, Moscow **732**
Bombardier beetle 124
Bombay, India 445, 448
Bomb disposal robots 717
Bomber aircraft 43, 884
Bombs 887, 888
    volcanic 881
    warplanes 884
Bonds
    atoms and molecules 92
    compounds 559
    metallic 550
Bone tools 809
Bones
    bone marrow 766
    development 405
    fossils 354
    human body 436
    skeleton **765-6**
Boniface, St 381
Bonney, Anne 659
Bonsai 479
Bony fish 336
Booby traps 887
Book of the Dead 292
*Book of Kells* 192, 466

*Book of Kings, The* (Firdausi) 515
Books 143
    children's literature **203-5**
    literature **515-16**
    printing **691-2**
Boomerangs 888
Bora Bora, French Polynesia 679
Border terrier 271
Boreal forests 83, 353
Borglum, Gutzon 866
Borneo 449, 472, 523
Borodino, Battle of (1812) 595
Boron 925
Borosilicate glass 387
Borzoi 270
Bosnia and Herzegovina **106**
Bosporus Strait 160
Boston Tea Party 49
Boston terrier 271
Botanic gardens 374
Botany 131
    Linnaeus, Carolus **510**
Botany Bay, Australia 97, 238
Bothnia, Gulf of 816
Botswana **31**
Bottle tree 99
Boudicca 191
Boudin, Eugène 561
Bougainville Island 636
Boules 111, 357
Boulez, Pierre 589
Boulton, Matthew 306
Bourbon dynasty 358, 359
Bournonville, August 108
Boutros-Ghali, Boutros 862, 863
Bovidae 154
Bow drills 334
Bowls and bowling 110, 111
Bows *see* Archery
Bow Street Runners 676
Boxer (dog) 271
Boxer Rebellion (1900) 78, 210
Boxfish, spiny 338
Boxing 229
"Boxing"
    hares 694
    kangaroos 488
Boyacá, Battle of (1819) 140
Boyle, Robert 200, 375
Boyle's Law 375
Boyne, Battle of the (1690) 466
"Boz" (Charles Dickens) 263
Bozo people 36
Brachial plexus 144
Bracket clocks 839
Bracket fungus 903
    cinnabar 586
    many-zoned 586
Bragg, William Henry 778
Bragg, William Lawrence 778
Brahman 421
Braille 144
    watches 839
Brain **144-5**
    eyes and seeing 322
Brain fungus, yellow 586
Brain stem 145
Brain waves 145
Brakes
    bicycles and motorcycles 128
    friction 363
    hydraulic 690
Bramaputra River 114
Brambles 347
Bran the Blessed 192
Brandnames 763

Brandt, Willy 225, 311
Brandywine, Battle of (1777) 49
Brasília, Brazil 146, 216, 790
Brass 550
    Benin empire 127
Brass instruments 590, 592
Bratislava, Slovakia 314
Braun, Wernher von 796
Brazil **146-7**
    dance 254
    history of 790
    Portuguese empire 684
    slave trade 768
Brazil nuts 793
Brazzaville, Congo 22
Breadfruits 367
Breastplates, armour 70
Breaststroke, swimming 818
Breathing **519**
    first aid 335
    fish 336
    plants 665
Breccia 723
Brecht, Bertolt 272
Breeding
    Agricultural Revolution 326
    artificial selection 319
    conservation programmes 234
    see also Reproduction
Breezes 896
Bremen, Germany 380
Brer Rabbit 203
Brest-Litovsk, Treaty of (1918) 906
Brétigny, Peace of (1360) 439
Bretons 357
Breuer, Marcel 382
Brezhnev, Leonid 795
Brian Boru, King of Munster 466
Bricks, building material 157
Bridge (card game) 201
Bridges **148**
    longest suspension bridges 934
Bridgetown, Barbados 175
Briggs, Raymond 205
Brightness, stars 808
Brihadnatha, Emperor 539
Brine 13
Brisbane, Australia 94
Bristlecone pine 663
Bristleworms 750
Britain see United Kingdom
Britain, Battle of (1940) 907
British Army 68
British Broadcasting Company
    (BBC) 496, 830
British Columbia, Canada 171
British Empire 302, 861
    India 448
British Isles see United Kingdom
British shorthair cat 184, 185
Brittlestars 806
Broadcasting
    drama 273
    radio 696
    television 829-30
    video 875
Broad-leaved trees 847  848
    woodlands 316, 612
Broadsheet newspapers 603
Broadway, New York 272
Broca, Pierre Paul 145
Brome grass
    great 394
    soft 394
Bromeliads 699
Bromine 298, 925
Bronchioles 519
Bronchus 519

Brontë sisters **149**
Bronze 550
    casting 150, 745
    Benin empire 127
Bronze Age **150**
Brooklyn Bridge, New York City 148
Broom (shrub) 317
Brown, Clarence 373
Brown, James 719
Brown, Louise 542
Brown, Robert 375
Brownian motion 375
Brownie Hawkeye camera 164
Brown-veined white butterfly 159
Bruce, Mount 93
Brunei 523, **525**
Brunel, Isambard Kingdom 148
Brunel, Marc Isambard 851
Brunelleschi, Filippo 61
Brunhoff, Jean de 205
Brush lily, New Zealand 235
Brussels, Belgium 126
Brutus 161
Bryony, black 666
Bryophytes 573
Bubble shells 771
Bubonic plague 138
Bucephalus 47
Bucharest, Romania 728
Budapest, Hungary 314
Buddha **151**, 152
    Sacred Tooth 446
Buddhism **152-3**
    architecture 62
    Asian history 77
    Buddha **151**
    Gupta Empire 410
    in India 447
    in Laos 877
    Mauryan Empire 539
    monasteries 560
    shrines 762
Budgerigar 644
Buenos Aires, Argentina 66
Buffalo **154**, 643
    Cape 154
    water 154
Buffalo grass 616
Buff-tip moth 159
Buganda 27
Bugs **155**, 460
Building and construction **156-7**
    architecture **61-3**
    bridges 148
    castles **182-3**
    churches and cathedrals 215
    earthquake proofing 281
    houses and homes 434
    roads 716
    tunnels 851
    urban wildlife 872
Bujumbura, Burundi 23
Bulbils 668
Bulbs (plants) 665
Bulgaria **403-4**
Bulldog 271
Bulldog bat 118
Bull elephants 300
"Bullet" trains 479, 842
Bullet-proof vests 69
Bullets 409
Bullfighting 683
Bullfinch 779
    Eurasian 134
Bullfrogs
    African 365
    American 533
Bull jumping, Minoans 557

Bull Run, Battle of (1861) 48
Bulrushes 316, 393
Bumblebee 460
Bumtang 114
Buoys 598
Burbage, Richard 753
Burdock 367
Burgoyne, General John 49
Burgundy, France 439, 588
Buriganga River 115
Burke, Robert O'Hara 97, 98, 320
Burkina Faso **36**
Burle Marx, Roberto 374
Burma **833-4**
    Anglo-Burmese wars 78
    Death Railway 79
Burmese cat 185
Burning 40, 334
Burrowing toad, Mexican 365
Burrows **599-600**
    mongooses 567
    rabbit warrens 694
Burundi **23**
Bush dog 899, 900
Bushbaby 609
    greater 570
Bushido code 738
Bushmen see San people
Bushnell, David 812
Bustard, greater 397
Butane 626
Butterfish 338
Butterflies **158-9**, 460
    adaptation 318
    Australian 100
    metamorphosis 458
    migration 556
    rainforest 700
Butterfly stroke, swimming 818
Butterworts 177
Buttress dams 252
Buttresses 215
Buzzards 135
    turkey 136
Byrd, Richard E 673
Byzantine empire **160**, 631, 724

# C

Cabbage 665
Cabbage white butterfly 420
Cabinets 369
Cable-stay bridges 148
Cabot, John 171, 613, 614
Cacti 261, 284, 667
    Knowlton 235
    saguaro 615
Caddis flies 342
Cadmium 925
Caecilians 50
Caerphilly Castle, Wales 182
Caesar, Julius **161**
    conquers France 358
    on Druids 191
    invades Britain 860, 861
Caesium 924
Caetano, Marcello 684
Cage, John 589
Caimans 245, 711
    spectacled 534, 711
    yacare 793
Cairn terrier 271
Cairns birdwing butterfly 159
Cairo, Egypt 25
Calais, France 439
Calcite 249
Calcium 298

in Earth 279
    periodic table 924
Calculators 462
    electronics 297
    liquid crystal displays (LCDs) 508
Calcutta, India 448
Calderas 881
Calendar festivals 328
Calendars 837
Calgary Stampede 170
California, USA 867
    earthquakes 281
    Gold Rush 614
California spangled cat 185
Californium 925
Caliphs 470
Calligraphy 910
    China and Japan 73, 209
    Islamic 572
Callisto 661
Calvin, Jean 704
Camargue horse 432
Cambodia **876-7**
    independence 79
    Khmer Empire **490**
Cambrian period 378, 687
Cambyses, King of Persia 103
Camcorders 164, 875
Camelot 593
Camels 162, 260, 325
    animal symbols 764
    Bactrian 83, 162
    caravans 526
    in Chad 21
    dromedary 162, 529
"Camera obscura" 163
Cameras **163-4**
    camcorders 875
    photography 653
Cameron Highlands, Malaysia 523
Cameroon **21**
Camouflage **165-6**
    amphibians 50
    Batesian mimicry 158
    butterflies and moths 158
    chameleons 700
    deer and antelopes 257
    fish 337
    insects 459
    nightjars 633
    octopuses and squids 624
    rodents 702
    sloths 57
    tigers 511
Campaign for Nuclear
    Disarmament (CND) 646
Camp David Accords (1978) 646
Camping and hiking **167-8**
Campion, Jane 332
Campion, red 347
Cams 520
Camshafts 305
Canaan 427
Canada **169-71**, 611
    banknotes 564
    clothes 219
    crafts 243
    history of **171**, 614
    prime ministers 946
Canadian canoes 736
Canals 681
    aqueducts 148
    history of 844
    Netherlands 601
    Panama Canal 193, 195, 196,
        681, 844, 869
    Suez Canal 25, 406, 844
Canary Islands 90, 472

Canberra, Australia 95, 98
Cancer 190
    drugs 274
    radiotherapy 697
Candle-snuff fungus 586
Candles, clock 838
Cane toads 365
Canidae 899
Canine teeth 824
Cannons 409
Cano, Sebastián del 521
Canoes 736
    Aboriginal 97
    canoe hiking 168
    Polynesia 679
Canopy, rainforest 699
Canova, Antonio 746
Cantilever bridges 148
Canton, China 78
Canute, King of Denmark and
    England 51, 740, 860, 861
Canyons, submarine 620
Capacitors 297
Cape Colony 786
Cape Cod, USA 658
Capek, Karel 717
Cape Province, South Africa 786
Cape Town, South Africa 784
Cape Verde Islands 90
Capilla del Salvador, Ubeda 63
Capillaries 415, 519
Capital 840
Capitalism 392
    Marx, Karl 535
Capital punishment 244
Capitol, Washington DC 504
Capone, Al 244
Captaincy General 196
Capuchin, black-capped 570
Capybara 533, 702, 703
Carabobo, Battle of (1821) 140
Caracal 512, 513
Caracara 137
    crested 794
Caracas, Venezuela 791, 792
Caravaggio, Michelangelo 72
Caravans 168, 435
Caravans, camel 526
Carbines 888
Carbohydrates 264
Carbon
    carbon cycle 284
    element 298
    organic chemistry 200
    periodic table 925
Carbon dating 697
Carbon dioxide
    in air 40, 91
    greenhouse effect 91, 217, 678
    lungs and breathing 519
    photosynthesis 654
Carbon steel 467
Carbonate rocks, caves 188
Carbonic acid 188
Carboniferous limestone 723
Carboniferous period 378, 687
Carcassonne, France 216
Carcharocles 355
Card games 201
Cardiac muscle 582
Cardinal beetle 458, 903
Cardinal spiders 802
Cardon 794
Cargo aircraft 43
Cargo ships 757
Caribbean Sea **172-6**
    Columbus visits 228
    festivals 328

history of **176**
pirates 659
Caribou 257, 615
Caribs 172, 175, 176
Car industry
France 357
Germany 380
Japan 479
Malaysia 524
Spain 799
United Kingdom 859
United States 865, 869
Carline thistle 347
Carloman 197
Carnac, France 689
Carnegie, Andrew 205
Carnegie Medal 205
Carnelian 249
Carnivals 328
*Carnevale* 476
Rio de Janeiro 147
Carnivores 53
arthropods 74
beetles 125
food webs and chains 350
lizards 518
teeth 527
Carnivorous plants **177**, 534
Carolingian Empire 197
Carp, European 336
Carpathian Mountains 105, 308, 312, 727
Carpenter bee 122
Carpets
*kilims* 853
Moroccan 29
Persian 464
Turkmenistan 81
Carriage clocks 839
Carriages, transport history 843
Carrier waves
telecommunications 825
Carrion, vultures 135, 136
Carroll, Lewis 204
Cars **178-80**
catalytic converters 199
design 262
facts 934
"green" cars 147
history of 843
motor sports **575-6**
roads 716
*see also* Car industry
Carson, Rachel 131
Carter, Howard 59
Carthage 652
Cartier, Jacques 171, 613, 614
Cartilage 405, 436
Cartilaginous fish 336, **754-5**
Cartography 532
Cartoons and animation **181**
Disney, Walt **269**
Car transporters 179
Carts, transport history 843
Carvings
sculpture 745
wood 243
Casamance River 34
Cascade Range 611
Casein 200
Cashew nuts 34
Casini, Giovanni 661
Casinos, Monaco 357
Caspian Sea 75, 186, 308, 501
Cassava 346
*Cassini* space probe 797
*Cassiopeia* 483
Cassius 161

Cassowary 345
southern 290
Cast iron 467
Caste system 775
Hinduism 421
El Castillo, Chichen Itza 693
Castillon, Battle of (1453) 439
Casting
bronze 150, 745
metals 550
sculptures 745
Castles **182-3**
Norman 610
Castor 725
Castor oil 545, 667
Castries, St Lucia 175
Castro, Fidel 173, 176
Casts, bone fractures 766
"Cat and Mouse Act" (1913) 641
CAT scans 544, 744
Catalans 799
Catalaunian Plains, Battle of (451) 116
Catal Hüyük 216
Catalogues, mail order 760
Catalysts 199
Catalytic converters 179, 199
Catamarans 757
Catania, Sicily 475
Catapults 183
Catchment area, rivers 715
Caterpillars 158
leaf miners 600
metamorphosis 458
warning signals 166
Catfish 500
Cathedrals **215**
Norman 610
Catherine de Médicis 108
Catherine the Great, Empress of Russia **730**
Catherine of Valois 439
Cathode-ray tubes 829
Catholic Church *see* Roman Catholic Church
Cats **184-5**
behaviour 53
eyes 609
lions and other wild cats **511-13**
reproduction 528
whiskers 527
Cattle *see* Cows
Cauca River 791
Caucasus Republics **186-7**
Cavalry 68
Cave crab 189
Caverns 188
Caves **188**
cave paintings 71, 358, 638, 809
prehistoric people 689
shrines 410
wildlife **189**
Cave spiders 802
Caviar **733**
Cavies 701, 703
Cavour, Count 477
Cayman Islands 172
Cays 239
CD Roms 143
CDs (compact discs) 232, 462, 719, 783
Ceauçescu, Nicolae 728, 829
Cecil, William, Lord Burghley 301
Cedar, incense 848
Cefalù Cathedral, Sicily 610
Cel animation 181
Celery 545
Celestial sphere 85

Cellini, Benvenuto 708
Cello 592
Cells **190**
brain 145
division 190
DNA 376
drugs 274
eggs 289
genetic engineering 377
neurons 144
protists 554
Cellulose 190
Celsius scale 416
Celsus, Aulus 544
Celts **191-2**, 310
crosses 215
gods and goddesses 388, 389
in Ireland 466
Cenozoic era 378, 688
Centipedes 74
giant tiger 700
Central Africa **20-3**
Central African Republic (CAR) 21
Central America **193-6**
dance 254
exploration 320
history of **196**
Maya Empire **540**
Mesoamericans **549**
Olmecs **627**
pyramids 693
sculpture 746
Central Asia **80-1**
history of 77
Central Europe **312-14**
collapse of Communism 311
Central nervous system (CNS) 144
Central processing units (CPUs), computers 231
Centrifuges 558
Centripetal force 352
Century Tower, Tokyo 63
Cephalopods 624, 770, 771
Cepheid stars 808
Ceramics *see* Pottery and ceramics
Cerberus 389
Cerebellum 145
Cerebrum 145
Ceremonies 775
Christian 214
dances 253
Ceres 230, 389
Cerium 924
Cernunnos 191
Cerro Aconcagua 65
Cervantes, Miguel de 516
Cervical nerve 144
Cestius, Caius 693
Cetacea 893
Ceylon *see* Sri Lanka
Cézanne, Paul 72
CFCs (chlorofluorocarbons) 91, 678
Chaco 787
Chad **21**
Chafer beetle 125
Chahine, Youssef 332
Chain, Ernst 275
Chain mail 69
Chairs 368, 369
Chaka 786
Chalcedony 249
Chalk 279, 723
Chalky soils 777
Chamber music 123, 630
Chamber orchestras 630
Chameleons 711
flap-necked 517
Jackson's 518

Parson's 700
Cham people 490
Champlain, Samuel de 171, 614
Champollion, Jean-François 910
Chancay culture 790
Chandragupta I, Emperor 410
Chandragupta II, Emperor 410
Chandragupta Maurya 447, 539
Chanel, Gabrielle "Coco" 219
Chang Jiang River 75
Channel Islands 858
Channel Tunnel 851, 859
Chantries 138
Chao Phraya River 833
Chaos theory 537, 655
Chapels, castles 182
Chaplin, Charlie 331
Chappe, Claude 825
Characin, blind cave 189
Charge-coupled devices (CCDs) 87
Chariots 425
Chari River 21
Charlemagne, Emperor **197**, 329, 358
Charles, Jacques 375
Charles, Ray 718
Charles I, King of England 861
Charles I, King of Spain 521
Charles III, King of France 610
Charles III, King of Spain 790
Charles IV, King of Spain 790
Charles V, Emperor 428, 800, 874
Charles VI, Emperor 428
Charles VI, King of France 439
Charles VII, King of France 439
Charles' Law 375
Charles Martel, King of the Franks 358
Charnley, John 544
Chartists 861
Chartreux cat 185
Charts
navigation 598
statistics 537
Chaucer, Geoffrey 515
Chavín culture **198**
Chavín de Huántar, Peru 198
Chechnya, Russian Federation **732**
Cheese, French 357
Cheetah 53 , 512, 513
Cheke, Sir John 708
Chemical energy 303
Chemicals
analysis 559
animal behaviour 54
engineering 823
formulae 92
plant defences 667
pollution 677
reactions 199, 416
weapons 887
Chemistry **199-200**
acids and alkalis **12-13**
atoms and molecules **92**
elements **298**
mixtures and compounds **558-9**
periodic table **924-5**
Chemoreceptors, smell and taste 769
Chequer bloom 666
Chequered skipper butterfly 159
Cheques 562
Chernobyl nuclear power station 113, 618
Cherries 367
Chess **201-2, 732**
Chestnuts, sweet 367
Chewing 824
Cheyenne tribe 224

Chhukha Dam 114
Chiang Kai-shek 212
Chicago, USA 865
Chichen Itza 549, 552, 693
Chicken 325
Chicken-of-the-woods 586
Chickenpox 555
Chicory 666
Chihuahua 552
Chihuahua dog 270
Chihuahuan Desert 612
Childbirth 544, 710
Children
child labour 453
children's literature **203-5**
education 288
families 774
growth and development **405**
hospitals 433
Japan 479
schools and colleges 741
Children's Crusade 247
Children's Day 328
Chile 65, 67
banknotes 564
history of 790
Chilean four-eyed frogs 365
Chilean racer 794
Chimpanzee 568, 570
comparative anatomy 319
Goodall, Jane **390**
human evolution 437
tool-using 390, 568
China **206-12**
arts and crafts 73, **211**
astrology 85
and barbarians 116
books 143
calendar 837
Chinese Revolution **212**
Communism 79
Confucius **233**
dance 253
dynasties and republics 942
earthquakes 281
education 741
food 349
gardens 374
history of 77, 78, **209-12**
household shrines 762
and Japan 480
kites 494
Kublai Khan 498
medicine 543
music 587
mythology 593
paper 143
porcelain **686**
rockets 720
writing 910
Chinchilla 325, 702, 703
Chinese lanterns (plant) 82
Chinese opera 208, 273
Chinook wind 896
Chipmunk 703
eastern 902
Chiroptera 117
Chisinau, Moldavia 728
Chitons 770
Chivalry, Code of 495
Chlorine 298, 925
Chlorofluorocarbons (CFCs) 91, 678
Chlorophyll 584
algae 751
photosynthesis 654, 663
plant cells 190
Chloroplasts 190
Chocolate 346

Chocolate Hills, Philippines 650
Chola dynasty 77, 447
Chomsky, Noam 502
Chondrite meteorites 279
Chordates 54
Chough, Alpine 134, 317
Christ see Jesus Christ
Christian X, King of Denmark 740
Christianity 213-14
  African missions 18
  Byzantine church 160
  Celtic Church 192
  churches and cathedrals 215
  European history 310
  festivals 214, 328
  in Germany 381
  Holy Land 427
  in Ireland 466
  Jesus Christ 484
  knights 495
  monasteries 51, 560
  Reformation 704
  in Russia 729
  in Scandinavia 740
  signs and symbols 764
  witch hunts 898
Christmas 214, 328
Christmas Carol, A (Dickens) 263
Christmas Island 450
Chromatic aberration 828
Chromatography 559
Chromium 924
Chromosomes
  cell division 190
  genetics 376
  sex chromosomes 377
Chromosphere, Sun 814
Chrysalises, metamorphosis 458
Chrysler 865
Chrysler Building, New York 63
Chün-tzu 233
Chuquicamata 67
Church and state
  medieval Europe 546
  Normans 610
Churches 215
  architecture 61, 116
  Byzantine 160
  Scandinavian 740
Churchill, Winston 225, 908
Church of England 301, 658, 861
Churchyards 215
Churún River 791
Cicada 155, 460
Cicero 707, 725
Cichlids 38, 500
  mouth-brooding 289
Cidade de Praia, Cape Verde 90
Cider gum 848
Cigarettes 275
Cigars 173
Cine 8 cameras 164
Cinema see Films and film-making
CinemaScope 331
Cinquefoil, marsh 347
Ciphers 224
Circles
  mathematics 926
  pi 536
Circuit boards 297, 462
Circuits, electricity 295
Circular motion 352
Circulatory system 414-15, 436
  first aid 335
Circumpolar stars 808
Circuses 273
Cirrostratus clouds 221
Cirrus clouds 221

Cities 216
  flats and apartments 434
  human societies 774
  Indus Valley civilization 455
  Islamic Empire 470
  maps 532
  pollution 678
  populations 930
  Sumerian 813
  traffic 716
  urban myths and legends 593
  urban wildlife 872
  see also individual cities
Citlaltépetl 551
Citroen DS 180
Citroen Traction Avant 180
Citrus fruits 785
Civets 567
Civil engineering 823
Civil law 504
Civil rights 438
  black rights 948
  King, Martin Luther 491
Civil service 391
Civil wars 882
  American Civil War 48, 868, 869, 883
  English Civil War 861
  Russian Civil War 734
  Spanish Civil War 800
Clams 239, 770
  giant 289, 635, 771
Clarinets 590
Clark, William 614
Class, social stratification 775
Classes, classification 914
Classical architecture 61
Classical art 71
Classical music 589
Classical physics 655
Classification, living things 131, 914-15
  animals 54
  plants 510
Claudius, Emperor 724, 725
Clausewitz, Karl von 882
Claves 592
Clawed toad, African 365
Claws
  armadillos 57
  cats 184
  lions and other wild cats 511
  woodpeckers 904
Clay 723
  pottery and ceramics 685
  soils 777
Cleaner fish 337
Cleaner-shrimps 241
Cleisthenes 402
Clemens, Samuel Langhorne see Twain, Mark
Clement VI, Pope 138
Clement X, Pope 496
Cleopatra VII, Queen of Egypt 161, 292
Click beetle 125
Clifford, George 510
Cliffs 223
  cliff diving 818
  sea caves 188
Climate 217
  climatology 282
  deserts 259
  ice ages 688
  see also Weather and individual continents and countries
Clocks 837-9
Clones, plants 668

Close-up photography 653
Clothes 218-20
  medieval 547
  prehistoric people 689
  theatrical costumes 836
  see also Uniforms
Clots, blood 415
Clouds 221, 890
  rain 698
  thunderstorms 810
Clover, red 347, 666
Clown fish 284, 337, 483
Clown triggerfish 338
Club fungi 584, 586
Club mosses 327
Clubs (weapons) 69
Cluedo (board game) 202
Clusters
  galaxies 370
  stars 807
Clutches, eggs 289
Clydesdale horse 432
Cnidarians 54
Cnut the Great, King see Canute, King of Denmark and England
Coal 222, 932
Coal tar 222
Coasts 223
Coati 640
Coats-of-arms 495, 496
Cobalt 31, 924
Cobra, monocled 773
Cobwebs 801
Coca 285
Coca-Cola 262, 763
Cocaine 141, 285
Cochise 383
Cochlea 278
Cockatoos 644
Cockchafer beetle 124, 343
Cockcroft, John 742
Cockerell, Christopher 363
Cockles 770
Cockroaches 289, 872
Cocksfoot grass 394
Cocoa 35
Coconuts 367
  dispersal 366
  island wildlife 472
  Pacific islands 635, 636
  Polynesia 679
Cocoons, spiders 801
Cod 289
Codes and ciphers 224
  bar codes 760
Codex Justinianus 160
Coelenterata 483
Coffee
  Central America 196
  Costa Rica 195
  Yemen 407
Coffee houses, Turkey 853
Coins 562
  medieval 547
  Roman 725
  Viking 878
Coke 222
  iron smelting 467
Cold-blooded animals 917
Cold fronts, weather 890
Cold War 225, 795, 869
Collage 638
Collagen, bones 766
Collective bargaining, trade unions 857
Colleges 288, 741
Collenia 355
Collie, border 271

Collins, Wilkie 263
Collodi, Carlo 205
Colloids 558
Colobus monkeys
  black and white 569
  red 39
Colombia 791, 792
  banknotes 564
  independence 140
Colombo, Sri Lanka 446
Colon 264
Colonialism
  Africa 18
  Asia 78
Colonies
  ants and termites 58
  bees and wasps 122
Colorado River 611
Colosseum, Rome 725
Colossus of Rhodes 752
Colour 226-7
  animals 165-6
  birds 132
  chromatic aberration 828
  dyes and paints 71, 277
  fish 337
  flowers 346
  horses 431
  printing 691
  spectrum 605
  television 829
  see also Camouflage
Colour blindness 322
Colour pointed British shorthair cat 185
Colour pointed longhair cat 185
Coltrane, John 482
Columbarium 215
Columbus, Christopher 176, 228, 614
Columns, architecture 61
Comanche tribe 224
Comaneci, Nadia 411
Combat sports 229, 803
Combustion 334
Comedy films 331
Comenius, John Amos 205
Comets 230
  space probes 796
Comet West 230
Comics 604
Commercial Revolution 841
Committee of Public Safety 361
Common Agricultural Policy (CAP) 315
Commune, Paris 535
Communication
  animal behaviour 54
  ants and termites 58
  chimpanzees 568
  codes and ciphers 224
  communications industry 840
  elephants 300
  flags 340-1
  information technology 456-7
  languages 502
  newspapers and magazines 603-4
  radio 696
  satellites 739
  scent glands 528
  signs and symbols 763
  telecommunications 825
  telephones 826
  television 829-30
  writing 910
Communism 392
  in Asia 79
  in China 206, 210, 212

Cold War 225
  collapse of 311
  in Europe 311
  Marx, Karl 535
  Russian Revolution 734
  in Soviet Union 795
Communist Manifesto, The 535
Communities, wildlife 283
Comoros 32, 450
Compact discs (CDs) 232, 462, 719, 783
Companies
  advertising and marketing 14
  stocks and shares 563
Companion dogs 271
Compasses
  hiking 168
  magnetism 522
  navigation 321, 598
Compendiums, board games 202
Composers 939
  Beethoven, Ludwig van 123
  Mozart, Wolfgang Amadeus 579
  Stravinsky, Igor 811
Composite volcanoes 880
Composites, plastics 670
Compound microscopes 553
Compounds 558-9
Compressed air 40
Compression
  internal combustion engines 305
  sound waves 782
Compsognathus 267
Computers 231-2, 744, 869
  astronomy 87
  cartoons and animation 181
  CD Roms 143
  chess 201
  codes 224
  colour printing 691
  computer-aided design 262
  films and film-making 331
  games 462
  information technology 456-7
  photography 653
  robots 717
Conakry, Guinea 35
Conan Doyle, Arthur 516
Concave lenses 509
Concave mirrors 509
Concentration camps 426, 908
Concertos 630
  Mozart, Wolfgang Amadeus 579
Concerts, rock and pop 719
Concorde 41
Concrete 61, 157
Concretions, fossils 354
Condell, Henry 753
Condensation 375, 538
  clouds 221
Condors
  Andean 136, 137, 578, 794
  Californian 235
Conduction, heat 417
Conductors, electricity 295
Conductors, orchestras 630
Cone cells, eyes 226, 322
Cone shell 770
Cones, pine trees 847, 903
Cones, volcanic 881
Confederacy, American Civil War 48
Confucius 209, 233, 587
Conglomerate, rocks 723
Congo 22
Congo (Zaire) 23
Congo Basin 15
Congo River 20

Congress of Industrial Organizations (CIO) 857
Conical projection, maps 532
Coniferous forests 353
  North America 612, 616
  wildlife 317
Coniferous trees 663, 847, 848
*Connecticut Yankee in King Arthur's Court, A* (Twain) 856
Connemara, Ireland 465
Connemara pony 432
*Conquistadores* 101, 789
Conscientious objectors 646
Consciousness 651
Consciousness raising, women's movement 901
Conservation, matter 538
Conservation, wildlife 234-5
  zoos 912
Constance, Lake 379, 819
Constantine the Great, Emperor 160, 213, 725
Constantinople 160, 725
Constantius I, Emperor 725
Constellations, stars 808, 921
Constitution (US) 438, 504, 868
Constitutional law 504
Construction *see* Building and construction
Consumerism 869
Consumption, world resources 932
Container ships 759
Contemporary dance 254
Continental climate 217
Continental Congress 49, 886
Continental drift 236
Continental shelf 620
Continents 236-7
  Africa 15-39
  Antarctica 56
  Asia 75-83
  Australia 95-100
  Europe 308-17
  North America 611-16
  South America 787_94
Contraception 275, 709
Contras 196
Convection, heat 417
Convention on International Trade in Endangered Species (CITES) 234
Conversion tables 927
Convex lenses 509
Convex mirrors 509
Convicts, transportation to Australia 97
Cook, Captain James 238, 320
  and Australia 97, 98
  and New Zealand 607
Cook Islands 680
Cooking 334, 346
Cook, Mount 606
Cook, Thomas 845
Co-operative movement 454
  Africa 19
Copenhagen, Denmark 258
Copepods 241
Copernican Universe 871
Copernicus, Nicolas 371, 707, 871
Copper 924
  in Chile 67
  metalwork 150
  periodic table 925
  in Zambia 31
Copper butterfly, small 159
Copperbelt, Zambia 31
Copperhead snake 773
Coprolites 265

Coral
  fossils 354
  gemstone 249
  symbiosis 555
Coral fungus, meadow 586
Coral islands
  Caribbean Sea 172
  formation 471
  Pacific Ocean 93, 635, 679
Coral reefs 93, 239
  formation 471
  Great Barrier Reef 95
  Indian Ocean 450
Coral Sea, Battle of (1942) 908
Coral snake 165
Cor anglais 592
Corbusier, Le 62, 262
Corinthian order 61
Coriolis effect 896
Coriolis, Gustave 303
Cork 669, 683
Cormorants 747
Corn dollies 328
Cornea 322
Corneille, Pierre 358
Cornet 592
Cornflower 347
Cornish rex cat 185
Corn marigold 347
Corno, Mount 475
Cornsnake 712, 773
Corona, Sun 814
Corporal punishment 244
Corroborres 11
Corsairs 659
Corsica 356, 357
Cortés, Hernán 101
*Corystrosaurus* 267
Cosmetics 669
Cosmology 655, 744
Costa Rica 193, 195, 196
Costumes, theatre 836
Cotopaxi, Mount 285
Cottage industry 840
Cotton
  Burkina Faso 36
  Central African Republic 21
  Egypt 25
  farming 323, 768
  Pakistan 639
  Syria 822
  Tanzania 27
  textiles 832
  United States 866
  Uzbekistan 81
Cottontails 694
Cotyledons 663
Coubertin, Pierre de 628
Couch grass 394
Cougar 616
Coughing 519
Counter-Reformation 704
Counting 619
Countries, political world 928-9
  *see also individual countries*
Courtrooms 505
Courtship
  animals 53 , 166
  songbirds 780
Couscous 29
Cousteau, Jacques 621
Covalent bonds 92
Covalent compounds 559
Cowboys 866
  gauchos 66
Cows
  in Brazil 147
  buffalo and other wild cattle 154

farming 323, 324, 325
  ranching 142
  sacred cows 422
  in Switzerland 820
  in United States 867
Coyotes 899
Coypu 527
Crabs 74, 240
Crab spiders 802
Cracking, oil refining 626
Craft, Robert 811
Craft guilds, Benin Empire 127
Crafts 242-3
  Chinese 211
  Inca 443
  Indus Valley civilization 455
  Stone Age 809
  Toltec 549
Cramp balls 586
Cranach, Lucas the Younger 704
Cranberries 865
Crane, crowned 133
Crane fly 460
Cranesbill
  dusky 666
  meadow 664
Cranks 520
Crankshafts 305
Crassula 666
Crassus, Marcus 161
Crater Lake 501
Craters
  on Mercury 660
  meteorite 230
  on Moon 571
  volcanoes 881
Crayfish 241
Crazy Horse 596
Creation myths 593
Creation theories 319
Crécy, Battle of (1346) 439
Credit cards 562
Creoles 790
Crested dogstail 394
Cretaceous period 265, 378, 687, 688
Crete 403
  Minoans 557
Crevasses 385, 386
Crick, Francis 376
Cricket 109, 111, 859
  champions 937
Crickets 395
  cave 189
  desert 261, 460
Crime 244
  novels 516
  police 676
Crimea 727
Crimean War (1853-56) 608
Criminal law 504
*Criorhynchus* 687
Cristofori, Bartolomeo 591
Criterium racer bicycle 129
Croaking, frogs and toads 364
Croatia 106
Crocodiles 245
  animal symbols 764
  Nile 245, 499
  saltwater 82
Crocodilians 711, 712
*Crocuta crocuta* 440
Cronos 401
Crop rotation 326
Crops *see* Farming
Cross, Christianity 213
Crossbill 779
  common 317

Crossbows 183, 439, 887
Cross-country events, horse riding 430
Croton 666
Crows 246
  Cape 290
  carrion 246
Crucifixion 484
Cruise liners 757
Crusades 160, 247, 883
Crust, Earth's 279
Crustaceans 74, 240-1, 750
Cryogenics 416
Cryoturbation 850
Cryptic coloration 165
Crystal glass 387
Crystalline solids 778
Crystal Palace, London 861
Crystals and gems 248
Cuba 173
  Columbus visits 228
  history of 176
Cuban missile crisis (1962) 176, 225
Cuban War (1898) 176
Cubic system, crystals 248
Cubism 73, 656
Cuchulain 192
Cuckoo
  didric 134
  guira 290
Cuckoo clocks 839
Cue-and-ball games 110
Cuirasses 70
Cultural Revolution, China 210, 212
*Cumbia* 792
Cumulonimbus clouds 221, 810
Cumulus clouds 221
Cuneiform script 813
Cupid 389
Curie, Marie 250, 548, 697
Curie, Pierre 250, 697
Curium 924
Curlew 761
Currency 562
Current electricity 295
Currents 621
  Atlantic Ocean 89
  Indian Ocean 449
  Pacific Ocean 634
Customs duties 841
Cut and cover tunnels 851
Cuttlefish 624, 771
Cuvier, Georges 319, 354
Cuzco, Peru 442
Cyclades Islands 471
Cycles in nature 284
Cycling 128-9, 251
  sport 803
  Tour de France 357
Cyclocross 251
Cyclones 810
Cylindrical projection 532
Cyprus 821, 822
Cyrus the Great, King of Persia 103, 648, 649, 804
Cytoplasm, cells 190
Cytosine 376
Cytotoxic drugs 274
Czechoslovakia 313
Czech Republic 312, 313
  coat of arms 496

**D**

D-Day (1944) 908
Dachshund 271
Daddy-longlegs 801
Da Gama, Vasco 320, 684, 707

Dagda 192
Daggers 888
Daguerre, Louis 163, 653
Daguerrotypes 164
Dahl, Roald 204
Daimler, Gottlieb 128
Daimler cars 179
Daimyos 738
Dairy farming 323, 324, 820
Dakar, Senegal 34
Dalai Lama 153
Daleeda 332
Dali, Salvador 72
Dalmatian 271
Dalton, John 200
Damascus, Syria 470, 822
Damba 254
Dams 252
Damselfly 458
Damsons 367
Dance 253-4
  ballet 108
  Ballets Russes 656
  Cambodian 877
  facts 939
  flamenco 799
  Indonesia 452
  jazz dance 482
  Micronesia 637
Dandelions 367
Danelaw 860
Dante Alighieri 515, 707
Danube, River 312
  in Austria 819
  in Bulgaria 403
  Iron Gate 105
*Dapedium* 355
Dapper, Olfert 127
Da Ponte, Lorenzo 579
Darby, Abraham 453, 454
Dar es Salaam, Tanzania 27
Darius I the Great, King of Persia 103, 648, 649
Darius III, King of Persia 47, 648
Dark Ages 197, 424
Darkling beetle 125
Dark matter 870
Darling River 97
Dartmoor pony 432
Darwin, Charles 255, 909
  Galápagos finches 318
  theory of evolution 255, 319, 744
Darwin, Erasmus 255
Darwin's beetle 460
Dasht-e Kavir, Iran 463
Dasht-e Lut, Iran 463
Dashur pyramid 693
Dates (fruit) 29
Dating, carbon 697
Daubenton's bat 235
David, Jacques-Louis 776
David, King of Israel 427
David, Père 256
*David Copperfield* (Dickens) 263
Davis, Miles 482
Davison, Emily 641
Davy, Humphry 200, 222
Day, Lewis F 369
Day and night
  Earth's orbit 815
  time 837
Day of the Dead 328, 552
Deadly nightshade 667
Dean, James 805
Dead Sea 75, 473, 474, 501, 822
Dead Sea Scrolls 214
Death
  gods and goddesses 389

major causes of 931
rituals 775
Death cap 585
Death Railway 79
Death Valley 611, 612
De Beers Mining Company 248
De Brazza's monkey 570
Debro pavro camera 164
Debt, world economy 933
Debussy, Claude 589
Decathlon 88
Decibels (dBs) 782
Deciduous forests 847
  Asia 76
  Australia 94
  Europe 309
  North America 612
  South America 788
Decimal numbers 619, 926
Declaration of Human Rights 768
Declaration of Independence 49,
  360, 504, 868
Declaration of the Rights of
  Man 438
Decopoda 240
Decorator crab 240
Dedicated computers 232
Deer 256-7, 325
  fallow 256, 316
  Père David's 256
  red 256, 257
  roe 902
Defences
  animal warning signals 166
  ants and termites 58
  arthropods 74
  beetles 124
  bugs 155
  butterflies and moths 158
  castles 182-3
  crabs 240
  deer and antelopes 257
  dinosaurs 266
  fish 337
  frogs and toads 364
  grasshoppers and crickets 395
  insects 459
  lizards 517
  lobsters 241
  octopuses and squids 624
  plants 667
  rodents 702
  salamanders and newts 737
  sea urchins 806
  skunks 104
  spiders 801
Defoe, Daniel 516
Deforestation 142, 194, 353
Degas, Edgar 561, 746
De Gaulle, Charles 359
De Havilland Comet 844
Deinonychus 267
De Klerk, FW 530, 786
Delhi, India 447
Delian League 402
Delphic oracle 388, 401
Deltas 714
Demeter 401
Democracy 391, 392
Democritus 655, 743
Demoiselles d'Avignon, Les
  (Picasso) 656
Demonstrations, peace
  movements 646
Denali 611
Denary system, numbers 619
Dendritic crystals 248
Denim 832

Denmark 258
  history of 740
Density, matter 538
Dentine 824
Dentistry 824
Department stores 760
Depression, Great 399
Depressions, weather 890, 896
Dermatology 541
Dermis 767
Dervishes 469, 631
Des Prez, Josquin 588
Desaguliers, John Theophilus 744
Descartes, René 651
Desert holly 261
Desertification 34, 259
Deserts 259
  Africa 15, 16
  Asia 76
  Australia 94
  climate 217
  dust devils 810
  facts 922
  North America 612
  wadis 577
Desert scorpion 802
Desert wildlife 260-1
  Africa 39
  Asia 83
  Australia 99
  camels 162
  ecosystems 283
  insects 459
  lizards 517
  North America 615
  rodents 702
  South America 794
  wild cats 513
Design 262
Design engineering 823
Desktop publishing (DTP) 456
Desna, River 728
Detectives 676
Détente, Cold War 225
Detergents 13
Detroit, USA 865
Development and growth 405
Devil 898
Devil's finger 586
Devonian period 378
Devon rex cat 184
Dewey, John 288
Dhaka, Bangladesh 115
Dharmapada 153
Dhole 899
  Indian 900
Diabetes 429
Diaghilev, Serge 108, 656, 811
Diagnosis, medicine 541
Dialects 502
Dialysis, renal 873
Diamonds 248, 249
  in Angola 31
  in Australia 96
  element 298
  in Israel 474
Diamond Sutra 692
Diapause 420
Diaphragm 519
Diaspora, African 18
Diatoms 622
Diaz, Bartolomeu 707
Dickens, Charles 263
Dicotyledons 663, 664, 666
Dictatorship 391
Dido, Queen of Carthage 652
Didymograptus 355
Diesel, Rudolf 306

Diesel engines 179, 306, 842
Diesel fuel 625
Diet see Feeding; Food
Diffusion, gases 375
Digestion 264, 436
  acids 13
  teeth and jaws 824
  urinary system 873
Digital audio tape (DAT)
  sound recording 783
Digital cameras 163
Digital circuits 297
Digital clocks 839
Digital recordings 783
Dilophosaurus 267
Dimerocrinites 355
Dimetrodon 355
Dinaric Alps 105
Dinghies 759
Dingo 899, 900
Dinka people 24
Dinosaurs 265-7, 687
  evolution 711
  extinction 688
Diocletian, Emperor 725
Diodes 297
Diorite 723
Dior, Christian 219, 220
Dipper (bird) 779
Diptera 342
Directors
  films and film-making 330, 940
  theatre 836
Disabled people
  education 288
  Paralympics 628
Disarmament conferences 646
Disc brakes 363
Disco dancing 254
Disco music 719
Discus throwing 88
Diseases 268
  Black Death 138, 546
  immune and lymphatic system
    441
  microbial 555
  Pasteur, Louis 645
Disks, computers 232
Disney, Walt 269
Disney Club 269
Disneyland, USA 269
Disney World, USA 269, 866
Displays, animals 166
Disposable cameras 164
Disruptive coloration 165
Dissection, corpses 874
Dissolution of the monasteries 704
Distances
  astronomical 871
  measuring 892
Distillation
  oil 626
  separating mixtures 558
Distribution, trade and industry 841
Distributors, engines 305
Diving 818
  submarines 812
Diving beetle, great 125
Diwali 328
Djebel Toubkal 28
Djenné, Mali 526, 781
Djibouti 26
Dmitri, Prince of Moscow 730
DNA (deoxyribonucleic acid)
  cells 190
  and evolution 319
  genetics 376, 377
  natural selection 318

structure 744
Dnieper, River 728
Dobrowolski, Christopher 745
Doctors 541
  check-ups 413
  Flying Doctor 96
  hospitals 433
  living standards 931
Dodder 643
Dodo 688
Dodoma, Tanzania 27
Dogfish 755
Dogon people 36
Dogs 270-1
  sense of smell 769
  teeth 527
  wolves and wild dogs 899-900
Doha, Qatar 408
Dolerite 723
Dolomite 188
Dolomites 475
Dolphins 622, 893-5
  Amazon River 895
  dusky 895
  echolocation 695
  fishing industry 339
  Hector's 895
  La Plata 895
  long-snouted spinner 895
  Yangtze River 895
Domains, magnetic 522
Dome of the Rock, Jerusalem 427
Domes, architecture 61
Domesday Book 329, 610, 861
Dome volcanoes 880
Dominant genes 377
Dominica 175
Dominican Republic 174
Domino beetle 261
Donbass Basin, Ukraine 728
Donkeys 325, 431
Doppler, Christian 782
Doppler effect 782
Doric order 61
Dormancy, animals 420
Dormouse 420, 600
Double bonds, atoms 92
Double stars 807
Douro, Rio 682
Douroucouli 570
Dover, England 858
Dracula, Count 728
Dragon dances, China 253
"Dragon" economies 79
Dragonflies 342, 343, 460
  emperor 534
Dragons 593
Drag racing 575
Drainage basins, rivers 715
Drake, Sir Francis 301, 659
Drakensberg 16, 784
Drama 272-3
  Shakespeare, William 753
  theatres 835-6
Dramatic poetry 671
Draughts (board game) 202
Drawing 638
Dreams 145, 362
Dreamtime 11
Dredgers (ships) 759
Dress see Clothes
Dressage 430
Dreyfus, Alfred 359
Dreyse, Nikolaus von 887
Dried foods 168
Drilling, for oil 625

Drills
  electric 296
  pneumatic 690
Drinks, from plants 669
Dromedary camel 162, 529
Drones, bees and wasps 122
Drowned coasts 223
Drugs 274-5
  drug abuse 275
  early medicine 545
  modern medicine 544
Druids 191
Drumlins 385
Drums 590
  African 22
Drupes 366, 367
Dry fruits 366, 367
Dry rot 585
Dryad's saddle 586
Duaflex camera 164
Dubai, United Arab Emirates 408
Dublin, Ireland 465
Dubnium 924
Ducks 276, 325
Dufay, Guillaume 588, 589
Dugong 235, 894
Duiker, yellow-backed 39
Duma 730
Dumb cane 667
Dunant, Henri 883
Duncan, Isadora 254
Dunes 259
Dung beetle 125, 396
Dunstan, St 51
Duodenum 264
Durango, Mexico 552
Dürer, Albrecht 381, 708
Durga 388
Durham Cathedral, England 610
Dushanbe, Tajikistan 81
Dust, interstellar material 870
Dust Bowl 399
Dust devils 810
Dutch people see Netherlands
Duyvenbode's lory 134
Dyes and paints 277, 669
  batik 452
  Phoenician 652
Dylan, Bob 718
Dynamic friction 363
Dynamics 352
Dynamite 851
Dysprosium 925

E

Eagles 135, 137
  bald 764
  black 137
  crowned hawk 39
  golden 137
  harpy 699
  imperial 137
  tawny 82, 137
Earhart, Amelia 344
Ears and hearing 53, 278
  animal hearing ranges 917
  cats 184
  crickets 395
  elephants 299
  horses 431
  nocturnal animals 609
Earth 279-80
  atmosphere 91
  continents 236-7
  Coriolis effect 896
  crust 925
  facts 921, 922-3

geochemistry 200
geology **378**
geophysics 655
gravity 398
magnetism 522
maps and mapping 532
mountains and valleys **577**
oceans and seas **621**
orbit 815
as a planet 660
rivers **714-15**
scale of the Universe 871
Solar System 815
and the Sun 814
time 837
Earthenware 685
Earthquakes 281, 923
Earth's structure 279
Lisbon 684
Earth sciences **282**
Earthstar, barometer 586
Earth Summit (1992) 863
Earth-tongue, scaly 586
Earthworms 53, 909
Earwig 289
East Africa **24-7**
East India Companies 79, 302, 448, 602
East Indies 525
Magellan, Ferdinand 521
East Pakistan *see* Bangladesh East Timor 451
Easter 214
Easter Island 73, 531, 635, 679
Eastern Europe *see* Central Europe
Eastern Orthodox Church 213, 310
Balkan States 105
Byzantine Empire 160
ceremonies 214
Greece 403, **729**
Romania, Ukraine and Moldavia 727
Serbia 107
Easter Rising (1916) 466
Eastman, George 163
Ebers Papyrus 543
Ebeye Island 637
Echidna, short-beaked 99, 529
Echinoderms 54 , 750, 806
Echoes 782
Echolocation 695
bats 117, 609
whales 894
Eclipses
Moon 571
Sun 814
Ecliptic 814
Ecology and ecosystems 131, **283-4**
conservation 234
food webs and chains 350
forests 353
Economic and Social Council, United Nations 862
Economics
"dragon" economies 79
global economy 311
Great Depression **399**
Marx, Karl 535
money **562-4**
Russia **731**
trade and industry **840-1**
warfare 883
world economy **933**
Ecotourism 845
Ecuador 140, **285-6**
Eddington, Arthur 398, 814
Edentates 57
Ederle, Gertrude 818

Edinburgh festival 328
Edison, Thomas **287**, 509, 783
Editing suites, television 830
Edmund, King of East Anglia 878
Education **288**
Argentina 66
Christian Church and 310
humanism 708
Islam 469
Kuwait 408
Mauritius 450
schools and colleges **741**
Songhai Empire 781
Sri Lanka 446
television 829
Edward, Black Prince 439
Edward I, King of England 183, 860
Edward III, King of England 439
Edward the Confessor, King of England 51
Edwards, Robert 542
Edwin, King of Northumbria 51
Eels 556
blue-ribbon 338
Efficiency, energy 303
Effort, simple machines 520
Egbert, King of Wessex 51
Eggs **289-90**
amphibians 50
bees and wasps 122
birds 133
crocodiles 245
dinosaurs 266
fish 337
flies 342
as food 349
frogs and toads 364
grasshoppers and crickets 395
human reproduction 709-10
lizards 517
ostriches 345
parasites 643
reptiles 712
salamanders and newts 737
sex chromosomes 377
turtles and tortoises 854
Egg tempera 71
Egret, cattle 419
Egypt **25**
banknotes 564
Camp David Accords (1978) 646
Egypt, Ancient **291-3**
Alexander the Great and 47
boats 844
crime 244
dance 253
gods and goddesses 388, 389
hieroglyphics 910
medicine 543
music 587
mythology 593, 935
papyrus scrolls 143
periods and dynasties 942
pyramids **693**, 752
sculpture 746
weights and measures 892
Egyptian mau cat 185
Ehrlich, Paul 274, 275
Eichmann, Adolf 426
Eightfold Path, Buddhism 152
Einstein, Albert **294**
on energy 303
on light 509
on mass and energy 538
theories of relativity 398, 655, 744, 837
and time 838
Einstein, Mileva 294

Einsteinium 925
Eisenhower, Dwight D. 491
Eisenstein, Sergei 331
Elasticity 778
Elat 473
Elba 594
Elbe, River 380
El'brus, Mount 186, 308
Elburz Mountains 463
Elder, dwarf 347
El Dorado 789, 791
Eleanor of Aquitaine 546
Elections
democracy 392
Pankhurst family 641
women's movement 901
Electric trains 842, 843
Electrical musical instruments 591
Electricity **295**
circuits 295
current 295
Franklin, Benjamin 360
friction and 363
heat and 416
hydroelectricity 67, 252
lightbulbs 287
motors 296, 306
power 303
power stations 304
solar power 306
Electrochemistry 200
Electroencephalographs (EEG) 145
Electroluminescence 508
Electrolysis 200
Electrolytes, batteries 13
Electromagnetic spectrum **911**
light 508
Electromagnetism **296**
Electromotive force 295
Electron guns, television 829
Electronic music 591, 719
Electron microscopes 553
Electronics **297**
computers **231-2**
in Japan 479
in Malaysia 524
navigation 598
Electrons 92
electricity 295
metallic bonds 550
static electricity 363
subatomic physics 744
Electrosense, sharks 755
Elements **298**, 870
atoms and molecules **92**
four elements 743
names 925
periodic table **924-5**
Elephantiasis 909
Elephants **299-300**, 325
African 299, 529
Asian 299
Khmer Empire 490
teeth 527
temperature control 528
Elevators, aircraft 42
Elf cups, curly-haired 586
Elizabeth I, Queen of England **301**, 861
Elizabeth II, Queen of England 531
El Lanzon 198
Ellington, "Duke" 482
Elliptical galaxies 370
Elm bark beetle 460
El Salvador 193, **194**, 196
civil war 882
El Teniente 67
E-mail 224, 457

Embroidery 242, 243
Embryo 528, 709-10
Emerald 249
"Emerald Isle" 465
Emergencies, hospitals 433
Emergent layer, rainforest 699
Emigration 176, 845
Emi Koussi 20
Emission spectrum 226
Emotions 144
Emperor butterfly, Japanese 82
Empires 302, 321
Alexander the Great 47
Assyrian Empire **84**
Babylonian Empire **103**
European 310, 311
Gupta Empire **410**
Holy Roman Empire **428**
Islamic Empire **470**
Khmer Empire **490**
Mali Empire **526**
Maya Empire **540**
Minoans **557**
Mongol Empire **565**
Ottoman Empire **631**
Safavid Empire **735**
*see also* Roman Empire
Empire State Building, New York 62
Employment, child labour 453
Empty Quarter 406, 407
Emu 99, 345, 397
Emulsions 558
Enamel, teeth 824
Enclosures, medieval farming 326
Encyclopedias 143
Endangered wildlife **234-5, 920**
*Endeavour* 238
Endocrine system **429**, 436
Endoplasmic reticulum 190
Endoscopes 542, 544, 553
Endothermic reactions 199
*Energia* rockets 721
Energy **303-4**
animal needs 917
coal **222**
consumption 932
Earth sciences 280, 282
geothermal power 90
heat 416
industry 840
lasers 503
light 508
matter and 538
nuclear power **618**
Sun 814
X-rays 911
Engels, Friedrich 535, **730**
Engineering 823
facts **934**
structural 156
Engines and motors **305-6**
aircraft 42
cars 178
motorcycles 128
ships and boats 758
submarines 812
trucks 179
England 858-9
*see also* United Kingdom
English Channel 858
cross-Channel swimming 818
World War II 908
English Civil War 861
Engraving 692
ENIAC 232
Enigma cipher machine 224
Enkidu 671
Enlightenment, Buddhism 151

Enriquillo, Lake 174
Ensign camera 164
Entertainment
cities 216
dance 253-4
films and film-making **330-2**
radio 696
television 829-30
video 875
Entre Rios 65
Environment
airports and 44
conservation 234
disasters 920
Earth system 280
environmental organizations 920
and evolution 318
United Nations and 863
warfare and 883
Enzymes 264, 584
Eocene epoch 378
*Eoraptor* 266
Ephesus, Turkey 752
Epicentre, earthquakes 281
*Epic of Gilgamesh, The* 671
Epic poetry 671
Epics 515
Epidemics, Black Death **138**, 546
Epidemiology 268
Epidermis 767
Epidermis, teeth 264, 519
Epiglottis 264, 519
Epiphytes 699
ferns 327
Epistemology 651
Epoxies 670
Epstein, Brian 121
Equal rights, women's movement 901
Equations
algebra 537, 619
chemical 199
Equator
Central Africa 20
climate 217
Equatorial Guinea 22
*Equidae* 431
Equilibrium, forces 352
Equinoxes 837
*Equus* 318
Erasmus, Desiderius 708
Erbium 925
Erebus, Mount 56
Erg of Bilma 16
Erie, Lake 611
Eritrea **26**
Ermine 889
*Eroica* symphony (Beethoven) 123
Erosion
coastlines 223
glaciation 385
rivers 715
rocks 722
soil 777
Eruptions, volcanoes 880
Escapement, clocks 838
Escape velocity 720
Esigie, Oba of Benin 127
Eskimos *see* Inuit
Esterházy, Prince Paul 589
Estonia 112, **113**
Estuaries 223, 714
Ethane 200
Ethanol 147, 626
Ethene 200, 626
Ethics, philosophy 651
Ethiopia 18, **26**
Ethiopian Orthodox Church 26

Ethnic groups, social
  stratification 775
Ethnology 131
Etna, Mount 475
Etruria *see* Etruscans
Etruscans **307**, 310, 725
Eucalyptus 94, 489, 683
Eucharist 214
Euchromiid moth 460
Euclid 536
*Euoplocephalus* 266
Euphrates, River
  Babylonian Empire 103
  Mesopotamia 463
  Sumeria 813
  Turkey 852
*Euplocephalus* 267
Euripides 402
Europa 661
European Atomic Energy
  Community (Euratom) 315
European Coal and Steel
  Community (ECSC) 315
European Community (EC) 315
European Court of Human
  Rights 438
European Economic Community
  (EEC) 315, 841
European Monetary System
  (EMS) 315
European Space Agency
  (ESA) 720, 792
European Union (EU) **315**
  Brussels 126
  formation of 311
  Luxembourg City 126
  Scandinavia and 740
Europe 236, **308-17**
  Balkan States **105-7**
  Baltic States **112-13**
  banknotes 564
  Belgium **126**
  Central Europe **312-14**
  Cold War **225**
  Denmark **258**
  feudalism 329
  film posters 332
  Finland **333**
  folk dance 253
  France **356-7**
  Germany **379-82**
  Greece and Bulgaria **403-4**
  history of **310-11**
  Holy Roman Empire **428**
  Ireland **465-6**
  Italy **475-7**
  medieval **546-7**
  Napoleonic Wars **595**
  Netherlands **601-2**
  Norway **617**
  Portugal **682-4**
  Romania, Ukraine and
    Moldavia **727-8**
  Russian Federation **731-33**
  Soviet Union **795**
  Spain **798-9**
  Sweden **816**
  Switzerland and Austria **819-20**
  Turkey **852-3**
  United Kingdom **858-61**
  wildlife **316-17**
  World War I **905-6**
  World War II **907-8**
  *see also* Medieval Europe
Europium 924
Eurostar 843
Eustachio, Bartolomeo 278
Evaporation 514, 538

separating mixtures 558
Evening primrose 664
Eventing, horse riding 430
Everest, Mount 75, 114
Everglades 612
Evergreen trees 847
Evidence, trials 505
Evolution **318-19**, 744
  Darwin, Charles 255
  human **437**
Ewé people 36
Ewuare the Great, Oba of Benin 127
Excavation, archaeology 59
Exchanges, telephone 826
Executive, government 391
Exercise, health and fitness 413
Exmoor pony 432
Exodus 427
Exoskeleton, arthropods 74
Exosphere, atmosphere 91
Exothermic reactions 199
Exotic cat 185
Expansion, thermal 416
Experiments
  physics 655
  scientific method 742
Exploration **320-1**
  Australia 97
  Columbus, Christopher **228**
  Cook, James **238**
  Magellan, Ferdinand **521**
  North America 614
  polar exploration **673**
  Portugal 684
  Renaissance 707
  Vikings 878
Explosives 887
Exports 841, 933
Exposure time, cameras 163
Express trains 842
Extended families 774
External skeletons 53
Extinction
  animals and plants 688
  reptiles 712
  volcanoes 880
Eyck, Jan van 71
Eyed lizard 517, 518
Eyes **322**
  birds 133
  birds of prey 135
  cats 184
  colour vision 226
  crocodiles 245
  eye clinics 433
  genetics 376
  insects 458
  light and 508
  nocturnal animals 609
  owls 633
  vision 53
Eyots 471
Eyre, Lake 93, 501
Ezama, King of Aksum 19

# F

Fabergé, Carl **730**
Fables 203
Fabrics *see* Textiles
Face, muscles 767
Factories, Industrial Revolution 453
Faeces 264
Fahrenheit scale 416
Fa-Hsien 410
Fairies 593
Fairy-ring champignon 585, 586
Fairy tales 203

Falabella horse 432
Falaise Castle, France 610
Falcons 135, 137
Falkland Islands 66, 90
Falklands War (1982) 790
False fox sedge 394
False fruits 366, 367
Falster, Denmark 258
"Familiars", witches 898
Families 774
  classification 914
Family law 504
Family stories 204
Famines 346
  Ireland 466
Fang people 22
Fangs, snakes 772
Fantasy stories 204
Faraday, Michael 295, 296
Farming **323-5**
  Albania 107
  Ancient Egypt 291
  Argentina 66
  Armenia 187
  Australia 96
  Bhutan 115
  Bolivia 142
  Bosnia and Herzegovina 106
  Brazil 147
  Bulgaria 404
  Burundi 23
  Canada 170
  Central African Republic 21
  Colombia 792
  Congo 22
  Czech Republic 313
  Denmark 258
  Dominican Republic 174
  Ecuador 286
  Egypt 25
  Eritrea 26
  European Union 315
  Finland 333
  France 357
  Germany 380
  Great Zimbabwe 400
  Greece 404
  Guatemala 194
  Guinea 35
  Guinea-Bissau 34
  history of **326**
  Incas 442
  India 445
  Indonesia 452
  Iran 464
  Iraq 464
  Ireland 465
  Israel 474
  Italy 476
  Japan 479
  Jordan 822
  Kazakhstan **733**
  Kenya 27
  Khmer Empire 490
  Latvia 113
  Malawi 32
  Maya Empire 540
  Mexico 552
  Moldavia 728
  Mongolia 566
  Nepal 115
  Netherlands 601
  New Zealand 606
  Nicaragua 195
  Nigeria 37
  North Korea 497
  organic farming 678
  Philippines 650

Poland 313
Portugal 683
Russian Federation **732**
Saudi Arabia 407
Senegal 34
South Africa 785
Spain 799
Sri Lanka 446
Sumerian 813
Sweden 816
Switzerland 820
Tajikistan 81
Thailand 834
Togo 36
Turkey 853
Uganda 27
United Kingdom 858, 859
United States 866, 867
world resources 932
Faroe Islands 258
Fascism 311, 392
  Great Depression 399
  in Italy 477
  Spanish Civil War 800
Fashion **218-20**
Fasilidas Castle, Ethiopia 183
Fast breeders, nuclear power 618
Fathpur Sikri, India 580
Fatimid dynasty 470
Fats
  digestion 264
  food 349
  organic chemistry 200
Faults
  earthquakes 281
  mountain building 577
Fax machines 825
Feathers 132
  camouflage and colour 165
  ducks 276
  owls 633
  seabirds 747
Feather stars 806
February Revolution (1917) 734
Federal Bureau of Investigation
  (FBI) 676
Feeding
  animals 53
  ants and termites 58
  arthropods 74
  bats 118
  bears 120
  beetles 124
  birds 133
  bugs 155
  chimpanzees 568
  crocodiles 245
  fish 337
  flies 342
  grasshoppers and crickets 395
  insects 459
  lizards 517
  mongooses and civets 567
  orangutans 569
  parrots 644
  pigs and peccaries 657
  rodents 701
  seabirds 747
  sharks and rays 755
  shorebirds 761
  snakes 772
  songbirds 779
  spiders 801
  teeth and jaws **824**
Feet
  birds 132
  camels 162
  reflexology 542

seabirds 747
songbirds 779
*see also* Claws; Hooves
Feminism **901**
Fencing (sport) 229
Fennec fox 39, 260
Fens, England 858
Ferdinand, Emperor 428
Ferdinand II, King of Aragon 800
Ferdinand VII, King of Spain 140
Fermentation 645
Fermium 925
Fermi, Enrico 618
Ferns **327**, 663, 903
Ferries 759
Fertile Crescent 813
Fertility
  fertility stones 762
  gods and goddesses 389
  world population 930
Fertilization
  human reproduction 709
  plants 668
Fès, Morocco 29
Festivals **328**
  in Bahamas 173
  Christian 214, 328
  drama festivals 273
  Hindu 328, 422
  Islamic 469
  Jewish 474, 487
  Mexico 552
Feudalism **329**
Fiat 500 D 180
Fibreglass 387, 670
Fibres
  from plants 669
  textiles 832
Fibrin 415
Fiction 516
*Ficus* 355
Fiddler crab 240, 534
Field events, champions 936
Fieldmice 703
Field of the Cloth of Gold 708
Fieldwork, science 742
Fiestas, Spain 799
Fifth Republic, France 359
Fighter aircraft 884
Fighting
  beetles 124
  elephants 300
  giraffes 384
  hippopotamuses 423
  sheep and goats 756
  *see also* Armies; Soldiers; Warfare
Fighting ships 759
Figs 367
Figure skating 897
Fiji 472, **637**
Filaments, light-bulbs 508
Films and film-making **330-2**
  advertisements 14
  cameras 163, 164
  cartoons and animation **181**
  Disney, Walt **269**
  facts **940**
  Garbo, Greta **373**
  Hollywood 867
  in India 445
  movie cameras 164
Filter feeders 53
Filters 558
Finches 318
  Gouldian 779, 780
  woodpecker 779
Finger-nails 767
Fingerprints 676, 767

Finland 333
  banknotes 564
  history of 740
Fins, fish 336
Firdausi 515
Fire 334
  teepee fires 167
Firearms 409, 888
Fire-bellied toad 364
Firebird, The (Stravinsky) 811
Fir, giant 848
Fire clocks 839
First aid 335
First International Working Men's
  Association 535
First World War see World War I
Fish 336-8
  cave wildlife 189
  coral reefs 239
  flight 343
  as food 349
  homes 599
  lake and river wildlife 500
  marsh and swamp wildlife 534
  migration 556
  movement 53
  ocean wildlife 622
  poisonous 672
  prehistoric 687
  rainforest wildlife 699
  records 919
  sharks and rays 754-5
  shoals 53
  see also Fishing
Fish-eating bats 118
Fish-eating birds 134
Fisher (marten) 889
Fisheye lenses 163
Fishing 339
  Arctic Ocean 64
  bears 120
  Benin 37
  boats 757, 759
  Burma 834
  Chile 67
  fish farming 339, 635
  herons 419
  Iceland 90
  Indian Ocean 450
  Japan 479
  Kiribati 680
  Mauritania 34
  Mozambique 32
  Oman 407
  Pacific Ocean 635
  Peru 286
  Portugal 683
  prehistoric people 689
  Sumerian 813
  Surinam 792
  Taiwan 208
  United Arab Emirates 408
  United States 865
  Vietnam 877
  world resources 932
  see also Fish
Fishing cat 513
Fission, nuclear 548, 618
Fissure caves 188
Fissure volcanoes 880
Fitness and health 413
Fitzgerald, Ella 482
Fizeau, Armand Hippolyte 509
Fjord pony 432
Fjords 223, 385, 617
Flags 340-1
  codes 224
  pirates 659

Flamenco 253, 799
Flame tests, chemical analysis 559
Flamingos 38, 134, 419, 499
Flares, Sun 814
Flashes, photography 163
Flatfish 336
Flat racing 430
Flats 434
Flat shapes 536
Flat-water racing, canoes 736
Flatworms 54 , 643, 909
Flavours, taste 769
Flax 106, 113, 832
Fleas 131, 643
  Black Death 138
Flehmen 511
Fleming, Alexander 544
Flies 342, 458, 460
Flight
  aircraft 42
  airships and balloons 45-6
  bats 117, 343
  beetles 124
  birds 53, 132, 133, 343
  birds of prey 135
  flies 342
  gliding animals 343
  helicopters 42
  history of 344
  hummingbirds 817
  insects 343
  kites 493-4
  Leonardo da Vinci 507
  swifts 817
Flightless birds 133, 345
Flight paths, aircraft 44
Flinders Ranges 93
Flint carvings, Maya Empire 540
Flint tools 809
Float glass 387
Floating 690
  ships and boats 757
Flood barriers 252
Floods, rivers 715
Floors, building and
  construction 156
Floppy disks, computers 232
Florence, Italy 477, 708
Florey, Howard 275
Flowers 346-7
  anatomy 665
  prehistoric 687
  records 918
Flowstone 188
Fluids, pressure 690
  see also Liquids
Flukes 909
Fluking, whales 894
Fluorescence 508
Fluorescent light 509
Fluorine 925
Flushing, blood vessels 415
Fluted bird's nest 586
Flutes 592
Fly agaric 585, 586
Flycatchers 134
  ochre-bellied 134
  spotted 779
Flyer I 344
Flying see Flight
Flying boats 43
Flying buttresses 61
Flying Doctor 96
Flying fish 343
Flying foxes 117
  spectacled 118
Flying squirrel 343
Flywheels 520

Foam-nesting frogs 365
Foams 558
Foetus 710
Fog 221
Fold mountains 577
Folk dance 253
Folk music 587, 718
Folk tales 203
Follicles, hair 767
Fongafale, Tuvalu 680
Food 348-9
  Algeria 29
  Argentina 66
  Armenia 187
  astronauts 86
  Australia 96
  Belorussia 113
  Botswana 31
  camping 168
  Central African Republic 21
  China 207
  cooking 334
  digestion 264
  Earth sciences 282
  ecosystems 284
  Egypt 25
  energy 303
  Ethiopia 26
  food technology 823
  food webs and chains 350
  France 357
  fruits and seeds 366-7
  genetic engineering 377
  Germany 380
  Ghana 36
  Greece 404
  halal food 469
  health and fitness 413
  Hittites 425
  India 445
  Indonesia 452
  Iraq 464
  Israel 474
  Italy 476
  Japan 479
  kosher 487
  Lebanon 822
  living standards 931
  Mexico 552
  micro-organisms in 555
  Native Americans 613
  Nicaragua 195
  nutritional diseases 268
  Olmecs 627
  packaging 760
  plants 669
  prehistoric people 689
  Russia 732
  Spain 799
  Tunisia 29
  Turkey 853
  Ukraine 728
  United Kingdom 859
  World War II 908
  Yugoslavia 107
  see also Feeding
Food mixers 462
Food stores, plants 665
Foot, Phillipa 651
Football 111, 351
  Brazil 147
  Cameroon 21
  flags 340
  Germany 380
Footbinding, China 210
Footprints, hominid 506
Forbidden City, Beijing 216
Force and motion 352

friction 363
  gravity 398
  magnetism 522
  metallic bonds 550
Forces of nature 744
Ford GT40 180
Ford, Henry
  assembly lines 461, 841
  mass production 869
  Model T Ford 178, 844
Ford Motor Company 178, 865, 901
Ford Mustang 180
Ford Thunderbird 180
Forebrain 145
Forecasting weather 891
Foreign aid, world economy 933
Foreign debt, world economy 933
Forensic science 676
Forest hog, giant 657
Forests 353
  Baltic States 112
  Bhutan 114
  broad-leaved woodlands 316
  Canada 170
  Central Europe 312
  deciduous 76
  endangered 920
  Finland 333
  mountain wildlife 578
  North American wildlife 616
  taiga 76, 309
  teak logging 834
  wild cats 512, 513
  see also Boreal forests; Coniferous
  forests; Temperate forests;
  Rainforests; Woodlands
Forging, metals 550
Formula, chemical 92
Formula One racing 575
  champions 937
Fort Knox, USA 563
Fort Still, USA 383
Fortune telling 85
Fossey, Dian 568
Fossil fuels 304
  coal 222
  oil 625-6
  world resources 932
Fossils 354-5
  continental drift 236
  Darwin, Charles 255
  dinosaurs 265-6
  and evolution 318, 319
  Leakey family 506
  palaeontology 282
  prehistoric life 687
Foundations, buildings 156, 157
Fourth Republic, France 359
Fox and cubs (flower) 347
Foxes 899
  Arctic 528, 615, 674, 900
  bat-eared 900
  fennec 900
  grey 900
  red 316, 528, 899, 900
  Ruppell's sand 900
Foxglove 347, 667
Fox Talbot, William 163, 164
Fox terrier, smooth 271
Fractals 655
Fractional distillation 40
Fractions 619
Fractures, bones 766
Fragonard, Jean Honoré 358
Frames, building
  and construction 156
France 356-7
  castles 182, 183

crafts 243
  drama 272
  European Union 311, 315
  food 349
  French Revolution 361
  history of 358-9
  human rights 438
  Hundred Years' War 439
  kings 945
  Monet, Claude 562
  Napoleon Bonaparte 594
  Napoleonic Wars 595
  Normans 610
  nuclear tests 680
  Paris Commune 535
  post boxes 805
  presidents 945
  and Quebec 171
  sculpture 746
  World War I 905
Francis I, King of France 171, 708
Francis II, Emperor 428
Francis Xavier, St 480, 481
Francium 924
Franco, General 800
Franco-Prussian War 359, 382
Frank, Anne 426, 516
Franklin, Aretha 718
Franklin, Benjamin 295, 360, 493
Franklin, John 673
Franklin, Rosalind 376
Franks 358
  Charlemagne 197
Franz Ferdinand, Archduke 905
Fraunhofer, Joseph von 226
Frederick I, Emperor 247
Frederick II, Emperor 546
Frederick the Great, King of
  Prussia 381, 382
Fredericksburg, Battle of (1862) 48
Freedom of expression 438
Freedom satellite 739
Freestyle skiing 897
Freetown, Sierra Leone 35
Freezing 514, 538
Freighters (aircraft) 41, 43
French Guiana 792
French-Indian War (1753) 886
French Open Tennis
  Championship 357
French Polynesia 679, 680
French Revolution 45, 359, 361,
  901
Frequency
  hearing 278
  radio waves 696
  sound 782
Frequency modulation (FM) 825
Freshwater fish 336, 338, 339
Fresnel, Augustin 508, 509
Freud, Anna 362
Freud, Sigmund 362, 544
Friction 363
Friedman, William 224
Friedrich, Caspar David 72
Friendship Bridge, Mekong
  River 877
Frigatebirds 747
Frigates 885
Frilled lizard, Australian 517
Fringe-toed lizard 261
Frisch, Otto 548
Fritillary butterfly, great spangled
  159
Froebel, Friedrich 741
Frog beetle 460
  Malaysian 125
Frogbit 666

Froghopper, red and black 166
Frogs 50, **364-5**
　animal symbols 764
　edible 316
　eggs 289
　European common 50
　poisonous 50, 672, 700
　rainforest wildlife 700
　urban wildlife 872
　water-holding 99, 261
　White's tree 50
Front crawl, swimming 818
Fronts, weather 890
Frost 698
Frowning 582
Frozen food 346
Fruit bats 117, 118
　Borneo 119
　Franquet's 119
　Mexican 119
　New World 119
Fruits **366-7**
　citrus fruits 785
　farming 324
　food 349
　fruit-eating birds 134
Fuchsia 347
Fuels
　coal **222**
　fire 334
　fossil 304
　natural gas 29, 625, 626
　oil **625-6**
　from plants 669
　rockets 720
　world resources 932
Fujairah, United Arab
　Emirates 408
Fuji, Mount 75, 478
Fukuyama, Frances 424
Fulani people 21, 35, 36, 69
*Ful medames* 25
Fulcrum 520
Functions, algebra 537
Fundamentalism, Islamic 469
Funerals 775
Funerary amulets, Ancient
　Egypt 293
Fungi 131, **584-6**
　classification 914
　fungal diseases 555
　microscopic 554
　records 918
　woodland wildlife 903
Fungus gardens, termite nests 58
Funk music 719
Funnel-eared bat 119
Funnelweb spiders 802
　Sydney 801
Fur
　cats 184
　mammals 527
　otters 104
　trade 171, 878
Furniture **368-9**
Furniture beetle 459
Fur seal, northern 556
Fusion, nuclear 618
Futuna 680
Fyn, Denmark 258

# G

Gabbro 722, 723
Gabon **22**
Gaborone, Botswana 31
Gabriel, Angel 468, 469, 581
Gabrieli, Andrea 588

Gabrieli, Giovanni 588
Gaddafi, Colonel 29
Gadolinium 924
Gaelic football 351
Gagarin, Yuri 86, 795
Gage, Phineas 145
Gaia theory 280
Galah 99
Gálapagos Islands 255, 286, 318
Galaxies **370**
　Big Bang 130
　black holes 139
　gravity 398
　Great Wall 870
　scale of the Universe 871
Galen 543, 874
Galilee, Sea of 501
Galileo Galilei **371**, 743, 805
　and gravity 398
　Jupiter's moons 661
　pendululum clock 838
　telescopes 828
*Galileo* space probe 796, 797
Gall bladder 264
Gallic Wars 161
*Gallimimus* 265, 267
Gallipoli, Battle of (1915) 98
Gallium 925
Gambia **34**
　banknotes 564
Gambia River 33, 34
*Gamelan* orchestras 452
Games
　chess and other board games
　**201-2**
　*see also* Sport
Gamma rays 697
　astronomy 870
　electromagnetic spectrum 911
Gandhi, Indira 448
Gandhi, Mohandas (Mahatma)
　**372**, 448, 491
Gandhi, Rajiv 448
Ganesha 421
Ganges, River 75
　in Bangladesh 114
　delta 114
　hydroelectricity 114
　in India 444
Gangsters 244
Gannets 747
　northern 747
Ganymede 661
Gao 781
Gaodong, Emperor of China 320
Ga people 36
Garbo, Greta **373**
Gardens **374**
　United Kingdom 859
Garden spiders 802
Gargoyles 215
Garibaldi, Giuseppe 477
Garnet 722
Garnier, Charles 835
*Garrigue* 309
Gases **375**
　air 40, 91
　convection 417
　elements 298
　interstellar material 870
　latent heat 417
　laws 375
　noble gases 925
　pressure 690
　states of matter 538
Gas lighting 454
Gas, natural *see* Natural gas
Gaskell, Elizabeth 263

Gas planets 661-2
Gaspra 230
Gastropods 770, 771
Gas turbine engines 306
Gates, Bill 457
Gauchos 66
Gaugamela-Arbela, Battle of
　(331 BC) 648, 649
Gaul 161, 358
Gauntlets 70
Gautama Siddhartha 152
Gears 520
　bicycles and motorcycles 128
　cars 178
Geckos 517, 711
　flying 343, 518
　leopard 289, 518
　Tokay 518
Geese **276**, 325
　African pygmy 134
　greylag 54
　snow 556
　white-fronted 276
Geiger, Hans 697
Geiger-Müller counters 697
Gelada 39
Gels 558
Gemmae, liverworts 573
Gems **248-9**, 446
Gender, social stratification 775
General Agreement on Tariffs and
　Trade (GATT) 841
General Assembly, United Nations
　862
General Motors 865
General practitioners (GPs) 541
General Strike (1926) 857
Generators, electricity 295
Genes 376
　heredity 377
　sex chromosomes 377
Genet, small spotted 39
Genetics 131, **376-7**, 744
　artificial selection 319
　DNA 190
　genetic engineering 377
　natural selection 318
　plant reproduction 668
Geneva, Lake 819
Geneva Convention (1864) 646,
　883
Genghis Khan 79, 498, 565
Genotype 376
Gentian, spring 664
Gentileschi, Artemisia 708
Genus, classification 914
Geochemistry 200
Geodes 248
Geoffroy's cat 513
Geography 282
Geology 282, **378**
Geometry 536
Geomorphology 282
Geophysics 655
Georgetown, Guyana 792
Georgia (Caucasus) 186, **187**
Geostationary satellites 739
Geothermal power 90, 304
Gerbils 703
　Mongolian 83
　pallid 703
Germanium 925
German measles 555
German shepherd dog 271
Germany **379-82**
　banknotes 564
　Berlin Olympics (1936) 632
　castles 182, 183

European Union 311, 315
　history of **381-2**
　Holocaust **426**
　Iron Curtain 311
　Nürnberg Trials 883
　re-unification 225
　World War I 311, 905-6
　World War II 907-8
Germs 268, 441
Geronimo **383**
Gershwin, George 629
Gestation periods 917
Gestures 502
Gettysburg Address 48
Gettysburg, Battle of (1863) 868
Geysers 93, 881
Ghana 19, **36**
Ghana Empire 17
Gharials 245
Ghettos 487
Giant's Causeway, Northern
　Ireland 881
Gibbon, John Jr 544
Gibbons 569
　Lar 570
Gibraltar, Strait of 798
Gila monster 261
　banded 518
Gilbert, William 522
Gilgamesh 103, 671, 813
Gill rakers, sharks 755
Gills, fish 336
Ginger 665
*Ginkgo* 687
*Giotto* space probe 796, 797
Giraffes 38, **384**
　reticulated 384
Girondins 361
*Giselle* 108
Giverny, France 561
Giza pyramids 693
Glaciation **385-6**
　ice caves 188
　Iceland 90
　lakes 501
　meltwater 715
　valleys 577
Glaciers *see* Glaciation
Gladiators 725
Glaisher, James 91
Glands
　hormones and the endocrine
　system **429**
　scent 528
　sweat 528
Glasnost 795
Glass **387**
　Bohemian 313
　glassblowing 387
　Phoenician 652
　stained-glass windows 547
Glass lizard, Yugoslavian 518
Glazes, pottery and ceramics 685,
　686
Glial cells 145
Gliders 41
Gliding
　animals 343
　birds 343
Global Positioning System (GPS)
　598
Global warming 217, 678
Globe Theatre, London 753, 835
Glomeruli, kidneys 873
Glossophagine bat 118
Glow-worm, New Zealand 189
Glucose, photosynthesis 654
Gluons 92

Glycogen 190
Glyphs, Maya Empire 540
Gneisses 723
Go (board game) 201
Goat moth 159
Goats 325, **756**, 853
　mountain 616
　Rocky Mountain 756
Goat's rue 666
Gobelins tapestries 358
Gobi Desert 75, 76, 566
　camels 162
　wildlife 83
God
　Christianity 213
　Islam 468
　Judaism 486
　*see also* Gods and goddesses
Goddard, Robert 721
Gods and goddesses **388-9**, 705
　ancient Egypt 291
　ancient Greece 401
　Hinduism 421
　Indus Valley civilization 455
　mythology 935
　Roman 725
　shrines 762
Godthaab, Greenland 64
Goethe, Johann Wolfgang von 515,
　671
Gold 550
　in Australia 96
　element 298
　Fort Knox 563
　Gold Rush 97, 216, 614, 868
　hallmarks 763
　Inca arts and crafts 443
　periodic table 925
　in South Africa 785
　in United States 866
Gold Coast 19, 36
　*see also* Ghana
Golden beetle 125
Golden Horn, Constantinople 160
Golden Triangle 833
Goldfinch 779
　Eurasian 134
Gold standard 562
Golf 110, 111
　champions 937
　flags 340
　in Portugal 683
　in Singapore 525
Golgi apparatus 190
Goliath 427
Goliath beetle 125, 460
Gombe, Tanzania 390
Gongs 590, 592
Goodall, Jane **390**
Good Hope, Cape of 684
Goods trains 842
Goose *see* Geese
Gooseberries 367
Goosegrass 367
Gorbachev, Mikhail 225, **730**, 795
Gordon, General Charles 302
Gordy, Berry 865
Gorges 577
Gorillas 235, 568
　lowland 570
　mountain 39, 568
　western lowland 529
Goshawk 135, 137
Gospel music 587
Gospels 214, 484
Gothic architecture 61, 63, 116,
　547
Goths 116, 477

Gouldian finch, red-headed 165
Governments and politics **391-2**
　empires 302
　law **504-5**
　peace movements 646
　Roman 724
Graf, Steffi 803
Grahame, Kenneth 205
Gran Chaco 65, 141, 142, 788
Gran Chaco War (1932-35) 141
Gran Colombia 140
Grand Canal, China 210
Grand Canyon, USA 577, 611
Grand Casino, Monaco 357
Grand Coulee Dam, USA 252
"Grand Tour" 845
Grandfather clocks 839
Granite 723
Grant, Ulysses S. 48
Grape hyacinth 666
Grapes 96, 367, 476
Graphic design 262
　computer graphics 456
Graphite 298
Graphs, statistics 537
Grasses **393-4**
Grasshoppers 74, **395**
　common field 395
　lubber 616
Grasslands
　Australia 94
　Europe 309
　pampas 65
　South America 788
　see also Savannah
Grassland wildlife **396-7**
　Asia 82
　Australia 99
　ecosystems 283
　South America 794
　wild cats 513
Grass snake 397
Gravity **398**
　black holes 139
　Einstein, Albert 294
　galaxies 370
　Galileo's theory 371
　Newton, Isaac 605
　rockets 720
　space probes 796
　tides 621
　Universe 870
　weight 892
Gravity bombs 887
Gravity dams 252
Great Arch, Paris 63
Great Barrier Reef, Australia 95, 239
Great Britain see United Kingdom
Great Dane 271
Great Dark Spot, Neptune 662
Great Depression **399**, 869
Great Dividing Range, Australia 94, 95
Greater Caucasus Mountains 186
Great Famine, Ireland 466
"Great Game" 78
Great Lakes 501, 611, 864
Great Lakes states 865
Great Man-made River project, Libya 29
Great Mosque, Córdoba 572
Great Northern War 740
Great Plain of China 75
Great Plains, North America 611, 612, 866
Great Pyramid, Giza 693
Great raft spider 534
Great Red Spot, Jupiter 661

Great Rift Valley 15, 24, 236
Great Salt Lake 501, 611
Great Schism (1054) 160
Great Trek (1836-46) 786
Great Victoria Desert, Australia 93
Great Wall (Universe) 870
Great Wall of China 79, 206, 210
Great War see World War I
Great Western (steamship) 844
Great Zimbabwe 32, **400**
Greaves 70
Grebes 499
Greco, El 800
Greece **403-4**
　roadside shrines 762
Greece, ancient 310, **401-2**
　Alexander the Great 47
　architecture 61
　armies 68
　art 71
　dance 253
　drama 272
　gods and goddesses 389
　medicine 543
　music 587
　mythology 935
　philosophy 651, 743
　Seven Wonders of the Ancient World 752
　slavery 768
　theatres 835
　view of the Universe 871
　writing 910
Greek Orthodox Church 403, **729**
Greenbul, yellow-streaked 290
Greengages 367
Greenham Common, England 646
Greenhouse effect 91, 678
"Greenhouse gases" 217
Greenland 64, 258, 471, 611
　ice cap 386
Green Revolution 326
Green stain fungus 586
Greenwich Mean Time (GMT) 838, 929
Greer, Germain 901
Gregorian calendar 837
Gregorian chant 588
Gregory I, Pope 588
Gregory VII, Pope 428
Grenada 175, 611
Grenadines 175
Grey, Tanni 628
Grey matter, brain 145
Greyhound 271
Greywracke 723
Gribble 241
Grieg, Edvard 589
Griffon, Himalayan 83
Grimm Brothers 203
Grooming, cats 184
Gropius, Walter 262
Grosbeak, black and yellow 290
Ground beetle 460
　sabre-toothed 125
Groundnuts 33
Ground snake 773
Ground squirrel, Kalahari 260
Groundwater 715
Grouper, panther 338
Grouse
　sage 234
　willow 290
Growth and development
　human body **405**
　plants 668
　reptiles 712
Growth hormone 429

Grünewald, Mathias 381
Gryloblattid 459
Guam 635
Guanaco 162
Guanaco Lake 625
Guanine 376
Guaraní Indians 142, 789
Guatemala 193, **194**
　Maya civilization 196
Guatemala City, Guatemala 194, 196
Guayana Highlands 787
Gucci 476
Guerillas 882, 887
Guernica (Picasso) 656
Guernica, Spain 800
Guggenheim Museum, New York 63, 583
Guillemots 747
　common 290
Guillotine 361
Guinea 35
Guinea-Bissau **34**
Guinea, Gulf of 37
Guinea pig 703
Guiscard, Robert 610
Guitarfish 754
Guitars 592
Gulf States **406-8**
Gulf Stream 89, 309, 465, 617
Gulf War (1990-91) 463, 678, 883
Gulls 675, 747
Gums, plant defences 667
Gums and teeth 824
Gum trees 94
Gundestrup Cauldron 191
Gunpowder 209, 887
Guns **409**
Guppy, uncoloured 338
Gupta Empire **410**, 447
Gustavus I, King of Sweden 740
Gustavus II Adolphus, King of Sweden 740
Gutenberg, Johannes 143, 691
Gutenberg discontinuity 279
Guttman, Dr Ludwig 628
Guyana **792**
Guyots 620
Gymnastics **411-12**, 803
Gymnosperms 663
Gynaecology 541
Gypsies 728
　Romany language 502
Gypsum 34, 723
Gyrocompasses 598

# H

Haber, Fritz 13
Habitats
　insects 459
　rodents 702
　wildlife 283
Habsburg Empire
　Holy Roman Empire 428
　and the Netherlands 602
　Thirty Years War 381
Hachas 549
Hackney horse 432
Hades 388, 389
Hadley, George 896
Hadley cells 896
Hadrian, Emperor 724
Hadrian's Wall 724
Haemoglobin 414
Hafnium 924
Hagia Sophia, Constantinople 160
Hague, The Netherlands 601

Hahn, Otto 548, 618
Hahn-Meitner Institute 548
Haikus 671
Haile Selassie, Emperor of Ethiopia 18, 176
Hailstones 698
Hair
　human body **767**
　mammals 527
Hair dryers 462
Hairgrass 675
Hairstreak butterfly, Hewitson's blue 159
Hairy sedge 394
Haiti **174**, 176
Hajj 468
Halal food 469
Hale telescope, Mount Palomar 828
Haley, Bill and His Comets 718
Half-life, radioactivity 697
Halftone printing 692
Halicarnassus 752
Halley, Edmond 230
Halley's Comet 230, 796
Hallmarks 763
Halloween 898
Hallstatt culture 191
Halogens 298, 925
Ha Long Bay, Vietnam 876
Hamada deserts 259
Hamburgers 865
Hamburg, Germany 380
Hammarskjöld, Dag 863
Hammers, antler 809
Hammer throwing 88
Hammurabi code 504
Hammurabi, King of Babylon 103
Hamsters
　Chinese 703
　dwarf 260, 703
　Russian 318
Han Chinese 207, 208
Handaxes 809
Handel, George Frideric 588, 589
Handstand dive 818
Han dynasty 78, 209
Hang-gliders 43
Hanna, Bill 181
Hanoi, Vietnam 877
Hanoverian horse 432
Hanseatic League 381, 382, 547
Hanukkah 487
Harappa 150, 455
Harare, Zimbabwe 32
Harbours **681**
Hardness
　Mohs' scale 722
　solids 778
Hares **694**
　Arctic 317, 674, 694
　mountain 694
　Patagonian 396
Hargreaves, James 453
Harley Davidson motorcycles 129
Harmonics 782
Harmony, music 587
Harold II, King of England 51, 610, 860
Harpoons 809
Harpsichords 591
Harrier GR5 jet 884
Harris, Joel Chandler 203
Harris's hawk 134, 137
Harrison, George 121
Harrison, John 598, 838
Hartebeest 256

Harvard, John 658
Harvard University 658
Harvest festivals 328
Harvesters 324
Harvestmen 801
Harvey, William 414, 544, 874
Harz Mountains 379
Hassaal Bolkiah, Sultan of Brunei 525
Hassium 924
Hastings, Battle of (1066) 51, 610, 860, 861
Hat Boi theatre 273
Hatchbacks 178
Hatchet fish 338, 623, 793
Hats 218-20
　Panama hats 286
Hatshepsut, Queen of Egypt 292
Hattusas 425
Hausa people 37
Havana, Cuba 173
Hawaii 635
　Cook, James 238
　kites 494
　tsunamis 281
　US state 864, 867
　volcanoes 471, 881
Hawkmoth caterpillar 166
Hawks 135, 137
Haworth, England 149
Haydn, Joseph 123, 589
Healing
　African medicine 22
　witches and witchcraft 898
　see also Medicine
Health and fitness **413**
Hearing 53, **278**
　animal hearing ranges 917
Hearst, William Randolph 603
Heart and circulatory system **414-15**
　animal heart rates 917
　pacemakers 462
　transplants 541
Heat **416-17**
　friction and 363, 416
Heat resistant glass 387
Heat sensitive pits, snakes 772
Heather, bell 347, 664
Heathrow Airport 859
Heavy horses 432
Hedgehog fungus 586
Hedgehogs **418**, 527, 872
　European 418
Hegira 581
Heinkle Perle motorcycles 129
Helicopters 42, 43
　helicopter cruisers 885
　history of 844
　warplanes 884
Helictites 188
Helios 752
Helium
　airships 45
　in natural gas 626
　periodic table 925
　stars 807
　in the Sun 814
Hellebore, green 666
Helmets 70
Helmholtz, Hermann von 303
Helsinki, Finland 333
Hemlock 666
Hemminges, John 753
Hemp 832
Henie, Sonja 897
Henna 669
Henry, Joseph 295

Henry I, King of England 610
Henry II, King of England 610
   Angevin empire 358
   invades Ireland 466
Henry III, King of England 610, 860
Henry IV, Emperor 428
Henry IV, King of France 310, 359
Henry V, King of England 439
Henry VII, King of England
   614, 861
Henry VIII, King of England
   Church of England 301
   dissolution of monasteries
   704, 861
   Field of the Cloth of Gold 708
Henry the Navigator, Prince 684
Henslow, John 255
Henson, Matthew 673
Hephaistos 389
Heptathlon 88
Hepworth, Barbara 745, 746
Hera 725
Heraldry 495-6
Herb gardens, monasteries 560
Herbaceous plants 665
Herbivores 53
   arthropods 74
   beetles 125
   food webs and chains 350
   grassland wildlife 396
   lizards 518
   plant defences 667
Herbs 349
   herbal remedies 543, 544,
   545, 547
Hercules 388
Hercules star cluster 807
Herding dogs 271
Herds
   elephants 300
   giraffes 384
   hippopotamuses 423
   horses 431
   pigs and peccaries 657
Heredity 318, 377
Hermes 725
*Hermes and Dionysus* (Praxiteles) 71
Hermit crabs 240, 750
Herodotus 424, 752
Hero of Alexandria 306, 509
Herons 419
   black 419
   black-crowned night 134
   goliath 419
   green 419
*Herrerasaurus* 267
Herschel, William 662, 828, 911
Hertz, Heinrich 696, 911
Hertz (Hz) 782
Hertzsprung-Russell diagram 808
Herzegovina *see* Bosnia and
   Herzegovina
Hesiod 402
*Heterodontosaurus* 267
Hexagonal system, crystals 248
Hibernation 420
   bats 117
   mammals 528
Hibiscus 347
Hideyoshi, Toyotomi 480
Hieratic script 292
Hieroglyphic moth 159
Hieroglyphics 292, 910
High bar, gymnastics 411
High jump 88
Highland coasts 223
Highland pony 432
High pressure

weather 890
winds 896
Hiking **168**
Hill tribes, Thailand and
   Burma 833
Hillforts 191
Himalayan balsam 664
Himalayas 75
   formation 577
   India 444
   Nepal 114, 115
   wildlife 83
Himba people 31
Himeji Castle, Japan 183
Hinduism 421-2
   Asian history 77
   calendar 837
   festivals 328, 422
   gods and goddesses 388
   in India 445, 447
   Khmer Empire 490
   monasteries 560
   signs and symbols 764
   weddings 775
Hindu Kush 639
Hines, Barry 204
Hinge joints 766
Hipparchus 807
*Hipparion* 318
Hippocrates 543
Hippopotamuses 38, **423**, 499
   common 423
   pygmy 423
Hirohito, Emperor of Japan 481
Hiroshima, Japan 481, 618, 908
Hispaniola 174, 228
History **424**, **942-7**
Hitler, Adolf 399
   Berlin Olympics 632
   Holocaust 426
   Nazis 382
   World War II 907, 908
Hittites 103, **425**
HIV (human immunodeficiency
   virus) 268, 441
Hoatzin 793
*Hobbit, The* (Tolkien) 204
Hockey 109
   champions 936
Hoggar Mountains 28
Hognose snake, giant Madagascan
   773
Hogs *see* Pigs and peccaries
Hogweed 367
Hojo family 738
Hokkaido, Japan 478
Hokusai, Katsushika 73
Holbein, Hans 381, 708
Holi 422
Holidays 845
Holland *see* Netherlands
Holly 667
   common 666
Hollywood, USA
   Disney, Walt 269
   film industry 331, 867
   Garbo, Greta 373
Holmium 925
Holocaust **426**
Holocene epoch 378
Holograms **503**
Holy days, Judaism 487
Holy Land
   Crusades 247, 883
   history of **427**
Holy objects and places **706**
Holy Roman Empire 197, 302,
   310, 381, **428**

Holy Sepulchre Church, Jerusalem
   427
Holy Spirit 213
Holy Trinity 213
Homeopathy 542
Homer 401
Homes *see* Houses and homes
Homestead Act (1862) 868
Hominids 437, 506
*Homo erectus* 437, 506, 809
*Homo habilis* 437, 506, 688
*Homo sapiens* 437, 688
*Homo sapiens sapiens* 689
Honda motorcycles 129
Honduras **194**, 196
Honesty (plant) 367, 664
Honey 122, 349
Honeyeater, blue-faced 780
Honey fungus 585
   fine-scaled 586
Honeysuckle 347
Hong Kong 206, **208**
   container port 635
   "dragon" economy 79
   trams 842
Hong Wu 210
Honiara, Solomon Islands 637
Honshu, Japan 478
Hooke, Robert 553
Hoop pine moth 159
Hoover, Herbert 399
Hooves
   buffalo 154
   horses 431
   sheep and goats 756
Hopewell people 613
Horace 402
Hormones and the endocrine
   system
   human body **429**
   plants 668
Hornbills **492**
   rhinoceros 82
   trumpeter 492
Horn, Cape 65
Horned lizard, Texas 518
Horned toads
   Asian 365
   ornate 365
Hornet moth 159
Hornets 122
Hornfels 723
Horns
   antelopes 256
   giraffes 384
   rhinoceroses 713
   sheep and goats 756
Horoscopes 85
Horror films 331
Horror novels 516
Horse boxes 179
Horse chestnut 667
Horses **431-2**
   armour 69
   Celts and 191
   evolution 318
   farming 325
   knights 495
   riding **430**, 803
   skeleton 527
   warfare 882
Horseshoe bat 117
   greater 118
   lesser 119, 189
Horsetails 327
Hospitals **433**

Hossein (Muhammad's grandson)
   735
Hossein, Shah 735
Hot-air ballooning 45
Hot-blooded animals 917
Hot springs 881
Hottentot fig 664
Hounds 271
Hours 837
Households 774
Household shrines 762
*Household Words* 263
Houses and homes **434-5**
   ancient Egypt 292
   building and construction 156
   cities 216
   electricity 295
   Elizabethan 301
   inventions 461, 462
   Native Americans 596
   stilt houses 115
   urban wildlife 872
House spiders 802
Hovercraft 363, 758
Hoverfly 459, 460
Hovering birds 343
   hummingbirds 817
   kestrels 135
Howard, Luke 221
Howitzers 409
Howler monkey, red 569, 570
Howlin' Wolf 718
Hoyle, Fred 87, 130
Huancayo, Peru 286
Huang He River 75, 206
Huari culture 198
Huaxtecs 549
Hubble, Edwin 370
Hubble Space Telescope 87, 321,
   739, 797, 828
*Huckleberry Finn* (Twain) 204, 856
Hudson, Henry 673
Hudson's Bay Company 171, 614
Hughes, Howard 41
Hughes, Thomas 204
Huguenots 358, 704
Hulls, ships, and boats 757
Human body **436**
   brain and nervous system **144-5**
   digestion **264**
   diseases **268**
   drugs **274-5**
   ears and hearing **278**
   eyes and seeing **322**
   food **348**
   genetics **376-7**
   growth and development **405**
   health and fitness **413**
   heart and circulatory system
   **414-15**
   hormones and the endocrine
   system **429**
   immune and lymphatic
   system **441**
   lungs and breathing **519**
   medicine **541-5**
   muscles and movement **582**
   reproduction **709-10**
   skeleton **765-6**
   skin, hair, and nails **767**
   smell and taste **769**
   teeth and jaws **824**
   urinary system **873**
Human evolution 437, 688
   Leakey family **506**
Human Genome Project 377
Human rights **438**
   black rights 948

King, Martin Luther **491**
Truth, Sojourner **849**
   women's movement 901
   women's voting rights 948
Human sacrifices 101, 705
Human societies **774-5**
Humanism 708
Humanitarian aid, United Nations
   863
Humayun, Emperor 580
Humidity, weather 890
Hummingbirds 343, 420, **817**
   rufous 134
Humours 543
Humus 777
Hundred Years' War **439**
Hungary 312, **314**
Hunger 346
Huns 116, 381
Hunting
   Aboriginal Australians 11
   lions and other wild cats 511,
   512
   Maya Empire 540
   prehistoric people 689
   wolves and wild dogs 899
Hunting wasps 122
Hurdling 88
Hurling 109
Huron, Lake 611
Huron Indians 614
Hurricanes 810, 896
   Caribbean Sea 172
   Pacific Ocean 635
Hus, Jan 704
Husky, Siberian 270
Husqvarna Motocross 129
Hussein, Saddam 391, 464
Hussites 704
Hutton, James 378
Hutu people 23
Huygens, Christiaan 838
*Huygens* space probe 797
Hydraulics 690
Hydrocarbons 626
Hydroelectricity 304
   Austria 820
   Bangladesh and Nepal 114
   dams 252
   Uruguay 67
Hydrofoils 758
Hydrogen
   acids and alkalis 12
   airships 45
   covalent bonds 92
   element 298
   periodic table 924
   stars 807
   in the Sun 814
   water 514
Hydrometers 514
Hydrostatic skeletons 53
Hydrothermal vents 620
Hyenas **440**, 528
   aardwolf 440
   brown 440
   spotted 440, 529
   striped 440
Hygieia 543
Hygrometers 890, 891
Hypothalamus 145, 429
Hypotheses, scientific method 742
*Hypsilophodon* 267
*Hyracotherium* 318

I

Ibadi sect 407

Iberian peninsula
  Portugal **682-4**
  Spain **798-800**
Ibex
  Alpine 578
  Himalayan 756
Ibis, glossy 290
Ibiza 798
IBM computers 232, 457
Ibn-an-Nafis 543
Ibn Battuta 526
Ibn Khaldun 424
Ibn Saud, King of Saudi Arabia 407
Ibn Sina (Avicenna) 247, 470
Ibo people 37
Ibsen, Henrik 272
Ice 514
  Antarctica 56
  Arctic Ocean 64
  clouds 221
  glaciation **385-6**
  ice caves 188
  ice sheets and caps 385, 386
  snow 698
  tundra 850
Ice ages 688
  fjords 617
  glaciation 386
  North America 613
Ice hockey 111, 897
Ice skates 690
Ice speedway races 576
Icebergs 56, 64, 386
Iceland **90**
Icelandic horse 432
Iceni tribe 191
*I Ching* 233
Ichimura, Uzaemo 836
*Ichthyosaurus* 355
*Ichthyostega* 688
Icons 160
Id al-Adha festival 469
Id al-Fitr festival 469
Identical twins 710
Identification, scent glands 528
Ides of March 161
Ieyasu Tokugawa 738
Ife people 73
Ightham Mote, England 329
Igloos 435, 596
Ignatius Loyola, St 704
Igneous rocks 722, 723
Iguanas
  common green 518
  marine 711
*Iguanodon* 265, 266, 267
Ileum 264
*Iliad* 515
Illinois, USA 865
Illuminated manuscripts 547
Illustrations, books 143
Imhotep 693
Immigration 845
  Australia 98
  Canada 171
  United Kingdom 859, 861
  United States 864, 868
Immune system 268, **441**
Immunization 413, 441, 544
Imperfect fungi 584
Imperialism 302, 311
Imperial scorpion 802
Imperial system, weights and measures 892
Imports 841
Impressionism 72, 73, 359
  Monet, Claude **562**
Imprinting, animal behaviour 54

*In vitro* fertilization (IVF) 542, 710
Incandescence 508
Incas 285, **442-3**, 789
Incisors 824
Inclined plane 520
Independence movements
  Africa 19
  Asia 79
  Bolívar, Simon 140
  India 448
India **444-5**
  banknotes 564
  clothes 219
  dance 253
  exploration 320, 321
  festivals 774
  food 349
  Gandhi, Mohandas (Mahatma) **372**
  Gupta Empire **410**
  Hinduism 421-2
  history of 77, 78, **447-8**
  independence 79, 448
  Jainism 705
  kites 494
  Mauryan Empire **539**
  Mother Teresa **574**
  Mughal Empire **580**
  music 587
Indiana, USA 865
Indianapolis 500 race 575
Indian bean tree 848
Indian Mutiny (1857-58) 448
Indian National Congress Party 448, 372
Indian Ocean 75, **449-50**, 621
  cyclones 810
  pirates 659
Indian Wars 596
Indigestion 13
Indium 925
Indochina 876
Indonesia 75, **451-2**
  banknotes 564
  independence 79
Indri 570
Induction
  internal combustion engines 305
  magnetic 522
Inductors 297
Induráin, Miguel 251
Indus River 75, 639
Indus Valley civilization 78, 447, **455**
Industrial boards, trade union 857
Industrial diseases 268
Industrial Revolution 310, **453-4**
  Marx, Karl 535
  steam power 744, 841
  technology 823
  textile industry 832
  trade unions 857
  United Kingdom 861
  and world imperialism 311
Industry **840-1**
  acids and alkalis 12, 13
  Argentina 66
  Australia 96
  Belgium 126
  Brazil 147
  Canada 170
  chemical industry 199
  China 207
  cities 216
  clothing manufacture 218
  Congo 22
  Czech Republic 313
  Denmark 258

design 262
Finland 333
France 357
Germany 380, 382
India 445, 448
Indonesia 452
inventions 461, 462
Iraq 464
Ireland 465
iron and steel **467**
Israel 474
Italy 476
Japan 479, 481
Jordan 822
Mexico 552
Mongolia 566
Netherlands 601
New Zealand 606
Norway 617
Philippines 650
Poland 313
pollution 841
Portugal 683
robots 717
Russian Federation **732**
Sierra Leone 35
South Africa 785
South Korea 497
Spain 799
Sweden 816
Switzerland 820
Taiwan 208
Thailand 834
Turkey 853
Ukraine 728
United Kingdom 859
United States 869
Yugoslavia 107
Indy car racing 575
Inertia 352
Infantry 68
Infectious diseases 268
Infertility 710
Infiltration, rainwater 715
Inflation 563
Information
  information superhighway 457
  information technology (IT) **456-7**, 823
  newspapers and magazines **603-4**
  signs and symbols 763, 764
Infrared rays 417
  electromagnetic spectrum 911
  infrared telescopes 870
Ingenhousz, Jan 654
Ingots, bronze 150
Ingrassia, Giovanni 766
Ink 910
Inquisition 371
Insect-eating birds 133, 134, 779
Insectivorous animals **418**
  lizards 518
Insect-pollinated flowers 347
Insects **458-60**
  antennae 53
  ants and termites **58**
  arthropods 74
  bees and wasps **122**
  bugs **155**
  butterflies and moths **158-9**
  camouflage and colour 165
  carnivorous plants **177**
  classification 915
  desert wildlife 261
  diapause 420
  flies **342**
  flight 343
  grasshoppers and crickets **395**

homes 600
marsh and swamp wildlife 534
parasites 643
pollination of flowers 346
rainforest wildlife 700
records 919
social behaviour 53
spreading diseases 268
stings 13
warning signals 166
woodland wildlife 903
Insight learning 54
Instincts 54
Insulators
  electricity 295
  heat 417
Insulin 274, 429
Intaglio printing 692
Integumentary system 436
Intelligence, artificial (AI) 457, 717
Intensive care units, hospitals 433
Interference, colours 227
Interior design 368
Intermediates, evolution 319
Internal combustion engine 305
Internal skeletons 53
International Code of Signals 340, **341**
International Confederation of Free Trade Unions 857
International Congress of Women 646
International Court of Justice 862
International date line 634, 929
International Labour Organization (ILO) 857, 863
International law 504
International Modernism, architecture 62, 63
International Monetary Fund (IMF) 863
International Olympic Committee (IOC) 628
International Red Cross 340, 646, 883
International time zones 929
International trade, world economy 933
International Union for Conservation of Nature and Natural Resources (IUCN) 234
International Women's Day 901
Internet 143, 457
Interpol 676
Interstellar material 870
Intestines 264
Inuit 64
  Canada 170, 171
  clothes 219
  igloos 435, 596
Inventions **461-2**
  China 209
  Edison, Thomas **287**
  Franklin, Benjamin 360
  Leonardo da Vinci 507
  technology **823**
Invertebrates
  arthropods **74**
  cave wildlife 189
  coral reefs 239
  desert wildlife 261
  fossils 355
  grassland wildlife 396
  island wildlife 472
  jellyfish, sea anemones, and sponges **483**
  lake and river wildlife 500
  marsh and swamp wildlife 534

ocean wildlife 622
prehistoric 687
rainforest wildlife 700
Investments, stock markets 563
Io 661
Iodine 298, 924, 925
Iona, Scotland 192
Ionic bonds 92
Ionic compounds 559
Ionic order 61
Ions, electrochemistry 200
Iran 281, **463-4**
  *see also* Persian Empires
Iran-Iraq war (1980-88) 79, 882
Iraq **463-4**, 883
Ireland **465-6**
  banknotes 564
  Celtic Church 192
  history of **466**
Irian Jaya 451
Iridium 924
Iris, eyes 322
Irish dancing 253
Irish draught horse 432
Irish Free State 466
Iron and steel **467**
  in Earth 279
  Industrial Revolution 454
  periodic table 924
  rust 199, 550
Iron Age 150
Iron Curtain 225, 311
Iron Gate 105
Ironbridge, England 453
Iroquois tribe 596
Irrawaddy River 833
Irregular galaxies 370
Irrigation 326, 474
Isaac 469, 486
Isabella, Queen of Castille 800
Isfahan, Iran 735
Isis 388
Islam and Muslims **468-9**
  architecture 62
  Asian history 77
  Bosnia and Herzegovina 106
  calendar 837
  Crusades 247
  gardens 374
  Gulf States 406
  Holy Land 427
  India 447
  Islamic Empire **470**
  Kazakhstan **733**
  law code 505
  Mecca 407
  medicine 247, 543
  mosques 464, **572**
  Mughal Empire 580
  Muhammad **581**
  North Africa 17
  Ottoman Empire 631
  Pakistan 639
  Safavid Empire 735
  science 743
Islamabad, Pakistan 639
Islamic Empire 470
Islands **471**
  Asia 75
  Atlantic Ocean 90
  coral islands 93
  Indian Ocean 449
  island arcs 471
  Pacific Ocean 635
  Philippines 650
  wildlife **472**
Ismail I, Shah 735
Isobars 890

Isotopes 92
Israel **473-4**
    Camp David Accords (1978) 646
    creation of 79
    Six-Day War 883
    wars with Arabs 79
    Zionism 486
    *see also* Holy Land
Israelites 486
Issar people 26
Issus, Battle of (333 BC) 47,
    648, 649
Istanbul, Turkey 631, 853
Itaipu Dam, Paraguay 142
Italy **475-7**
    crafts 243
    Etruscans **307**
    food 349
    history of **477**
    post boxes 805
    Renaissance 707
Ivan III, Tsar **730**
Ivan IV (Ivan the Terrible), Tsar
    **729**, **730**
Ivanov, Lev 108
Ivory
    Benin Empire 127
    carvings 652
    ivory trade 299
    organic gems 249
Ivory Coast **35**

# J

Jacana 761
Jackals 899
    golden 900
Jackdaw 246
Jackrabbits 694
    black-tailed 615
Jackson, General Andrew 48
Jacob 486
Jacobin Club 361
Jade
    Chinese arts and crafts 211
    Olmec art 627
Jade fish 627
Jaffna, Sri Lanka 446
Jaguar 512, 513
    endangered animals 235
    Olmecs worship 627
    rainforest wildlife 700
Jaguar XK120 car 180
Jahangir, Emperor 580
Jainism 560, 705
Jakarta, Indonesia 451
Jamaica **173**
    Columbus visits 228
    Rastafarians 176
James I, King of England 861
James II, King of England 466
Jamestown, USA 614
*Jane Eyre* (Brontë) 149
Janissaries 631
Jansky, Karl 828
Jansz, Willem 97
Japan **478-81**, 593
    banknotes 564
    and barbarians 116
    "bullet" trains 479, 842
    castles 183
    Death Railway 79
    drama 273
    earthquakes 281
    food 349
    gardens 374
    gods and goddesses 389
    history of **480-1**, 942

houses 434
invasion of China 210
Kabuki theatre 836
kites 494
mythology 935
samurai and shoguns 69, **738**
Shinto 705
World War II 481, 869, 907, 908
Japan, Sea of 75, 497
Japanese Alps 478
Japanese bobtail cat 185
Japanese emperor butterfly 159
Jardin Anglais style 374
Jarrow March (1936) 399
Jason and the Argonauts 402
Java 451, 452
Javanese cat 185
Javan garden lizard 712
Java Trench 449
Javelin, athletics 88
Jawless fish 336
Jaws
    human body **824**
    mammals 527
Jay
    blue 246
    Eurasian 134
Jayavarman II, Emperor 490
Jayavarman VII, Emperor 490
Jazz **482**, 866
Jazz Age 869
Jazz dance 254
Jeans 218
Jebel esh Sharqi Mountains 821
Jebel Liban Mountains 821
Jefferson, Thomas 49, 886
Jejunum 264
Jelly babies (fungus) 586
Jellyfish **483**
    mangrove 483
Jenner, Edward 544, 645
Jericho 216, 427
Jerome, St 725
Jerusalem, Israel 247, 427, 473
Jesuits
    Counter-Reformation 704
    in Paraguay 142
    South American missionaries 789
Jesus Christ **484**
    Christianity 213-14
    Holy Land 427
    signs and symbols 764
"Jesus lizard" 517, 518
Jet (fossilized wood) 249, 355
JET (Joint European Torus) 618
Jet aircraft 344
Jet engines 42, 306
Jet streams 896
Jewellery
    Anglo-Saxon 51
    body decoration 219
    Celtic 192
    Etruscan 307
    Viking 878, 879
Jewish Revolt 725
Jews
    calendar 837
    creation of Israel 79
    Holocaust **426**
    Holy Land 427
    Israel **473-4**
    Judaism **486-7**
    World War II 907, 908
Jezebel butterfly 460
Jigs, dance 253
Jihad 468
Jin dynasty 686
Jinnah, Muhammad 448

Jivaro Indians 286
Joan of Arc 358, 439, 898
Jobs, Steve 232
Johanson, Donald 59
John, King of England 610, 860
John VI, King of Portugal 790
John of Braganza 684
John the Baptist 484
John Dory 338
Johnson, Amy **485**
Johnston atoll 635
Joints, skeleton 766
Joliot, Frédéric 250, 697
Joliot-Curie, Irène 250, 697
Jolly Roger 659
Jolson, Al 331
Jones, Chuck 181
Joplin, Scott 482
Jordan **821-2**
Jordan, River 473, 821, 822
Joseph Bonaparte, King of Spain
    790
Josephine, Empress 594
Jostedal Glacier 617
Joule, James 303, 655, 744
Joules 303
Juan Carlos, King of Spain 800
Judah 427
Judaism **486-7**
    Holy Land 427
    signs and symbols 764
Judges 391, 505
Judiciary, government 391
Judo 229
July Days (1917) 734
"Jumbo jets" 344
Jumping
    athletics 88
    horse riding 430
Jumping spiders 802
Jung, Carl Gustav 362
Jung Chang 516
Jungle cat 513
Jungle fowl, red 699
Junkanoo Festival 173
Juno 389, 725
Jupiter (god) 725
Jupiter (planet) **661**
    asteroid belt 230
    facts 921
    moons 371
    Solar System 815
    space probes 796
Jurassic period 378
Juries 505
Justice 504
Justinian I, Emperor 160, 504, 724
Jute 115
Jutes 51, 116
Jutland, Battle of (1916) 906
Jylland peninsula, Denmark 258

# K

K2 639
Kabuki theatre 836
Kabul, Afghanistan 81
Kadesh, Battle of (1286 BC) 425
Kafka, Franz 516
Kakapo 235, 644
Kalahari Bushmen *see* San people
Kalahari Desert 15, 16, 30, 31, 784
Kalidasa 410
Kalimantan 451
Kalmar, Union of (1397) 740
Kamakura, Japan 480
Kamakura shoguns 738

Kamikaze 498
Kamikaze pilots 481
Kampala, Uganda 27
Kandy, Sri Lanka 446
Kane, Bob 604
Kangaroo rat 609
Kangaroos **488**
    red 260, 488, 489
    tree 100, 488
Kanimbo people 21
*Kapital, Das* (Marx) 535
Karachi, Pakistan 639
Karakorum 321, 639
Kara Kum Canal 80
Karakumy Desert 80
Karate 229
Kariba dam 32
Karma, Buddhism 152
Karting 575
Karueein University 29
Kashmir, India/Pakistan 445, 639
Kasparov, Gary 201
Kassites 103
Kästner, Erich 205
Katabatic winds 896
Katmandu, Nepal 115
Kay, John 454
Kayaks 736
Kazakhstan **731**, **733**
Kea 644
Keating, Paul 98
Keck telescope, Mauna Kea 828
Kellogg, John Harvey 461
Kellogg, William Keith 461
Kelly, Gene 254
Kelly, Grace 805
Kelly, Ned 97
Kelp 554
    giant 751
Kempe, Will 753
Kendo 229
Kennedy, John F. 491, 869
Kenning, Chavín culture 198
Kent, William 374
Kentucky coffee 666
Kenya **27**
    banknotes 564
    crafts 243
    Maasai people 216
    Olduvai Gorge 506
Kepler, Johannes 815
Keratin 767
Kern, Jerome 629
Kerosene 625, 626
Kestrels 135, 137
    American 137
Keyboard instruments 591
Keyboards, computers 231
KGB 795
Khadija 581
Khafre, Pharaoh 752
Khaki Campbell duck 276
Khalkh Mongols 566
Kha people 877
Khartoum, Sudan 25, 302
Khmer Empire 79, **490**
Khmer Rouge 877
Khomeini, Ayatollah 464
Khrushchev, Nikita 795
Khufu, Pharaoh 752
*Kibbutzim* 474
Kibo, Mount 24
Kidneys 873
Kiev, Ukraine 565, 728, **731**
Kigali, Rwanda 23
Kilimanjaro, Mount 15, 24
*Kilims* 853

Kilns 685
Kinetic energy 303
Kinetoscope 287
King, Martin Luther **491**
King Charles spaniel 271
King snakes
    Californian 773
    grey-banded 773
Kingcycle Bean bicycle 129
Kingdoms, classification 914
Kingfishers **492**
    belted 492
    common 492
    European 316
    malachite 533
Kinglet, golden-crowned 780
Kings and queens 391
    British 943
    feudalism 329
    French 945
    pharaohs 291
    Russia 944
    Spain 945
Kingsley, Mary 321
Kingston, Jamaica 173
Kingstown, St Vincent and the
    Grenadines 175
Kinkajou 640
Kinship 774
Kipling, Rudyard 205, 671
Kiribati **680**
Kirov Ballet, St Petersburg **732**
Kites 493-4, 524
Kites (birds)
    black-shouldered 290
    snail 136
Kitt Peak National Observatory 87
Kittens 184
Kittiwake 53 , 747
Kiwanos 367
Kiwi 345, 367
*Klebsiella* 554
Knights and heraldry **495-6**
    armour 69
    feudalism 329
    Crusades 247, 883
Knights of Malta 70
Knights of St John 247
Knossos, Crete 557
Knowledge, epistemology 651
Koala 100, 489, 529
Kobe earthquake, Japan 281
Kodak cameras 163, 164
Koguryo dynasty 77
Kolonia, Micronesia 637
Komodo dragon 518
Kongo people 22
Kookaburra 134, 492
    laughing 100
Koran *see* Qur'an
Korat cat 185
Korea
    early history 77
    *see also* North Korea; South
    Korea
Korean War (1950-53) 79, 225,
    497
Koror, Palau 637
Kosher food 487
Krafft, Katia and Maurice 880
Krak des Chevaliers, Syria 182
Krakatoa 281, 451, 472
Kramer, Heinrich 898
Krasnohorska Cave, Slovakia 188
Kremlin, Moscow **729**
Krill 241, 675, 893
Krishna 421
"Kristallnacht" (1938) 426

Krypton 925
Ku Klux Klan 491
Kuala Lumpur, Malaysia 523, 524
Kuba people 23
Kublai Khan **498**
  attacks Japan 481
  conquers China 210
  and Marco Polo 320
  Mongol Empire 565
Kudu, greater 256
Kultarr 99
Kumaragupta, Emperor 410
Kuomintang 212
Kura River 186, 187
Kurds 463, 853
Kushan Empire 77
Kushites 17
Kuwait 406, **408**
  Gulf War 883
Kuwait City, Kuwait 408
Kyoto, Japan 480
Kyrgyzstan **81**
Kyushu, Japan 478
Kyzyl Kum Desert 80

# L

Labdah 29
Laboratories 742
Labour
  childbirth 710
  industry 840
  trade unions **857**
Labour camps, World War II 908
Labradorite 249
Laburnum 367
Lacewings 342
  thread 460
Ladoga, Lake 308
Ladybirds 124, 460
Laetoli 506
La Fontaine 358
Lagomorpha 694
Lagos, Nigeria 37
Lakes **501**
  facts 922
  Finland 333
  oxbow 714
  Switzerland 819
  wildlife **499-500**
Lalibela, Ethiopia 26
Lamarck, Jean Baptiste de 319
Lamellicorn beetle 125
Lammergeier 317
Lamprey, sea 336
Lancaster, House of 861
Land, Edwin 163
Land breezes 896
Land speed record 576
Landers, space probes 796
Landscapes
  glaciation **385-6**
  photography 653
Landsteiner, Karl 415
Langevin, Paul 695
Languages **502**
  ancient Greek 402
  Celtic 192
  computer 456
  Etruscan 307
  Latin 725
  Southwest Pacific 636
Lanner falcon 135, 136, 260
Lantern bug 155
Lantern clocks 839
Lanthanides, periodic table 924-5
Lanthanum 924
Laos 79, **876-7**

La Paz, Bolivia 142
Lapilli 881
Lapis lazuli 249
Lapland 333, 510, 816
Lapps 617
Laptop computers 232
Lapwing 165, 761
Larch, Japanese 848
Larkspur 367
Larvae
  amphibians 50
  bees and wasps 122
  beetles 124
  flies 342
  metamorphosis 458
  salamanders and newts 737
Laryngoscopes 541
Larynx 519
La Salle, René Cavelier de 614
Las Casas, Bartolomé de 789
Lascaux cave paintings 59, 71,
  188, 358
Lasers 462, **503**
Last Supper 214, 484
Las Vegas, USA 867
La Tène culture 191
Latent heat 417
Latex 670
Latin language 725
Latitude 532, 598
Latvia 112, **113**
Lauren, Ralph 219
Lava
  plate tectonics 237
  volcanoes 880, 881
Lava caves 188
La Venta, Mexico 627
Lavoisier, Antoine 199, 200
Lavoisier, Marie 199
Law **504-5**
Law of Conservation of Energy 303
Lawn tennis 831
Lawrence, Thomas Edward
  (Lawrence of Arabia) 18
Lawrencium 925
Laws **504-5**
  legislature 391
  police 676
  Roman 724
Lawyers 505
Le Mans 24-hour race 576
Leaching, soil erosion 777
Lead 550
  periodic table 925
Lead glass 387
Leadbelly 718
Leaf insects 459, 460, 700
Leaf miners 600
Leafhoppers 155
  red-banded 155
Leafy liverworts 573
League of Arab States 19
League of Nations 862
  International Labour
  Organization (ILO) 857
Leakey, Louis 59, 390, **506**
Leakey family **506**
Leap years 837
Lear, Edward 205
Learned behaviour 54
Learning *see* Education
Leatherhead 289
Leaves **666**
  anatomy 665
  broad-leaved trees 847
  cotyledons 663
  grasses 393
  records 918

trees 846, 847
Lebanon 821, **822**
Leclanché, Georges 295
Lee, Robert E 48
Leeches 500, 643, 909
Leeuwenhoek, Antony van 553, 555
Leeward Islands 90, 174
Lefkosia, Cyprus 822
Legends **593**
Legislation 504
Legislature, government 391
Leica cameras 164
Leif Ericsson 878
Leisure 775
Lemaître, Georges 130
Lemming 674
Lemons 367, 799
Lemurs
  black-and-white ruffed 570
  ring-tailed 166, 529, 569
Length
  conversion tables 927
  measuring 892, 927
Lenin, Vladimir I 734, 795
Leningrad *see* St Petersburg
Lennon, John 121
Lenses **509**
  cameras 163
  eyes 322
  microscopes 553
  telescopes 828
Lent 328
Leo III, Pope 197
Leonardo da Vinci **507**, 707, 708
Léonin 589
Leonov, Alexey 797
Leopard cat 513
Leopards 511, 512, 513
  black 54
Lepage, Robert 273
Lepanto, Battle of (1571) 631
Leptis Magna 29
Leroy, Louis 561
Lesotho 784, **785**
Lesseps, Ferdinand de 844
Lessivage, soil erosion 777
Letters, typography 691
*Leuchochloridium macrostomum* 643
Leutgeb, Ignaz 579
Levallois technique, flint tools 809
Levant 652
Levers **520**
Levi Strauss jeans 218
Lewis, Carl 88
Lewis, Meriwether 614
Lexington and Concorde, Battle of
  (1775) 49
Liao dynasty 686
Liberation Army (China) 212
Liberia **35**
Liberty ships 759
Librettos, opera 629
Libreville, Gabon 22
Libya **29**
Lice 643
  human head 643
Lichens
  polar wildlife 675
  seashore life 749
  symbiosis 585
Lie, Trygve 863
Lieber, Francis 883
Liebig, Justus von 559
Liebniz, Konrad 537
Liechtenstein 819, **820**
Life
  biology 131
  cells **190**

conservation **234-5**
Earth system 280
genetics **376-7**
prehistoric **687-8**
Life expectancy 931
Life rafts 759
Lifespans
  animal 916
  plants 663, 916
Ligaments 766
Light **508-9**
  chromatic aberration 828
  colour **226-7**
  electromagnetic spectrum 911
  eyes and seeing 322
  General Theory of Relativity 294
  Impressionist paintings 561
  lasers and holograms **503**
  measuring the Universe 871
  photons 911
  photosynthesis 654
  plant growth 668
  spectrum 605
  telescopes 828
Lightbulbs 287, 508
Light Emitting Diodes (LEDs) 297
Lighthouses 598, 752
Lighting 369
  gas 454
  theatre 836
Lightning 810
  electricity 295
  Franklin, Benjamin 360
  speed of sound 782
Light years (ly) 871
Lignite 222
Lilongwe, Malawi 32
Lima, Peru 286
Limbic system 145
Limericks 205
Limestone 723
  caves 188, 189
Limpets 749
Limpkin 290
Lincoln, Abraham
  American Civil War 48
  Gettysburg Address 48
  and Sojourner Truth 849
Lind, Jenny 629
Lindisfarne, England 878
Lindisfarne Gospels 192
Line graphs 537
Linear A script 557
Linear B script 557
Linen 106, 113
Liners 757
*Lingula* 355
Linnaeus, Carolus **510**
Lionfish 338, 672
Lion 38, **511-13**
  mountain 616
  teeth 527
Lipizzaner horse 432
Lippershey, Hans 828
Liquid crystal displays (LCDs) 508
Liquid gas 626
Liquids **514**
  condensation 375
  convection 417
  latent heat 417
  pressure 690
  states of matter 538
Lisbon, Portugal 682
  earthquake (1755) 281, 684
Lister, Joseph 544, 545
Liszt, Franz 589
Literacy 931
Literature **515-16**

ancient Greek 402
Babylonian 103
books 143
Brontë sisters **149**
children's literature **203-5**
Dickens, Charles **263**
great writers **941**
Gupta Empire 410
Hittite 425
poetry **671**
science fiction 742
Shakespeare, William **753**
Twain, Mark **856**
Lithium 924
Lithography 692
Lithuania 112, **113**
Little Rock, USA 491
Little Surtsey, Iceland 90
*Little Women* (Alcott) 204
Live Aid concert (1985) 719
Liver 190, 264
Liver flukes 643
Liverworts 573, 663
Livestock, farming 323, 325
Living matter 538
Living standards **931**
Living things
  classification **914-15**
  how they work **916-17**
Livingstone, Dr David 321
Lizards **517-18**, 711
  common 317
  desert wildlife 261
  eggs 289, 712
  grassland wildlife 397
  plated 711
  rainforest wildlife 700
Ljubljana, Slovenia 106
Llama 162
Load, simple machines 520
Loam 777
Lobelia, giant 39
Lobsters 74, 241, 339, 750
  spiny 556
Local Group galaxies 370, 871
Locks, canals 681
Locomotives 842, 843
Locusts 395, 556
Lodestone 321, 522
Loganberries 367
Logan, Mount 169
Logarithms 537, 619
Log cabins 435
Logging industry
  Cameroon 21
  teak logging 834
  United States 867
Logic
  mathematics 537
  philosophy 651
Logos 262
Logs, navigation 598
Loki 388
Lolland, Denmark 258
Lollards 704
Lombardy 197
Lomé, Togo 36
London, England 858, 860
  Dickens' London 263
London Underground 262
London Zoo 912
Longbows 439, 888
Long-haired cats 185
Longhorn beetle 125, 460
Longhouses 596
Longitude 532, 598
Long, Lutz 632
Long March (China) 212

Money **562-4**
  medieval Europe 547
  Viking 878
Mongol Empire 77, **565**, 883
  expelled from China 210
  Kublai Khan **498**
Mongolia 76, **566**
Mongooses 567
  banded (*Mungos mungo*) 567
  dwarf 528
  marsh 567
*Monitor* 48
Monitor lizard 712
  Bosc 518
Monitor tegu, spotted 794
Monitors, computers 231
Monkey King 203
Monkey puzzle tree 848
Monkeys **568-70**
Monks
  Buddhist 153
  Celtic Church 192
  medieval Europe 546
  military orders 247
  monasteries 560
Monk's hood (plant) 664
Monnet, Jean 315
Monoclinic system, crystals 248
Monocotyledons 393, 663, 664
  leaves 666
Monopoly (board game) 202
Monoprints 692
Monotremes 99, 528
Monrovia, Liberia 35
Monsoon 217, 449, 698
Monsoon rainforest, Thailand
  and Burma 833
Mont Blanc 308
Mont Cenis tunnel 851
Montagu, Lady Mary Wortley 441
Montaigne, Michel Eyquem de 358
Montana, USA 866
Montcalm, Marquis Louis 171
Monte Carlo, Monaco 357
Monte Carlo Rally 576
Montenegro 107
Monterrey, Mexico 552
Montessori, Maria 288
Montessori system 288
Monteverdi, Claudio 629
Montevideo, Uruguay 67
Montezuma II, Emperor 101
Montgolfier brothers 45
Montgomery, General Bernard 907
Months 837
Montreal, Canada 171, 614
Monument Valley, USA 864
Moon **571**
  astronauts 86, 321,
    571, 797
  craters 371
  eclipses 814
  facts 921
  gravity 398
  tides 621
  and time 837
Moon moth, African 159
Moons
  Galileo observes 371
  Jupiter 661
  Neptune 662
  Saturn 661
  Uranus 662
Moore, Henry 746
Moors
  gardens 374
  Mauritania 34
  in Portugal 684

in Spain 800
Moose 616
Mopeds 128
Moraine 385
Morals, philosophy 651
Moravia, Czech Republic 313
More, Sir Thomas 708
Morgan horse 432
Morganite 249
Morisot, Berthe 561
Morocco **29**
  food 349
  and Songhai Empire 781
Moroni, Comoros 32
Morris, William 368
Morrison, Toni 516
Morrison, Warren 838
Morse code 224, 825
Morse, Samuel 224, 825
Mortar bombs 888
Morton, William 544
Mosaics 160, 215
Moscow Canal 732
Moscow, Russia 732, **729**
Moses 427, 486, 487
Mosna River 198
Mosques 62, 464, **572**
Mosquito Coast 193
Mosquitoes 342
Mosses **573**, 663
Mother goddess 388
Mother-of-pearl 249
Mother Teresa **574**
Motherboard, computers 231
Moths **158-9**, 460, 609
Motion 352
Motion pictures *see* Films and
  film-making
Motocross racing 576
Motor industry *see* Car industry
Motor neurons 144
Motor sports **575-6**, 803
Motor yachts 759
Motorcycles **128-9**
  racing 576
Motors 296, **305-6**
Motorways, Germany 380
Motown records 865
Motte-and-bailey castles 182
Mouflon 317, 756
Mouhot, Henri 490
Moulds
  bronze casting 150
  moulding plastics 670
Moulds (fungi) 584
Moulting, arthropods 74
Mount Palomar 828
Mount Vernon, USA 886
Mount Wilson telescope,
  California 828
Mountain bikes 129, 251
Mountains **577**
  Africa 16
  climate 217
  facts 922
  glaciation 385
  mountain walking 168
  plate tectonics 237
  pressure 690
  undersea 620
  winds 896
Mountain wildlife **578**
  Africa 39
  Asia 83
  cats 512, 513
  Europe 317
  North America 616
  South America 794

Mourning dove 134
Mouse *see* Mice
Mouse, computer 231
Mouse-tailed bat 119
Mouth
  digestion 264
  smell and taste 769
  teeth and jaws 824
Movement **582**
  animals 53
  forces and motion **352**
  octopuses and squids 624
  skeleton 765
Movies *see* Films and film-making
Mozambique **32**
Mozart, Leopold 579
Mozart, Maria Anna 579
Mozart, Wolfgang Amadeus **579**,
  589
  armonica 360
  operas 629
Mud houses 435
Mudskipper 336, 534
Mudstone 723
Mughal Empire 79, 447, **580**
  art 73
Muhammad, Elijah 491
Muhammad, Prophet 427, **581**
  Islam 406, **468-9**
  Islamic law 505
  mosques 572
Muhammad II, Sultan 631
Muhammad V, Sultan 631
Muharram 735
Mules 325
Mulgara 99
Müller, Walther 697
Multi-purpose vehicles (MPVs) 178
Mummification 292, 293
Munsell colour system 226
Muntjak 257
Murasaki Shikibu 480, 516
Murder 244
Murdock, William 509
Murillo, Bartolomé Esteban 800
Murray River 93, 97
Mursili I, King of the Hittites 425
Mururoa Atoll 680
Musa 781
Musa, Mansa 526
Muscat, Oman 407
Muscles 436, **582**, 765
Muscovy **729**
Museums **583**
Mushrooms **584-6**
Music **587-90**
  Austria 820
  Beatles, The 121
  Beethoven, Ludwig van **123**
  Bolivia 142
  Cameroon 21
  dance **253-4**
  facts **939**
  *gamelan* orchestras 452
  India 445
  jazz **482**, 866
  Motown 865
  Mozart, Wolfgang Amadeus 579
  music industry 719
  opera **629**
  orchestras **630**
  reggae 173
  religions 705
  rock and pop **718-19**
  Senegal 34
  steel bands 175
  Stravinsky, Igor **811**
Musical instruments **590-2**

Musicals 629
Musk, civets 567
Musk ox 674
Muslim League 448
Muslims *see* Islam
Mussels 749
  green 771
Mussel shrimp 241
Mussolini, Benito 399, 477, 908
Mustelidae 104
Musth, elephants 300
Mutations
  genetics 376
  natural selection 318
Mutualism 643
Muwatallis, King of the Hittites
  425
Myanmar *see* Burma
Mycenaean civilization 311, 401,
  402
Myriapods 74
Myrrh 545
Myths **593**, **935**
  Celtic 192
  fire 334
  gods and goddesses **388-9**
  Hittite 425

# N

Nabatean Arabs 822
Nabopolasser, King of Babylon 103
Nader Qoli Beg 735
Nagasaki, Japan 78, 481, 618, 908
Nagorno-Karabakh 187
Nails, human body 767
Nairobi, Kenya 27
Najd Desert 406
Nakhichevan 187
Nakhla meteorite 230
Nakuru, Lake 38
Names, scientific 914
Namib Desert 16, 30, 784
Namibia **31**
Nana Benz 36
Nanatuks 386
Nanking, China 212
Nantes, Edict of (1598) 358
Napier, John 537, 619
Napoleon III, Emperor (Louis-
  Napoleon) 359
Napoleon Bonaparte 358, **594**
  *Eroica* symphony (Beethoven)
    123
  French Revolution 361
  invades Italy 477
  Napoleonic Wars **595**
Napoleonic Wars (1797-1815) **595**
Nara, Japan 480
Narodnaïa 308
Narrative poetry 671
Narwhal 893, 895
Nash, Paul 906
Nassau, Bahamas 173
Nasser, Lake 501
Nasturtium 347
Natal, South Africa 786
Nation states 310
National Theatre, London 835
National Union of Women's
  Suffrage Societies (NUWSS) 901
National Woman Suffrage
  Association 901
Nationalism 311
  Asia 79
  Europe 311
  India 372
  music 589

Native Americans **596-7**
  art 73
  Canada 171
  food 613
  Geronimo **383**
  Mexico 552
  North America 612
  smoke signals 224
  South America 789
  trade 614
NATO (North Atlantic Treaty
  Organization) 225
Natterer's bat 117, 420
Natterjack toads 365
Natural gas 29, 625, 626
Natural philosophy 743
Natural selection 255. 318
Nature spirits 762
Nauru **637**
Nautiluses 624, 771
Navajo tribe 867
  art 73
  mythology 593
Naval battles 882
Navies 885
Navigation **598**
  Columbus, Christopher 228
  compasses 522
  Cook, James 238
  explorers 321
  medieval 547
  nocturnal animals 609
  Polynesians 531
  radar 695
Navratilova, Martina 831
Nazis 382
  Berlin Olympics 632
  Holocaust **426**
  Nürnberg Trials 883
  World War II 311
Ndebele women 785
N'Djamena, Chad 21
Neanderthals 437
Nebuchadnezzar II, King of
  Babylon 84, 103, 752
Nectar 122
Nectar-eating bats 118
Nectar-eating birds 134, 779
Nectar-eating flies 342
Nectar-eating insects 459
Nectarines 367
Needle grass 394
Needleaf forest, North America
  612
Needles, pine trees 847
Nefertiti, Queen of Egypt 292
Negative numbers 619
Negev Desert 473
Negro, Río 67
Nehru, Jawaharlal 372, 448
Nelson, Lord 594, 595
Nematodes 54
Neoclassical architecture 62
Neoclassical music 811
Neodymium 924
Neo-Hittites 425
Neolithic age 326, 809
Neon, periodic table 925
Neotony 737
Nepal **114-15**
Nephrons, kidneys 873
Neptune **662**
  facts 921
  Solar System 815
  space probes 797
Neptunium 924
Neruda, Pablo 805
Nerva, Emperor 724

Nerves 144
Nervous system **144-5**, 436
Nestlé, Henri 820
Nests **599-600**
  ants and termites 58
  ducks 276
  insects 459
  orangutans 569
  seabirds 747
  songbirds 780
  storks 419
  swans 276
  swifts 817
  toucans 904
  wasps and bees 122
Netball 110, 111
Netherlands **601-2**
  history of **602**
  post boxes 805
Nettles 347, 667
Neumann, John von 457
Neural networks 457
Neurology 541
Neurons 144, 145, 190
Neutralizing acids 13
Neutron stars 294, 807
Neutrons 92, 744
Nevis 174
New Brunswick, Canada 171
New Deal 399, 869
New Delhi, India 445
New Economic Policy (NEP) 734
New England 658
New Forest pony 432
New Granada 789, 790
New Orleans, USA 482, 866
New South Wales, Australia 94
New Stone Age 326
New Testament 214
"New Wave" films 331
New Year, Chinese 207
New York City 216, 865
  Broadway 272
New York Stock Exchange 399,
  563, 869
*New York Times, The* 603
New Zealand 93, **606**, 679
  climate 94
  history of **607**
  Maoris 531
  prime ministers 946
Newbery, John 205
Newbery Medal 205
Newcomen, Thomas 841
News
  photography 653
  television 829, 830
  video 875
Newspapers **603-4**
  Argentina 66
  facts 940
  United States 865
Newsprint 642
*Newsround* 830
Newton, Sir Isaac **605**, 743, 911
  and gravity 398
  laws of motion 352
  mathematics 537
  and physics 655
  telescopes 828
Newtons 398
Newts 50, **737**
  great crested 50, 235, 737
  Iberian ribbed 737
  marbled 50
Nezami 735
Ngata, Apirana 607
"Niagara Fruit Belt", Canada 170

Niamey, Niger 37
Nicaragua 193, **195**, 196
Nicaragua, Lake 193
Nicholas II, Tsar **730**, 734
Nickel 279, 925
Nicosia, Cyprus 822
Nicotine 275
Niepce, Joseph 163, 653
Niger **37**
Niger River 15, 33, 526, 781
Nigeria **37**
  Benin Empire **127**
  sculpture 746
Night and day
  Earth's orbit 815
  time 837
Nightingale 780
Nightingale, Florence 548, **608**
Nightjars **633**
  common 902
  Manila 290
  Nacunda 290
Nightshade, deadly 545
Nijinsky, Vaslav 108
Nile, River 15, 24, 25, 291
Nimbostratus clouds 221
Nimrud 84
Nineveh 84
Nieh, El 84
Niobium 924
Nitric acid 12
Nitrogen
  in air 40
  atmosphere 91
  periodic table 925
Niue 680
Nixon, Richard 805
Nkimba people 388
Nkrumah, Kwame 19
Nobel, Alfred 200
  dynamite 851
  Nobel Prizes 646, 744
Nobel Peace Prize 646, 941
Nobel Prizes 200, 744
Nobelium 925
Noble gases 298, 925
  periodic table 924
Noble, Richard 576
Noctule bat 119
Nocturnal animals **609**
Noh theatre 273
Noise *see* Sound
Nok culture 17, 73
Nomads 774
  Bedouins 821
  camels 162
  Central Asia 80
  East Africa 24
  slash and burn farming 353
Non-fiction 516
Non-metals, periodic table 924
Nong Kai, Thailand 877
Nonsilicates 722
Nordenskjöld, Nils 673
Nordic Council 740
Nordic skiing 897
Norman Conquest (1066) 860
Normandy, France 439
Normans **610**
  Bayeux Tapestry 424
  castles 182, 183
Norrland 816
Norse mythology 388, 593, 935
North Africa **28-9**
  ancient empires 17
  crafts 243
  Islam 17
North America 236, **611-16**

Canada **169-71**
  Columbus visits 228
  crafts 243
  history of **613-14**
  Mexico **551-2**
  Native Americans **596-7**
  Pilgrim Fathers **658**
  religions 705
  sculpture 746
  United States **864-9**
  wildlife **615-16**
North Atlantic Ridge 237
North Atlantic Treaty Organization
  (NATO) 225
North European Plain 308
North Island, New Zealand 606
North Korea **497**
  banknotes 564
North Pole 64
  polar exploration 321, **673**
Northeast Passage 673
Northern bat 83
Northern Ireland (Ulster) 466
  *see also* United Kingdom
Northern leopard frog 364
Northern lights 64
Northern Song dynasty 686
Northumbria 51
Northwest Africa **28-9**
Northwest Passage 673
Northwest Territories, Canada 171
Norway **617**
  history of 740
Nose, smell, and taste 769
Nostrils, elephants 299
Notation, music 588, 589
Notre Dame, Paris 63
*Nouvelle Vague* films 331
Nova Scotia, Canada 171
Novels 516
  Brontë sisters **149**
Nuclear families 774
Nuclear fission 548
Nuclear Freeze 646
Nuclear power **618**
  Meitner, Lise **548**
Nuclear submarines 812
Nuclear weapons 887
  Cuban missile crisis (1962) 176
  disarmament conferences 646
  Einstein, Albert 294
  Hiroshima 908
  peace movements 646
  tests 680
Nucleosynthesis, stars 807
Nucleus
  atoms 92
  cells 190
Nuku'alofa, Tonga 680
Numbat 489
Numbers **619**
  Arabic 470
  International Code of Signals 341

  mathematics **536-7**, **926**
  Roman 725
  terminology 927
Nunataks 850
Nuns 546, 560
Nürnberg Trials 883
Nursery rhymes 205, 671
Nurses 433
  Mother Teresa 574
  Nightingale, Florence **608**
Nutmeg 452
Nutrition *see* Feeding; Food
Nuts, food 349

Nuuk, Greenland 64
Nyala 256
Nyasa, Lake 501
Nylon 670, 832
Nymphs, metamorphosis 458

# O

Oak eggar moth 159
Oak galls 903
Oak trees 316, 846, 847
  acorns 367, 847
  Armenian 347
  white 848
Oases 259, 260
Oats 669
Oboes 590, 592
Observation, scientific method 742
Observation satellites 739
Observatories, astronomy 87
Ocean trenches 621
Oceania **93-4**
  art 73
  climatic zones 94
  film posters 332
  physical features 93
  *see also* Pacific Ocean
Oceanic climate 217
Oceans and seas 621
  Arctic Ocean 64
  Atlantic Ocean **89-90**
  coasts **223**
  coral reefs **239**
  exploration 321
  facts 922
  fish 336, 338
  fishing industry 339
  islands 471
  ocean floor **620**
  oceanography 282
  Pacific Ocean **634-7**
  pirates **659**
  pressure 690
  tides 398
  tsunamis 281
  wildlife **622-3**
Ocelot 513
Octavian *see* Augustus I, Emperor
October Revolution (1917) 734
Octopuses 624, 771
  blue-ringed 672
  common 624
  coral reefs 239
  eggs 289
  as symbol 764
Oda Nobunaga 480, 738
Odin 388, 593
Oedipus 388
Oersted, Hans Christian 296
Oesophagus 264
Offa, King of Mercia 51
Officers, armies 68
Off-road racing
  cycling 251
  motorcycles 576
Offset lithography 692
Oglala tribe 596
Ogodai Khan 565
O'Higgins, Bernardo 790
Ohio, USA 865
Ohrid, Lake 107
Oil **625-6**
  Angola 31
  Azerbaijan 187
  Brunei 525
  Ecuador 286
  engines 305
  Indonesia 452

  Iraq 464
  Kuwait 408
  Libya 29
  Mexico 552
  Nigeria 37
  pollution 13, 625, 678
  Saudi Arabia 407
  United States 867
  Venezuela 792
  world resources 932
Oil paints 71, 277
Oil rigs 625
Oil tankers 759
Oilbird 189, 633
Oils
  food 349
  organic chemistry 200
Okapi 384
Okavango Delta 15, 31, 533
Okefenokee Swamp 612
Oklahoma, USA 866
Oktas, cloud cover 221
Old Faithful geyser 866
Old lady moth 903
Old St Paul's Cathedral, London
  61
Old Testament 213, 214
Oldham, Richard 279
Olduvai Gorge 59, 506
Olfactory membrane 769
Olgas, Australia 94
Oligocene epoch 378
*Oliver Twist* (Dickens) 263
Olives 799
Olmecs **627**
  pyramids 693
Olympic Games **628**
  athletics 88
  champions 936
  Owens, Jesse 632
  water sports 736
Olympus, Mount 401, 403, 821
Olympus Mons, Mars 660
Om (sacred syllable) 764
Oman 406, **407**
Omar Khayyam 516, 671
Ometepe 193
Omnivores, lizards 518
Omsk, Russian Federation **732**
Onagers 83
Onions 665
Ontario, Canada 171
Ontario, Lake 611
Oolitic limestone 723
Oort Cloud 230
Opal 249
Opal butterfly 159
Opaque substances 509
Opera **629**, 939
  Chinese 208, 273
  Mozart, Wolfgang Amadeus 579
Opera House, Sydney 62
Operating systems (OS), computers
  232
Operating theatres 542
Ophthalmology 433
Ophthalmoscopes 541
Opium Wars (1839–42) 79, 210
Opossum, Virginia 489
Optical fibres, telecommunications
  825
Optical glass 387
Optical mini-disks, computers 232
Oracles 388
Oral history 424
Oral literature 515
Orange-barred giant sulphur
  butterfly 159

Orange caterpillar fungus 586
Orange Free State, South Africa 786
Orange peel fungus 586
Orange tip butterfly, great 159
Oranges 799
Orangutans 569, 570
Orbiters, space probes 796
Orbits
  planets 815
  satellites 739
Orchards 324
Orchestras **630**
Orchids 664
  insect mimicry 346
  lady 666
  mirror 347
  nurseries 525
Orders, architecture 61
Orders, classification 914
Ordovician period 378
Oregon, USA 867
Oregon Trail 868
Ores 550
Organelles 190
Organic chemistry 200
Organic farming 678
Organic gems 249
Organization of African Unity (OAU) 19
Organizations, coats of arms 496
Organized crime 244
Organs *see* Human body
Organs (musical instrument) 591
Oriental shorthair cat 185
Oriente, Bolivia 141
*Origin of Species* (Darwin) 255
"Original Dixieland Jazz Band" 866
Orinoco River 791, 792
Orioles
  Baltimore 599
  northern 780
Orion constellation 808
Orion Nebula 807
Orlov trotter 432
Ornament, architecture 61
Ornithischians 265, 267
*Orodromeus* 266
Ortega, Daniel 196
Orthodox churches *see* Eastern Orthodox Church; Greek Orthodox Church; Russian Orthodox Church
Orthopaedics 541
Orthorhombic system, crystals 248
Orvieto, Italy 307
Oryx
  Arabian 234
  fringe-eared 256
Oscars 331, 940
Oscilloscopes 782
Osiris 291
Oslo, Norway 617
Osmium 924
Osmosis 514
Ossicles 278
Ostrich 325, 345
Ostrogoths 116, 752
Otavalo, Ecuador 286
Otoscopes 541
Ottawa, Canada 169
Otters **104**, 499
  European 316
  giant 793
  hair 527
  pollution and 678
  sea 54

Otto, Nikolaus 306
Otto I, Emperor 381, 382, 428
Ottoman Empire 302, **631**
  and the Byzantine Empire 160
  collapse 852
  and the Safavid Empire 735
  World War I 18
Ouagadougou, Burkina Faso 36
Oulin, Mansa 526
Outback, Australia 94, 95
Ova 709-10
Ovambo people 31
Ovaries 429, 709
Over-the-counter drugs 275
Ovules 668
Owen, Richard 266
Owen, Robert 454
Owen, Wilfred 671, 906
Owen Falls, Uganda 27
Owens, Jesse **632**
Owl butterfly 159
Owl moth 159
Owls 133, **633**
  barn 633
  buffy fish 633
  burrowing 616
  elf 633
  great grey 83
  snowy 615, 675
  spectacled 134
  tawny 633, 902
Oxbow lakes 501, 714
Oxen 154
Oxenstierna, Axel 740
Oxidation 199
Oxpecker 643, 713
Oxygen
  in air 40, 91, 279
  element 298
  heart and circulatory system 414, 415
  lungs and breathing **519**
  oxygen cycle 91
  periodic table 925
  photosynthesis 654
  steel refining 467
  water 514
Oystercatcher 761
  Eurasian 761
Oysters 770, 771
  spiny 771
Ozone layer 91
  holes in 678

# P

Pacemakers 462
Pachacuti Inca 442
Pachisi 201
Pacific Ocean 621, **634-7**
  Cook, James **238**
  Magellan, Ferdinand 521
  Maoris and Polynesians **531**
  New Zealand **606**
  Polynesia **679-80**
  Southwest Pacific **636-7**
  tsunamis 281
  typhoons 810
  World War II 907
  *see also* Oceania
Package holidays 845
Packaging 760
Pacu 699
Padmasambhava 77
Padua University 543
Paediatrics 541
Pagodas 62
Pahoehoe lava 881

Pain
  anaesthetics 542
  painkillers 274
Painted frogs, Asian 365
Painting **638**
  body painting 219
  cave paintings 71, 358, 638, 809
  facts 938
  Gupta Empire 410
  history of art 71-3
  icons 160
  Monet, Claude **562**
  museums 583
  Picasso, Pablo **656**
  Pointillism 227
  restoration 583
  rock paintings 17
  Safavid Empire 735
  Stone Age 809
Paints 71, **277**
  pigments 227
Pakistan **639**
  creation of 372, 447, 448
  independence 79
  and Kashmir 445
Palace of the Statues, Rome 63
Palacio de las Cadenas, Ubeda 63
Palaeocene epoch 378
Palaeolithic age 809
Palaeontology 282, 354
Palaeozoic era 378, 687
Palau **637**
Palenque 540
Palestine 473
  Crusades 247, 883
  Holy Land 427
  Jesus Christ 484
Palestinians 474
Palestrina, Giovanni 587
Palettes, artist's 638
Pale tussock moth 159
Pali Canon 153
Palisade mesophyll cells 190
Palk Strait 446
Palladium 925
Palm oil 524
Palm trees 847
  coconuts 636, 679
Palmer, Nat 673
Palmistry 85
Pampas 65, 396, 787, 788
Pampas grass 397
Panama 140, **195**, 196
Panama Canal 193, 195, 196, 681, 844, 869
Panama City, Panama 195, 196
Panama hats 286
Pan-American highway 67, 193
Pancreas 264, 429
Pandas **640**
  giant 235, 640
  red 640
Pangaea 236, 280, 687
Pangolin 57
Pankhurst family **641**
P'an-ku 593
Panoramic cameras 164
Panpipes 592
Pansies 347, 664
Pantanal, Brazil 793
Pantheon, Rome 61
Panther, black 513
Papacy *see* Popes
Paparazzi 603
Paper **642**, 669
  books 143
  history of 209
  painting and drawing 638

Paperback books 143
Papier-mâché 242
Papillae, tongue 769
Papillon 271
Papua New Guinea 93, 94, 636
Papyrus 38, 143, 642
Parables 484
*Parade* (Satie) 656
Paradise fish 599
Paradoxical frogs 365
Paraguay **141-2**
Paraguay River 141, 142
Parallax, measuring the Universe 871
Parallel bars, gymnastics 411
Paralympics 628
Paramaribo, Surinam 792
Paraná River 141, 142
Paranthropines 437
*Parasaurolophus* 265
Parasites 131, 284, 459, **643**
  fungi 585
  worms 909
Parasols, shaggy 585
Parathyroid gland 429
*Parc des volcans*, Rwanda 23
Parchment worm 750
Parent bug 458
Parental care, mammals 528
Paris, France 356
Paris Commune 535
Paris Opera House 835
Parking meters 462
Parkinson, Sydney 238
Parks, cities 216
Parks, Rosa 491
Parliament
  British 860
  European Union 315
Parliamentary democracy 391
Parrotfish 599
Parrots **644**
  blue-crowned hanging 134
  St Vincent 235
Parsis 649
Parson Jack Russell terrier 271
Parsons, Charles 303, 304
Parthenogenesis, bugs 155
Parthenon, Athens 401
Parthian Empire 648, 649
Particles
  compounds 559
  gases 375
  gravity 398
  liquids 514
  matter 538
  mixtures 558
  particle accelerators 298
  particle physics 655
  solids 778
  subatomic 744
  thermal motion 417
Pascal, Blaise 232, 690
Pashtuns 81
Passchendaele, Battle of (1917) 905, 906
*Passeggiata* 476
Passenger aircraft 43
Passenger ferries 759
Passerine birds 779
  eggs 290
Passionflower 347, 667
Passports 44
Pasteur, Louis 544, **645**
Pasteur Institute 250, 645
Pasteurization 645
*Pastoral* symphony (Beethoven) 123
Patagonia 65, 787, 788, 794

Patagonian conure 134
Patents 461
Patients, hospitals 433
Patrick, St 192, 466
Patronage, Renaissance 708
Paul, St 213, 214, 484
Pauling, Linus 92, 200
Pavarotti, Luciano 629
Pavlof Volcano 634
Pavlova, Anna 108
Paws
  badgers, otters, and skunks 104
  bears 120
Pax Romana 724
Payne-Gaposchkin, Cecilia 808
Peace movements **646**
Peace Pledge Union 646
Peacekeeping, United Nations 68, 863, 882
Peaches 367
Peacock 166, 318, 325
Peacock butterfly 159
Peacock worm 623, 909
Peanuts 33
Peanut worms 750
Pearl Harbor 869, 907
Pearls 249
Pearse, Patrick 466
Peary, Robert 673
Peas 663
  broad-leaved everlasting 666
Peasants, feudalism 329
Peasant's Revolt (1381) 546
Peasants' War (1524-26) 381
Peat 222, 669, 777
Pebbles, beaches 223
Peccaries **657**
Pedestrians 716
Pedro I, Emperor of Brazil 790
Pedro II, Emperor of Brazil 684
Peipus, Lake 112
Pekingese 271
Pelé 351
Pele's hair 881
Pelicans 747
Pellets, owls 633
Peloponnese 403
Peloponnesian League 402
Peloponnesian Wars 402
Pelvis 765
Penda 27
Pendulous sedge 394
Pendulum clocks 838, 839
Penguins **647**, 675
  Adélie 647
  emperor 647, 674, 675
  Galapagos 647
  Humboldt 647
  king 647
  macaroni 647
  rockhopper 647
Penicillium moulds 585
Peninsular War (1808-14) 595
Penis 709, 873
Pennsylvanian epoch 378
Penrose, Roger 139
Pens 910
Penzias, Arno 838
Peon 191
People carriers 178
Péotin 589
Pepin, King of the Franks 358
Pepper 23
Peppered moth 319, 678
Pepys, Samuel 516
Percentages 619
Percheron horse 432
Percussion instruments 590, 592

Père David's deer 235
Peregrine falcon 137
Perennial plants 663
Perentie 397
Perestroika 795
Pérez de Cuéllar, Javier 863
Perfume, French 357
Pericles 402
Peridotite 723
Periglacial landscapes 850
Periodic comets 230
Periodic table 298, **924-5**
Peripheral nervous system 144
Peristalsis 264
Periwinkle, greater (plant) 347
Periwinkles (molluscs) 771
Perkin, William Henry 277
Permafrost 76, 850
Permian period 378, 687
Perrault, Charles 203
Perry, Commodore Matthew 481
Persephone 388
Persepolis 648
Persian Empires **648-9**
    Alexander the Great and 47
    Safavid Empire **735**
    wars with Greece 402
    *see also* Iran
Persian Gulf 406
Persian longhair cat 184, 185
Persimmons 367
Personal computers (PCs) 231, 232
Personality, brain and 145
Perspective 71, 507, 707
Peru **285-6**
    Chavín culture **198**
    Inca Empire **442-3**, 789
    independence 140
Pesach 487
PET scans 542
Pétain, Marshal 359
Petals 346
Peter I the Great, Tsar **729**, **730**
Peter III, Tsar 730
Peter the Hermit 247
*Peter Pan* (Barrie) 204
Peter Rabbit's Race Game 202
Petipa, Marius 108
Petra, Jordan 822
Petrarch 707
Petrification, fossils 354
Petrochemicals 625, 626, 670
Petrograd *see* St Petersburg
Petrograph microscopes 553
Petrol 625, 626
Petroleum 625
Petrology 378
Peugeot bicycles 129
pH scale 12
    soil 777
Phalarope, grey 761
Phaneric coloration 165
Pharaohs 291
Pharmacies 275
Pharos of Alexandria 752
Pharsalus, Battle of (48 BC) 161
Pheasants 289
Phenotype 376
Pheromones 54, 58
Phidias 752
Philately 804
Philip I, King of Spain 428
Philip II, King of Macedon 47, 402
Philip II, King of Spain 800, 874
    and Madrid 798
    Portuguese revolt 684
    Spanish Armada 301

Philip VI, King of France 329
Philip the Good, Duke of
    Burgundy 439
Philippines 75, 78, **650**
Philistines 427
Philosophy **651**
    humanism 708
    key philosophers 941
    Socrates 776
Phloem 654, 665, 846
Phnom Penh, Cambodia 877
Phoebus butterfly 234
Phoenicians 320, **652**
Phones *see* Telephones
Phonograph 287
Phosphates 637
Phosphorus 925
Photochemical smog 40
Photography **653**
    aerial 59
    cameras **163-4**
    facts 938
    holograms 503
    paparazzi 603
    *see also* Films and film-making
Photons 911
Photosphere, Sun 814
Photosynthesis 131, 303, **654**, 663
Phototropism 668
Phreatic water 715
Phylum, classification 914
Physics **655**
    atoms and molecules **92**
    Einstein, Albert **294**
    electricity 295
    electromagnetism **296**
    energy **303-4**
    force and motion **352**
    friction **363**
    gases **375**
    gravity **398**
    heat and temperature **416-17**
    light **508-9**
    magnetism **522**
    matter **538**
    Meitner, Lise **548**
    "modern" physics 744
    Newton, Isaac **605**
    pressure **690**
    radioactivity **697**
    solids **778**
    time **837**
Physiology 131
Phytoplankton 554, 622
Pi 536
Pianos 591
Picasso, Pablo **656**
Piccard, Auguste 321
Piccard, Jacques 321
Piccolo 592
Pickup trucks 180
Pico Duarte 174
Picture books 205
Picture signs 763
Pie charts 537
Pigeons 132
Pigments 227
    paints 277
    skin 767
Pigs 325, **657**
Pikas 694
Pilate, Pontius 484
Pilgrimages 762
    Hinduism 422
Pilgrim Fathers 614, **658**
Pillars of Islam 468
Pinacate National Park 551
Pinatubo, Mount 650

Pincers, arthropods 74
Pineal gland 429
Pine marten 317
Pine trees 847
    stone 848
    whitebark 616
Pingos 850
Pinnacles Desert 93
Pinnipedia 748
Pinochet, Augusto 790
Pinocytes 190
Pinto horse 432
*Pioneer 10* space probe 797
Piranha 337, 500, 699
Pirates 307, **659**
Pissarro, Camille 72, 561
Pistols 409, 888
Piston engines 42, 305
Pit props 851
Pitahui bird 672
Pitcairn Island 680
Pitch
    hearing 278
    sound 782
Pitch Lake 625
Pitchblende 250
Pitcher plant 177, 534
Pituitary gland 145, 429
Pitvipers 772
Pius II, Pope 496
Pizarro, Francisco 442, 789
Place-value number systems 619
Placenta 528, 710
Plagues, Black Death **138**
Plaice 337, 338
Plains wanderer 290
Planarians 909
Plane shapes, mathematics 926
Planes *see* Aircraft
Planets **660-2**
    astrology 85
    astronomy 87
    beyond Solar System 280
    Earth **279-80**
    facts 921
    Galileo observes 371
    gravity **398**
    Solar System 815
    space probes 796
Plankton 241, 554, 622
Plantain, greater 347
Plantations
    rubber 790
    slavery 768
    sugar 176
Plants **663-9**
    anatomy **665**
    Asian wildlife 82-3
    Australian wildlife 99-100
    botany 131
    carnivorous plants **177**
    cave wildlife 189
    cells **190**
    classification 510, **914-15**
    conservation 234, 235
    defence **667**
    desert wildlife 261
    drugs 274
    dyes 277
    endangered 920
    European wildlife 316-17
    evolution **318-19**
    extinction 688
    farming 323
    ferns 327
    flowers **346-7**
    food webs and chains **350**
    forests **353**

fossils 354, 355
    fruits and seeds **366-7**
    gardens **374**
    grasses, rushes, and sedges **393-4**
    grassland wildlife 397
    island wildlife 472
    lake and river wildlife 500
    leaves **666**
    legends 593
    lifespans 916
    Linnaeus, Carolus **510**
    marsh and swamp wildlife 534
    mosses and liverworts **573**
    mountain wildlife 578
    North American wildlife 615-16
    ocean wildlife 622
    oxygen cycle 91
    parasites 643
    photosynthesis **654**
    polar wildlife 675
    pollution **677-8**
    postage stamps 805
    prehistoric 687
    propagators 417
    rainforest wildlife 699
    records **918**
    reproduction **668**
    seashore life 749
    seaweeds and other algae **751**
    South American wildlife **793-4**
    trees **846-8**
    tundra 850
    uses **669**
    woodland wildlife 903
Plaque, teeth 824
Plasma
    blood 414
    matter 538
Plasma membrane, cells 190
Plasticity 778
Plastics **670**
    oil products 626
    polymers 200
Plata, Río de la 66
Platelets 414, 415
Plate tectonics 236-7
Plath, Sylvia 671
Platinum 550, 925
Plato 402
    Academy 776
    Atlantis 593
    *Dialogues* 776
    on education 288
    and the Renaissance 707
Platypus, duck-billed 100, 528, 672
Playa 259
Play, chimpanzees 568
Playing cards 201
Plays
    drama **272-3**
    theatres 835-6
Pleasure boats 759
Pleiades 807
Pleistocene epoch 378
Pliocene epoch 378
Ploughs 324, 461
Plover, blacksmith 761
Plums 367
Plural societies 523
Pluto **660**
    facts 921
    Solar System 815
Plutonium 924
    nuclear power 618
Plymouth, USA 658
Pneumatic drills 690
Po, River 475
Pobedy Peak 80

Poe, Edgar Allen 516
Poetry **671**
    children's 205
    epics 515
    key poets 941
    Shakespeare, William 753
Pogroms 487
Pointer 271
Pointillism 227
Poison dart frogs 364, 672
    green and black 365
    yellow and black 365
Poison ivy 667
Poisons
    animals 166, **672**, 918
    caterpillars 158
    fish 337
    frogs 364
    fungi 585
    jellyfish 483
    plant defences 667
    salamanders 737
    snakes 772
    spiders and scorpions 801
    warning signs 166, 764
Poitiers, Battle of (1356) 439
Poker (card game) 201
Pol Pot 877
Poland 312, **313**
    Walesa, Lech 857
    Warsaw Ghetto 426
Polar bear *see* Bears, polar
Polar climate 217
Polar exploration **673**
Polar wildlife **674-5**
Polarized light 508
Polaroid cameras 163, 164
Pole vault 88
Polecat 889
Poles, magnets 522
Polhem, Christopher 520
Poliakov, Valeri 86
Police **676**
    armour 69
    law 504
    riverboats 759
Polisario Front 29
Politics **391-2**
    festivals 328
    flags 340
    political parties 392
    political world **928-9**
    politicians 392
Pollen 668
Pollination 122, 346
Pollock, Jackson 72
Pollution **677-8**
    acid rain 12
    air 40, 678
    and artificial selection 319
    cars and trucks 178
    catalytic converters 179
    global warming 217
    industrial 841
    in Japan 481
    nuclear power 618
    oil 13, 625, 678
Pollux 725
Polo 111, 430
Polo, Marco 320, 477, 498
Polonium 250, 925
Polygons 536, 926
Polyhedra 536
Polymers 200, 670
Polynesia 93, 94, **679-80**
    Maoris 531, 607
Polyphony 587
Polyps, coral 239

Polystyrene 670
Polythene 670
Polyvinyl chloride (PVC) 670
Pombal, Marqués de 684
Pommel horse, gymnastics 411
Pompeii, Italy 59, 71, 354
Pompey the Great 161
Pond sedge, greater 394
Pond skater 155
Pondweed, broad-leaved 347
Ponies 432
Pont du Gard, Nîmes 725
Pontic Mountains 852
Poodle 271
Pool (game) 110
Poor metals 550
    periodic table 924
Poorwill 633
Pop Art 73
Popes 310
    key popes 942
    medieval Europe 546
Poplar, white 666, 848
Pop music **718-19**
Popocatapetl 101, 551
Popper, Karl 742
Poppies 367, 664
Popular culture
    literature 516
    rock and pop music **718-19**
Popular protest, peace movements
    646
Population
    facts **930**
    food webs and chains 350
    living standards **931**
*Populus* 355
Porcelain 685
    Chinese **686**
Porcupine fish 53
Porcupine grass 99
Porcupines 702, 703
    American 616
Porifera 483
Porpoises 893
    Dall's 895
    harbour 895
Porsche Carrera 911 RS 180
Port-au-Prince, Haiti 174
Port Louis, Mauritius 450
Port Moresby, Papua New Guinea
    636
Port-of-Spain, Trinidad and Tobago
    175
Port Royal, Nova Scotia, Canada
    171
Port Vila, Vanuatu 637
Port wine 683
Porto-Novo, Benin 37
Ports **681**
    facts 934
    Pacific Ocean 635
Portugal **682-4**
    Angola War 19
    history of **684**
    slave trade 768
    and South America 787, 789
Portuguese-man-of-war 623
Poseidon 389, 401
Postal services **804-5**
Posters, film 332
Postmodernism, architecture 62
Potassium 298, 924
Potassium permanganate 558
Potatoes, Irish famine 466
Potential energy 303
Potholes 188
Potosí, Bolivia 789

Potter, Beatrix 202, 203, 205
Pottery and ceramics **685-6**
    Belorussia 113
    Chavín culture 198
    Minoan 557
    Portugal 683
    Stone Age 809
Poulsen, Valdemar 783
Poverty
    Mother Teresa 574
    world economy 933
Power *see* Energy
Power stations 304
    coal-fired 222
    electricity supply 295
    nuclear power 618
Powerboats 759
Powers, numbers 619
Prague, Czech Republic 313, 496
Prairie chicken 290
Prairies 612
    Canada 169
    wildlife 396, 616
Praise poetry 671
Praseodymium 924
Prawns 241
Praxiteles 71
Prayers, Islam 468
Precambrian time 378
Precious metals 550
Precious stones 249
Predators
    birds of prey 135
    food webs and chains 350
Pregnancy 710
    gynaecology 541
    *in vitro* fertilization (IVF) 542,
    710
Prehistoric life **687-8**
Prehistoric people 424, **689**
    in Africa 17
    archaeology **59-60**
    art 71
    Bronze Age **150**
    cave paintings 638
    education 288
    in Europe 310
    in France 358
    Leakey family **506**
    medicine 543
    Stone Age **809**
    technology 823
Premolars 824
Prescription drugs 275
Preservation, environment 234
Presidents
    democracy 391
    France 945
    United States 944
    women 948
Presley, Elvis 718
Prespa, Lake 107
Presses, printing 691
Pressure **690**
    air 40, 890
    Pressure Law 375
    and winds 896
Pressure cookers 690
Pressure groups 392
Pretoria, South Africa 784
Prevailing winds 896
Priapus 389
Prickly pear 664
Priestley, Joseph 40, 654
Priests 388
    ancient Egypt 291
    Christianity 214
    Hinduism 421

Indus Valley civilization 455
Primary colours 227
Primary industry 840
Primates **568-70**
Prime ministers
    Australia 946
    Britain 943
    Canada 946
    New Zealand 946
    women 948
Prime numbers 619, 926
Primrose 347
Principe *see* São Tomé Principe
*Principia Mathematica* (Newton)
    605, 743
Printers, computers 231
Printing **691-2**
    books 143
    colour printing 227
    Franklin, Benjamin 360
Pripet Marshes, Belorussia 112
Prism, white light spectrum 226
Prismatic crystals 248
Prisoners of war (POWs) 883
Prisons 244
    Pankhurst family 641
Privateers 659
Prizes
    children's literature 205
    Nobel Prizes 200, 646, 744, 941
Probability, statistics 537
Proboscis bat 119
Proboscis monkey 533
*Proconsul* 437
Producers, films and film-
    making 330
Product design 262
Programs, computer 456
Prohibition 869
Projections, maps and mapping 532
Prokaryotes 687
Prolactin 429
Prometheus 334
Promethium 924
Prominences, Sun 814
Pronghorn 616
Pronking 257
Propaganda 424
    World War I 906
Propagators 417
Propane 626
Property crime 244
Props, theatre 836
Proserpina 389
Protactinium 548, 924
Proteins 264
Protest groups 392
Protestantism 213
    in Ireland 466
    Reformation **704**
    religious wars 310
Protists 554
    classification 131, 914
    evolution 280
Proton cars 524
Protons 92, 744
Protostars 807
Protozoa 554, 555
Provence burnet moth 159
Proxima Centauri 871
Prussia 381-2
    Franco-Prussian War 359
Pruta do Janelão, Brazil 188
Przewalski's horse 235, 431
Psychiatry 541
    Freud, Sigmund **362**
Psychoanalysis 362
Psychotherapy 544

Pteridophytes 327
Pterosaurs 687
Ptolemaic Universe 871
Ptolemy, Claudius 532, 870
Ptolemy I, Pharaoh 143, 752
Puberty 405
Public health 413
Public pressure, politics 392
Public relations 14
Publishing
    books 143
    desktop publishing 456
Pueblo Bonito 613
Puerto Limito 613
Puerto Rico 174
Puerto Rico Trench 89
Puffball 584, 586
Pufferfish 672
Puffin 747
Pug 271
Puissance, horse riding 430
Pulleys 520
Pulsars 294, 807
Pulse, first aid 335
Pulses (beans) 349
Puma 513, 616
Pundits 321
Punishment **244**
Punjab, Pakistan 639
Punk 719
Punta Arenas, Chile 67
Pupae
    butterflies and moths 158
    metamorphosis 458
Pupils, eyes 322
Pupin, Michael 911
Puppetry 273
Puritans 658, 704
Pygmy hog 657
Pyloric sphincter 264
Pyongyang, North Korea 497
Pyramids **693**
    Aztec 62
    Egypt 25, 752
    Maya Empire 540
Pyrenees 308, 309, 798
Pyroclastic debris 881
Pythagoras 587
Pythagoras' theorem 536
Python 711, 772
    Burmese rock 712, 773
    Calabar ground 712

**Q**
Qatar 406, **408**
Qianlong, Emperor of China 79
Qin dynasty 209
Qin Shih Huangdi, Emperor of
    China 209
Qing dynasty 210
Qolleh-ye-Damävand, Iran 463
Quaking grass, large 394
Quantum physics 744
Quarks 92
Quarter horse 432
Quartz 248
    gold veins 298
    semi-precious stones 249
    watches 838
Quasars 87, 370, 870
Quaternary period 378
Québec, Canada 170, 171, 614
Quechua Indians 67, 141
Queen Alexandra's birdwing
    100, 235
Queens
    ants and termites 58

bees and wasps 122
    *see also* Kings and queens
Queensland, Australia 94
Quelea, red-billed 780
*Quercus* 355
Quetzalcoatl 101, 549, 593
Quinces 367
Quipu 442
Quisling, Vidkun 740
Quito, Ecuador 286
Quorn 585
Qur'an (Koran) 407, 468
    and daily life 469
    Muhammad 581
    mosques 572
    religious law 505
    writing 910

**R**
Ra 593
Rabat, Morocco 29
Rabbis 487
Rabbits **694**
    European 529, 694
Rabies 645
Raccoon dog 899, 900
Raccoons **640**, 872
    common 529
Race, social stratification 775
Racer, red-tailed 772
Races
    athletics 88
    board games 201
    cycling 251
    horse 430
    motor sports 178, **575-6**
    sailing and other water sports
    736
    swimming 818
    winter sports 897
Racine, Jean 272, 358
Racing *see* Races
Racism, apartheid 784
Racket sports 803, **831**
Racket-tail, booted 134, 817
Rackham, Jack 659
Racquetball 831
Radar **695**
    airports 44
    navigation 598
    weather forecasting 891
Radiation
    Big Bang 130
    heat 417
    radioactivity 697
    X-rays and the electromagnetic
    spectrum **911**
"Radiation" fog 221
Radio 589, **696**, 825
    drama 273
    facts 940
Radioactivity **697**
    Curie, Marie **250**
    Meitner, Lise 548
Radioisotopes 697
Radiosonde balloons 891
Radiotherapy 697
Radio waves
    electromagnetic spectrum 911
    radio galaxies 370
    radio telescopes 87, 828, 870
    telecommunications 825
Radium 250, 924
Radium Institute, Paris 250
Radon 925
Raffia 669
Raffles, Sir Stamford 525

Rafts 844
Raft spiders 802
Ragdoll cat 185
Ragged robin 664
Ragtime music 482
Ragworms 750, 909
　king 909
Railways *see* Trains and railways
Rain 698, 890
　acid rain 12, 677
　cave formation 188
　climate 217
　deserts 259
　monsoon 217, 449
　rivers 715
　storms 810
Rainbows 226
Rainforest wildlife 699-700
　Africa 39
　Asia 82
　Australia 100
　ecosystems 283
　lizards 517
　South America 793
Rainforests 353
　Africa 16, 20
　Asia 76
　Australasia and Oceania 94
　Brazil 146, 147
　deforestation 142, 194
　Indonesia 451
　South America 788, 791
　Southeast Asia 876
　Thailand and Burma 833
Raised beaches 223
Rajang River 523
Rally driving 576
RAM (random-access memory) 231
Rama V (Chulalongkorn), King of Siam 78
Ramadan 469
*Ramayana* 421
Rambutans 367
Rameses II, Pharaoh 25, 291, 292, 425
Ramon y Cajal, Santiago 144
*Rana* 355
Rangoon, Burma 834
Rankine, William 303
Raphael 707, 708, 776
*Raphidonema* 355
*Raphus* 355
Rapids 715
Rarefactions, sound waves 782
Rarotonga, Treaty of (1986) 607
Ras al Khaimah, United Arab Emirates 408
Raspberries 366
Rastafarians 173, 176
Rationing, World War II 908
Rats 701
　black 702, 703
　Black Death 138
　black-headed 703
Rat snake 903
Rattlesnakes 609, 712
Raven 133
　common 246
Rays (fish) 623, 754-5
　blue spotted 754
　electric 755
　spotted 755
Ray, Satyajit 332
Razdan, River 187
Razor-strop fungus 586
Reactions, chemical 199, 416
Reactors, nuclear power 618

Reagan, Ronald 225
Real de Manzanares castle, Spain 183
Realism, drama 272, 273
Real tennis 831
Rearmament 399
Reber, Grote 828
Receivers, radio 696
Recessive genes 377
Reconnaissance aircraft 43, 884
Record companies 719
Recorders (musical instruments) 592
Recording
　sound 783
　video 875
Records, animal and plant 918-19
Records (music), best-selling 939
Recovery position 335
Recruitment
　armies 68
　World War I 905
Rectum 264
Recycling
　glass 387
　paper 642
　plastics 670
Red Army (China) 212
Red Army (Russia) 734
Red Basin, China 75
Red blood cells 414, 415
Red Cross 340, 646, 883
Redcurrants 367
Red giant stars 807
Redgrave, Steven 736
Red Guard 212
Red mullet 336, 338
Red river hog 657
"Red Scare", USA 225
Red Sea 406, 473, 621
Redonda 174
Redshift
　galaxies 130
　measuring the Universe 871
Reduction, chemical reactions 199
Redwoods 846
　dawn 235
Reedbuck 165
Reed mace 393
Reeds 500, 534
Reefs, coral 93, 95, 239, 450, 471
Reefshark, black tip 239
Refining
　oil 626
　steel 467
Reflecting telescopes 828
Reflection 509
Reflex actions 144
Reflexology 542
Reformation 358, 382, 704
Refracting telescopes 828
Refraction 509
Refrigerators 416, 462
Refugees 845, 883, 930
Reggae 173, 718
Regolith 777
Reincarnation, Buddhism 152
Reindeer 257, 529, 615
Reinforced concrete 157
Relativity, theories of 294, 398, 837, 870
Relaxation 413
Relief maps 532
Relief printing 692
Religions 705-6
　Aboriginal Australians 11
　ancestor worship 17, 233, 400
　Ancient Egypt 291

Babylonians 103
Buddha 151
Buddhism 152-3
Byzantine Empire 160
Celtic Church 192
Chavín culture 198
Christianity 213-14
　churches and cathedrals 215
Druids 191
emigration to New World 614
gods and goddesses 388-9
Hinduism 421-2
holy objects 706
Incas 442
Indus Valley civilization 455
Islam 468-9
Judaism 486-7
Khmer Empire 490
Minoans 557
monasteries 560
Mughal Empire 580
Native Americans 597
Olmec 627
Polynesians 531
prehistoric people 689
Reformation 704
religious law 505
religious wars 310
Roman 725, 726
shrines 762
signs and symbols 763, 764
Songhai Empire 781
voodoo 18, 174
Reliquaries 546
REM sleep 145
Rembrandt van Rijn 602, 638
Remus 725
Renaissance 707-8
　architecture 63
　art 71
　cities 216
　drama 272
　gardens 374
　in France 358
　in Germany 381
　Leonardo da Vinci 507
　music 588
　science 743-4
　theatres 835
Renal dialysis 873
Renewable energy 304
Renoir, Pierre Auguste 72, 561
Reproduction 916
　arthropods 74
　bactria 554
　bats 118
　bears 120
　bees and wasps 122
　beetles 124
　birds 133
　bugs 155
　crocodiles 245
　deer 257
　dinosaurs 266
　dogs 270
　ferns 327
　fish 337
　flies 342
　frogs and toads 364
　grasshoppers and crickets 395
　hippopotamuses 423
　horses 431
　human 436, 709-10
　insects 458
　kangaroos 488
　leopards 512
　lizards 517
　mammals 528

and migration 556
　mosses and liverworts 573
　parasites 643
　penguins 647
　pigs and peccaries 657
　plants 668
　reptiles 712
　rhinoceroses 713
　rodents 701
　salamanders and newts 737
　scorpions 801
　seals 748
　sharks and rays 755
　sheep and goats 756
　snakes 772
　spiders 801
　tigers 511
　viruses 555
　whales 894
Reptiles 711-12
　coral reefs 239
　crocodiles 245
　desert wildlife 261
　eggs 289
　grassland wildlife 397
　island wildlife 472
　lake and river wildlife 499
　lizards 517-18
　marsh and swamp wildlife 534
　ocean wildlife 622
　prehistoric 687, 688
　rainforest wildlife 700
　records 919
　snakes 772-3
　South American wildlife 793-4
　turtles and tortoises 854-5
　woodland wildlife 903
Republics 391
*Requiem* (Mozart) 579
Research
　cars and trucks 179
　drugs 274
　market research 14
Reservations, Native American 383, 596
Reservoirs 252
Resin, pine trees 847
Resistance movement, World War II 908
Resistors 297
Resources
　conservation 234
　Earth sciences 282
　world 932
Respiratory system 436, 519
Resultant force 352
Retailers 841
Retina 322
Retriever, curly-coated 271
Réunion 450
Revere, Paul 49
Reversible reactions 199
Revolutions 947
　Agricultural Revolution 326
　American Revolution 49
　Chinese Revolution 212
　European revolutions of 1848 535
　French Revolution 359, 361
　Industrial Revolution 453-4
　Russian Revolution 734
Revolvers 888
Reykjavik, Iceland 90
Rheas 345
　lesser 794
Rhenium 924
Rhine, River 379, 380, 819
Rhinoceroses 713
　black 529, 713

great Indian 713
Javan 713
Sumatran 713
white 234, 235, 713
Rhizomes 665
　ferns 327
Rhodes, Cecil 248
Rhodes, Greece 752
Rhodesia *see* Zimbabwe
Rhodesian ridgeback 271
Rhodium 924
Rhodochrosite 249
Rhododendrons 83
Rhyolite 723, 881
Rhythm, music 587
Rhythm-and-blues 718
Rhythmic gymnastics 411, 412
Rias 223
Ribbon worms 909
Rice
　China 207
　farming 323
　food 349, 669
　Indonesia 452
　Japan 479
　Southeast Asia 876
　Thailand 834
　world resources 932
Richard I, King of England 247, 610
Richardson, Lewis 891
Richborough Fort 116
Richest countries 933
Richter scale, earthquakes 281, 923
Richthofen, Manfred von 905
Rickshaws 129
Rideau Canal 169
Riding 430
Riflebird, paradise 290
Rifles 409, 887, 888
Rift valleys 236, 577
*Rig Veda* 421
Riga, Gulf of 112
Riga, Latvia 113
Rigel 808
Right-angled triangles 536
Rights
　black rights 948
　human rights 438
　women's voting rights 948
*Rights of Man* 361
Riley, Charles 632
Rimsky Korsakov, Nicolai 811
Ringed snail-eating snake 773
Ring of Fire, Pacific Ocean 634, 650
Rings, gymnastics 411
Ringworm 555, 585
Rio de Janeiro, Brazil 146, 147, 790
Rio Muni 22
*Rite of Spring, The* (Stravinsky) 811
Ritter, Johann 911
Rituals 775
　Buddhism 152
　drama 273
　Hinduism 422
　Maya Empire 540
　Native Americans 597
　religions 705
Rivers 714-15
　dams 252
　eyots 471
　facts 922
　lakes 501
　valleys 577
　waterways 681
　wildlife 499-500
Riyadh, Saudi Arabia 407
Road racing, cycling 251
Roadrunner 260, 615

Roads **716**
  cities 216
  facts 934
  history of 843
  maps 532
Roadside shrines 762
Road trains 96
Roaring, lions 511
Robert of Valois 329
Robespierre, Maximilien 361
Robins 780
  American 289
Robinson, Mary 391, 466
Robots **717**
  space exploration 796
Rochester Castle, England 182
Rock and pop music **718-19**
  Beatles, The **121**
Rock crystal 249
Rockets 344, **720-1**
Rock hyrax 39
Rock paintings 17, 809
  *see also* Cave paintings
Rock pools 749
Rock-rose, common 347
Rocks **722-3**
  blasting tunnels 851
  caves 188
  earthquakes 281
  erosion by rivers 715
  fossils 354
  geology 282, **378**
  glaciation 385
  lava 881
  petrograph microscopes 553
  water content 715
Rocky Mountains 611, 612
  Canada 169
  Chinook wind 896
  United States 864
  wildlife 616
Rocky planets 660
Rodents **701-2**
  hibernation 420
  rabbits and hares **694**
  teeth 527
Rodríguez, Símon 140
Rods and cones, eyes 322
Roentgen, Wilhelm *see*
  Röntgen, Wilhelm
Roger I, King of Sicily 610
Roger II, King of Sicily 610
Rogers, Richard 859
Roller, racket-tailed 134
Rollers, friction 363
Rolling Stones 718
Roll-on-roll-off ferries 759
Rollo the Viking 610
Rolls Royce 180
ROM (read-only memory),
  computers 231
Roman Catholic Church 213
  Baroque art 72
  in Brazil 147
  and Carnival 328
  in Central Europe 312
  ceremonies 214
  Galileo Galilei and 371
  Henry VIII and 861
  in Ireland 465, 466
  Mother Teresa **574**
  nuns 560
  papacy 310
  Philippines 650
  Reformation 704
  Renaissance 708
  in South America 789
Roman Empire 310, **724-6**

alphabets 910
architecture 61
army 68
art 71
bridges 148
Britain 860
Byzantine Empire 160
Caesar, Julius **161**
Christianity 213, 310
end of 477
flags 340
flats and apartments 434
France 358
gardens 374
glassware 387
gods and goddesses 388, 389
Jesus Christ 484
law 504
Libya 29
medicine 543
mythology 935
Portugal 684
pyramids 693
roads 843
sculpture 746
Seven Wonders of the Ancient
  World 752
slavery 768
tunnels 851
Romania **727-8**
Romanies 728
  language 502
Romanov dynasty **730**, 734
Romanticism
  art 72
  ballets 108
  films 331
  music 123, 589
  novels 516
Rome, Italy 475, 476
Rome, Treaty of (1957) 311, 315
Romero, Archbishop Oscar 196
Rommel, Field Marshal 907
Romulus 725
Ronne Ice Shelf 56
Röntgen, Wilhelm 250, 655, 911
Roofs
  architecture 61
  building and construction 156
  thatched 157
Rook 246
Roosevelt, Eleanor 438
Roosevelt, Franklin D 399
  New Deal 399, 869
  nuclear weapons 294
  Yalta Conference (1945) 225
Roosevelt, Theodore 383, 868, 869
Roosting
  bats 117
  birds of prey 136
Root vegetables 349
Roots
  plants 665
  trees 846
Rose quartz 249
Roseau, Dominica 175
Rosetta Stone 59, 292
Roskilde festival 328
Ross, Diana 718, 865
Rossby waves 896
Ross Ice Shelf 56
Rössing Uranium Mine, Namibia
  31
Rossini, Gioacchino 629
Rothko, Mark 72
Rotterdam, Netherlands 602
Rounders 111
Round Table 593

Roundworms 52, 909
Rousseau, Jean Jacques 288
Rove beetle 125
Rowan 367, 848
Rowing 736
Royal Air Force (RAF) 884
Royal Ballet 108
Royal gramma fish 338
Royal jelly 122
Royal Road 648
Royal Society 605
Royal Society for the Prevention of
  Cruelty to Animals (RSPCA)
  496
Royal Society for the Promotion of
  Natural Knowledge 744
Royal Society of Victoria 97
Rub' al-Khali 406, 407
Rubber 669, **670**
  Malaysia 524
  South America 790
Rubbish trucks 179
Rubel, Ira W 692
Rubella 555
Rubicon, River 161
Rubidium 924
Ruby 249, 834
Rudders, aircraft 42
Ruddy daggerwing 460
Rudolf I, Emperor 428
Rufous patas monkey 570
Rugby football 351
  champions 937
  in South Africa 785
Ruhr, River 380
Rules of war 883
Runners, plants 668
Running, athletics 88
Runways, airports 44
Rus **729**
Rushes **393-4**
  flowering 664
  soft 394
Rushmore, Mount 866
Russell, William 604
Russia 75, 308, **731-32**
  ballet 108
  and Central Asia 78
  food 349
  history of **729-30**
  Iron Curtain 311
  leaders 944
  monarchs 944
  Napoleonic Wars 595
  World War I 905
  World War II 907, 908
  *see also* Soviet Union
Russian Orthodox Church **732**
Russian Revolution (1905) **730**
Russian Revolution (1917) **734**
Russian shorthair cat 185
Russo-Japanese War (1904-5) 481
Rust 199, 467, 550
Ruth, Babe 109
Ruthenium 924
Rutherford, Ernest 618, 697
Rutherfordium 924
Rutting 257
Ruwenzori Mountains 15, 16
Ruyter, Michiel de 602
Rwanda **23**
Rye 669
Ryukyu Islands 478

# S

Saab 99 Turbo car 180
Sabah 523

Sabatons 70
Sabbath 487
Sable 83
Sabres 69
Sac fungi 584, 586
Sacral nerve 144
Sacral plexus 144
Sacraments, Christian 214
Sacrifices
  Aztecs 101
  to gods and goddesses 388
  Maya Empire 540
  religions 705
Sadat, Anwar 646
Saddlebred horse 432
Saddle joints 766
Safari parks 912
Safavid Empire 735
Safety
  cars 179
  tunnels 851
Sagas 515
Sago palms 367, 847
  Japanese 235
Sahara Desert 15, 28, 33
  and African history 17
  trans-Saharan trade 781
  types of desert 259
  wildlife 260
Sahel region 33
  desertification 34
  droughts 259
  nomads 21
Sailing boats 759, 844
  ancient Egypt 291
  yachts 757, 758
St Bartholomew's Day Massacre
  (1572) 704
St Bernard 271
St Etienne Abbey, France 610
St George's, Grenada 175
St Gotthard tunnel 819
St Helena 90
St John's, Antigua, and
  Barbuda 174
St Kitts and Nevis 174
St Lawrence River 171, 614
St Lawrence Seaway 170, 611
St Lucia 172, **175**
St Mark's, Venice 588
St Paul's Cathedral, London 63
St Peter's, Rome 63
St Petersburg, Russia (Leningrad)
  **729**, **730**, **732**, 734
  siege of (1941) 795
St Sabina, Rome 215
St Vincent and the Grenadines
  172, **175**
Saints
  reliquaries 546
  saints' days 214
Sakura 526
Saladin 247
Salamanders 50, **737**
  European fire 737
  mandarin 50, 737
  mountain dusky 578
  spotted 737, 903
Salamis, Battle of (480 BC) 402
Salat 468
Salazar, Antonio 684
Salem witch trials 898
Salginatobel Bridge, Switzerland
  148
Salieri, Antonio 579
Salim, Sheikh 580
Salinas Grandes, Argentina 787
Salinization 777

Salisbury, Rhodesia *see* Harare,
  Zimbabwe
Salisbury Cathedral, England 215
Salk, Jonas 275
Salmon
  Atlantic Ocean 89
  migration 556
  reproduction 337
*Salmonella* 555
Saloon cars 178
Salt
  Indian Ocean 449
  salinization 777
  salt water lakes 501
  sea water 621
Salt glands, seabirds 747
Salt march (India, 1930) 372
Saltmarshes 223
Salts 12
Saluki 271
*Salyut 1* space station 797
Samarium 924
Samarkand, Uzbekistan 77, 81
Sami people 617
Sammurammat, Queen of
  Assyria 84
Samoa **680**
Samudragupta, Emperor 410
Samurai **738**
  armour 69, 70, 738
  swords 888
Sana, Yemen 407
San Andreas Fault 237
San Carlos reservation, Arizona 383
Sand
  beaches 223
  deserts 259
  glass 387
  shores 749
  soils 777
Sand cat 513
Sand clocks 838
Sand couch 347
Sand dollar 750
Sand paintings, Native American 73
Sandanistas 196
Sandbars 223
Sandfish 261
Sandglasses 839
Sandgrouse 39
Sandstone 722, 723
Sandwich Islands 238
SANE 646
San Fernando Fault, USA 281
San Francisco, USA 281, 867
San Francisco Conference
  (1945) 863
Sanger, Margaret 710
Sangha people 22
Sanitation 268, 413
San José, Costa Rica 195, 196
San Juan, Puerto Rico 174
San Juan River 193
San Marino **476**
San Martín, General José de
  140, 790
San people 31
San Salvador, El Salvador 194, 196
Sanskrit language 410
Santiago, Chile 67
Santiago de Compostela, Spain 762
Santo Domingo, Dominican
  Republic 174
São Nicolau, Windward Islands 90
São Paulo, Brazil 146, 147
São Tomé, São Tomé e Principe 23
São Tomé e Principe 17, **23**
Sapphire 249

Saprophytes 585
Sapsucker, yellow-bellied 616
Saqqara pyramid, Egypt 25, 693
Sarajevo, Bosnia and
   Herzegovina 106
Sarak national park 816
Sarawak 523
Sarawak Chamber 188, 523
Sardinia 475
Sargassum weed 622
Sargon II, King of Assyria 84
Sargon of Akkad 813
Saris 219
Sarnath, India 151
Saro-Wiwa, Ken 19
Saskatchewan, Canada 171
Sassanian dynasty 648, 649
Satellites 739
   astronauts and 86
   maps 532
   navigation 598
   rockets 720
   telephone networks 452, 826
   weather 891
Satie, Erik 656
Satrapies 649
Saturn 661
   facts 921
   rings 371
   Solar System 815
   space probes 797
Satyagraha 372, 491
Saudi Arabia 406, 407
Saul, King of Israel 427
Saurischians 265, 267
Savannah 16, 396
   East Africa 24
   Southern Central Africa 30
   wildlife 38
Savery, Thomas 306
Sawfish 755
Sax, Adolphe 591
Saxifrage, purple 675
Saxons 51, 116
Saxophone 592
Scabious, field 666
Scales
   fish 336
   measuring weight 892
   music 588
   reptiles 711
   snakes 772
Scallops 770
   queen 623, 771
Scandinavia
   Denmark 258
   history of 740
   Norway 617
   Sweden 816
   Vikings 878-9
Scandium 924
Scanners
   colour printing 691
   computers 231
Scarab beetle 459
Scattering, colours 227
Scavengers, lizards 518
Scelidosaurus 267
Scent, flowers 346
Scent glands, mammals 528
Schiller, Friedrich von 273
Schist 722, 723
Schoenberg, Arnold 589
School stories 204
Schools, whales 894
Schools and colleges 741
   see also Education
Schuman, Robert 315

Sciatic nerve 144
Science 742
   Babylonians 103
   chemistry 199-200
   Curie, Marie 250
   Einstein, Albert 294
   electronics 297
   history of 743-4
   inventions 461, 462
   Islamic Empire 470
   Linnaeus, Carolus 510
   medieval 547
   microscopes 553
   Newton, Isaac 605
   notation 619
   physics 655
   Scientific Revolution 544
   technology 823
Science fiction 742
   robots in 717
Scientific names 914
Scooters 128, 129
Scorpion fish 239, 672
Scorpions 74, 261, 801-2
   poisons 672
Scorpius constellation 808
Scotland 858-9
   history of 861
   kings and queens 943
   see also United Kingdom
Scott, Dred 768
Scott, Captain Robert Falcon 673
Scottish fold cat 185
Scottish terrier 270
Scrabble 202
"Scramble for Africa" 18
Scrapers, flint tools 809
Screen printing 692
Screws 520
Scripts see Writing
Scrubland
   Africa 16
   Australia 94, 99
   South America 788
Sculling 736
Sculpture 745-6
   African 73
   Celtic 192
   Chavín culture 198
   church decoration 215
   Easter Island statues 531
   Etruscan 307
   facts 938
   Greek 402
   Gupta Empire 410
   medieval 547
   Olmec 627
   Stone Age 809
Scurvy 238
Scutari Hospital 608
Sea anemones 284, 483
Seabirds 747
Sea breezes 896
Sea caves 188
Seacole, Mary 608
Sea cows 894
Sea cucumbers 239, 806
Sea-floor spreading 237
Seagram Building, New York 63
Sea grasses 622
Seahorses 239, 337
Sea kale 664
Sea-life centres 912
Sea lilies 806
Sea lions 622, 748
   Californian 748
Seals 674, 748
   elephant 748

grey 748
   hunting 339
   reproduction 528
Seals and badges 763
Sea mist 221
Seamounts 620
Sea mouse 750
Sea pea 664
Sea Peoples 427
Sea potato 750
Seas see Oceans and seas
Seashore wildlife 749-50
   ecosystems 283
Seaside holidays 845
Sea slater 750
Sea slugs 239, 749, 771
Sea snakes 239, 772
Seasons 837
   animals and 166
   Earth's orbit 815
Sea spiders 623
Sea turtles 854
Sea urchins 239, 750, 806
Sea water 621
Seaweeds 622, 751
   maerl 751
   seashore life 749
Seaborgium 924
Secondary colours 227
Second Republic, France 359
Seconds 837
Secretariat, United Nations 862
Secretary bird 38, 136
Secretary-General, United Nations
   862
Secret police 676
Security Council, United Nations
   862
Security videos 875
Sedatives 275
Sedges 393-4
Sedimentary rocks 722, 723
Seeds 366-7, 668
   food 349
   records 918
   seed-bearing plants 663
   seed-eating birds 133, 134, 779
Seeing 322
Segmented worms 909
Seif dunes 259
Seikan Tunnel 851
Seine fishing 339
Seine, River 356, 471
Seismic waves 281
Seismographs 378
Seismometers 281
Selenium 925
Seleucid dynasty 648, 649
Seleucus 648
Seljuk Turks 247
Semaphore 340, 825
Semen 709
Semiconductors 297
Semimetals 550
   periodic table 924
Semi-precious stones 249
Semiramis, Queen of Assyria 84
Semitrailers 180
Semmelweis, Ignaz 544
Sen no Rikyu 738
Senate, Roman 724
Sendak, Maurice 205
Senefelder, Alois 692
Senegal 34
Senegal River 33, 34
Sennacherib, King of Assyria 84
Senses
   animal 53

birds 133
   cats 184
   dogs 270
   ears and hearing 278
   eyes and seeing 322
   smell and taste 769
Sensory neurons 144
Sensory receptors 144
Seoul, South Korea 497
Sepak raga 524
Separatists 658
Sephardic Jews 474, 486
Sepoy Rebellion (1857) 78
Serapis 389
Serbia 107
Serbian Orthodox Church 107
Serbo-Croatian language 107
Serfs, Russia 730
Sermon on the Mount 484
Serpents (musical instruments) 590
Serval 512, 513
Service industries 840
Sets, films and film-making 330
Sets, mathematics 537
Setter, English 270
Setts, badger 104
Seuss, Dr 205
Sevan, Lake 186
Seven Days Battle (1862) 48
Seven Wonders of the Ancient
   World 693, 752
Sèvres porcelain 358
Sewell, Anna 205
Sewing machines 218
Sex cells, division 190
Sex chromosomes 377
Sex Pistols, The 719
Sexism 775
Sextants 598
Sexual intercourse 709
Sexual reproduction, plants 668
Sexual selection, evolution 318
Seychelles 15, 450
Shackleton, Ernest 673
Shadows, colour 227
Shaffer, Peter 273
Shaggy ink-cap 584
Shah Jahan 580
Shakespeare, William 272, 301,
   516, 753
   Globe Theatre, London 835
   Henry V 439
   King Lear 332
Shakuhachi 592
Shale 723
Shamans 762, 898
Shang dynasty 78, 209, 210
Shanghai, China 207
Shannon, River 465
Shanty towns 791, 868
Shapes, mathematics 926
Sharjah, United Arab Emirates 408
Sharks 754-5
   angel 754
   eggs 289
   great white 235, 336, 754, 755
   lantern 755
   lemon 755
   leopard 754
   nurse 754
   Port Jackson 338, 754, 755
   spinner 623, 754
   thresher 754
   whale 755
Sharon, Plain of 473
Shar pei dog 319
Sharpeville massacre (1960) 530
Shatt-al-Arab 464

Shaw, Percy 598
Sheep 756
   farming 323, 325
   in Portugal 683
   in Turkey 853
   in Uruguay 67
Sheepdogs
   Old English 271
   Shetland 270
Sheet glass 387
Shelley, Mary 516
Shellfish, as food 349
Shells
   crabs 240
   crustaceans 241
   eggs 289
   snails and other molluscs 770
   turtles and tortoises 854
Sheng 590
Shepard, Alan 721
Sherman, General 48
Sherpas 115
Sherry 799
Shetland pony 432
   American 432
Shi'ah Islam 469, 470
   Safavid Empire 735
Shield bugs 155, 460
Shields 69
Shield volcanoes 880
Shikoku, Japan 478
Shining Path group 286
Shinto 705, 935
Ships and boats 757-9
   ancient Egypt 291
   Endeavour 238
   fishing industry 339
   flag codes 224
   Germany 380
   Greece 404
   history of 844
   Indonesia 452
   Mayflower 658
   navigation 598
   Norman 610
   oil tankers 625
   Pacific Ocean 635
   Phoenician 652
   pirates 659
   ports and waterways 681
   Portugal 683
   sailing and other water sports 736
   shipbuilding 758
   slave trade 768
   sonar 695
   submarines 812
   Viking 878
   warships 885
   weather stations 891
Shire horse 432
Shirts 218
Shiva 421
Shoals, fish 53
Shockley, William 297
Shoes 218-20
   astronauts 86
Shofar 590
Shoguns 738
Shona people 400
Shopboards 763
Shops 760
   marketing 14
   wholesalers 841
Shorebirds 761
Shore crab 240
Shores 223
Short-haired cats 185
Shorthand 910

Short sight 322
Short stories 516
Short-tailed leaf-nosed bat 119
Shot putting 88
Show jumping 430
Show trials, Soviet Union 795
Shrews 418
Shrimps 195, 241
Shrines 762
  Hindu 422
Shrubs 665
Shujai, Shah 580
SI Units 927
Siam see Thailand
Siamang 569
Siamese cat 184, 185
Siberia 731
  steppes 76
  taiga 76
  Trans-Siberian Express 732
  tundra 76
Siboney people 172
Sicily 475, 610
Siddhartha Gautama (Buddha) 77, 151
Sieges, castles 183
Siemens, Werner von 841
Sienna, Italy 496
Sierra Leone 35
  sculpture 746
Sierra Madre (Guatemala and El Salvador) 193
Sierra Madre (Mexico) 551
Sierra Nevada, USA 867
Sifaka, Coquerel's 570
Sight 322
  light and 508
Signals
  animals 166
  flags 340
  semaphore 340
  smoke 224
Sign language 502
Sign stimulus, instinctive behaviour 54
Signs and symbols 763-4
Sikhism 705
  symbols 763
Sikorsky, Igor Ivan 42
Silica, glass 387
Silicates 722
Silicon
  in Earth 279
  periodic table 925
Silicon chips 297, 869
"Silicon Valley", USA 867
Silk
  spiders' webs 801
  textiles 832
Silk Road 77, 78, 79, 80, 320
  Mongol Empire 210, 565
  trade 841
Silkworms 645
Silozwane Cave, Zimbabwe 689
Silser, Lake 819
Siltstone 723
Silurian period 378, 687
Silvanus 389
Silver 550, 552
  periodic table 925
  South American 789
Silversword 235
Simen Mountains 15
Simple microscopes 553
Simulation, computer 456
Sinan 572
Sind, Pakistan 639
Singapore 449, 523, 525

banknotes 564
"dragon" economy 79
Singapore City, Singapore 525
Singing, opera 629
Single-lens reflex (SLR) cameras 163, 164
Singles, best-selling 939
Sinkholes 188
Sinking 690
Sino-Japanese War (1894-95) 481
Sioux tribe 224, 596
Sip Canal 105
Sirenians 893, 894
Sisulu, Walter 530
Sitars 445, 592
Sitatunga 257
Six-Day War (1967) 883
Sixtus V, Pope 496
Sjaelland, Denmark 258
Skating 690, 897
Skeletal muscle 582
Skeleton
  animals 53
  birds 132
  human body 436, 765-6
  mammals 527
  penguins 647
Skeleton Coast, Namibia 30
Sketches, drawing 638
Skiing 897
  Austria 820
  Germany 380
Ski jumping 897
Skin
  amphibians 50
  elephants 299
  hippopotamuses 423
  human body 767
  reptiles 711, 712
  snakes 772
Skinks 517, 711, 712
  blue-tongued 518
  eyed 518
  sand 39
  tree 518
Skopje, Macedonia 107
Skulls 766
Skunks 104
Sky
  clouds 221
  colour 227
Skylab space station 797
Skyscrapers 62
Slash and burn farming 353
Slate 723
Slavery 768
  African history 17, 18
  American Civil War 48
  Brazil 790
  Caribbean 176
  music 482
  Truth, Sojourner 849
Sled racing 897
Sleep 145
  animal requirements 917
Sleeping sickness 555
Sliders
  red-eared 855
  yellow-bellied 855
Slime moulds 554
Sloths 57
  two-toed 793
Slovakia 312, 314
Slovenia 106
SLR cameras 164
Slugs 770, 771
  lettuce 771
Slums, Argentina 66

Sly and the Family Stone 719
"Smart" bombs 887
"Smart cards" 562
Smell, sense of 769
  nocturnal animals 609
Smellie, William 544
Smelting
  bronze 150
  iron 467
Smiling 582
Smog 40
Smoke detectors 697
Smoke signals 224
Smooth green snake 773
Smooth muscle 582
Snails 770
  apple 771
  banded 318
  brown-lipped 771
  garden 771
  giant African 770
  great pond 500
  land 771
  partula 771
  pond 771
Snake maiden 557
Snakes 711, 772-3
  Australia 100
  camouflage and colour 165
  desert wildlife 261
  eggs 712
  grassland wildlife 397
  mongooses and 567
  rainforest wildlife 700
  records 919
  sea snakes 623
  senses 609
  venom 672
Snakes and Ladders 202
Snapdragon vine, little 261
Sneezing 519
Snipe 133
Snooker 110
Snow 698
  avalanches 386
  meltwater 715
  snow-line 386
Snow, John 544
Snowfields, insects 459
Snow leopard 511, 512, 513, 578
Snow-ploughs 170
Snowshoes 690
Snow White and the Seven Dwarfs 269
Soap operas 273
Soaps 13, 454
Soares, Mario 684
Sobaek-Sanmaek Mountains 497
Soccer 351, 937
  flags 340
  in Germany 380
Social behaviour, animals 53
Social displays, animals 166
Social groups
  elephants 300
  giraffes 384
  hippopotamuses 423
  horses 431
  lions 511
  mongooses 567
  pigs and peccaries 657
  sheep and goats 756
  see also Colonies
Socialism 392
Socialization 288
Social policy, European Union 315
Social stratification 775

Societies, human 774-5
  human rights 438
Society of Harmonious Fists 210
Society of Jesus see Jesuits
Sociology 774
Socrates 776
Soda-lime glass 387
Sodium 298, 924
Sodium chloride 92, 559
Sodium hydroxide 13
Sofia, Bulgaria 404
Softball 111
Software, computer 456
Sognefjord 617
Soil 777
  acidity 13
  woodlands 902
  soil creep 777
Solar power 304, 306
Solar prominences 522
Solar System 814-15
  astronomy 87
  comets and asteroids 230
  gravity 398
  magnetic fields 522
  planets 660-2
Soldiers
  American Civil War 48
  American Revolution 49
  armies 68
  arms and armour 69-70
  Napoleonic Wars 595
  Norman 610
  Ottoman Empire 631
  Roman 724
  World War I 905
  see also Armies; Warfare
Soldier's Tale, The (Stravinsky) 811
Solenoids 296
Solidarity 857
Solid shapes, mathematics 536, 926
Solids 778
  pressure 690
  states of matter 538
Solitaire (game) 202
Solomon Islands 94, 637
Solomon, King of Israel 427
Solomon's Temple, Jerusalem 427, 652
Solstices 837
Solutions 558
Solvay, Ernest 13
Somali cat 185
Somalia 26
Somatic nervous system 144
Somba people 37
Somme, Battle of the (1916) 905, 906
Somoza, Anastasio 196
Sonar 695
  navigation 598
  ocean floor mapping 620
Songbirds 779-80
Song dynasty 209, 210, 498
Songhai Empire 127, 526, 781
Songhai people 36
Songthrush 599, 780
Sonni Ali 781
Sonni Baare 781
Sonoran Desert 551, 612, 615
Sony Corporation 783, 830
Sophocles 402
Sorbonne 250
Soto, Hernando de 614
Soufrière, St Lucia 172
Souks 29, 760

Soul music 718
Sound 782
  animal behaviour 54
  hearing 278
  musical instruments 590
  recording 783
  sound waves 782
Soup kitchens 399
South Africa 784-6
  apartheid 19, 530, 784, 786
  banknotes 564
  Boer Wars 98, 786
  crafts 243
  history of 786
  Mandela, Nelson 530
South African Students Organisation (SASO) 786
South America 236, 787-94
  Argentina, Chile and Uruguay 65
  Bolívar, Simon 140
  Bolivia and Paraguay 141-2
  Brazil 146-7
  dance 254
  Ecuador and Peru 285-6
  exploration 320
  history of 789-90
  Incas 442-3
  Northern 791-2
  wildlife 793-4
South China Sea, pirates 659
Southeast Asia
  architecture 62
  dance 253
  history of 77
  Kublai Khan 498
  Malaysia and Singapore 523-5
  Philippines 650
  shadow puppetry 273
  Thailand and Burma 833-4
  Vietnam, Cambodia, and Laos 876-7
Southern Alps, New Zealand 93
Southern Central Africa 30-2
Southern Ocean 621
South Island, New Zealand 606
South Korea 497
  clothes 219
  "dragon" economy 79
South Pole 56
  Cook, James and 238
  explorers 321
  ozone hole 678
  polar exploration 673
Southwest Pacific 636-7
Soviet Union 795
  Cold War 225, 869
  history of 729, 730
  Iron Curtain 311
  peace movements 646
  propaganda 424
  space exploration 797
  Russian Revolution 734
  see also Russia
Soweto, South Africa 785, 786
Space
  astronomy 87
  Big Bang 130
  black holes 139
  General Theory of Relativity 294
  gravity 398
  magnetic fields 522
  see also Astronomy; Universe
Space, measuring 892
Space exploration 796-7
  astronauts 86
  rockets 344, 720-1
  satellites 739

Soviet Union space programme 733, 795
space probes 87, 717, 796
space shuttle 685, 720, 721
space stations 797
spacesuits 86, 690
Spain **798-800**
banknotes 564
Caribbean history 176
castles 182
coat of arms 496
conquistadors 101, 442
drama 272
flamenco 253
food 349
history of **800**
kings and queens 945
and South America 787, 789
Spanish Armada 301
Spanish Civil War 656, 800
Spanish festoon butterfly 317
Spanish Main 659, 791
Sparrows 134
house 780
Sparta 401
Spartacus 768
Spawn 50
Spear-nosed bat 119
Spearwort, lesser 666
Special effects, films 331
Special needs education 288
Species
classification 914
evolution 318
Spectroscopes 226
Spectrum
electromagnetic **911**
light 226, 605
stellar 808
Speech 502
Speech synthesizers 457
Speed 352
animals 916
land speed record 576
of light 508
of sound 782
time and 837
Speedboats 757
Speed skating 897
Speedway races 576
Spenser, Edmund 301
Sperm 709
sex chromosomes 377
Sphagnum moss 573
Spice Islands 320, 521
Spices 349, 669
Grenada 175
Indonesia 452
trade 602
Spider crabs
Japanese 240
spiny 240, 241
Spider monkey, black 700
Spiders 74, **801-2**
poisonous 672
records 919
webs 52
Spies 224, 225
Spinal cord 144, 145
Spindle, yellow 586
Spines, plant defences 667
Spinnerets, spiders 801
Spinning jenny 453
Spiny orb weavers 802
Spiral galaxies 370
Spiral staircases 520
Spirits of nature 762
Spits, coasts 223

Spitz, Mark 818
Spleen 441
Sponges 54 , 239, **483**
breadcrumb 750
glass-rope 623
Sponsorship
sport 803
television 829
Spoonbill, roseate 793
Spores 663
ferns 327
mosses and liverworts 573
mushrooms 584
Sport **803**
aircraft 43
athletics **88**
ball games **109-11**
boats 757
combat sports **229**
facts **936-7**
flags 340
football **351**
Germany 380
gymnastics **411-12**
Japan 479
motor sports **575-6**
Olympic Games **628**
Owens, Jesse **632**
Portugal 683
postage stamps 805
Roman Empire 725, 726
sailing and other water sports **736**
South Africa 785
swimming and diving **818**
tennis and other racket sports **831**
United Kingdom 859
winter sports **897**
Sporting dogs 271
Sports acrobatics 411, 412
Sports cars 178
Spraints, otters 104
Spreadsheets, computer 456
Sprenger, Jacob 898
Springbok 257
Springer spaniel, English 271
Springs 715
Spring tides 749
Spruce, Norway 83, 317
Spurge-laurel 666
Sputnik 739
Spyrogyra 751
Squash (racket sport) 111, 831
Squid **624**, 771
Squires 495
Squirrel monkey 570
Squirrels 600, 701, 703
grey 319, 703
Sri Lanka, 444, **446**
Stadium, athletics 88
Stadler, Anton 579
Staffordshire bull terrier 271
Stag beetle 124, 125, 460, 903
Stage sets 836
Stained glass 215, 387, 547
Stainless steel 467
Staircases, spiral 520
Stalactites and stalagmites 188
Stalin, Joseph 225, 424, 795
Stalingrad, Russia 908
Stalinism 795
Stamens 346
Stamp tax, American Revolution 49
Stamps **804-5**
Standard units, weights and measures 892

Standing stones 762
Stanford University 867
Stanhope, Charles, 3rd Earl 692
Stanley, Henry 321
Stanley, Mount 15
Stanley, William 296
Stanton, Elizabeth Cady 901
Star dials 838
Starfish **806**
Bloody Henry 750
common 806
spiny 750
Starley, James 128
Starlings 779, 872
long-tailed 134
splendid glossy 134
Star-of-Bethlehem (plant) 664
Star of David 426, 764
Starr, Ringo 121
*Starry Messenger, The* (Galileo) 371
Stars **807-8**, 870
astrology 85
astronomy 87
black holes 139
colour 226
constellations 921
galaxies 370
General Theory of Relativity 294
gravity 398
scale of the Universe 871
State *see* Church and state
States of matter 538
Static electricity 295, 363
Static friction 363
Statics 352
Statistics 537
Statues *see* Sculpture
Steady State theory 130
"Stealth" bomber 882
Steam, state of matter 514
Steam engines 306
Industrial Revolution 744
railways 843
ships 844
Steel **467**
in Brazil 147
building material 62, 157
Steel bands 175
*Stegoceras* 267
*Stegosaurus* 267
Steinbeck, John 399, 516
Stems, plants 665
*Stenogaster* wasps 122, 600
Sten submachine guns 888
Stephen, John 874
Stephenson, George 842
Steppes 76
Romania, Ukraine, and Moldavia 727
Russian Federation and Kazakhstan **731**
wildlife 396
Step Pyramid, Saqqara 25, 693
Steptoe, Patrick 542
Stereos, personal 462
Steroids 274
Stevenson, Robert Louis 204
Stevenson screens 891
Stick insects 165, 460
Sticklebacks 337
three-spined 599
Stigma 668
*Stigmaria* 355
Stiller, Mauritz 373
Stills cameras 164
Stilt houses 115, 216, 435
Stimulants, drugs 275
Stings

arthropods 74
bees and wasps 13, 122
plants 667
Stinkhorn, common 584
Stirrups 882
Stoat 166, 889
Stock car racing 576
Stockholm, Sweden 816
Stock markets 563, 933
Stockton to Darlington Railway 844
Stomach 13, 264
Stone Age **809**
Stonehenge 689, 743
Stone houses 435
Stone stripes, tundra 850
Stone tools 809
Stoneware 685
Stonework 242, 243
Stopwatches 839
Stories
children's literature **203-5**
literature **515-16**
myths and legends **593**
Storks **419**
marabou 419
wood 793
Storm petrels 747
Storms **810**, 890
storm beaches 223
tropical 635
Storyboards
advertisements 14
films and film-making 330
Stoves 360
Stowe, Harriet Beecher 516, 768
Strabo 192, 320
Stradivari, Antonio 591
Strangler fig 643, 699
Strategic Arms Limitation Talks (SALT) 646
Strategy games 201
Stratigraphy 59, 378
Stratocumulus clouds 221
Stratopause 91
Stratosphere 91
Stratus clouds 221
Strauss, Johann the younger 254
Stravinsky, Igor 589, 656, **811**
Strawberries 367
Streamlining 363
Streams 715
Strength, solids 778
Stridulation, grasshoppers and crickets 395
Strikes, trade union 857
Strindberg, August 272
Stringed instruments 591, 592
Stromatolites 687
Stromboli 475
Strontium 924
Structural engineers 156
Stuart, John 97
Stuart dynasty 861
Studios
radio 696
recording 783
television 830
Stupas 539
Sturgeon, William 296
Sturt, Charles 98, 321
Styluses 910
*Styracosaurus* 267
Subatomic particles 92
artificial elements 298
subatomic physics 744
Sublimation 538, 778
Submachine guns 888

Submarines **812**, 882
Submersibles 621, 690, 759, **812**
Subsistence farming 323
Subsoil 777
Sucellos 192
Sucking, air pressure 40
Sucre, Antonio José de 140
Sudan 15, **25**
Sudeten Mountains 312
Suez Canal 25, 406, 844
Suffolk punch horse 432
Suffragettes 641
Sufis 469
Sugar and sugar cane
Cuba 173
"green" cars 147
food 349
Mauritius 450
photosynthesis 654
plantations 176
St Kitts and Nevis 174
Sui dynasty 210
Sukkot 487
Sulawesi 451, 472
Sulayman, Mansa 526
Sulfides 722
Sulphite 925
Sulphur
in Earth 279
in natural gas 626
periodic table 925
smog 40
Sulphuric acid 12
Sulphur tufts 586
Sultans, Ottoman Empire 631
Sumatra 216, 451
Sumerians 77, **813**
art 71
writing 910
Summer, Donna 719
Sumo wrestling 229
Sun **814-15**
and air temperature 890
climates 217
electromagnetic radiation 911
energy 303
facts 921
formation 130
Galileo's theory 371
magnetic fields 522
photosynthesis 654
scale of the Universe 871
solar power 304, 306
as a star 807, 808
sunspots 814
and time 837, 838
Sunbird 779
olive 290
Sundews 177
Sundials 838, 839
Sundiata 526
Sunflowers 668
Sunglasses 508
Sunlight *see* Sun
Sun Moon Lake, Taiwan 208
Sunni Islam 469, 470
Sunspots 814
Sunstar, purple 750
Sun Yat-sen 212
Superclusters, galaxies 370
Supercomputers 232
"Supercontinent" 236, 280
Supercooled liquids 387
Superhero comics 604
Superior, Lake 611
Supermarkets 760

Supernovae 87, 139, 807
Superpowers, Soviet Union 795
Suppiluliumas I, King of the
  Hittites 425
Supreme Court (USA) 768
Supremes, The 718
Surface tension 514
Surfing 736
Surgeon fish 337
Surgery 542, 544
  laser 503
  microscopic 553
Surinam 792
Surrealism 72, 73
Surtees, John 575
Surveying, Earth sciences 282
Surveyor 3 spacecraft 797
Surveyors 156
Suryavarman II, Emperor 490
Susa 648
Suspension bridges 148, 934
Suspensions, mixtures 558
Süssmayr, Franz Xaver 579
Susu people 35
Suva, Fiji 637
Swallowing 264
Swallowtail butterfly 158, 159
  African giant 159
Swamps
  mangrove 76
  wildlife 533-4
Swan, Joseph 287, 509
Swans 276, 343
  mute 276
Swastika 764
Swaziland 784, 785
Swazis 785
Sweat glands 528, 767
Sweden 816
  coat of arms 496
  history of 740
Sweet potato 665
Sweet vernal grass 394
Swiftlet, cave 817
Swifts 817
  chimney 817
  common 817
Swim bladder 336
Swimming 818
  champions 936
  ducks 276
  penguins 647
  sea turtles 854
  seals 748
  sharks and rays 755
Swing, jazz 482
Swiss cheese plant 666
Switzerland 819-20
Swords 69, 888
Sycamore 367
Sydney funnelweb spider 672
Sydney Harbour Bridge,
  Australia 148
Sydney Opera House, Australia 98
Syenite 723
Symbiosis
  clown fish and sea anemones
    294, 483
  fungi 585
  micro-organisms 555
Symbols 763-4
  arithmetic 619
  chemical 924
  codes and ciphers 224
  equations 619
  flags 340
  mathematical 926
  music 588

Symmetry 536
Symphonies 589
  Beethoven, Ludwig van 123
  Mozart, Wolfgang Amadeus 579
Symphony orchestras 630
Symptoms, medicine 541
Synagogues 487
Synapses, neurons 144
Syncom 2 satellite 739
Syncopation 482
Synoptic charts 891
Synthesizers, musical 591
SyQuest disks, computers 232
Syr Daraya River 733
Syria 821-2
  gods and goddesses 389
Syrian Desert 75
Syrinx, songbirds 779
Szent-Györgyi, Albert von 582

# T

T-Rex 719
Tabla 592
Tables 369
Table tennis 111, 831
Tabloid newspapers 603
Tadpoles 50, 364, 499
T'aebaek-Sanmaek Mountains 497
Taglione, Marie 108
Tagus, River 682
Tahiti 238
Tahmasp I, Shah 735
Tahmasp III, Shah 735
Taiga 76, 309, 353
  wildlife 83
Tails
  birds 132
  reptiles 712
  whales 894
  woodpeckers 904
Taipan 100
Taipei, Taiwan 208
Taiwan 79, 206, 208
Tajikistan 81
Tajmulco 193
Takamine, Jokichi 429
Takla Makan Desert 76
Talking watches 839
Tallinn, Estonia 113
Tallis, Thomas 301
Talmud 486
Talons, birds of prey 135
Tamarau 154
Tamarins
  cotton-top 570
  golden lion 569
Tambourine 592
Tamerlaine 565
Tamils 446
Tamil Tigers 446
Tamla Motown 718, 865
Tanagers
  red-throated ant 134
  scarlet 780
Tandems 129
Tanganyika 27
Tanganyika, Lake 23, 38
Tang dynasty 73, 79, 210, 686
Tango 254
Tanks, warfare 888
Tanshan earthquake, China 281
Tantalum 924
Tanzania 27, 219
Taoism
  funerals 775
  monasteries 560
Tap dance 254

Tape recorders 462
Tapes people 789
Tapetum 609
Tapeworms 643, 909
Tapirs 713
Tara brooch 192
Tarahumara Indians 552
Tarantulas
  Chilean rose 802
  red-kneed 801
  red-legged 802
  red-rumped 802
Tariffs 841
Tarmac roads 716
Tarot cards 85
Tarquinia, Italy 307
Tarsier, eastern 570
Tashkent, Uzbekistan 81
Tasman, Abel 97, 98, 607
Tasmania 94, 97
Tasmanian devil 489
Taste buds 769
Taste, sense of 769
Tatra Mountains 312
Taurus Mountains 852
Taxonomy 131
Tbilisi, Georgia 187
Tchaikovsky, Petr 108
Tea
  Boston Tea Party 49
  in Georgia 187
  in Malaysia 524
  mint tea 29
  in Sri Lanka 446
  tea ceremony 738
  tea-makers 462
Teach, Edward (Blackbeard) 659
Teaching
  education 288
  schools and colleges 741
Teak logging 834
Team pursuit, cycling 251
Tears 322
Teasel 318
Technetium 924
Technical drawings 638
Technicolor 331
  cameras 164
Technology 742, 823
  farming 324
  medical 542
Tectonic lakes 501
Tectonic plates 236-7
  earthquakes 281
  mountain building 577
Teenagers, music 718
Teepee fires 167
Teeth 824
  digestion 264
  elephants 299
  horses 431
  lions and other wild cats 511
  mammals 527
  rabbits and hares 694
  rodents 701
  sharks 755
  walruses 748
  whales 893
Tegucigalpa, Honduras 194, 196
Tegu lizard 518
Tehran, Iran 464
Te Kanawa, Kiri 629
Tel Aviv, Israel 474
Telecommunications 825
Telegraph 224, 825
Telephones 825, 826-7
  satellites 452
Telephoto lenses 163

Telescopes 828
  astronomy 87
  Galileo Galilei 371
  Hubble Space Telescope 321,
    739, 797
  observing Universe 870
Television 829-30
  advertisements 14
  colour television 227
  drama 273
  facts 940
  invention of 461, 462
  remote control 297
  video 875
Telex machines 825
Tellins 749
Tellurium 925
Telstar satellite 739, 830
Temne people 35
Tempera 71
Temperate climate 217
Temperate forests 353
  Asia 82
  Australia 217
  North America 616
Temperature 416-17
  air 890
  body 917
  boiling point 416, 417, 514, 924
  climate 217
  colour and 226
  conversion tables 927
  gases 375
  melting point 416, 924
  scales 416
Temperature control
  mammals 528
  skin 767
Templars 247
Temples
  ancient Egypt 291
  architecture 62
  Buddhist 152, 153
  Hinduism 422
  Maya Empire 540
  Temple of Artemis, Ephesus 752
  Temple of the Inscriptions,
    Palenque 693
Ten Commandments 486
Tenakh 486
Tendons 582
Tendrils, plants 665
Tennessee walking horse 432
Tennis 111, 831
  champions 937
  French Open Tennis
    Championship 357
Tenochtitlán 101
Tenor horns 592
Tenpin bowling 110
Tenrecs 418
Tentacles, octopuses and squid 624
Tents
  camping 167
  tepees 435, 596
  yurts 565
Tepees 435, 596
Tephra 881
Terauchi, Yoki 72
Terbium 925
Terebratula 355
Teresa, Mother see Mother Teresa
Terminal velocity 352
Termites 58, 396
Terns 747
  Arctic 556, 675
  Inca 134
Terraces, Philippines 650

Terracotta army 209
Terrapins 854
  European pond 855
Terriers 271
Territory
  animals 53
  songbirds 780
  tigers 511
Terrorism
  airports 44
  armies 68
Tertiary period 378
Tesla, Nikola 296
Test Ban Treaty 646
Testes 429, 709
Tests, medical 541
Tetra, neon 338
Tetragonal system, crystals 248
Texcoco, Lake 101
Textiles and weaving 832
  in Bangladesh 115
  batik 452
  dyes 277
  from plants 669
  Georgian 187
  Industrial Revolution 453
  Mexican 552
  Nigerian 37
  printing 692
Tezcatlipoca 388
TGV (Train à Grande Vitesse) 357
Thabana Ntlenyana 16, 784
Thailand 833-4
  crafts 243
  dance 253
  Death Railway 79
  food 349
  history of 77
  kites 494
Thalamus 145
Thallium 925
Thallose liverworts 573
Thanksgiving 658
Thant, U 863
Thar Desert 444, 639
Tharp, Marie 620
Thatched roofs 157
"Theatre of the Absurd" 272, 273
Theatre Royal, Haymarket,
  London 835
Theatres 835-6
  dance 253
  drama 272-3
  facts 939
  Greek 402
  opera 629
Theodolites 156
Theodosius, Emperor 724
Theories, scientific method 742
Thera 557
Theravada Buddhism 153, 877
Thermal expansion 416
Thermal motion 417
Thermals 221
Thermometers 416
  meteorology 890, 891
Thermoplastics 670
Thermosetting plastics 670
Thermosphere, atmosphere 91
Thimphu, Bhutan 115
Thinking 144
Third Republic, France 359
Thirty Years' War 381, 382, 740
Thistle, slender 666
Thompson, Benjamin 416
Thompson, EP 424
Thomson, Joseph John 295
Thor 388

Thoracic nerve 144
Thorium 924
Thorny devil 99
Thoroughbred horses 432
Thorow-wax 347
Thoughts 144
*Thousand and One Nights, A*
  470, 515
Threat displays, elephants 300
Throughflow, rainwater 715
Throwing events, athletics 88
Thrushes
  song 599, 780
  Swainson's 134
*Thrust 2* 576
Thucydides 402
Thulium 925
Thunderstorms 810
  speed of sound 782
Thurber, James 203
Thymine 376
Thymus gland 429
Thyroid gland 429
Tiahuanaco culture 198
Tiananmen Square 210
Tiber, River 475
Tibesti Mountains 20
Tibet 207
Tibetan Buddhism 153
Tibial nerve 144
Ticks 643, 801
Tides
  coasts 223
  and gravity 398
  oceans and seas 621
  spring tides 749
  tidal barrages 252, 304
Tien Shan Mountains 80
Tierra del Fuego 65, 521
Tiger beetles 125
  tropical 125
Tiger moths
  garden 159
  virgin 460
Tigers 511, 513
  camouflage 165
  endangered animals 235
  Indian 529
  rainforest wildlife 82
  Siberian 234
Tiglath-Pileser III, King of Assyria 84
Tigris, River 463, 813, 852
Tikal 540
Tiles, Islamic 572
Tilling, grasses 393
Timber *see* Wood
Timberworm beetle, Malaysian 125
Timbuktu, Mali *see* Tombouctou
Time 837-9
  black holes 139
  international date line 634
  international time zones 837, 929
  Special Theory of Relativity 294
Time-trials, cycling 251
Timothy grass 394
Timur 77
Tin 550, 925
Tinamou, elegant 290
Tinder 334
Tin Pan Alley 718
Tirana, Albania 107
Titan 661, 797
*Titanic* 386, 812
Titanium 924
Titans 401
Titian 707
Titicaca, Lake 141, 285, 787
Titration 559

Tits, blue 780
Tlaltelolco 760
Tlaxcala 101
Toads 50, **364-5**
  Asian horned 700
  Couch's spadefoot 50
  eggs 289
  European common 166
  poisonous 672
  rainforest wildlife 700
  square marked 50
  Surinam 793
  urban wildlife 872
Toadstools 584
Toasters 462
Tobacco 275
Tobago 175
Toboggans 897
Todd, Mark 430
Tody, Jamaican 290
Toenails 767
Togo **36**
Toilets, astronauts 86
Tokelau 680
Tokugawa Ieyasu 480
Tokugawa shoguns 480, 481, 738
Tokyo, Japan 478
Tolkien, JRR 204
Tollán 549
Tolpuddle Martyrs 857
Tolstoy, Leo 373, 516
Toltecs 101, 196, 549
  pyramids 693
*Tom Brown's Schooldays* (Hughes)
  204
Tomahawks 888
Tomatoes 367
Tomato frogs 365
Tombaugh, Clyde 660
Tombolos 223
Tombouctou, Mali 36, 781
Tombs
  Black Death 138
  churchyards 215
  Etruscan 307
  pyramids 693
  Tomb of the Unknown Soldier
  883
Tondibi, Battle of (1591) 781
Tonga **680**
Tongues
  anteaters 57
  snakes 772
  swallowing 264
  taste 769
  woodpeckers 904
Tonkinese cat 185
Tonle Sap 876
Tonsils 441
Tools
  animal behaviour 54
  birds and 779
  building and construction 157
  chimpanzees 390, 568
  crafts 242
  gardening 374
  painting and drawing 638
  sculpture 745
  Stone Age 809
Tooth *see* Teeth
Topa Inca 442
Topkapi Palace, Istanbul 631
Topsoil 777
Torah 486
Torch, Operation 18
Torches 508
Torcs 192
Tornadoes 810

Torpedo boats 759
Torpedoes 812, 888
Torres, Luis Vaez de 97
Tortoises 711, **854-5**
  desert 615
  eggs 712
  Herman's 855
  hinge-back 854, 855
  leopard 711, 854, 855
  radiated 855
  red-legged 855
  starred 854, 855
Torture, witches 898
Torus 618
Total internal reflection 509
Totem poles 73, 597
Toucans **904**
  Ariel 904
  Cuvier's 699
  red-billed 904
  toco 904
Tour de France 251, 357
Tourism 845
  Africa 19
  Antarctica 56
  Australia 96
  Barbados 175
  Bulgaria 404
  Costa Rica 195
  Cyprus 822
  Dominican Republic 174
  Estonia 113
  Gambia 34
  Greece 404
  Indonesia 452
  Italy 476
  Kenya 27
  Macao 208
  Maldives 450
  Mexico 552
  Pacific Ocean 635
  St Lucia 175
  San Marino 476
  Slovenia 106
  Spain 799
  Sri Lanka 446
  Thailand 834
  Tonga 680
  Turkey 853
  United Arab Emirates 408
  United Kingdom 859
  United States 865
  Zimbabwe 32
Tournaments 495
Toussaint L'Ouverture, Pierre 176
Tower of London 610
Townes, Charles 503
Towns
  Industrial Revolution 453
  medieval Europe 547
  *see also* Cities
Townshend, Charles "Turnip" 326
Townships, South Africa 785
Toyota, Shoichiro 843
Toyota Motor Corporation 843
Toyota Praevia 180
*Trachyphyllia* 355
Trachyte 723
Track and field events 88
  champions 936
Track races, cycling 251
Tracks, railway 842
Traction trebuchet 183
Trade **840-1**
  Asian history 78
  Benin Empire 127
  Etruscans 307
  furs 171

Great Zimbabwe 400
Mali Empire 526
medieval Europe 547
Minoans 557
Pacific Ocean 635
Phoenicians 652
shops **760**
slave trade 768
spices 602
trans-Saharan trade 781
Vikings 878
world economy 933
Trademarks 763
Trade unions *see* Unions, trade
Trades Union Congress
  (TUC) 857
Trafalgar, Battle of (1805) 595
Traffic 716
Traffic control, police 676
Trainers (shoes) 218
Trains and railways **842**
  "bullet train" 479, 842
  facts **934**
  history of 843
  in India 445
  Industrial Revolution 453
  maglev trains 522
  Peru 286
  TGV (Train à Grande Vitesse)
  357
  United States 868
  urban wildlife 872
Trajan, Emperor 724, 725
Trampolining 411
Tramp steamers 759
Trams 842
Transcaucasia 186
Transformers, electricity 296
Transforms, plate tectonics 237
Trans-Gabon Railway 22
Trans-Siberian Express **732**
Transistors 297, 462
Transition metals 298
  periodic table 924-5
Translucent substances 509
Transmitters, radio 696
Transparent substances 509
Transpiration 654
Transplants, heart 541
Transport *see* Travel
Transport aircraft 41
Transvaal 786
Transylvania, Romania 727, 728
Trapdoor spiders 802
Traps, carnivorous plants 177
Traquair House, Scotland 183
Travel **845**
  aircraft 41-3
  airports **44**
  airships and balloons **45-6**
  in Albania 107
  in Australia 96
  bicycles and motorcycles
  **128-9**, 251
  in Canada 170
  cars and trucks **178-80**
  facts **934**
  in Germany 380
  history of **843-4**
  in India 445
  Industrial Revolution 453
  in Israel 474
  in Japan 479
  in Portugal 683
  postage stamps 805
  roads **716**
  trains and railways **842**
  in Turkey 853

  in United Kingdom 859
  in Vietnam 877
Travel agents 845
Travertine 881
Trawlers 339, 759
*Treasure Island* (Stevenson) 204
Treblinka 908
Tree ferns 327
Tree frogs 50, 364
  green 615
  North American 903
  White's 365
Treehopper 155
Trees **846-8**
  anatomy 665
  bonsai 479
  and climate change 217
  European wildlife 316-17
  forests **353**
  fossils 354
  lifespans 663
  logging industry 834, 867
  rainforest 699
  records 918
  wood 669
  woodland wildlife 902
Tree snakes 772
Tree toads, Asian 365
Trekking, Himalayas 115
Trenches, ocean 620, 621
Trenton, Battle of (1776) 886
Trevithick, Richard 844
Trial and error learning 54
Trials
  courtrooms 505
  motorcycle racing 576
  witches and witchcraft 898
Triangles 926
  right-angled 536
Triassic period 265, 378
Tributaries, rivers 714
*Triceratops* 266
Triclinic system, crystals 248
Tricycles 129
*Trieste* bathyscaphe 321
Trigger plant 100
Trigonal system, crystals 248
*Trigonocarpus* 355
Trigonometry 536
Trilobites 354
Trinidad and Tobago 175, 228
Triple junctions, continental
  drift 236
Tripoli, Libya 29
Triptychs 215
Triton 662
Trivial Pursuit 202
Troglodyte houses 435
Trojan asteroids 230
Trojan War 401
Trombones 592
Trondheim, Norway 740
Troodos Mountains 821
Trophic pyramids 350
Tropical climate 217
Tropical rainforests *see* Rainforests
Tropical storms 635
Tropics 837
Tropopause, atmosphere 91
Troposphere, atmosphere 91
Trotsky, Leon 424, 734, 795
Troubadours 588
Trout 500
  rainbow 336
Troy 401
Trucks 178-80, 843
Truffles 585
  summer 586

Trumpets 590, 592
Trunks, elephants 299
Trunks, tree 846
Truth, Sojourner **849**
Tsiolkovsky, Konstantin 721, 739
Tsunamis 281
Tswana people 31
Tuareg people 36
Tuataras 711
Tubas 592
Tubers 665
Tubman, Harriet 768
Tudhaliyas II, King of the Hittites 425
Tudor dynasty 861
Tufa 723
Tuff 723
Tufted hair grass 394
Tumours 190
Tuna 339
　skipjack 635
Tundra **850**
　Asia 76
　Europe 309
　North America 612
　wildlife 615
Tungsten 924
Tuning forks 782
Tunis, Tunisia 29
Tunisia **29**
Tunnels **851**
　rail tunnels 934
*Tuojiangosaurus* 266
Turbines
　gas 306
　power stations 304
Turbofan engines 42, 306
Turbojet engines 42, 306
Turboprop engines 42
Turboshaft engines 306
Turing, Alan 456
Turkana, Lake 506
Turkey **852-3**, 906
Turkish angora cat 185
Turkish van cat 185
Turkmenistan **81**
Turks
　Crusades 247
　Ottoman Empire **631**
Turner, Nat 768
Turquoise 249
*Turtle* (submersible) 812
Turtles 623, 711, **854-5**
　alligator snapping 855
　big-headed 855
　big-headed mud 855
　common snapping 855
　coral reefs 239
　eggs 712
　green sea 855
　matamata 712
　Mississippi map 855
　painted 855
　sea 750
　snake-necked 854, 855
　snapping 534
　spiny soft-shelled 855
　white-lipped mud 855
Tusks
　elephants 299
　narwhals 893
　pigs and peccaries 657
　walruses 748
Tusk shells 770
Tussock sedge, greater 394
Tutankhamun, Pharaoh 59, 292
Tutsi people 23
Tuvalu **680**

Twain, Mark 204, **856**
Twelve Bens mountain range 465
Twenty-four-hour clock 838
Twins 710
Tyler, Wat 546
Typefaces 691
Typhoons 635, 810
Typography 691
*Tyrannosaurus* 265, 267
Tyres
　bicycles and motorcycles 128
　cars 178
Tyrrhenian Sea 307

# U

Ubar 407
U-boats 812
Uccello, Paolo 707
'Ud 591, 592
Udall, Nicholas 708
Uffington horse 191
Uganda **27**
Ugarit 425
Ukraine **727-8**
Ulan Bator, Mongolia 566
Ulster 466
　*see also* United Kingdom
Ultrasound 695, 782
Ultraviolet radiation
　astronomy 870
　electromagnetic spectrum 911
　ozone layer 91
Uluru (Ayers Rock), Australia 11, 94, 95
Umar 469
Umayyad dynasty 470
Umbilical cord 710
Umm al Quaiwain, United Arab Emirates 408
*Uncle Remus* stories (Harris) 203
Underground Railway 768
Underground railways 934
Understorey, rainforest 699
Underwater archaeology 59
Underwater cameras 164
Underwear 220
Unemployment 399
UNESCO (United Nations Educational, Scientific and Cultural Organization) 863
UNICEF (United Nations Children's Emergency Fund) 863
"Unified Theory", physics 655
Uniforms
　Napoleonic Wars 595
　navies 885
Union of Soviet Socialist Republics (USSR) *see* Soviet Union
Unions, trade 841, **857**
United Arab Emirates 406, **408**
United Kingdom **858-61**
　American Revolution 49
　Anglo-Saxons 51
　and Asian history 78
　and Canada 171
　castles 182, 183
　crafts 243
　Domesday Book 329
　Elizabeth I **301**
　food 349
　furniture 369
　history of **860-1**
　Hundred Years' War **439**
　Industrial Revolution 453-4
　and Ireland 466
　kings and queens 943
　Napoleonic Wars 595

and New Zealand 607
　Normans 610
　post boxes 805
　prime ministers 943
　sculpture 746
　slave trade 768
　World War II 907
United Nations (UN) **862-3**
　Commission on Human Rights 438
　Declaration of Human Rights 768
　flag 340
　High Commissioner for Refugees 863
　human rights 438
　international law 504
　peacekeeping role 68, 863, 882
　refugees 883
United States of America 611, **864-9**
　American Revolution **49**
　banknotes 564
　and Central America 196
　Cold War **225**, 869
　Constitution 360, 504
　film posters 332
　food 349
　Franklin, Benjamin 360
　Geronimo **383**
　Great Depression **399**, 869
　history of **868-9**
　immigration 845
　jazz 482
　King, Martin Luther **491**
　law 504
　peace movements 646
　police 676
　post boxes 805
　presidents 944
　slave trade 768
　space exploration 796-7
　Truth, Sojourner **849**
　Washington, George **886**
　World War II 907, 908
Universal Postal Union 804
Universe **870-1**
　astrophysics 655
　Big Bang **130**, 870, 871
　black holes **139**
　creation myths 593
　Einstein, Albert 294
　elements 298
　galaxies **370**
　gravity 605
　measuring 871
　planets **660-2**
　scale of 871
　space exploration **796-7**
　stars **807-8**
　statistics **921**
　Steady State theory 130
　structure 870
Universities 310, 741
Unknown Soldier, Tomb of 883
*Upanishads* 421
Upholstery 368
Upthrust 690
Ur, Mesopotamia 150, 216, 813
Ur-Nammu of Ur 813
Ural Mountains 75, 308, **731**
Uranium 81
　Namibia 31
　nuclear fission 548
　nuclear power 618
　periodic table 924
Uranus **662**
　facts 921

Solar System 815
　space probes 797
Urban II, Pope 247
Urban VIII, Pope 496
Urban myths and legends 593
Urban population, facts 930
Urban wildlife **872**
Ureters 873
Urethra 873
Urinary system 436, **873**
Urine 873
Urn plant 347, 664
Uros people 285
Uruguay **65**, **67**
Uruguay River 67
Uruk 813
Ushabti figures 293
USSR *see* Soviet Union
U-shaped valleys 385
Uterus 709-10
Uthman 469
Utility boats 759
Utrecht, Union of (1579) 602
Uzbekistan **81**

# V

V1 rockets 888
V2 rockets 720, 721
Vaccination
　immune system 441
　Jenner, Edward 544
　Pasteur, Louis 645
　vaccines 275
Vacuoles 190
Vacuum cleaners 462
Vacuum flasks 417
Vacuums 538
Vadose water 715
Vaduz, Liechtenstein 820
Vagina 709
Valerian, red 347
Valley Forge, USA 886
Valley of the Kings, Egypt 25
Valley of the Queens, Egypt 25
Valleys **577**
　formation 714
　glaciation 385
Valves, engines 305
Vampire bats 118
　common 119
Van, Lake 852
Vanadium 924
Van Castle, Turkey 183
Vandals 116
Van der Waal's forces 92
*Vänern*, Lake 816
Vanilla 32
Vanuatu 636, **637**
Van Wijnen 128
Vapours 375
Variable stars 808
Variation
　genetics 376
　natural selection 318
Vasari, Giorgio 507
Vassals 329
Vatican City State 308, **476**
Vaulting, gymnastics 411
Vaults, architecture 61, 215
*Vedas* 421
Vega, Lope de 272
Vegetables 173, 349
Vegetative reproduction 668
Veii, Italy 307
Veins 415
Velasquez, Diego de Silva y 800

*Veld*, South Africa 784
Velocar 129
Velocity 352
Venezuela 791, **792**
　banknotes 564
　independence 140
Venice, Italy 477
　Carnival 328
　Renaissance music 588
Venn, John 537
Venn diagrams 537
Venom 672
　snakes 672, 772
Ventilation, tunnels 851
Venus (goddess) 389
Venus (planet) **660**
　facts 921
　Solar System 815
　space probes 796
Venus figures 388
Venus flytrap 177, 235
Veracruz, Mexico 101
Verdant sphinx moth 159
Verdi, Giuseppe 629
Verdun, Battle of (1916) 906
Verge watches 839
Vermeer, Jan 602, 638
Verne, Jules 516
Versailles 358
Versailles, Treaty of (1919) 906
Vertebrae 527, 765
Vertebral column 765
Vertebrates
　fossils 355
　prehistoric 687
Vesalius, Andreas 544, **874**
Vesuvius, Mount 475
Vibraphone 592
Vibrations, sound recording 783
Viceroy butterfly 159, 318
Vichy France 359
Victor Emmanuel II, King of Italy 477
Victoria, Hong Kong 208
Victoria, Lake 15, 27
Victoria, Queen of England 302, 861
Victoria, Seychelles 450
Victoria Falls 32
Video **875**
　camcorders 164
　rock and pop music 719
　video games 297
　videophones 826
Vienna, Austria 123, 428, 820
Vientiane, Laos 877
Vietnam **876-7**
　clothes 219
　food 349
　independence 79
Vietnam War (1954-75) 79, 869, 882, 883
*Viking* space probes 717, 796
Vikings 740, **878-9**
　invade Britain 860
　in Ireland 466
　Normans 610
　in North America 613
　in Russia **729**
　sculpture 746
Village co-operatives, Africa 19
Villages 216
Villard, Paul 911
Villi 264
Vilnius, Lithuania 113
Vindhya Range 75
Vineyards *see* Wine and vineyards
Vinland 878

Vinson Massif 56
Vinyl records 719, 783
Viola 592
Violet, dog 347
Violin beetle 125, 460
Violins 591, 592
Vipers 772
  carpet 672
  Gaboon 773
  sand 261
Virgil 707, 725
*Virgin and Child, The* (Leonardo
  da Vinci) 507
Virgo Cluster 370
Virtual reality 456
Viruses 268, 555
Viscosity, liquids 514
Vishnu 421
Visible spectrum 911
Visigoths 116
  in Portugal 684
  sack Rome 477, 725
Vision 53, **322**
  birds 133
  colour vision 226
  light and 508
Visual signals, animal behaviour 54
*Vittoria* 521
*Viviparus* 355
Vladivostok **732**
Vlad the Impaler, Prince 728
Vocal cords 519
Vocational education 288
Volcanoes **880-1**
  Caribbean islands 172
  facts 923
  Iceland 90
  Indonesia 451
  islands 471, 635
  Italy 475
  Japan 478
  lakes 501
  Micronesia and Melanesia 636
  Polynesia 679
  Ring of Fire 634, 650
  volcanic mountains 577
  volcanology 282
Voles 703
  meadow 702
  water 316
Volga, River 308, **731**, **732**
Volkswagen Beetle 180
Vollard, Ambroise 72
Volleyball 110
Volta, Alessandro 295
Volta, Lake 36
Volta River 33
Voltage 295
Volume
  conversion tables 927
  measuring 892, 927
Voodoo 18
  dance 254
  Haiti 174
*Vostok* rockets 721
Voting
  elections 392
  women's voting rights 641,
    901, 948
*Voyager* space probes 662, 797
VTOL (vertical take-off and
  landing) aircraft 884
Vultures 135, 136, 137
  black 137
  Egyptian 136
  Indian white-backed 397
  palm-nut 136
  turkey 137

white-backed 136, 137

# W

Waders **761**
Wadi Rum 821
Wadis 259, 577
Wagner, Richard 629
Wagon trails, United States 868
Wagtails
  grey 499
  pied 599
Waitangi, Treaty of (1840) 607
*Waiting for Godot* (Becket) 272
Walata 781
Waldheim, Kurt 863
Wales **858-9**
  castles 183
  history of 860
  *see also* United Kingdom
Walesa, Lech 857
Walking, hiking 168
Wallabies 528
  red-necked 529
Wallace, Alfred Russel 255
Wallcreeper 578
Wallis and Futuna 680
Walloon dialect 126
Walls, building and construction 156
Wall Street *see* New York Stock
  Exchange
Wall Street Crash (1929) 399
Walnut, black 848
Walrus 622, 748
Walsegg, Count Franz von 579
Walsh, Lieutenant Donald 321
Walton, Ernest 742
Waltz 254, 589
Wampanoag tribe 658
Wandering spiders 802
Wapiti 234
Warblers
  Cetti's 290
  Kentucky 134
  reed 599
Warfare **882-3**
  aircraft 344
  chariots 425
  gods and goddesses 389
  knights **495**
  Leonardo da Vinci 507
  major wars 947
  Mongol Empire 565
  Napoleonic Wars **595**
  Ottoman Empire 631
  peace movements **646**
  radio 696
  refugees 845
  religious wars 310
  ships 759
  weapons **887**
  *see also* Armies; Soldiers
War hammers 888
Warm fronts, weather 890
Warner Brothers 181
Warning signs 764
  animals 166
War of Jenkins' Ear (1739) 614
Warplanes **884**
War poetry 671
Warrens, rabbits 694
Warriors, Viking 878
Wars of the Roses (1455-85) 861
Warsaw, Poland 313
Warsaw Ghetto 426
Warsaw Pact 225
Warships 757, **885**
Warthogs 657

Washington, George 868, **886**
  American Revolution 49
  public holiday 328
Washington, Martha 886
Washington DC, USA 864
Washington state, USA 867
Wasps **122**, 460
  eggs 289
  field digger 458
  nests 600
  paper 459
  stings 13
  tarantula hawk 460
  tree 903
Watches **837-9**
Water 514
  aqueducts 148, 681
  camels 162
  camping and hiking 168
  dams **252**
  Earth sciences 282
  ecosystems 283
  insects 459
  irrigation 326, 474
  lake and river wildlife **499-500**
  lakes **501**
  oceans and seas **622**
  photosynthesis 654
  pollination of flowers 346
  rain **698**
  rivers **714-15**
  safe drinking water 931
  seed dispersal 366
  swimming and diving **818**
  urinary system 873
  volcanic landscapes 881
  water cycle 284
  waves 223
Water beetles 124
Water boatman 500
Water bugs 155
Watercolour paints 277
Water dragon, Thai 518, 711
Waterfowl 276
Water ferns 327
Water fleas 241, 643
Waterfalls 714, 715
  facts 922
Water frame 453
Water-lily 500, 664
Waterloo, Battle of (1815) 595
Watermarks, paper 642
Waterproofed textiles 832
Waters, Muddy 718
Water-skiing 736
Water snakes 772
Water sports **736**, 803
Waterspouts 810
Water table 715
Water transport 844
Water vapour
  in air 40
  clouds 221
Waterways **681**
Watson, James 376
Watson-Watt, Robert 598, 695
Watt, James 306, 454, 823
Watteau, Antoine 358
Wattle, silver 100, 347
Watts 303
Waveforms, sound waves 782
Wavelengths, colour 226
Waves
  coasts 223
  electromagntic 911
  radio waves 696
  wave power 304
Waxbill, common 134

Wealth, world economy 933
Weapons **887-8**
  arms and armour **69-70**
  fencing 229
  from the *Mary Rose* 60
  guns **409**
  Napoleonic Wars 595
  Native Americans 596
  peace movements 646
  torpedoes 812
  Viking 878, 879
  World War I 906
Weasels **889**
  common 529, 889
Weather **890**
  air pressure 40
  clouds 221
  facts 923
  frost 698
  meteorology 282
  and migration 556
  rain **698**
  research balloons 45
  satellites 739
  seasons 815, 837
  snow 698
  storms 810
  symbols 764
  weather forecasting **891**
  winds **896**
  *see also* Climate
Weaver birds 599
  black-headed 290
Weaving **832**
Webs, spiders 54, 801
Webster, Charles and Co 856
Weddings 775
Weever fish 337
Weevils **125**
  nut 316
Wegener, Alfred 236
Weights and measures **892**
  of air 40
  conversion tables 927
  facts **927**
  gravity 398
  Indus Valley civilization 455
  measuring 892, 927
  Viking 878
Weimar Republic 382
Weirs 252
Weizmann, Chaim 79
Welding 334, 550
Welfare state, United Kingdom 861
Well dressing 762
Welles, Orson 331, 836
Wellington, New Zealand 606, 607
Welsh cob 432
Welsh mountain pony 432
Welwitschia 261
Weser, River 380
Wessex 51
West Africa **33-7**
  slave trade 768
  Songhai Empire **781**
Western Ghats 444
Western long-nosed snake 773
Western Sahara 29
Western Samoa *see* Samoa
West Indies *see* Caribbean Sea
*Westlothiana* 687
Westphalia, Treaties of (1648) 381,
  602
Weta 459
  Stephen's Island 235
Wetland wildlife
  Africa 38
  Europe 316

  marshes and swamps 534
  North America 615
  South America 793
  wild cats 513
Wetlands
  Asia 76
  North America 612
Whalebone 893
Whales 622, **893-5**
  animal symbols 764
  Baird's beaked 895
  blue 235, 893, 894, 895
  bowhead 895
  Bryde's 895
  Cuvier's beaked 235
  false killer 895
  grey 556, 674, 893, 894
  humpback 622, 895
  killer 893, 895, 912
  migration 556
  minke 895
  movement 53
  polar wildlife 674
  pygmy right 895
  right 895
  sperm 622, 893, 894, 895
  whaling 339
Wheat
  Canada 170
  food 349, 669
  in Poland 313
  world resources 932
Wheeler, Mortimer 59
Wheels 520
  bicycles 128, 251
  cars 178
  invention 461, 843
  motorcycles 128
Whelks 771
  dog 749, 771
*Where the Wild Things Are* (Sendak)
  205
Whippet 271
Whirligig beetle 124
Whirling dervishes 469
Whiskers, cats 184, 527
Whiskey Rebellion (1794) 886
White, EB 205
White blood cells 414, 415
White dwarf stars 807
White Huns 116
White light spectrum 226
White-lined bat 119
White matter, brain 145
White Nile 25
"White Russia" *see* Belorussia
White saddles, common (fungus)
  586
White Tower, London 610
White water racing, canoes 736
Whittle, Frank 306
Wholesalers 841
Wide-angle lenses 163
Wight, Isle of, England 471
Wild boars 657
Wild cats **511-13**
  European 512, 513
Wild dogs **899-900**
  African 53 , 396
Wildebeest 556
Wildlife **396-7**
  African **38-9**
  Asian **82-3**
  Australia **99-100**
  cave **189**
  coral reefs **239**
  in danger **920**
  desert **260-1**

ecology and ecosystems **283-4**
European **316-17**
islands **472**
lake and river **499-500**
marsh and swamp **533-4**
mountain **578**
North American **615-16**
ocean **621-2**
polar **674-5**
pollution **677-8**
postage stamps 805
rainforest **699-700**
records **918-19**
seashore **749-50**
South America **793-4**
trees **846-8**
tundra 850
urban **872**
wildlife gardens 374
wildlife parks 912
woodland **902-3**
zoos **912**
*Wild Swans* (Jung Chang) 516
Wilhelm, Mount 93
Wilhelm I, Kaiser 382
Wilhelm II, Kaiser 382
Wilkins, Maurice 376
William I the Conqueror, King of
  England
  Battle of Hastings 51, 861
  Domesday Book 329
  Norman Conquest 610, 860
William II, King of England 610
William III (William of Orange),
  King of England 466, 746
William the Silent 602
Willow, Arctic 675
Wills, William J 97, 98, 320
Willy-willies 635
Wilson, Robert 838
Windhoek, Namibia 31
Windmills 247, 601
Windows
  castles 183
  stained-glass 215, 547
Winds 890, **896**
  Beaufort scale 923
  monsoons 217, 449
  pollination of flowers 346, 347
  sailing boats 758
  seed dispersal 366
  storms **810**
  tropical storms 635
  wind power 304
Windsurfing 736
Windward Islands 90, 175
Wine and vineyards
  Chile 67
  France 357
  Moldavia 728
  pasteurization 645
  port 683
  sherry 799
  South Africa 785
Wings
  aircraft 42, 344
  bats 117
  beetles 124

birds 132, 133, 343
butterflies and moths 158
flies 342
hummingbirds 817
insects 343, 458
Winter, hibernation **420**
Winter Olympics 628, 897
Winter sports 170, 803, **897**
Wireless 462
Wisconsin, USA 865
Wisdom teeth 824
"Wise women" 543
Wisent 154
Witches and witchcraft **898**
*Wizard of Oz, The* (Baum) 204
Wodaabé people 37
Wolfe, General James 171
Wolfe Crater, Australia 230
Wolfhound, Irish 271
Wollstonecraft, Mary 901
Wolverine 889
Wolves 270, **899-900**
  grey 899, 900
  maned 794, 899, 900
  red 899
Womb *see* Uterus
Wombat, common 489
Women
  in Africa 30
  Curie, Marie **250**
  Elizabeth I **301**
  in Jamaica 173
  in Lesotho 785
  Meitner, Lise **548**
  Pankhurst family **641**
  pirates 659
  prime ministers and presidents 948
  in Russia **731**
  Truth, Sojourner **849**
  voting rights 641, 901, 948
  women's movement **901**
  World War I 906
Women's Social and Political Union
  (WSPU) 641
Wonder, Stevie 718, 865
Wonders of the Ancient World
  693, **752**
Wood (timber) 669, 846
  building material 157
  houses 435
  logging industry 21, 834, 867
  papermaking 642
Wood-boring insects 124, 459
Wood engraving 692
Woodcarving 243
Woodcock 761
Wooden percussion instruments 590
Woodlands
  broad-leaved 316
  South America 788
  wildlife **902-3**
  *see also* Forests
Woodlice 240
Woodmice 600
  yellow-necked 703
Woodpeckers **904**
  acorn 904
  Gila 260

green 902, 904
  yellow-fronted 134
Woodrush 394
Woodstock 869
Woodwind instruments 590, 592
Wool 67, 832
Woolly monkey, Humboldt's 570
Woolworth, FW 760
Work
  employment 775
  energy 303
Working classes 454
Working dogs 271
Workshops, crafts 242
World Cup (football) 937
World Disarmament Conference 646
World economy **933**
World Federation of Trade
  Unions 857
World Health Organization
  (WHO) 863
World Meteorological Organization
  891
World population 930
World resources **932**
World Trade Organization 841
World War I 882, **905-6**
  aerial bombing 887
  Africa 18
  aircraft 344
  balloon reconnaissance 45
  casualties 883
  conscientious objectors 646
  Europe 311
  Gallipoli 98
  Russia 734
  submarines 812
  war poetry 671
  warplanes 884
World War II 882, **907-8**
  Africa 18
  Asia 79
  balloon reconnaissance 45
  casualties 883
  conscientious objectors 646
  Enigma cipher machine 224
  Europe 311
  Holocaust **426**
  Japan 481, 869, 907, 908
  Scandinavia and 740
  Soviet Union 795
  submarines 812
  United Kingdom 861
  United States 869
  Vichy France 359
Worldwide Fund for Nature
  (WWF) 234
World Wide Web 457
Worm lizards 517
Worms **909**
  seashore life 750
Worship *see* Religions
Wozniak, Steve 232
Wrack 751
Wragge, Clement 810
Wrasses
  cleaner 337
  cuckoo 338

Wrestling
  greased 853
  sumo 229
Wright, Frank Lloyd 63
Wright, Orville and Wilbur 344,
  844
Writers **941**
Writing **910**
  ancient Egypt 292
  cuneiform script 813
  glyphs 540
  Indus Valley civilization 455
  Linear A script 557
  Linear B script 557
  literature **515-16**
  newspapers and magazines **603-4**
Wu Cheng'en 203
*Wuthering Heights* (Brontë) 149
Wyclif, John 704

# X

X-rays **911**
  Curie, Marie 250
  medical use 542, 544, 744, 765
  security scanners 44
  telescopes 870
Xenon 925
Xenophon 776
Xerox Corporation 232
Xerxes I, King of Persia 648
Xhosa people 785
Xuan Zang 320
Xylem 654, 665
Xylophones 590

# Y

Yachts 736, 757, 758, 759
Yak 83, 154
Yalta Conference (1945) 225
al-Yaman 781
Yamoussoukro, Ivory Coast 35
Yan'an soviet 212
Yangôn, Burma 834
Yangtse River 207
Yaoundé, Cameroon 21
Yarns 832
Yawning 519
Year
  seasons 815
  time 837
Yeast 555, 585
  fermentation 645
Yellow flag (plant) 664
Yellow Sea 75, 497
Yellow-shouldered bat 119
Yellowstone National Park, USA
  234, 866
Yeltsin, Boris **730**
Yemen 406, **407**
Yerevan, Armenia 187
Yersin, Alexander 138
Yeti 593
Yew, plum-fruited 848
Yiezhi clan 77
Ylang-ylang 32
Yoga 422

York, House of 861
Yorkshire fog 393
Yorkshire terrier 271
Yorktown, Battle of (1781) 49
Yoruba people 37, 671
Young, Thomas 227
Ytterbium 925
Yttrium 924
Yüan dynasty 498, 686
Yucatan Peninsula, Mexico 552
Yucca moth 261
Yugoslavia 105, **107**
Yuhina, striated 134
Yuit people 64
Yukon Territory, Canada 171
Yu'pik people 64
Yurts 435, 565

# Z

Zagreb, Croatia 106
Zagros Mountains 463
Zaire *see* Congo (Zaire)
Zaïre River *see* Congo River
Zambezi River 31
Zambia 31
Zanzibar 27
Zebra pipe fish 338
Zebras 38, 431
  common 529
Zen Buddhism 153
Zeppelin, Ferdinand von 45
Zeugen 259
Zeus 401, 725
  fire myths 334
  statue of 752
Zheng Ho, Admiral 210
Zhou dynasty 233
Zimbabwe **32**
  banknotes 564
  independence 19
  *see also* Great Zimbabwe
Zinc 925
Zindel, Paul 205
Zinjanthropus 506
Zion 427
Zionism 79, 486
Zodiac
  astrology 85
  constellations 808
Zola, Emile 359
Zoo Check 912
Zoology 131
  Goodall, Jane **390**
Zoom lenses 163
Zooplankton 554, 622
Zoos **912**
Zooxanthellae 555
Zorilla 889
Zoroaster 649
Zoroastrianism 649, 705
Zorros 899
Zoser, Pharaoh 25, 693
Zulus 785, 786
Zwingli, Ulrich 704
Zworykin, Vladimir 829, 830
Zygaenid moth 158

# GAZETTEER

## HOW TO USE THE GAZETTEER

The gazetteer helps you to find places on the maps in the encyclopedia. For identification, all places that are not cities or towns are followed by a brief description.

Grid references help locate the names on the maps. For example, if you look up Nairobi in the gazetteer, you will see the reference 24 D9. The first number, 24, is the page number of the map on which Nairobi appears. The second number, D9, shows that it is in the square D9 of the grid printed over the map. Turn to page 24. Trace down from the letter D at the top of the grid and across from the number 9 along the side of the grid. You will find Nairobi in the square where the letter and number meet.

The following abbreviations have been used in the gazetteer:

| | | | | |
|---|---|---|---|---|
| abbrev. | = | abbreviation | N | = North |
| Ben. | = | Bengali | off. | = officially |
| Cam. | = | Cambodian | prev. | = previously |
| C | = | Central | Rus. | = Russian |
| E | = | East | S | = South |
| Fr. | = | French | St | = Saint |
| Ger. | = | German | W | = West |
| L. | = | Lake, Lago, Lac | Wel. | = Welsh |
| Mts. | = | Mountains | | |

## A

Aachen Germany 379 A6
Aalst Belgium 126 C2
Aarau Switzerland 819 C5
Aare *River* Switzerland 819 B5
Aba Nigeria 33 I9
Ābādān Iran 463 E6
Abashiri Japan 478 G2
Abéché Chad 20 E4
Abengourou Ivory Coast 33 F8
Åbenrå Denmark 258 B6
Abeokuta Nigeria 33 H8
Aberdeen Scotland, UK 858 D4
Aberystwyth Wales, UK 858 C9
Abhā Saudi Arabia 406 C7
Abidjan Ivory Coast 33 F9
Abu Dhabi *Capital* United Arab
  Emirates 406 H4
Abuja *Capital* Nigeria 33 I7
Abū Kamāl Syria 821 I4
Åybybro Denmark 258 C2
Acapulco Mexico 551 H7
Acarai Mountains *Mountain range*
  Brazil/Guyana 791 H5
Acarigua Venezuela 791 E2
Accra *Capital* Ghana 33 G9
Achacachi Bolivia 141 B4
Acharnés Greece 403 D7
Acklins Island *Island* Bahamas
  172 E3
Aconcagua *Peak* Argentina 787
A Coruña Spain 798 B2
'Adan Yemen *var.* Aden 406 D9
  449 B3
Adare, Cape *Coastal feature*
  Antarctica 56 F7
Ad Dahnā' *Desert region* Saudi
  Arabia 406 D3
Ad Dakhla Western Sahara 28 A5
Addis Ababa *Capital* Ethiopia
  24 H4
Adelaide Australia 95 F7
Adélie, Terre d' *Territory* Antarctica
  56 H7
Aden *see* 'Adan
Aden, Gulf of *Sea feature* Indian
  Ocean 449 B3
Adige *River* Italy 475 D3

Adriatic Sea Mediterranean Sea
  475 E4
Aegean Sea Mediterranean Sea
  403 E7
Ærø *Island* Denmark 258 C6
Afghanistan *Country* C Asia 80
Africa 15
Afrin *River* Syria/Turkey 821 E2
'Afula Israel 473 C3
Agadez Niger 33 J5
Agadir Morocco 28 C3
Agaña Guam 636 C2
Agartala India 444 H5
Ağcabädi Azerbaijan 186 I5
Ağdam Azerbaijan 186 I5
Agen France 356 D7
Āgra India 444 D4
Agrigento Italy 475 D10
Agrínio Greece 403 B7
Aguarico *River* Ecuador/Peru
  285 D2
Aguascalientes Mexico 551 F5
Ahaggar *Mountains* Algeria 28 G6
Ahmadābād India 444 B5
Ahvāz Iran 463 E5
Aïr *Region* Niger 33 J4
Aix-en-Provence France 356 F8
Āīzawl India 444 I5
Ajaccio Corsica, France 356 H9
Ajdābiyā Libya 28 K3
Ajmer India 444 C4
Akanthou Cyprus 821 B3
Akhalts'ikhe Georgia 186 D4
Akita Japan 478 F5
'Akko Israel 473 C2
Akmola Kazakhstan 731 D5
Akola India 444 D6
Akpatok Island *Island* Canada
  169 I6
Aksai Chin *Disputed region*
  China/India 444 D1
Aktau Kazakhstan 731 B5
Alabama *River* Alabama, USA
  864 H8
Alabama *State* USA 864 H8
Alajuela Costa Rica 193 G8
Al 'Amārah Iraq 463 D5
Åland Islands *Island group* Finland
  333 A9
Al 'Aqabah Jordan 821 D10

Alaska Peninsula *Peninsula* Alaska,
  USA 864 B3
Alaska Range *Mountain range*
  Alaska, USA 864 B2
Alaska *State* USA 864 B2
Alaska, Gulf of *Sea feature* Pacific
  Ocean 611
Alaverdi Armenia 186 F4
Alazani *River* Azerbaijan/Georgia
  186 G3
Alba Iulia Romania 727 C6
Albacete Spain 798 F5
Albania *Country* SE Europe 105
Albany Australia 95 B7
Albany New York, USA 864 K6
Albany *River* Canada 169 H8
Al Başrah Iraq 463 D6
Albatross Plateau *Undersea feature*
  Pacific Ocean 634 J5
Al Bayda' Libya 28 K2
Albert, Lake *Lake* Uganda/Congo
  (Zaire) 20 H8 24 C9
Alberta *Province* Canada 169 D8
Albi France 356 D7
Ålborg Denmark 258 C2
Ålborg Bugt *Sea feature* Denmark
  258 D3
Alcácer do Sal Portugal 682 C9
Alcalá de Henares Spain 798 E4
Alchevs'k Ukraine 727 K4
Aldabra Group *Island group*
  Seychelles 449 B4
Aleg Mauritania 33 B5
Aleksinac Yugoslavia 105 I5
Alençon France 356 D3
Alessandria Italy 475 B3
Ålesund Norway 617 B6
Aleutian Islands *Islands* Alaska,
  USA 864 B3
Aleutian Trench *Undersea feature*
  Pacific Ocean 634 F3
Alexandria Egypt 24 C1
Alexandroúpoli Greece 403 F5
Alföld Plain Hungary 312 E10
Algarve *Region* Portugal 682 C11
Algeciras Spain 798 D8
Algeria *Country* N Africa 28
Alghero Italy 475 A6
Algiers *Capital* Algeria 28 F1
Al Hufūf Saudi Arabia 406 F4
Al Hasakah Syria 821 H2
Al Hillah Iraq 463 C5
Al Hudaydah Yemen 406 D8
Alicante Spain 798 G6
Alice Springs Australia 95 E4
Aligarh India 444 D4
Al Jaghbūb Libya 28 L3
Al Jawf Saudi Arabia 406 C2
Al Jazirah *Region* Iraq/Syria
  821 H3
Al Karak Jordan 821 D8
Alkmaar Netherlands 601 C3
Al Khums Libya 28 I3
Al Kufrah Libya 28 L5
Al Lādhiqiyah Syria 821 D2
Allāhābād India 444 E5
Alma-Ata *Capital* Kazakhstan
  731 E7
Al Madinah Saudi Arabia 406 B4
Al Mafraq Jordan 821 E7
Almalyk Uzbekistan 80 H4
Al Marj Libya 28 K2
Al Mawşil Iraq 463 C3
Almelo Netherlands 601 E4
Almería Spain 798 F7
Al Mukallā Yemen 406 F8
Alofi *Capital* Niue 679 D6
Alor, Kepulauan *Island group*
  Indonesia 451 H5
Alps *Mountain range* C Europe
  308
Al Qāmishli Syria 821 I1
Al Qunayţirah Syria 821 D6

Altai Mountains *Mountain range*
  C Asia 75
Al Tall al Abyaḍ Syria 821 G2
Altamura Italy 475 G7
Altay Mongolia 566 C3
Altdorf Switzerland 819 D5
Altun Mountains *Mountain range*
  China 75
Al Wajh Saudi Arabia 406 B3
Alytus Lithuania 112 C6
Amakusa-shotō *Island group* Japan
  478 B9
Amami-Ō-shima *Island* Japan
  478 B11
Amazon Delta *Wetland* Brazil
  787
Amazon *River* South America
  787
Amazonia *Region* C South
  America 146 C3
Ambanja Madagascar 30 K4
Ambarchik Russian Federation
  731 J2
Ambato Ecuador 285 C2
Ambon Indonesia 451 I4
Ambositra Madagascar 30 K6
Ambovombe Madagascar 30 J7
Ambriz Angola 30 A2
Ameland *Island* Netherlands
  601 D1
American Samoa *External territory*
  USA, Pacific Ocean 679 E5
Amersfoort Netherlands 601 D5
Amery Ice Shelf *Coastal feature*
  Antarctica, Indian Ocean 449
  D10
Amiens France 356 D2
Amman *Capital* Jordan 821 D7
Āmol Iran 463 F3
Amorgós *Island* Greece 403 F9
Amritsar India 444 C3
Amsterdam *Capital* Netherland
  601 C4
Amstetten Austria 819 J3
Am Timan Chad 20 E5
Amu Darya *River* C Asia 80 F5
Amundsen Gulf *Sea feature*
  Canada 169 C5
Amundsen Sea Antarctica 56 B6
Amur *River* E Asia 75
Anadyr' Russian Federation 731
  K1
Anambas, Kepulauan *Island group*
  Indonesia 451 D2
Anchorage Alaska, USA 864 C2
Ancona Italy 475 E4
Andalucía *Region* Spain 798 D7
Andaman Islands *Island group*
  India 449 E3
Andaman Sea Indian Ocean 449
  E3
Andes *Mountain range* South
  America 787
Andizhan Uzbekistan 80 I4
Andong South Korea 497 D6
Andorra *Country* SW Europe 798
Andorra la Vella *Capital* Andorra
  798 H2
Ándros *Island* Greece 403 E8
Andros Island *Island* Bahamas
  172 D2
Angara *River* C Asia 75
Ángel de la Guarda, Isla *Island*
  Mexico 551 B2
Angeles Philippines 650 C4
Angel Falls *Waterfall* Venezuela
  791 G4
Ångerman *River* Sweden 816 C4
Angers France 356 C4
Anglesey *Island* Wales, UK 858 C8
Angola *Country* C Africa 30
Angola Basin *Undersea feature*
  Atlantic Ocean 89 F8

Angoulême France 356 D6
Angren Uzbekistan 80 H3
Anguilla *External territory* UK,
  West Indies 172 K4
Anjouan *Island* Comoros 30 J3
Annaba Algeria 28 G1
An Nafūd *Desert region* Saudi
  Arabia 406 C2
An Najaf Iraq 463 C5
Annapolis Maryland, USA
  864 J7
An Nāşiriyah Iraq 463 D6
Annecy France 356 G6
Anshan China 206 H4
Antalaha Madagascar 30 L4
Antananarivo *Capital* Madagascar
  30 K6
Antarctic Peninsula *Peninsula*
  Antarctica 56 A3
Antarctica 56
Antequera Spain 798 D7
Antigua *Island* Antigua &
  Barbuda 172 K5
Antigua & Barbuda *Country* West
  Indies 172
Antofagasta Chile 65 B3
Antsiranana Madagascar 30 L4
Antsohihy Madagascar 30 K4
Antwerpen Belgium 126 D2
Anyang South Korea 497 C6
Aomori Japan 478 F4
Aosta Italy 475 A2
Aparri Philippines 650 C2
Apeldoorn Netherlands 601 D4
Apennines *Mountain range* Italy
  475 C4
Apia *Capital* Samoa 679 D5
Appalachian Mountains *Mountain
  range* E USA 864 I7
Appenzell Switzerland 819 D5
Apure *River* Venezuela
  791 D3
Apurímac *River* Peru 285 E8
Aqaba, Gulf of *Sea feature* Red
  Sea 473 C12 821 C10
Āqchah Afghanistan 80 F5
Arabah, Wādi al Israel/Jordan
  473 D8
Arabian Peninsula *Peninsula*
  Asia 75
Arabian Sea Indian Ocean 449 C2
Aracaju Brazil 146 I5
'Arad Israel 473 C7
Arad Romania 727 A5
Arafura Sea Asia/Australasia
  634 C7
Araguaia *River* Brazil 146 F5
Arāk Iran 463 E4
Aral Sea *Inland sea*
  Kazakhstan/Uzbekistan 75
Aran Islands *Islands* Ireland 465 B5
Ararat Armenia 186 F6
Ararat, Mount *Peak* Turkey 75
Aras *River* SW Asia 186 I6
Arauca Colombia 791 D4
Arauca *River* Colombia/Venezuela
  791 D3
Arbatax Italy 475 B7
Arbil Iraq 463 C3
Arctic Ocean 64
Arda *River* Bulgaria/Greece 403 E4
Ardennes *Region* W Europe
  126 E4
Arendal Norway 617 B9
Arequipa Peru 285 G10
Arezzo Italy 475 D4
Argentina *Country* S South
  America 65
Argentine Basin *Undersea feature*
  Atlantic Ocean 89 C10
Argentino, Lago *Lake* Argentina
  65 B10
Århus Denmark 258 C4

Arica Chile 65 B2
Arizona *State* USA 864 D8
Arkansas *River* C USA 864 G7
Arkansas *State* USA 864 G8
Arkhangel'sk Russian Federation 731 D2
Arles France 356 F8
Arlon Belgium 126 F6
Armenia *Country* SW Asia 186
Armenia Colombia 791 B4
Arnhem Netherlands 601 D5
Arnhem Land *Region* Australia 95 E2
Arno *River* Italy 475 C4
Ar Ramādī Iraq 463 C4
Arran *Island* Scotland, UK 858 B5
Ar Raqqah Syria 821 G3
Arras France 356 F2
Ar Rub' al Khali *Desert* SW Asia 406 F6
Ar Rustāq Oman 406 I4
Artashat Armenia 186 F6
Artigas Uruguay 65 E5
Artyk Turkmenistan 80 D5
Aru, Kepulauan *Island group* Indonesia 451 J4
Arua Uganda 24 C8
Aruba *External territory* Netherlands, West Indies 172 H7
Årup Denmark 258 C5
Arusha Tanzania 24 D10
Arvayheer Mongolia 566 E3
Arvidsjaur Sweden 816 D3
Asadābād Afghanistan 80 H6
Asahikawa Japan 478 F2
Asamankese Ghana 33 G9
Āsānsol India 444 G5
Ascension Island *Island* Atlantic Ocean 89 E8
Ascoli Piceno Italy 475 E5
Ashburton New Zealand 606 D7
Ashdod Israel 473 B5
Ashgabat *Capital* Turkmenistan 80 C5
Ashqelon Israel 473 B6
Ashtarak Armenia 186 F5
Asia 75
Asmara *Capital* Eritrea 24 E5
Assab Eritrea 24 F6
Assad, Lake *Lake* Syria 821 F3
Assal, Lake *Lake* Djibouti 15
Aş Şalţ Jordan 821 D7
Assen Netherlands 601 E3
Assisi Italy 475 D5
As Sulaymānīyah Iraq 463 C3
As Sulayyil Saudi Arabia 406 E6
As Suwaydā' Syria 821 E6
Astrakhan' Russian Federation 731 B5
Astypálaia *Island* Greece 403 F9
Asunción *Capital* Paraguay 141 G9
Aswân Egypt 24 D3
Asyût Egypt 24 C2
Atacama Desert *Desert* Chile 65 B2
Atakpamé Togo 33 G8
Atâr Mauritania 33 C3
Athabasca, Lake *Lake* Canada 169 D7
Athens *Capital* Greece 403 D8
Athlone Ireland 465 D4
Ati Chad 20 D4
Atlanta Georgia, USA 864 I8
Atlantic Ocean 89
Atlantic-Indian Basin *Undersea feature* Atlantic Ocean 89 F12
Atlas Mountains *Mountain range* Morocco 28 D3
Aţ Ţafīlah Jordan 821 D8
Aţ Ţā'if Saudi Arabia 406 C5
Attapu Laos 876 F7
Attawapiskat Canada 169 H8
Attawapiskat *River* Canada 169 H8

Atter, L. *Lake* Austria 819 I4
Auch France 356 D7
Auckland Islands *Island group* New Zealand 93
Auckland New Zealand 606 E3
Augsburg Germany 379 E9
Augusta Italy 475 E10
Augusta Maine, USA 864 L5
Aurillac France 356 E7
Austin Texas, USA 864 F9
Australia *Country* Pacific Ocean 95
Australian Territory *Territory* Australia 95 H7
Austria *Country* C Europe 819
Auxerre France 356 F4
Avarua *Capital* Cook Islands 679 F7
Aveiro Portugal 682 C4
Avignon France 356 F8
Ávila Spain 798 D4
Avilés Spain 798 C1
Awbārī Libya 28 I4
Axel Heiberg Island *Island* Canada 169 E2
Ayacucho Peru 285 E8
Aydarkul', Ozero *Lake* Uzbekistan 80 G3
Ayers Rock *see* Uluru
'Ayn ath Tha'lab Libya 28 K4
Ayr Scotland, UK 858 C6
Ayutthaya Thailand 833 E9
Azaouad *Physical region* Mali 33 F4
A'zāz Syria 821 E2
Azerbaijan *Country* SW Asia 186
Azores *External territory* Portugal, Atlantic Ocean 89 E5
Azov, Sea of Black Sea 727 J6
Azuero, Peninsula de *Peninsula* Panama 193 I10
Azul Argentina 65 D6
Azur, Côte d' *Coastal region* France 356 G8
Az Zarqā' Jordan 821 E7
Az Zāwiyah Libya 28 I3

# B

Ba'abda Lebanon 821 D5
Baalbek Lebanon 821 E5
Bab el Mandeb *Sea feature* Djibouti/Yemen 406 C9
Babahoyo Ecuador 285 B3
Bābol Iran 463 F3
Babruysk Belorussia 112 F8
Babuyan Island *Island* Philippines 650 C2
Bacan, Pulau *Island* Indonesia 451 I3
Bacău Romania 727 E6
Bačka Topola Yugoslavia 105 G3
Bacolod Philippines 650 D7
Badajoz Spain 798 C6
Badalona Spain 798 I3
Baden Austria 819 K3
Badgastein Austria 819 H5
Bad Ischl Austria 819 K3
Bafatá Guinea-Bissau 33 B6
Baffin Bay *Sea feature* Atlantic Ocean 89 C2
Baffin Island *Island* Canada 169 G4
Baffin Island *Island* Canada 611
Bafoussam Cameroon 20 B6
Baganuur Mongolia 566 G2
Baghdad *Capital* Iraq 463 C4
Bagherhat Bangladesh 114 I9
Baghlān Afghanistan 80 G6
Baglung Nepal 114 D4
Baguio Philippines 650 C3
Bahamas *Country* West Indies 172
Bahāwalpur Pakistan 639 F5
Bahía Blanca Argentina 65 D7

Bahía, Islas de la *Islands* Honduras 193 E3
Bahir Dar Ethiopia 24 E6
Bahrain *Country* SW Asia 406
Baia Mare Romania 727 C5
Baikal, Lake *Lake* Russian Federation 75
Bairiki *Capital* Kiribati 679 B2
Baitadi Nepal 114 A2
Baja California *Peninsula* Mexico 551 B2
Baja Hungary 312 E10
Baker & Howland Islands *External territory* USA, Pacific Ocean 679 D2
Bakherden Turkmenistan 80 C4
Bākhtarān Iran 463 D4
Baku *Capital* Azerbaijan 186 K4
Balabac Island *Island* Philippines 650 A8
Balabac Strait *Sea feature* South China Sea/Sulu Sea 523 J1
Balā Morghāb Afghanistan 80 E6
Balaton Lake Hungary 312 D9
Balbina Represa *Reservoir* Brazil 146 D3
Balearic Islands *Island group* Spain 798 I5
Bali *Island* Indonesia 451 F5
Balikpapan Indonesia 451 F3
Balkan Mountains *Mountain range* Bulgaria 105 D4
Balkhash Kazakhstan 731 E6
Balkhash, Ozero *Lake* Kazakhstan 731 D6
Balsas *River* Mexico 551 G6
Baltic Sea Atlantic Ocean 308
Bālţi Moldavia 727 E5
Baltiysk Kalingrad, Russian Federation 112 A5
Bamako *Capital* Mali 33 D6
Bambari Central African Republic 20 E6
Bamenda Cameroon 20 B6
Banaba *Island* Kiribati 679 A2
Banda Sea Pacific Ocean 451 I4
Bandaaceh Indonesia 451 A2
Bandar-e 'Abbās Iran 463 H7
Bandar-e Būshehr Iran 463 F7
Bandarlampung Indonesia 451 C4
Bandar Seri Begawan *Capital* Brunei 523 J3
Bandundu Congo (Zaire) 20 D9
Bandung Indonesia 451 D5
Bangalore India 444 D9
Banggai, Kepulauan *Island group* Indonesia 451 H3
Banghāzī Libya 28 J2
Bangka, Pulau *Island* Indonesia 451 C3
Bangkok *Capital* Thailand 833 E9
Bangladesh *Country* S Asia 114
Bangor Northern Ireland, UK 858 B6
Bangui *Capital* Central African Republic 20 E7
Bangweulu, Lake *Lake* Zambia 30 F3
Bani *River* Mali 33 E6
Banja Luka Bosnia & Herzegovina 105 D4
Banjarmasin Indonesia 451 F4
Banjul *Capital* Gambia 33 A6
Banks Island *Island* Canada 169 D4
Banks Islands *Island group* Vanuatu 636 F7
Banská Bystrica Slovakia 312 E7
Bantry Bay *Sea feature* Ireland 465 B7
Bantry Ireland 465 B7
Banyak, Kepulauan *Island group* Indonesia 451 A3

Banyo Cameroon 20 C6
Ba'qūbah Iraq 463 C4
Baracaldo Spain 798 E2
Baranavichy Belorussia 112 D7
Barbados *Country* West Indies 172
Barbuda *Island* Antigua & Barbuda 172 K5
Barcelona Spain 798 I3
Barcelona Venezuela 791 F2
Bārdā Azerbaijan 186 I5
Bareilly India 444 D4
Barents Sea Arctic Ocean 64 G8
Bari Italy 475 G7
Barinas Venezuela 791 D3
Barisal Bangladesh 114 J9
Barisan, Pegunungan *Mountains* Indonesia 451 B3
Barito *River* Indonesia 451 F3
Bar-le-Duc France 356 G3
Barlee, Lake *Lake* Australia 93
Barnaul Russian Federation 731 F6
Barnstaple England, UK 858 C10
Barquisimeto Venezuela 791 E2
Barra *Island* Scotland, UK 858 A4
Barranquilla Colombia 791 B2
Barreiras Brazil 146 G6
Barrow *River* Ireland 465 E6
Bartang *River* Tajikistan 80 I5
Bartica Guyana 791 I4
Baruun-Urt Mongolia 566 H2
Barysaw Belorussia 112 F7
Basarabeasca Moldavia 727 F6
Basilan *Island* Philippines 650 D9
Basle Switzerland 819 C4
Basque Provinces *Region* Spain 798 E2
Basse-Terre *Capital* Guadeloupe 172 K5
Basseterre *Capital* St Kitts & Nevis 172 K5
Bass Strait *Sea feature* Australia 93
Bastia Corsica, France 356 I9
Bastogne Belgium 126 F5
Bata Equatorial Guinea 20 B7
Batan Islands *Islands* Philippines 650 C1
Batangas Philippines 650 C5
Bātdâmbâng Cambodia 876 C9
Bath England, UK 858 D10
Bathurst Canada 169 K8
Bathurst Island *Island* Australia 93
Bathurst Island *Island* Canada 64 B5
Batna Algeria 28 G2
Baton Rouge Louisiana, USA 864 H9
Batticaloa Sri Lanka 444 E11
Bat'umi Georgia 186 C3
Batu Pahat Malaysia 523 C4
Bat Yam Israel 473 B5
Bauchi Nigeria 33 J7
Bavarian Alps *Mountains* Austria/Germany 379 E10
Bayamo Cuba 172 E4
Bayanhongor Mongolia 566 D3
Baydhabo Eritrea 24 F8
Baykal, Ozero *Lake* Russian Federation 731 H6
Bayonne France 356 B7
Bayramaly Turkmenistan 80 E5
Beaufort Sea Arctic Ocean 64 C3
Beauvais France 356 E3
Béchar Algeria 28 E3
Be'ér Sheva' Israel 473 B7
Begamganj Bangladesh 114 K8
Beijing *Capital* China 206 I4
Beira Mozambique 30 H6
Beirut *Capital* Lebanon 821 D5
Beja Portugal 682 C9
Béjaïa Algeria 28 G1
Békéscsaba Hungary 312 G9
Belau *see* Palau

Belarus *see* Belorussia
Belcher Islands *Islands* Canada 169 H7
Beledweyne Eritrea 24 F8
Belém Brazil 146 G3
Belfast Northern Ireland, UK 858 B6
Belfort France 356 H5
Belgaum India 444 C8
Belgium *Country* W Europe 126
Belgrade *Capital* Yugoslavia 308 G4
Belitung, Pulau *Island* Indonesia 451 D4
Belize *Country* Central America 193
Belize City Belize 193 D2
Bella Unión Uruguay 65 E5
Belle Île *Island* France 356 B4
Belle Isle, Strait of *Sea feature* Canada 611
Bellingshausen Sea Antarctica 56 A4
Bellinzona Switzerland 819 D7
Bello Colombia 791 B4
Belluno Italy 475 D2
Bellville South Africa 784 C8
Belmopan *Capital* Belize 193 D2
Belmullet Ireland 465 B3
Belo Horizonte Brazil 146 G7
Belorussia *Country* E Europe *var.* Belarus 112
Benevento Italy 475 E6
Bengal, Bay of *Sea feature* Indian Ocean 449 E2
Bengkulu Indonesia 451 C4
Benguela Angola 30 A4
Beni *River* Bolivia 141 B2
Benidorm Spain 798 G6
Beni-Mellal Morocco 28 D3
Beni Suef Egypt 24 C2
Benin *Country* N Africa *prev.* Dahomey 33
Benin, Bight of *Sea feature* W Africa 33 H9
Benue *River* Cameroon/Nigeria 33 J8
Berat Albania 105 G9
Berbera Somalia 24 F6
Berbérati Central African Republic 20 D7
Berdyans'k Ukraine 727 J6
Bergamo Italy 475 C2
Bergen Norway 617 A7
Bering Sea Pacific Ocean 634 E2
Bering Strait *Sea feature* Bering Sea/Chukchi Sea 634 F1
Berkner Island *Island* Antarctica 56 D3
Berlin *Capital* Germany 379 F4
Bermejo *River* Argentina 65 E4
Bermuda *External territory* UK, Atlantic Ocean 89 C5
Bern *Capital* Switzerland 819 B5
Bertoua Cameroon 20 C7
Besançon France 356 G5
Bethlehem West Bank 473 C6
Bethlehem South Africa 784 H5
Bet Shemesh Israel 473 C5
Béziers France 356 E8
Bhairab Bazar Bangladesh 114 J7
Bhairahawa Nepal 114 D4
Bhaktapur Nepal 114 F4
Bhamo Burma 833 C4
Bhangtar Bhutan 114 K5
Bhātāpāra India 444 E6
Bhāvnagar India 444 B6
Bheri *River* Nepal 114 C3
Bhimphedi Nepal 114 E4
Bhojpur Nepal 114 G5
Bhopal India 444 D5
Bhubaneswar India 444 F6
Bhutan *Country* S Asia 114

Biak, Pulau *Island* Indonesia 451 K3

Białystok Poland 312 G3

Biel Switzerland 819 B5

Bielsko-Biała Poland 312 E6

Bihać Bosnia & Herzegovina 105 C4

Bijelo Polje Yugoslavia 105 G6

Biläsuvar Azerbaijan 186 J6

Bila Tserkva Ukraine 727 G3

Bilbao Spain 798 E2

Biltine Chad 20 E4

Bintulu Malaysia 523 I4

Bio Bio, Rio *River* Chile 65 B7

Birāk Libya 28 I4

Biratnagar Nepal 114 G5

Birendranagar Nepal 114 B3

Birmingham Alabama, USA 864 H8

Birmingham England, UK 858 E9

Birni-Nkonni Niger 33 I6

Biržai Lithuania 112 D4

Biscay, Bay of *Sea feature* Atlantic Ocean 308

Bishek *Capital* Kyrgyzstan 80 J3

Bisho South Africa 784 G8

Biskra Algeria 28 G2

Bislig Philippines 650 F8

Bismarck Archipelago *Island group* Papua New Guinea 636 D5

Bismarck North Dakota, USA 864 F5

Bissau *Capital* Guinea-Bissau 33 B6

Bitola Macedonia 105 H9

Biwa-ko *Lake* Japan 478 D7

Bizerte Tunisia 28 H1

Bjelovar Croatia 105 D2

Black Drin *River* Albania/Macedonia 105 G8

Black Forest *Forested mountain region* Germany 379 C9

Black Hills *Mountains* C USA 611

Blackpool England, UK 858 D7

Black River *River* China/Vietnam 876 C2

Black Sea Asia/Europe 75 308

Black Volta *River* Ghana/Ivory Coast 33 F7

Blackwater *River* Ireland 465 C6

Blagoevgrad Bulgaria 403 D4

Blagoveshchensk Russian Federation 731 J6

Blanca, Bahía *Sea feature* Argentina 65 D7

Blanca, Costa *Coastal region* Spain 798 G6

Blantyre Malawi 30 H4

Blenheim New Zealand 606 E6

Blida Algeria 28 F1

Bloemfontein South Africa 784 F6

Bloemhofdam *Reservoir* South Africa 784 F5

Blois France 356 D4

Blue Nile *River* Ethiopia/Sudan 24 D6

Bluefields Nicaragua 193 G6

Bo Sierra Leone 33 C8

Boa Vista Brazil 146 D2

Bobaomby, Cape *Cape* Madagascar 449 B5

Bobo-Dioulasso Burkina 33 E7

Bochum Germany 379 B5

Bodø Norway 617 D4

Bogor Indonesia 451 D5

Bogotá *Capital* Colombia 791 C4

Bogra Bangladesh 114 I7

Bohai, Gulf of *Sea feature* Yellow Sea 206 J4

Bohemian Forest *Region* Czech Republic/Germany 379 F8

Bohol *Island* Philippines 650 E7

Bohol Sea Philippines 650 E7

Boise Idaho, USA 864 C5

Bokāro India 444 G5

Bokna Fjord *Coastal feature* Norway 617 B8

Bol Chad 20 C4

Boldumsaz Turkmenistan 80 D3

Bolivia *Country* Central South America 141

Bologna Italy 475 D3

Bolton England, UK 858 D8

Bolzano Italy 475 D2

Boma Congo (Zaire) 20 C10

Bombay India 444 B7

Bomu *River* Central African Republic 20 E7

Bonete, Cerro *Peak* Chile 787

Bongo, Massif des *Upland* Central African Republic 20 E5

Bongor Chad 20 D5

Bonn Germany 379 B6

Boosaaso Eritrea 24 G6

Borås Sweden 816 B8

Borlänge Sweden 816 C7

Borneo *Island* SE Asia 449 G4

Bornholm *Island* Denmark 258 E3

Bosanski Šamac Bosnia & Herzegovina 105 F4

Bosna *River* Bosnia & Herzegovina 105 E4

Bosnia & Herzegovina *Country* SE Europe 105

Bosporus *Sea feature* Turkey 75

Bossangoa Central African Republic 20 D6

Boston Massachusetts, USA 864 K6

Botevgrad Bulgaria 403 D2

Bothnia, Gulf of *Sea feature* Baltic Sea 308

Botoşani Romania 727 E5

Botswana *Country* southern Africa 30

Bouaké Ivory Coast 33 D7

Bouar Central African Republic 20 D6

Bougainville Island *Island* Papua New Guinea 636 D5

Bougouni Mali 33 D7

Boulogne-sur-Mer France 356 D2

Bourges France 356 E5

Bournemouth England, UK 858 E11

Bouvet Island *External territory* Norway, Atlantic Ocean 89 F11

Brač *Island* Croatia 105 D6

Bradford England, UK 858 E7

Braga Portugal 682 C2

Bragança Portugal 682 E2

Brahmanbaria Bangladesh 114 J7

Brahmaputra *River* S Asia 114 I6 444 I4

Brăila Romania 727 E7

Brande Denmark 258 B4

Brandon Canada 169 F9

Brasília *Capital* Brazil 146 G6

Bratislava *Capital* Slovakia 312 D8

Bratsk Russian Federation 731 G5

Braunau am Inn Austria 819 H3

Braunschweig Germany 379 D4

Brava, Costa *Coastal region* Spain 798 I3

Bravura, Barragem da *Reservoir* Portugal 682 C10

Bray Ireland 465 F5

Brazil Basin *Undersea feature* Atlantic Ocean 89 E8

Brazil *Country* South America 146

Brazilian Highlands *Upland* Brazil 146 H7

Brazzaville *Capital* Congo 20 D9

Braşov Romania 727 D6

Brecon Beacons *Hills* Wales, UK 858 D9

Breda Netherlands 601 C6

Bregenz Austria 819 E4

Bremen Germany 379 C3

Bremerhaven Germany 379 C3

Brescia Italy 475 C2

Brest Belorussia 112 B8

Brest France 356 A3

Bria Central African Republic 20 F6

Bridgetown *Capital* Barbados 172 L7

Brig Switzerland 819 C6

Brighton England, UK 858 F11

Brindisi Italy 475 G7

Brisbane Australia 95 I5

Bristol England, UK 858 D10

British Columbia *Province* Canada 169 B7

British Indian Ocean Territory *External territory* UK, Indian Ocean 449 D4

British Isles *Islands* W Europe 89 F4

British Virgin Islands *External territory* UK, West Indies 172 J4

Brittany *Region* France 356 B3

Brno Czech Republic 312 D7

Broken Hill Australia 95 F6

Broken Ridge *Undersea feature* Indian Ocean 449 E6

Brønderslev Denmark 258 C2

Brooks Range *Mountains* Alaska, USA 864 B1

Broome Australia 95 C3

Brørup Denmark 258 B5

Brugge Belgium 126 B2

Brunei *Country* E Asia 523

Brussels *Capital* Belgium 126 D3

Bryansk Russian Federation 731 B3

Bucaramanga Colombia 791 C3

Buchanan Liberia 33 C8

Bucharest *Capital* Romania 727 D7

Budapest *Capital* Hungary 312 E8

Buenaventura Colombia 791 B5

Buenos Aires *Capital* Argentina 65 E6

Buenos Aires, Lago *Lake* Argentina/Chile 65 B9

Bug *River* E Europe 312 G3 727 C2

Bujumbura *Capital* Burundi 20 H9

Bukavu Congo (Zaire) 20 G9

Bukhara Uzbekistan 80 F4

Bulawayo Zimbabwe 30 F6

Bulgan Mongolia 566 F2

Bulgaria *Country* E Europe 403

Bumba Congo (Zaire) 20 F7

Bunia Congo (Zaire) 20 H8

Buraydah Saudi Arabia 406 D3

Burē Ethiopia 24 E6

Burgas Bulgaria 403 G3

Burgos Spain 798 E3

Burgundy *Region* France 356 F4

Burkina *Country* W Africa 33

Burma *var.* Myanmar *Country* SE Asia 833

Burqin China 206 D2

Burtnieku Ezers *Lake* Latvia 112 E3

Buru *Island* Indonesia 451 I4

Burundi *Country* C Africa 20

Butembo Congo (Zaire) 20 H8

Butuan Philippines 650 F7

Butwal Nepal 114 F4

Buyo Reservoir *Reservoir* Ivory Coast 33 E8

Buzău Romania 727 D7

Bydgoszcz Poland 312 E3

Byerazino *River* Belorussia 112 F7

Bykhaw Belorussia 112 G8

Bytom Poland 312 E6

Byuzmeyin Turkmenistan 80 C4

# C

Caaguazú Paraguay 141 H9

Cabanatuan Philippines 650 C4

Cabimas Venezuela 791 D2

Cabinda Angola 30 A1

Cabinda *Exclave* Angola 30 A1

Cabora Bassa, Lake *Reservoir* Mozambique 30 G4

Cabot Strait *Sea feature* Atlantic Ocean 169 K7

Čačak Yugoslavia 105 G5

Cáceres Spain 798 C5

Cadiz Philippines 650 D6

Cádiz Spain 798 C8

Caen France 356 D3

Caernarfon Wales, UK 858 C8

Cagayan de Oro Philippines 650 F8

Cagliari Italy 475 B8

Cahors France 356 D7

Cairns Australia 95 F3

Cairo *Capital* Egypt 24 C2

Cajamarca Peru 285 C5

Čakovec Croatia 105 D2

Calabar Nigeria 33 J9

Calabria *Region* Italy 475 F9

Calais France 356 E1

Calama Chile 65 B3

Calamian Group *Island group* Philippines 650 B6

Calbayog Philippines 650 E6

Calcutta India 444 G5

Caldas da Rainha Portugal 682 B6

Caleta Olivia Argentina 65 C9

Calgary Canada 169 D9

Cali Colombia 791 B5

Calicut India 444 C9

California *State* USA 864 B7

California, Golfo de *Sea feature* Pacific Ocean 551 C3 634 J5

Cälilabad Azerbaijan 186 J6

Callao Peru 285 D8

Caltagirone Italy 475 E10

Caltanissetta Italy 475 E10

Calvinia South Africa 784 C7

Camagüey Cuba 172 D3

Cambodia *Country* SE Asia *Cam.* Kampuchea 876

Cambridge England, UK 858 F9

Cameron Highlands *Mountain range* Malaysia 523 B3

Cameroon *Country* W Africa 20

Camiri Bolivia 141 D6

Campeche Bahía de *Sea feature* Mexico 551 J5

Campeche Mexico 551 K5

Campina Grande Brazil 146 I4

Campinas Brazil 146 G8

Campo Grande Brazil 146 E8

Canada *Country* North America 169

Canary Basin *Undersea feature* Atlantic Ocean 89 E6

Canary Islands *Islands* Spain 89 E6

Canberra *Capital* Australia 95

Cancún Mexico 551 L4

Caniapiscau, Réservoir *Reservoir* Canada 169 I7

Cannes France 356 G8

Canterbury England, UK 858 G10

Canterbury Bight *Sea feature* Pacific Ocean 606 D7

Canterbury Plains *Plain* New Zealand 606 D7

Cân Thơ Vietnam 876 E11

Cap-Haïtien Haiti 172 G4

Cape Basin *Undersea feature* Atlantic Ocean 89 G9

Cape Coast Ghana 33 G9

Cape Town South Africa 784 B9

Cape Verde *Country* Atlantic Ocean 89 E6

Cape Verde Basin *Undersea feature* Atlantic Ocean 89 E7

Cape York Peninsula *Peninsula* Australia 95 G2

Capri, Isola d' *Island* Italy 475 E7

Caquetá *River* Colombia 791 D7

CAR *see* Central African Republic

Caracas *Capital* Venezuela 791 F2

Caratasca, Laguna de *Coastal feature* Honduras 193 G4

Carcassonne France 356 E8

Cardiff Wales, UK 858 D10

Cardigan Bay *Sea feature* Wales, UK 858 C9

Caribbean Sea Atlantic Ocean 172 H5

Carlisle England, UK 858 D6

Carlow Ireland 465 E5

Carlsberg Ridge *Undersea feature* Indian Ocean 449 C3

Carnarvon South Africa 784 D7

Carnegie, Lake *Lake* Australia 93

Carolina Brazil 146 G5

Caroline Island *Island* Kiribati 679 H4

Caroline Islands *Island group* Micronesia 636 C3

Caroní *River* Venezuela 791 G4

Carpathian Mountains *Mountain range* E Europe 308

Carpaţii Meridionali *Mountain range* Romania 727 C6

Carpentaria, Gulf of *Sea feature* Australia 95 F2

Carra, Lough *Lake* Ireland 465 C3

Carson City Nevada, USA 864 B7

Cartagena Colombia 791 B2

Cartagena Spain 798 G7

Cartago Costa Rica 193 G8

Cartwright Canada 169 K6

Carúpano Venezuela 791 G2

Casablanca Morocco 28 D2

Cascade Range *Mountain range* Canada/USA 611

Cascais Portugal 682 A8

Caspian Sea *Inland sea* Asia/Europe 75 308

Castellón de la Plana Spain 798 G5

Castelo Branco Portugal 682 D6

Castlebar Ireland 465 C3

Castries *Capital* St Lucia 172 L6

Castro Chile 65 B8

Catalonia *Region* Spain 798 H3

Catanduanes Island *Island* Philippines 650 E5

Catania Italy 475 E10

Catanzaro Italy 475 F8

Cat Island *Island* Bahamas 172 E2

Cauca *River* Colombia 791 B3

Caucasus *Mountain range* Asia/Europe 186 E2

Cauquenes Chile 65 B6

Caura *River* Venezuela 791 F4

Cayenne *Capital* French Guiana 791 K4

Cayman Islands *External territory* UK, West Indies 172 C4

Cayman Trench *Undersea feature* Caribbean Sea 172 C4

Cebu *Island* Philippines 650 D7

Cebu Philippines 650 E7

Cedros, Isla *Island* Mexico 551 B3

Cefalù Italy 475 E9

Celebes *Island* Indonesia 449 G4

Celebes Sea Pacific Ocean 634 B6

Celje Slovenia 105 C2

Celtic Sea Atlantic Ocean 465 D8

Frankfurt an der Oder Germany 379 G4

Frantsa-Iosifa, Zemlya *Islands* Russian Federation 731 F1

Franz Josef Land *Islands* Russian Federation 64 F7

Fraser Island *Island* Australia 93

Frauenfeld Switzerland 819 D4

Fredericia Denmark 258 C5

Fredericton Canada 169 K8

Frederikshavn Denmark 258 D1

Fredrikstad Norway 617 C8

Freetown *Capital* Sierra Leone 33 C8

Freiburg im Breisgau Germany 379 B9

Freistadt Austria 819 I2

Fremantle Australia 95 B6

French Guiana *External territory* France, N South America 791 K5

French Polynesia *External territory* France, Pacific Ocean 679 G6

Fribourg Switzerland 819 B6

Frosinone Italy 475 E6

Fuerteventura *Island* Spain 28 B4

Fuji, Mount *Peak* Japan 478 E7

Fukui Japan 478 D7

Fukuoka Japan 478 B8

Fukushima Japan 478 F4

Fukushima Japan 478 F6

Fulda Germany 379 D6

Furnas Represa *Reservoir* Brazil 146 G8

Fuzhou China 206 J7

Füzuli Azerbaijan 186 I6

Fyn *Island* Denmark 258 C6

FYR Macedonia *see* Macedonia

# G

Gaalkacyo Eritrea 24 G7

Gabarone *Capital* Botswana 30 E7

Gabès Tunisia 28 H2

Gabon *Country* W Africa 20

Gabrovo Bulgaria 403 E2

Gaeta, Golfo di *Sea feature* Italy 475 E6

Gafsa Tunisia 28 H2

Gagnoa Ivory Coast 33 E8

Gagra Georgia 186 A1

Gaibanda Bangladesh 114 I6

Gairdner, Lake *Lake* Australia 95 E6

Galápagos Islands *Islands* Ecuador, Pacific Ocean 634 K6

Galaţi Romania 727 E7

Galicia *Region* Spain 798 B2

Galle Sri Lanka 444 E11

Gallipoli Italy 475 G8

Gällivare Sweden 816 D2

Galway Ireland 465 C4

Galway Bay *Sea feature* Ireland 465 C4

Gambia *Country* W Africa 33

Gamgadhi Nepal 114 C2

Gäncä Azerbaijan 186 H4

Gander Canada 169 L6

Gandi Reservoir *Reservoir* India 444 C5

Gandía Spain 798 G5

Ganges *River* S Asia *Ben.* Padma 114 I7 444 G5

Ganges, Mouths of the *Delta* Bangladesh/India 114 J9

Gangtok India 444 G4

Gao Mali 33 G5

Garda, Lago di *Lake* Italy 475 C2

Gardēz Afghanistan 80 H7

Garissa Kenya 24 E9

Garoowe Eritrea 24 G7

Garoua Cameroon 20 C5

Gasa Tashi Thongmen Bhutan 114 I4

Gaspé Canada 169 K7

Gävle Sweden 816 C7

Gaya India 444 F5

Gaza Gaza Strip 473 B6

Gaza Strip *Disputed territory* SW Asia 473 A7

Gazandzhyk Turkmenistan 80 B4

Gdańsk Poland 312 E2

Gdynia Poland 312 E2

Gedaref Sudan 24 D6

Gedser Denmark 258 E7

Geelong Australia 95 G7

Gëkdepe Turkmenistan 80 C4

Gelsenkirchen Germany 379 B5

Gemena Congo (Zaire) 20 E7

Geneina Sudan 24 A6

General Eugenio A. Garay Paraguay 141 E6

General Santos Philippines 650 E9

Geneva Switzerland 819 A7

Geneva, L. *Lake* France/Switzerland 356 G6 819 A6

Genk Belgium 126 E2

Genoa Italy 475 B3

Genova, Golfo di *Sea feature* Italy 475 B3

Gent Belgium 126 C2

George Town *Capital* Cayman Islands 172 B4

Georgetown Gambia 33 B6

Georgetown *Capital* Guyana 791 I4

George Town Malaysia 523 A2

Georgia *Country* SW Asia 186

Georgia *Country* SW Asia 75

Georgia *State* USA 864 I8

Gera Germany 379 E6

Geraldton Australia 95 A5

Gereshk Afghanistan 80 F8

Germany *Country* W Europe 379

Getafe Spain 798 E4

Gevgelija Macedonia 105 I9

Geylegphug Bhutan 114 J5

Ghadāmis Libya 28 H3

Ghana *Country* W Africa 33

Ghanzi Botswana 30 D6

Ghardaïa Algeria 28 F3

Gharyān Libya 28 I3

Ghāt Libya 28 H5

Ghaznī Afghanistan 80 G7

Gibraltar *External territory* UK, SW Europe 798 D8

Gibraltar, Strait of *Sea feature* Atlantic Ocean/Mediterranean Sea 798 D8

Gibson Desert *Desert region* Australia 95 D4

Gijón Spain 798 D1

Gilbert Islands *Islands* Kiribati 679 B2

Girona Spain 798 I3

Gisborne New Zealand 606 G4

Giurgiu Romania 727 D8

Give Denmark 258 B4

Gjirokastër Albania 105 G10

Gjøvik Norway 617 C7

Glåma *River* Norway 617 C7

Glarus Switzerland 819 D5

Glasgow Scotland, UK 858 C5

Gliwice Poland 312 E6

Gloucester England, UK 858 D9

Gmünd Austria 819 J2

Gmunden Austria 819 I4

Gobi *Desert* China/Mongolia 75

Godāvari *River* India 444 E7

Godoy Cruz Argentina 65 B5

Goiânia Brazil 146 F7

Golan Heights *Disputed territory* SW Asia 473 D1 821 D6

Goma Congo (Zaire) 20 H9

Gómez Palacio Mexico 551 F3

Gonaïves Haiti 172 F4

Gonder Ethiopia 24 E6

Good Hope, Cape of *Coastal feature* 784 C9

Gopalpur Bangladesh 114 I7

Gorakhpur India 444 F4

Goré Chad 20 D6

Gorē Ethiopia 24 D7

Gorgān Iran 463 G3

Gori Georgia 186 E3

Goris Armenia 186 H6

Gorontalo Indonesia 451 H3

Gorzów Wielkopolski Poland 312 C3

Gospić Croatia 105 C4

Gostivar Macedonia 105 H8

Göteborg Sweden 816 A8

Gotland *Island* Sweden 816 D9

Gotō-rettō *Island group* Japan 478 A9

Göttingen Germany 379 D5

Gouda Netherlands 601 C5

Gough Island *External territory* UK, Atlantic Ocean 89 F10

Gouin, Réservoir *Reservoir* Canada 169 I8

Govind Ballash Pant Reservoir *Reservoir* India 444 E5

Göyçay Azerbaijan 186 I4

Gozo *Island* Malta 475 E11

Graaf Reinet South Africa 784 E7

Gračanica Bosnia & Herzegovina 105 E4

Graham Land *Region* Antarctica 56 B4

Grahamstown South Africa 784 F8

Grampian Mountains *Mountains* Scotland, UK 858 C4

Granada Nicaragua 193 E6

Granada Spain 798 E7

Gran Canaria *Island* Spain 28 B4

Gran Chaco *Region* C South America 787

Grand Bahama *Island* Bahamas 172 C1

Grand Banks *Undersea feature* Atlantic Ocean 89 C5

Grand Canyon Valley SW USA 864 C7

Grande, Bahía *Sea feature* Argentina 787

Grande, Serra *Mountain range* Brazil 146 H4

Grande Comore *Island* Comoros 30 J3

Grande Prairie Canada 169 C8

Grand Erg Occidental *Desert region* Algeria 28 E3

Grand Erg Oriental *Desert region* Algeria/Tunisia 28 G4

Grand Falls Canada 169 K6

Gråsten Denmark 258 B6

Graz Austria 819 J5

Great Abaco *Island* Bahamas 172 D1

Great Australian Bight *Sea feature* Australia 95 D6

Great Bahama Bank *Undersea feature* Atlantic Ocean 172 D2

Great Barrier Reef *Coral reef* Coral Sea 95 H3

Great Basin *Region* USA 864 B6

Great Bear Lake *Lake* Canada 169 C6

Great Dividing Range *Mountain range* Australia 95 G3

Greater Antarctica *Region* Antarctica 56 G5

Greater Antilles *Island group* West Indies 172 D4

Greater Khingan *Mountain range* China 206 J3

Great Exuma *Island* Bahamas 172 E2

Great Inagua *Island* Bahamas 172 F3

Great Lakes *Lakes* North America 611

Great Man-made River Project Libya 28 K4

Great Plain of China *Region* China 206 I6

Great Plains *Region* N America 864 E5

Great Rift Valley *Valley* E Africa 24 D9

Great Salt Lake *Salt lake* Utah, USA 864 C6

Great Sand Sea *Desert region* Egypt/Libya 28 K3

Great Sandy Desert *Desert* Australia 93

Great Slave Lake *Lake* Canada 169 D7

Great Victoria Desert *Desert* Australia 95 C5

Gredos, Sierra de *Mountains* Spain 798 D4

Greece *Country* SE Europe 403

Greenland *External territory* Denmark, Atlantic Ocean 89 D2

Greenland Basin *Undersea feature* Arctic Ocean 64 D9

Greenland Sea Atlantic Ocean 89 F2

Greenock Scotland, UK 858 C5

Greifswald Germany 379 F2

Grenå Denmark 258 D3

Grenada *Country* West Indies 172

Grenoble France 356 G7

Greymouth New Zealand 606 C6

Grimsby England, UK 858 F8

Grindsted Denmark 258 B5

Groningen Netherlands 601 E2

Grootfontein Namibia 30 C6

Grosseto Italy 475 C5

Groznyy Russian Federation 731 A5

Grudziądz Poland 312 E3

Gstaad Switzerland 819 B6

Guadalajara Mexico 551 F5

Guadalquivir *River* Spain 798 D7

Guadeloupe *External territory* France, West Indies 172 K5

Guadiana *River* Portugal/Spain 682 D9 798 D5

Guainía *River* Colombia 791 E5

Guallatiri *Peak* Chile 787

Guam *External territory* USA, Pacific Ocean 636 C2

Guanare *River* Venezuela 791 E3

Guanare Venezuela 791 D3

Guangzhou China 206 H8

Guantánamo Cuba 172 E4

Guatemala *Country* Central America 193

Guatemala City *Capital* Guatemala 193 B4

Guaviare *River* Colombia 791 E5

Guayaquil Ecuador 285 B3

Guayaquil, Gulf of *Sea feature* Ecuador/Peru 285 B3

Gudenå *River* Denmark 258 C3

Guerguerat Western Sahara 28 A6

Guiana Basin *Undersea feature* Atlantic Ocean 89 D7

Guiana Highlands *Upland* N South America 791 F4

Guider Cameroon 20 C5

Guilin Hills *Hill range* China 206 H7

Guimarães Portugal 682 C3

Guinea *Country* W Africa 33

Guinea, Gulf of *Sea feature* Atlantic Ocean 89 F7

Guinea-Bissau *Country* W Africa 33

Guiyang China 206 G7

Gujrānwāla Pakistan 639 F3

Gujrāt Pakistan 639 F3

Gulariya Nepal 114 B4

Gulu Uganda 24 C8

Gunnbjørn Fjeld *Peak* Greenland 611

Guri, Embalse de *Reservoir* Venezuela 791 G3

Gusau Nigeria 33 I6

Gusev Kalingrad, Russian Federation 112 B5

Gushgy Turkmenistan 80 E6

Guwāhāti India 444 H4

Guyana *Country* NE South America 791

Gwādar Pakistan 639 A6

Gwalior India 444 D4

Győr Hungary 312 D8

Gyumri Armenia 186 E5

Gyzylarbat Turkmenistan 80 C4

# H

Ha Bhutan 114 I4

Ha'apai Group *Islands* Tonga 679 D6

Haapsalu Estonia 112 E1

Haarlem Netherlands 601 C4

Habiganj Bangladesh 114 K7

Habomai Islands *Islands* Japan/Russian Federation (disputed) 478 H2

Hachinohe Japan 478 F4

Hadejia *River* Nigeria 33 J6

Hadera Israel 473 C4

Haderslev Denmark 258 B6

Hadramawt *Region* Yemen 406 F8

Haeju North Korea 497 B5

Hagen Germany 379 B5

Hague, The *Capital* Netherlands 601 B5

Ha'il Saudi Arabia 406 C3

Hailuoto *Island* Finland 333 C5

Hainan *Island* China 206 H9

Hainburg Austria 819 L3

Hai Phong Vietnam 876 F3

Haiti *Country* West Indies 172

Hakodate Japan 478 F3

Halab Syria 821 E2

Halden Norway 617 C8

Halifax Canada 169 K8

Halle Germany 379 E5

Hallein Austria 819 H4

Halmahera *Island* Indonesia 451 I3

Halmstad Sweden 816 B9

Hamada Japan 478 C7

Hamah Syria 821 E3

Hamamatsu Japan 478 E7

Hamar Norway 617 C7

Hamburg Germany 379 D3

Hämeenlinna Finland 333 C8

Hamersley Range *Mountain range* Australia 95 A4

Hamgyöng-Sanmaek *Mountain range* North Korea 497 D3

Hamhüng North Korea 497 C4

Hamilton Canada 169 I10

Hamilton New Zealand 606 E3

Hamm Germany 379 B5

Hammār, Hawr al *Lake* Iraq 463 D6

Hammerfest Norway 617 F1

Hampden New Zealand 606 C8

Han *River* South Korea 497 D6

Handan China 206 I5

Hangayn Nuruu *Mountain range* Mongolia 566 D2
Hangzhou China 206 J6
Hannover Germany 379 D4
Hanoi *Capital* Vietnam 876 E3
Hansholm Denmark 258 B2
Happy Valley-Goose Bay Canada 169 J6
Ḥaraḍ Saudi Arabia 406 F4
Harare *Capital* Zimbabwe 30 F5
Harbin China 206 K3
Hardanger Fjord *Sea feature* Norway 617 B8
Hargeysa Eritrea 24 F7
Hari *River* Indonesia 451 C3
Haringhat *River* Bangladesh 114 I8
Harirūd *River* C Asia 80 E7
Härnösand Sweden 816 D5
Har Nuur *Lake* Mongolia 566 C2
Harper Liberia 33 D9
Harrisburg Pennsylvania, USA 864 J6
Harstad Norway 617 E3
Hartford Connecticut, USA 864 K6
Har Us Nuur *Lake* Mongolia 566 B2
Hasharon *Plain* Israel 473 C3
Hasselt Belgium 126 E2
Hässleholm Sweden 816 B10
Hastings New Zealand 606 F5
Hatia *River* Bangladesh 114 K8
Hatteras, Cape *Coastal feature* North Carolina, USA 611
Hat Yai Thailand 833 E12
Haugesund Norway 617 A8
Havana *Capital* Cuba 172 B2
Havre-Saint-Pierre Canada 169 K7
Hawaii *Island* Hawaii, USA 864 C10
Hawaii *State* USA 864 B9
Hay *River* Canada 169 D7
Heard & Mcdonald Islands *Dependent territory* Australia, Indian Ocean 449 D9
Hebron West Bank 473 C6
Heerenveen Netherlands 601 D3
Heerlen Netherlands 601 D8
Ḥefa Israel 473 C2
Hefei China 206 I6
Heidelberg Germany 379 C8
Heilbronn Germany 379 C8
Helena Montana, USA 864 D5
Helmand *River* Afghanistan 80 E9
Helmond Netherlands 601 D6
Helsingborg Sweden 816 B10
Helsingør Denmark 258 F4
Helsinki *Capital* Finland 333 C9
Ḥelwân Egypt 24 C2
Hendrik Verwoerdam *Reservoir* South Africa 784 F6
Hengelo Netherlands 601 F4
Henzada Burma 833 B7
Herāt Afghanistan 80 E7
Herisau Switzerland 819 D5
Hermansverk Norway 617 B7
Hermosillo Mexico 551 C2
Herning Denmark 258 B4
Herzliyya Israel 473 B4
Hetauda Nepal 114 E4
Hida-sammyaku *Mountains* Japan 478 E7
Hiiumaa *Island* Estonia 112 D1
Hijāz *Region* Saudi Arabia 406 B4
Hildesheim Germany 379 D5
Hillerød Denmark 258 F4
Hilversum Netherlands 601 C4
Himalayas *Mountain range* S Asia 75
Himora Ethiopia 24 D6
Ḥims Syria 821 E4

Hindu Kush *Mountain range* C Asia 75
Hinnøya *Island* Norway 617 E3
Hirakud Reservoir *Reservoir* India 444 F6
Hiroshima Japan 478 C8
Hitachi Japan 478 F6
Hitra *Island* Norway 617 C6
Hjørring Denmark 258 C1
Hlybokaye Belorussia 112 E6
Hobart Tasmania 95 G8
Hobro Denmark 258 C3
Hô Chi Minh Vietnam 876 F10
Hoek van Holland Netherlands 601 B5
Hokkaidō *Island* Japan 478 G2
Holguín Cuba 172 E3
Holland *see* Netherlands
Holon Israel 473 B5
Holot Ḥaluza *Historical site* Israel 473 B7
Holstebro Denmark 258 B3
Holyhead Wales, UK 858 C8
Homyel' Belorussia 112 G9
Honduras *Country* Central America 193
Honduras, Gulf of *Sea feature* Caribbean Sea 193 D3
Hønefoss Norway 617 C8
Hông Gai Vietnam 876 F3
Hong Kong China 206 I8
Hongshui *River* China 206 G8
Hongwŏn North Korea 497 C3
Honiara *Capital* Solomon Islands 636 E6
Honolulu Hawaii, USA 864 B9
Honshū *Island* Japan 478 F5
Hoorn Netherlands 601 C3
Hopedale Canada 169 J6
Horki Belorussia 112 G7
Horlivka Ukraine 727 K4
Hormuz, Strait of *Sea feature* Iran/Oman 406 H3 463 H8
Horn, Cape *Coastal feature* Chile 65 C12
Horsens Denmark 258 C4
Hørsholm Denmark 258 F5
Hotan China 206 B5
Hô Thác Bà *Lake* Vietnam 876 D2
Houston Texas, USA 864 G9
Hovd Mongolia 566 B3
Hövsgöl Nuur *Lake* Mongolia 566 E1
Howe, Cape *Coastal feature* Australia 93
Hradec Králové Czech Republic 312 C6
Hrazdan Armenia 186 F5
Hrodna Belorussia 112 C6
Huainan China 206 I6
Huambo Angola 30 B4
Huancayo Peru 285 E8
Huang He *see* Yellow River
Huánuco Peru 285 D7
Huaraz Peru 285 C7
Huascarán *Peak* Peru 787
Huddinge Sweden 816 C8
Hudiksvall Sweden 816 C6
Hudson Bay *Sea feature* Canada 169 G7
Hudson *River* NE USA 864 J5
Hudson Strait *Sea feature* Canada 169 H5
Huê Vietnam 876 F6
Huehuetenango Guatemala 193 B3
Huelva Spain 798 C7
Huesca Spain 798 G3
Hüich'ŏn North Korea 497 B3
Hulun Lake *Lake* China 206 I2
Hungary *Country* C Europe 312
Hŭngnam North Korea 497 C4

Hurghada Egypt 24 D2
Huron, Lake *Lake* Canada/USA 611
Hvar *Island* Croatia 105 D6
Hyargas Nuur *Lake* Mongolia 566 C2
Hyderābād India 444 D7
Hyderābād Pakistan 639 D7
Hyères, Îles d' *Islands* France 356 G8
Hyesan North Korea 497 C2
Hyvinkää Finland 333 C8

# I

Iași Romania 727 E5
Ibadan Nigeria 33 H8
Ibagué Colombia 791 B5
Ibarra Ecuador 285 C1
Iberian Peninsula *Peninsula* SW Europe 89 F5
Ibotirama Brazil 146 H6
Ica Peru 285 D9
Iceland *Country* Atlantic Ocean 89 E3
Idaho *State* USA 864 C5
Idfu Egypt 24 C3
Ieper Belgium 126 B2
Ifôghas, Adrar des *Upland* Mali 33 G4
Iglesias Italy 475 A7
Iguaçu Falls *Waterfall* Brazil 146 E9
Iguaçu *River* Argentina/Brazil 146 F9
Ihosy Madagascar 30 K7
Iisalmi Finland 333 C6
Ijebu-Ode Nigeria 33 H8
Ijssel *River* Netherlands 601 E4
Ijsselmeer *Lake* Netherlands 601 D3
Ikaría *Island* Greece 403 F8
Ikast Denmark 258 B4
Iki *Island* Japan 478 B8
Ilagan Philippines 650 C3
Ilam Nepal 114 H5
Ilebo Congo (Zaire) 20 E9
Ilha Solteira Represa *Reservoir* Brazil 146 F7
Iligan Philippines 650 E8
Illapel Chile 65 B5
Illinois *State* USA 864 H6
Ilo Peru 285 G11
Iloilo Philippines 650 D6
Ilorin Nigeria 33 I8
Imatra Finland 333 D8
Impfondo Congo 20 D8
Imphāl India 444 I5
Inari, L. *Lake* Finland 333 C2
Inch'ŏn South Korea 497 B6
India *Country* S Asia 444
Indian Ocean 449
Indiana *State* USA 864 H6
Indianapolis Indiana, USA 864 H6
Indonesia *Country* SE Asia 451
Indore India 444 C6
Indus *River* S Asia 639 E5
Indus Delta *Wetlands* Pakistan 639 D7
Ingolstadt Germany 379 E8
Inhambane Mozambique 30 H7
Inland Niger Delta *Wetlands* Mali 33 F5
Inn *River* C Europe 379 F9 819 F5
Innsbruck Austria 819 F5
In Salah Algeria 28 F4
Insein Burma 833 C7
Interlaken Switzerland 819 C6
Inukjuak Canada 169 H7
Inuvik Canada 169 B5
Invercargill New Zealand 606 B9

Inverness Scotland, UK 858 C3
Ioánnina Greece 403 B6
Ionian Islands *Island group* Greece 403 A7
Ionian Sea Mediterranean Sea 403 B9
Íos *Island* Greece 403 F9
Iowa *State* USA 864 G6
Ipoh Malaysia 523 B3
Ipswich England, UK 858 G9
Iqaluit Canada 169 H5
Iquique Chile 65 B2
Iquitos Peru 285 E3
Irákleio Greece 403 E11
Iran *Country* SW Asia 463
Iranian Plateau *Upland* Iran 463 H5
Irānshahr Iran 463 J7
Irapuato Mexico 551 G5
Iraq *Country* SW Asia 463
Irbid Jordan 821 D6
Ireland *Country* W Europe 465
Iri South Korea 497 C7
Irian Jaya *Province* Indonesia 451 K4
Iringa Tanzania 24 D11
Irish Sea Ireland/UK 465 F5 858 C7
Irkutsk Russian Federation 731 H6
Iron Gate *HEP station* Yugoslavia 105 I4
Irrawaddy *River* Burma 833 B6
Irrawaddy Delta *Wetlands* Burma 833 B8
Ischia, Isola d' *Island* Italy 475 E7
Ishikari *River* Japan 478 F2
Ishurdi Bangladesh 114 I7
Isiro Congo (Zaire) 20 G7
Iskŭr *River* Bulgaria 403 D2
Iskŭr, Yazovir *Reservoir* Bulgaria 403 D3
Islamabad *Capital* Pakistan 639 F3
Islay *Island* Scotland, UK 858 B5
Ismâ'ilîya Egypt 24 C1
Isna Egypt 24 C3
Israel *Country* SW Asia 473
Issyk-Kul' Kyrgyzstan 80 J3
Issyk-Kul', Ozero *Lake* Kyrgyzstan 80 K3
Itagüí Colombia 791 B4
Itaipú, Represa *Reservoir* Brazil/Paraguay 141 H9 146 E8
Italy *Country* S Europe 475
Itānagar India 444 I4
Ittoqqortoormiit Greenland 64 C9
Iturup *Island* Japan/Russian Federation *(disputed)* 478 H1
Ivalo Finland 333 C2
Ivano-Frankivs'k Ukraine 727 D4
Ivory Coast *Country* W Africa *Fr.* Côte d'Ivoire 33
Ivujivik Canada 169 H6
Iwaki Japan 478 F6
Iwŏn North Korea 497 D3
Izabal, Lago de Lake Guatemala 193 C3
Izhevsk Russian Federation 731 C4

# J

Jabalpur India 444 E5
Jackson Mississippi, USA 864 H8
Jacmel Haiti 172 F5
Jaén Spain 798 E7
Jaffna Sri Lanka 444 E10
Jaipur India 444 C4
Jaipur Hat Bangladesh 114 I6
Jaisalmer India 444 B4
Jajce Bosnia & Herzgovina 105 D4
Jakar Bhutan 114 J4
Jakarta *Capital* Indonesia 451 D4
Jakobstad Finland 333 B6
Jalālābād Afghanistan 80 H7
Jalandhar India 444 C3

Jalandhar India 444 C3
Jalapa Mexico 551 H6
Jamaame Eritrea 24 F9
Jamaica *Country* West Indies 172
Jamalpur Bangladesh 114 I6
Jambi Indonesia 451 C3
James Bay *Sea feature* Canada 169 H8
Jammerbugten *Sea feature* Denmark 258 B2
Jāmnagar India 444 A6
Jamshedpur India 444 F5
Jamuna *River* Bangladesh 114 I6
Janakpur Nepal 114 F5
Jan Mayen *External territory* Norway, Arctic Ocean 89 F2
Japan *Country* E Asia 478
Japan, Sea of Pacific Ocean 478 D5
Japan Trench *Undersea feature* Pacific Ocean 634 C4
Jari *River* Brazil/Surinam 146 E2
Järvenpää Finland 333 C8
Jarvis Island *External territory* USA, Pacific Ocean 679 F2
Java *Island* Indonesia 451 E5
Java Sea Pacific Ocean 451 D4
Java Trench *Undersea feature* Indian Ocean 634 A7
Jayapura Indonesia 451 L3
Jaz Mūriān, Hamun-e *Salt lake* Iran 463 J7
Jebel Liban *Mountains* Lebanon 821 D5
Jefferson City Missouri, USA 864 G7
Jēkabpils Latvia 112 E4
Jelgava Latvia 112 D4
Jember Indonesia 451 E5
Jena Germany 379 E6
Jenbach Austria 819 G5
Jenin West Bank 473 C3
Jérémie Haiti 172 F4
Jerez de la Frontera Spain 798 C8
Jericho West Bank 473 D5
Jerusalem *Capital* Israel 473 C5
Jesenice Slovenia 105 B2
Jessore Bangladesh 114 I8
Jhalakati Bangladesh 114 J9
Jhelum Pakistan 639 F3
Jhenida Bangladesh 114 I8
Jiddah Saudi Arabia 406 B5
Jihlava Czech Republic 312 C7
Jilin China 206 K3
Jima Ethiopia 24 D7
Jinan China 206 I5
Jinotega Nicaragua 193 E5
Jīzān Saudi Arabia 406 C7
João Pess Brazil 146 I4
Jodhpur India 444 B4
Joensuu Finland 333 D6
Johannesburg South Africa 784 H4
Johor Bharau Malaysia 523 C4
Joinville Brazil 146 F9
Jokkmokk Sweden 816 D3
Jolo *Island* Philippines 650 C9
Jolo Philippines 650 C9
Jomsom Nepal 114 D3
Jonglei Canal *Waterway* Sudan 24 C7
Jönköping Sweden 816 B8
Jonquière Canada 169 J8
Jordan *Country* SW Asia 821
Jordan *River* SW Asia 473 D4 821 D7
Jos Nigeria 33 J7
Juan Fernandez, Islas *Islands* Chile, Pacific Ocean 634 L8
Juàzeiro Brazil 146 H5
Juba Sudan 24 C8
Júcar *River* Spain 798 F5
Judenburg Austria 819 J5
Juigalpa Nicaragua 193 F6

991

Juiz de Fora Brazil 146 G8
Juliaca Peru 285 G10
Jumla Nepal 114 C3
Juneau Alaska, USA 864 D3
Junín Argentina 65 D6
Jura *Mountains*
 France/Switzerland 356 G5
Jura *Island* Scotland, UK 858 B5
Jurbarkas Lithuania 112 C5
Juruá *River* Brazil/Peru 146 B4
Juticalpa Honduras 193 E4
Juventud, Isla de la *Island* Cuba
 172 B3
Jylland *Peninsula* Denmark 258 B4
Jyväskylä Finland 333 C7

# K

K2 Peak China/Pakistan 639 G1
Kabale Uganda 24 C9
Kabalebo Reservoir *Reservoir*
 Surinam 791 I5
Kabinda Congo (Zaire) 20 F10
Kábul *Capital* Afghanistan 80
 H7
Kachch, Gulf of *Sea feature*
 Arabian Sea 444 A6
Kachch, Rann of *Wetland*
 India/Pakistan 444 A5
Kadugli Sudan 24 C6
Kaduna Nigeria 33 I7
Kaédi Mauritania 33 B5
Kaesong North Korea 497 B5
Kagoshima Japan 478 B9
Kai, Kepulauan *Island group*
 Indonesia 451 J4
Kaikoura New Zealand 606 D6
Kainji Reservoir *Reservoir* Nigeria
 33 H7
Kairouan Tunisia 28 H2
Kaitaia New Zealand 606 D2
Kajaani Finland 333 D5
K'ajaran Armenia 186 H6
Kakhovs'ka Vodoskhovyshche
 *Reservoir* Ukraine 727 I5
Kalahari Desert *Desert* southern
 Africa 15
Kalamariá Greece 403 D5
Kalámata Greece 403 C9
Kalāt Afghanistan 80 G8
Kalāt Pakistan 639 C5
Kalemie Congo (Zaire) 20 H10
Kalgoorlie Australia 95 C6
Kali Gandaki *River* Nepal 114 D4
Kaliningrad *External territory*
 Russian Federation 112 A4
 731 B2
Kaliningrad Kalingrad, Russian
 Federation 112 A5
Kalinkavichy Belorussia 112 F9
Kalisz Poland 312 E4
Kalmar Sweden 816 C9
Kalundborg Denmark 258 D5
Kam"yanets'-Podil's'kyy Ukraine
 727 E4
Kama *River* Russian Federation
 308
Kamarhati India 444 G5
Kamchatka *Peninsula* Russian
 Federation 731 K3
Kamchiya *River* Bulgaria 403 G2
Kamina Congo (Zaire) 20 F11
Kamloops Canada 169 C9
Kamo Armenia 186 G5
Kampala *Capital* Uganda 24 C9
Kâmpóng Cham Cambodia
 876 E10
Kâmpóng Chhnăng Cambodia
 876 D9
Kâmpóng Saôm Cambodia
 876 D11
Kâmpôt Cambodia 876 D11
Kampuchea *see* Cambodia

Kananga Congo (Zaire) 20 F10
Kanazawa Japan 478 E6
Kandahār Afghanistan 80 F8
Kandi Benin 33 H7
Kandla India 444 B5
Kandy Sri Lanka 444 E11
Kanestron, Ákra *Coastal feature*
 Greece 403 D5
Kangaroo Island *Island* Australia
 95 F7
Kanggye North Korea 497 B3
Kangnŭng South Korea 497 D5
Kanjiža Yugoslavia 105 G2
Kankan Guinea 33 D7
Kano Nigeria 33 J6
Kanpur India 444 E4
Kansas City Kansas, USA 864 G7
Kansas *State* USA 864 F7
Kansk Russian Federation 731 G5
Kaohsiung Taiwan 206 J8
Kaolack Senegal 33 B6
Kapan Armenia 186 H6
Kapchagay Kazakhstan 731 E7
Kapfenberg Austria 819 J4
Kaposvár Hungary 312 D10
Kapuas *River* Indonesia 451 E3
Kara Kum *see* Karakumy
Kara Sea Arctic Ocean 64 G7
Kara-Balta Kyrgyzstan 80 J3
Kara-Bogaz-Gol, Zaliv *Sea feature*
 Caspian Sea 80 B3
Karāchi Pakistan 639 C7
Karaganda Kazakhstan 731 E6
Karaj Iran 463 E3
Karakol Kyrgyzstan 80 K3
Karakoram Range *Mountain range*
 C Asia 639 G1
Karakumskiy Kanal *Canal*
 Turkmenistan 80 D5
Karakumy *Desert* Turkmenistan
 *var.* Kara Kum 80 D4
Karamay China 206 C3
Karasburg Namibia 30 C8
Karasjok Norway 617 G2
Karbalā' Iraq 463 C5
Kardítsa Greece 403 C6
Kariba, Lake *Lake*
 Zambia/Zimbabwe 30 F5
Karkinits'ka Zatoka *Sea feature*
 Black Sea 727 H6
Karlovac Croatia 105 C3
Karlovy Vary Czech Republic
 312 A6
Karlskrona Sweden 816 C9
Karlsruhe Germany 379 C8
Karlstad Sweden 816 B7
Karmi'él Israel 473 C2
Karnali *River* Nepal 114 B3
Karora Eritrea 24 E5
Kárpathos *Island* Greece 403 G10
Karshi Uzbekistan 80 F4
Karskoye More Arctic Ocean
 731 F2
Kasai *River* Congo (Zaire) 20 E9
Kasama Zambia 30 G3
Kāshān Iran 463 F4
Kashi China 206 B4
Kashmir *Disputed region*
 India/Pakistan 444 C2 639 G2
Kasongo Congo (Zaire) 20 G9
Kaspi Georgia 186 E3
Kassala Sudan 24 D5
Kassel Germany 379 D6
Kateríni Greece 403 C5
Katha Burma 833 C4
Katmandu *Capital* Nepal 114 E4
Katsina Nigeria 33 I6
Kattegat *Sea feature*
 Denmark/Sweden 816 A9
Kauai *Island* Hawaii, USA 864 B9
Kaunas Lithuania 112 C5
Kavadarci Macedonia 105 I8
Kavála Greece 403 E4

Kawasaki Japan 478 F7
Kayan *River* Indonesia 451 F2
Kayes Mali 33 C6
Kazakhstan *Country* C Asia 731
Kazakh Uplands *Upland*
 Kazakhstan 75
Kazan' Russian Federation 731 C4
Kazanlŭk Bulgaria 403 F3
Kéa *Island* Greece 403 E8
Kecskemét Hungary 312 F9
Kēdainiai Lithuania 112 D5
Kefallinía *Island* Greece 403 A7
Kefar Sava Israel 473 C4
Kelmė Lithuania 112 C4
Kelowna Canada 169 C9
Kemerovo Russian Federation
 731 F5
Kemi Finland 333 B4
Kemi *River* Finland 333 C4
Kemijärvi Finland 333 C4
Kendari Indonesia 451 H4
Kenema Sierra Leone 33 C8
Këneurgench Turkmenistan 80 D2
Kénitra Morocco 28 D2
Kenora Canada 169 G9
Kentucky *State* USA 864 I7
Kenya *Country* E Africa 24
Keramadec Trench *Undersea
 feature* Pacific Ocean 93
Kerch Ukraine 727 J7
Kerch Strait *Sea feature* Russian
 Federation/Ukraine 727 J7
Kerguelen *Island* Indian Ocean
 449 D8
Kerguelen Plateau *Undersea feature*
 Indian Ocean 449 D9
Kerki Turkmenistan 80 F5
Kérkyra Greece 403 A5
Kérkyra *Island* Greece 403 A6
Kermadec Trench *Undersea feature*
 Pacific Ocean 634 F8
Kermān Iran 463 H6
Kerulen *River* China/Mongolia
 566 G3
Khabarovsk Russian Federation
 731 K6
Khambhat, Gulf of *Sea feature*
 India 444 B6
Khān Yūnis Gaza Strip 473 A7
Khanthabouli Laos 876 D6
Kharkiv Ukraine 727 J3
Khartoum *Capital* Sudan 24 C5
Khartoum North Sudan 24 D5
Khāsh Iran 463 J6
Khaskovo Bulgaria 403 F3
Khaydarkan Kyrgyzstan 80 H4
Kherson Ukraine 727 H6
Khmel'-nyts'kyy Ukraine 727 E3
Kholm Afghanistan 80 G6
Khon Kaen Thailand 833 F7
Khorog Tajikistan 80 I5
Khorramshahr Iran 463 E6
Khouribga Morocco 28 D2
Khudzhand Tajikistan 80 H4
Khulna Bangladesh 114 I8
Khvoy Iran 463 C2
Khyber Pass *Mountain pass*
 Afghanistan/Pakistan 80 H7
Kičevo Macedonia 105 H8
Kiel Germany 379 D2
Kiel Bay *Sea feature* W Germany
 258 C7
Kielce Poland 312 F5
Kiev *Capital* Ukraine 727 G3
Kiffa Mauritania 33 C5
Kigali *Capital* Rwanda 20 H9
Kigoma Tanzania 24 C10
Kikwit Congo (Zaire) 20 E10
Kilchu North Korea 497 D3
Kilimanjaro *Peak* Tanzania 15
Kilkenny Ireland 465 D5
Kilkís Greece 403 C4

Killarney Ireland 465 B6
Kimberley South Africa 784 F5
Kimch'aek North Korea 497 D3
Kimch'ŏn South Korea 497 C7
Kimje South Korea 497 C7
Kindia Guinea 33 C7
Kindu Congo (Zaire) 20 G9
King Island *Island* Australia 93
Kingman Reef *External territory*
 USA, Pacific Ocean 679 F1
Kingston *Capital* Jamaica 172 D5
Kingston Canada 169 K9
Kingston upon Hull England, UK
 858 F7
Kingstown St Vincent & the
 Grenadines 172 K7
King William Island *Island*
 Canada 169 E5
Kinshasa *Capital* Congo (Zaire)
 20 D9
Kirghiz Steppe *Plain* Kazakhstan
 731 D5
Kirghizia *see* Kyrgyzstan
Kiribati *Country* Pacific Ocean 679
Kirinyaga *Peak* Kenya 15
Kiritimati *Island* Kiribati 679 G2
Kirkenes Norway 617 H2
Kirkland *Lake* Canada 169 I9
Kirkūk Iraq 463 C3
Kirkwall Scotland, UK 858 D2
Kirov Russian Federation 731 C3
Kirovohrad Ukraine 727 H4
Kīrthar Range *Mountain range*
 Pakistan 639 C6
Kiruna Sweden 816 D2
Kisangani Congo (Zaire) 20 F8
Kishorganj Bangladesh 114 J7
Kismaayo Eritrea 24 F9
Kisumu Kenya 24 D9
Kitakyūshū Japan 478 B8
Kitami Japan 478 G2
Kitchener Canada 169 I10
Kitwe Zambia 30 F3
Kitzbühel Austria 819 G4
Kivu, Lake *Lake* Rwanda/Congo
 (Zaire) 20 G9
Kladno Czech Republic 312 B6
Klagenfurt Austria 819 I6
Klaipėda Lithuania 112 B4
Klang Malaysia 523 B4
Klerksdorp South Africa 784 G4
Klerksdorp South Africa 784 G4
Ključ Bosnia & Herzegovina
 105 D4
Klosterneuburg Austria 819 K3
Knin Croatia 105 C5
Knittelfeld Austria 819 J5
Knud Rasmussen Land *Region*
 Greenland 64 C7
Kōbe Japan 478 D7
Koblenz Germany 379 B7
Kobryn Belorussia 112 C8
Kočani Macedonia 105 I8
Kōchi Japan 478 C8
Kodiak Island *Island* Alaska, USA
 864 B3
Køge Denmark 258 E5
Kohima India 444 I4
Kohtla-Järve Estonia 112 G2
Kohŭng South Korea 497 C8
Koilabas Nepal 114 C4
Kŏje-do *Island* South Korea
 497 D8
Kokand Uzbekistan 80 H4
Kokchetav Kazakhstan 731 D5
Kokkola Finland 333 B6
Kokshaal-Tau *Mountain range*
 Kyrgyzstan 80 K3
Kol'skiy Poluostrov *Peninsula*
 Russian Federation 731 D2
Kola Peninsula *Peninsula* Russian
 Federation 308
Kolda Senegal 33 B6
Kolding Denmark 258 C5

Kölen Mountains *Mountain range*
 Norway/Sweden 617 D5
Kolka Latvia 112 D2
Köln Germany 379 B6
Kolwezi Congo (Zaire) 20 F11
Kolyma Range *Mountain range*
 Russian Federation 75
Kolymskoye Nagor'ye *Mountain
 range* Russian Federation 731 K3
Komárno Slovakia 312 E8
Komoé *River* Ivory Coast 33 F8
Komotiní Greece 403 E4
Komsomol'sk Turkmenistan 80 E4
Komsomol'sk-na-Amure Russian
 Federation 731 K5
Komusan North Korea 497 D2
Kongsberg Norway 617 C8
Konispol Albania 105 G11
Konjic Bosnia & Herzegovina
 105 E5
Kopaonik *Mountains* Yugoslavia
 105 H6
Koper Slovenia 105 A3
Koprivnica Croatia 105 D2
Korçë Albania 105 H9
Korčula *Island* Croatia 105 D6
Korea Bay *Sea feature*
 China/North Korea 497 A4
Korea Strait *Sea feature*
 Japan/South Korea 75
Korhogo Ivory Coast 33 E7
Korinthiakós Kólpos *Sea feature*
 Greece 403 C7
Kórinthos Greece 403 C8
Kōriyama Japan 478 F6
Korla China 206 D4
Koror *Capital* Palau 636 B3
Körös *River* Hungary 312 F9
Korosten' Ukraine 727 F2
Korsør Denmark 258 D6
Kortrijk Belgium 126 B3
Kos *Island* Greece 403 G9
Kosan North Korea 497 C4
Kosciusko, Mount *Peak*
 Australia 93
Košice Slovakia 312 G7
Kosŏng North Korea 497 C5
Kosovo *Province* Yugoslavia
 105 H7
Kosovska Mitrovica Yugoslavia
 105 H6
Kosrae *Island* Micronesia 636 E3
Koszalin Poland 312 D2
Kota India 444 C5
Kota Bharu Malaysia 523 C2
Kota Kinabalu Malaysia 523 J2
Kotka Finland 333 D8
Kotto *River* C Africa 20 F6
Koudougou Burkina 33 F6
Kourou French Guiana 791 K4
Kousséri Cameroon 20 C4
Kouvola Finland 333 D8
Kovel' Ukraine 727 D2
Kozáni Greece 403 C5
Kra, Isthmus of *Coastal feature*
 Burma/Thailand 833 D11
Kragujevac Yugoslavia 105 H5
Krakatau *Peak* Indonesia 75
Kraków Poland 312 F6
Kraljevo Yugoslavia 105 H5
Kranj Slovenia 105 B2
Krasnoyarsk Russian Federation
 731 G5
Krasnyy Luch Ukraine 727 K5
Kremenchuk Ukraine 727 H4
Kremenchuts'ke Vodoskhovyshche
 *Reservoir* Ukraine 727 H4
Krems Austria 819 K3
Kretinga Lithuania 112 B4
Kribi Cameroon 20 B7
Krishna *River* India 444 C7
Kristiansand Norway 617 B9
Kristianstad Sweden 816 B10

Krk *Island* Croatia 105 B3
Kroonstad South Africa 784 G5
Kruševac Yugoslavia 105 H5
Krugersdorp South Africa 784 G4
Krychaw Belorussia 112 G8
Kryvyy Rih Ukraine 727 H5
Kuala Lumpur *Capital* Malaysia 523 B3
Kuala Terengganu Malaysia 523 C2
Kuantan Malaysia 523 C3
Kuching Malaysia 523 G4
Kuçovë Albania 105 G9
Kudat Malaysia 523 K1
Kufstein Austria 819 G4
Kuito Angola 30 C3
Kujang North Korea 497 B4
Kulai Malaysia 523 C4
Kuldiga Latvia 112 C3
Kulyab Tajikistan 80 H5
Kumamoto Japan 478 B9
Kumanovo Macedonia 105 I7
Kumasi Ghana 33 F8
Kumbo Cameroon 20 B6
Kümch'ŏn North Korea 497 B5
Kümho *River* South Korea 497 D7
Kumi South Korea 497 C7
Kumon Range *Mountain range* Burma 833 C2
Kümsong South Korea 497 B8
Kunashir *Island* Japan/Russian Federation *(disputed)* 478 G2
Kunduz Afghanistan 80 G6
Kungar Malaysia 523 A2
Kunlun Shan *Mountain range* China 206 C5
Kunming China 206 G8
Kunsan South Korea 497 B7
Kuopio Finland 333 D6
Kupang Indonesia 451 H5
Kura *River* Azerbaijan/Georgia 186 I5
Kurashiki Japan 478 C8
Kürdämir Azerbaijan 186 J4
Kuressaare Estonia 112 D2
Kurgan-Tyube Tajikistan 80 H5
Kurigram Bangladesh 114 I5
Kurile Islands *Islands* Pacific Ocean 634 D3
Kurile rench *Undersea feature* Pacific Ocean 634 D3
Kurmuk Sudan 24 D6
Kuršėnai Lithuania 112 C4
Kuru *River* Bhutan 114 J4
Kuruman South Africa 784 D5
Kushiro Japan 478 G3
Kushtia Bangladesh 114 I7
Kusŏng North Korea 497 B3
Kustanay Kazakhstan 731 D5
K'ut'aisi Georgia 186 D3
Kuujjuaq Canada 169 I6
Kuujjuarapik Canada 169 H7
Kuŭm North Korea 497 C4
Kuusamo Finland 333 D4
Kuusankoski Finland 333 D8
Kuwait *Country* SW Asia 406
Kuwait City *Capital* Kuwait 406 F2
Kværndrup Denmark 258 D6
Kwangju South Korea 497 C8
Kwango *River* Congo (Zaire) 20 D10
Kykládes *Islands* Greece 403 E8
Kyŏnggi-man *Sea feature* North Korea/South Korea 497 B6
Kyŏnghŭng North Korea 497 E1
Kyŏngju South Korea 497 D7
Kyōto Japan 478 D7
Kyrenia Cyprus 821 B3
Kyrgyzstan *Country* C Asia *var.* Kirghizia 80
Kýthira *Island* Greece 403 D10
Kyūshū *Island* Japan 478 B9

# L

Laâyoune *Capital* Western Sahara 28 B4
Labé Guinea 33 C7
Laborec *River* Slovakia 312 G7
Labrador City Canada 169 J7
Labrador *Region* Canada 611
Labrador Sea Atlantic Ocean 89 C3
Labuan Malaysia 523 J2
Laccadive Islands *Island group* India 449 D3
La Ceiba Honduras 193 E3
La Chau-de-Fonds Switzerland 819 B5
Ladoga, Lake *Lake* Russian Federation 308
Lae Papua New Guinea 636 C5
Læsø *Island* Denmark 258 E2
La Esperanza Honduras 193 D4
Lågen *River* Norway 617 C7
Laghouat Algeria 28 F2
Lagos Nigeria 33 H8
Lagos Portugal 682 B11
Lahore Pakistan 639 F4
Laï Chad 20 D5
Lake District *Region* England, UK 858 D7
Laksham Bangladesh 114 K8
Lakshmipur Bangladesh 114 J8
La Ligua Chile 65 B5
Lalitpur Nepal 114 E4
Lalmanir Hat Bangladesh 114 I5
La Louvière Belgium 126 D3
Lambaré Paraguay 141 G9
Lambaréné Gabon 20 B8
Lambert Glacier *Ice feature* Antarctica 56 I4
Lamía Greece 403 C7
Lampedusa *Island* Italy 475 D11
Lampione *Island* Italy 475 C11
Lanao, L. *Lake* Philippines 650 E8
Lancaster England, UK 858 D7
Lancaster Sound *Sea feature* Canada 784
Land's End *Coastal feature* England, UK 858 B11
Landeck Austria 819 F5
Langeland *Island* Denmark 258 D6
Langkawi, Pulau *Island* Malaysia 523 A2
Lang Sơn Vietnam 876 F2
Länkäran Azerbaijan 186 K7
Lansing Michigan, USA 864 I6
Lanzarote *Island* Spain 28 B3
Lanzhou China 206 G5
Laoag Philippines 650 C2
Laon France 356 F3
La Oroya Peru 285 D8
Laos *Country* SE Asia 876
La Palma *Island* Spain 28 A3
La Paz Bolivia 141 B4
La Paz Mexico 551 C4
La Perouse Strait *Sea feature* Japan 478 F1
La Plata Argentina 65 E6
Lapland *Region* N Europe 308
Lappeenranta Finland 333 D8
Laptev Sea Arctic Ocean *Rus.* Laptevykh, More 64 G4
Laptevykh, More *see* Laptev Sea
L'Aquila Italy 475 E5
La Rioja Argentina 65 C5
Lárisa Greece 403 C6
Lārkāna Pakistan 639 D5
Larnaca Cyprus 821 B4
la Roche-sur-Yon France 356 C5
la Rochelle France 356 C5

La Romana Dominican Republic 172 H4
La Serena Chile 65 B5
La Spezia Italy 475 C4
Las Piedras Uruguay 65 E6
Las Tablas Panama 193 J9
Las Vegas Nevada, USA 864 C7
Latacunga Ecuador 285 C2
Latvia *Country* NE Europe 112
Launceston Australia 95 G8
Laurentien Plateau *Upland* Canada 611
Lausanne Switzerland 819 A6
Laval France 356 C4
Laylā Saudi Arabia 406 E5
Lebanon *Country* SW Asia 821
Lebu Chile 65 A7
Lecce Italy 475 H7
Leduc Canada 169 D9
Leeds England, UK 858 E7
Leeuwarden Netherlands 601 D2
Leeuwin, Cape *Coastal feature* Australia 95 B6
Leeward Islands *Island group* West Indies 172 K4
Lefkáda *Island* Greece 403 B7
Legaspi Philippines 650 D5
Legnica Poland 312 C5
le Havre France 356 D2
Leicester England, UK 858 E9
Leiden Netherlands 601 B5
Leinster *Region* Ireland 465 E5
Leipzig Germany 379 E5
Leivádia Greece 403 C7
Lek *River* Netherlands 601 C5
Lelystad Netherlands 601 D4
le Mans France 356 D4
Lemvig Denmark 258 A3
Lena *River* Russian Federation 731 H3
Leoben Austria 819 J5
León Nicaragua 193 E6
León Mexico 551 G5
León Spain 798 D2
le Puy France 356 F7
Lerwick Scotland, UK 858 A1
Leskovac Yugoslavia 105 I6
Lesotho *Country* southern Africa 784
Lesser Antarctica *Region* Antarctica 56 C6
Lesser Antilles *Island group* West Indies 172 J6
Lesser Caucasus Mountains Asia 186 G3
Lésvos *Island* Greece 403 F6
Lethbridge Canada 169 D9
Leti, Kepulauan *Island group* Indonesia 451 I5
Leuven Belgium 126 D2
Leverkusen Germany 379 B6
Lewis *Island* Scotland, UK 858 B2
Leyte *Island* Philippines 650 E6
Lezhë Albania 105 G8
Lhasa China 206 E7
Lhuntshi Bhutan 114 J4
Liberec Czech Republic 312 C5
Liberia Costa Rica 193 D7
Liberia *Country* W Africa 33
Libya *Country* N Africa 28
Libyan Desert *Desert* N Africa 15
Liechtenstein *Country* C Europe 819
Liège Belgium 126 F3
Lienz Austria 819 H6
Liepāja Latvia 112 B3
Liestal Switzerland 819 C4
Liezen Austria 819 I4
Liffey *River* Ireland 465 E4
Ligurian Sea Mediterranean Sea 356 H8 475 B4
Likasi Congo (Zaire) 20 G11

Lille France 356 F2
Lillebælt *Sea feature* Denmark 258 C6
Lillehammer Norway 617 C7
Lilongwe *Capital* Malawi 30 G4
Lima *Capital* Peru 285 D8
Limassol Cyprus 821 B4
Limerick Ireland 465 C5
Limfjorden *Sea feature* Denmark 258 B2
Límnos *Island* Greece 403 E6
Limoges France 356 D6
Limón Costa Rica 193 H8
Limpopo *River* southern Africa 30 G6 784 G2
Linares Chile 65 B6
Linares Spain 798 E6
Lincoln England, UK 858 F8
Lincoln Nebraska, USA 864 F6
Lincoln Sea Arctic Ocean 64 D6
Linden Guyana 791 I4
Lindi Tanzania 24 E12
Line Islands *Island group* Kiribati 679 G3
Lingga, Kepulauan *Island group* Indonesia 451 C3
Linköping Sweden 816 C8
Linosa *Island* Italy 475 D11
Linz Austria 819 I3
Lion, Golfe du *Sea feature* Mediterranean Sea 356 F9
Lipa Philippines 650 C5
Lipari *Island* Italy 475 E9
Lira Uganda 24 C8
Lisbon *Capital* Portugal 682 B8
Lithuania *Country* E Europe 112
Little Minch *Sea feature* Scotland, UK 858 B3
Little Rock Arkansas, USA 864 G8
Liverpool England, UK 858 D8
Livingstone Zambia 30 E5
Livno Bosnia & Herzegovina 105 D5
Livorno Italy 475 C4
Ljubljana *Capital* Slovenia 308 B2
Ljungan *River* Sweden 816 B5
Ljusnan *River* Sweden 816 C6
Llanos *Region* Colombia/Venezuela 791 F3
Lleida Spain 798 H3
Lobatse Botswana 30 E7
Lobito Angola 30 B3
Locarno Switzerland 819 D7
Lod Israel 473 B5
Lodja Congo (Zaire) 20 F9
Łódź Poland 312 E4
Lofoten *Island group* Norway 617 D3
Logan, Mount *Peak* Canada 611
Logroño Spain 798 F2
Loire *River* France 356 D4
Loja Ecuador 285 B4
Lokitaung Kenya 24 D8
Løkken Denmark 258 C2
Loksa Estonia 112 F1
Lolland *Island* Denmark 258 E7
Lombok *Island* Indonesia 451 F5
Lomé *Capital* Togo 33 G8
Lomond, Loch *Lake* Scotland, UK 858 C5
Lomonosov Ridge *Undersea feature* Arctic Ocean *var.* Harris Ridge 64 E5
London Canada 169 I10
London *Capital* UK 858 F10
Londonderry Northern Ireland, UK 858 A6
Londonderry, Cape *Coastal feature* Australia 93
Londrina Brazil 146 F8
Long Beach California, USA 634 I4
Longford Ireland 465 D4

Long Island *Island* Bahamas 172 E2
Long Island *Island* NE USA 864 K6
Longyearbyen Svalbard 64 E8
Lop Nur Lake *Lake* China 206 D4
Lorca Spain 798 F7
Lord Howe Rise *Undersea feature* Pacific Ocean 634 D8
Lorient France 356 B4
Los Angeles California, USA 864 B8
Los Mochis Mexico 551 D4
Lot *River* France 356 D7
Louang Namtha Laos 876 B3
Louangphabang Laos 876 B4
Loubomo Congo 20 C9
Louisiana *State* USA 864 G9
Louisville Kentucky, USA 864 I7
Lovech Bulgaria 403 E2
Loyauté, Îles *Island group* New Caledonia 636 F8
Loznica Yugoslavia 105 F4
Luanda *Capital* Angola 30 A2
Luanshya Zambia 30 F4
Lubānas Ezers *Lake* Latvia 112 F4
Lubango Angola 30 B4
Lübeck Germany 379 D3
Lublin Poland 312 G5
Lubny Ukraine 727 H3
Lubumbashi Congo (Zaire) 20 G12
Lucan Ireland 465 E4
Lucapa Angola 30 D2
Lucena Philippines 650 C5
Lučenec Slovakia 312 F8
Lucerne Switzerland 819 C5
Lucerne, L. *Lake* Switzerland 819 C5
Lucknow India 444 E4
Lüderitz Namibia 30 B8
Ludhiāna India 444 C3
Lugano Switzerland 819 D7
Lugano, L. *Lake* Italy/Switzerland 819 D7
Lugo Spain 798 B2
Luhans'k Ukraine 727 L4
Lule *River* Sweden 816 C2
Luleå Sweden 816 E3
Lumsden New Zealand 606 B8
Luninyets Belorussia 112 D8
Lúrio *River* Mozambique 30 I4
Lusaka *Capital* Zambia 30 F4
Lushnjë Albania 105 G9
Lüt, Dasht-e *Desert* Iran 463 I5
Luts'k Ukraine 727 D2
Lutzow-Holm Bay *Sea feature* Antarctica 56 H2
Luxembourg *Capital* Luxembourg 126 F6
Luxembourg *Country* W Europe 126
Luxor Egypt 24 C3
Luzon *Island* Philippines 650 C3
Luzon Strait *Sea feature* Philippines/Taiwan 650 C1
L'viv Ukraine 727 C3
Lyepyel' Belorussia 112 F6
Lyon France 356 F6

# M

Ma'ān Jordan 821 D9
Maarianhamina Finland 333 A9
Maas *River* W Europe 601 E6
Maastricht Netherlands 601 D8
Macao *External territory* Portugal, E Asia 206 H8
Macapá Brazil 146 F2
Macdonnell Ranges *Mountains* Australia 93
Macedonia *Country* SE Europe *off.* Former Yugoslav Republic of Macedonia

*abbrev.* FYR Macedonia 105
Maceió Brazil 146 I5
Machakos Kenya 24 E10
Machala Ecuador 285 B3
Mackay Australia 95 H4
Mackay, Lake *Lake* Australia 93
Mackenzie *River* Canada 64 B3
Mackenzie Bay *Sea feature* Atlantic Ocean 56 I4
Mackenzie *River* Canada 169 C7
McKinley, Mount *see* Denali
McMurdo Sound *Sea feature* Antarctica 56 F7
Mâcon France 356 F6
Madagascar *Country* Indian Ocean 30
Madagascar Basin *Undersea feature* Indian Ocean 449 C6
Madagascar Ridge *Undersea feature* Indian Ocean 449 B7
Madang Papua New Guinea 636 C5
Madaripur Bangladesh 114 J8
Madeira *Island group* Portugal 89 E5
Madeira *River* Bolivia/Brazil 146 D4
Madison Wisconsin, USA 864 H6
Madona Latvia 112 E4
Madras India 444 E9
Madre de Dios *River* Bolivia/Peru 141 B2 285 G8
Madrid *Capital* Spain 798 E4
Madurai India 444 D10
Mae Nam Ping *River* Thailand 833 D7
Mafeteng Lesotho 784 G6
Magadan Russian Federation 731 K3
Magdalena *River* Colombia 791 C3
Magdeburg Germany 379 E5
Magellan, Strait of *Sea feature* S South America 787
Magerøy *Island* Norway 617 G1
Maggiore, L. *Lake* Italy/Switzerland 475 B2 819 D7
Magura Bangladesh 114 I8
Māhabalipuram India 444 E9
Mahajanga Madagascar 30 K5
Mahakali *River* India/Nepal 114 A2
Mahalapye Botswana 30 E7
Mahanādi *River* India 444 F6
Mahilyow Belorussia 112 G7
Maicao Colombia 791 C2
Maiduguri Nigeria 33 K6
Maine *State* USA 864 L5
Mainz Germany 379 C7
Maiquetía Venezuela 791 F2
Maitland Australia 95 H6
Majuro *Capital* Marshall Islands 636 F3
Makarska Croatia 105 D6
Makeni Sierra Leone 33 C7
Makgadikgadi *Salt pan* Botswana 30 E6
Makhachkala Russian Federation 731 B5
Makiyivka Ukraine 727 K5
Makkah Saudi Arabia 406 B5
Makkovik Canada 169 J6
Makurdi Nigeria 33 J8
Malabār Coast *Coastal region* India 444 C9
Malabo *Capital* Equatorial Guinea 20 B7
Malacca, Strait of *Sea feature* Indonesia/Malaysia 451 B2
Maladzyechna Belorussia 112 E6
Málaga Spain 798 D7
Malakal Sudan 24 C7
Malang Indonesia 451 E5

Malanje Angola 30 B3
Malawi *Country* southern Africa 30
Malaya Peninsula SE Asia 523 B3
Malaysia *Country* Asia 523
Maldive Ridge *Undersea feature* Indian Ocean 449 D4
Maldives *Country* Indian Ocean 449
Mali *Country* W Africa 33
Malindi Kenya 24 E10
Mallorca *Island* Spain 798 J5
Malmö Sweden 816 B10
Malmsbury South Africa 784 B8
Malta *Country* Mediterranean Sea 475
Maluku *Island group* Indonesia 451 H3
Mamberamo *River* Indonesia 451 K3
Mamoré *River* Bolivia 141 C3
Mamoudzou Mayotte 30 K4
Man Ivory Coast 33 D8
Man, Isle of *Island* UK 858 C7
Manado Indonesia 451 H3
Managua *Capital* Nicaragua 193 E6
Manama *Capital* Bahrain 406 F3
Mananjary Madagascar 30 K6
Manaus Brazil 146 D3
Manchester England, UK 858 D8
Manchurian Plain *Plain* E Asia 206 J3
Mandalay Burma 833 C5
Mandalgovĭ Mongolia 566 F4
Mangalia Romania 727 E8
Mangalore India 444 C9
Mangla Reservoir *Reservoir* India/Pakistan 444 C2
Manguéni, Plateau du *Upland* Niger 33 K3
Manicouagan, Réservoir *Reservoir* Canada 169 J7
Manikganj Bangladesh 114 J7
Manila *Capital* Philippines 650 C4
Manitoba *Province* Canada 169 F8
Manizales Colombia 791 B4
Mannar Sri Lanka 444 E10
Mannheim Germany 379 C8
Mannu *River* Italy 475 B7
Manono Congo (Zaire) 20 G10
Manp'o North Korea 497 B3
Mansel Island *Island* Canada 169 G6
Manta Ecuador 285 A2
Mantes-la-Jolie France 356 E3
Mantova Italy 475 C3
Manzanillo Mexico 551 F6
Manzini Swaziland 784 I4
Mao Chad 20 E4
Maoke, Pegunungan *Mountains* Indonesia 451 K4
Maputo *Capital* Mozambique 30 G7
Mar, Serra do *Mountains* Brazil 787
Maracaibo Venezuela 791 D2
Maracaibo, Lago de *Inlet* Venezuela 791 D2
Maracay Venezuela 791 E2
Maradi Niger 33 I6
Marajó, Ilha de *Island* Brazil 787
Maranhão, Barragem do Portugal 682 D7
Marañón *River* Peru 285 D4
Marbella Spain 798 D8
Mar Chiquita, Laguna *Salt lake* Argentina 65 D5
Mardān Pakistan 639 F2
Mar del Plata Argentina 65 E7
Margarita, Isla de *Island* Venezuela 791 G2

Margow, Dasht-e- *Desert* Afghanistan 80 E8
Mariana Trench *Undersea feature* Pacific Ocean 634 D5
Maribo Denmark 258 E7
Maribor Slovenia 105 C2
Marie Byrd Land *Region* Antarctica 56 D5
Mariestad Sweden 816 B8
Marijampolė Lithuania 112 C6
Marinduque *Island* Philippines 650 C5
Mariscal Estigarribia Paraguay 141 E7
Maritsa *River* SE Europe 403 F3
Mariupol' Ukraine 727 K5
Marka Eritrea 24 F9
Marne *River* France 356 F3
Marneuli Georgia 186 F4
Maroua Cameroon 20 C5
Marowijne *River* French Guiana/Surinam 791 K5
Marquesas Islands *Island group* French Polynesia 679 J4
Marrakech Morocco 28 D3
Marsala Italy 475 D9
Marseille France 356 F8
Marshall Islands *Country* Pacific Ocean 636
Martadi Nepal 114 B2
Martigny Switzerland 819 B7
Martin Slovakia 312 E7
Martinique *External territory* France, West Indies 172 L6
Mary Turkmenistan 80 E5
Maryland *State* USA 864 J7
Masan South Korea 497 D8
Masbate *Island* Philippines 650 D6
Masbate Philippines 650 D6
Mascarene Plateau *Undersea feature* Indian Ocean 449 C6
Maseru *Capital* Lesotho 784 G6
Mashhad Iran 463 I3
Masindi Uganda 24 C9
Masinloc Philippines 650 B4
Maṣīrah, Jazīrat *Island* Oman 406 J5
Mask, Lough *Lake* Ireland 465 B4
Massachusetts *State* USA 864 K6
Massalı Azerbaijan 186 K6
Massawa Eritrea 24 E5
Massif Central *Upland* France 356 E6
Massoukou Gabon 20 C9
Masterton New Zealand 606 E5
Matadi Congo (Zaire) 20 C10
Matagalpa Nicaragua 193 F5
Matamoros Mexico 551 H3
Matanzas Cuba 172 B2
Matara Sri Lanka 444 E11
Mataró Spain 798 I3
Mato Grosso *Physical region* Brazil 146 E5
Matosinhos Portugal 682 C3
Matrûh Egypt 24 B1
Matsue Japan 478 C7
Matsuyama Japan 478 C8
Matterhorn *Peak* Switzerland 819 B7
Maturín Venezuela 791 G2
Maui *Island* Hawaii, USA 864 B9
Maun Botswana 30 D6
Mauna Loa *Peak* Hawaii, USA 864 C10
Mauritania *Country* W Africa 33
Mauritius *Country* Indian Ocean 449
Mayaguana *Island* Bahamas 172 F3
Mayotte *External territory* France, Indian Ocean 449 B5
Mazār-e Sharif Afghanistan 80 G6
Mazatenango Guatemala 193 A4
Mazatlán Mexico 551 E5

Mažeikiai Lithuania 112 C4
Mazury *Region* Poland 312 F3
Mazyr Belorussia 112 E9
Mbabane *Capital* Swaziland 784 I4
Mbala Zambia 30 G2
Mbale Uganda 24 D9
Mbandaka Congo (Zaire) 20 D8
Mbeya Tanzania 24 D11
Mbuji-Mayi Congo (Zaire) 20 F10
Mechelen Belgium 126 D2
Medan Indonesia 451 B2
Medellín Colombia 791 B4
Médenine Tunisia 28 H2
Mediterranean Sea Atlantic Ocean 89 G5
Meerut India 444 D3
Meghna *River* Bangladesh 114 J8
Meherpur Bangladesh 114 H8
Mek'elē Ethiopia 24 E6
Meknès Morocco 28 D2
Mekong *River* SE Asia 75
Mekong Delta *Wetlands* Vietnam 876 F11
Melaka Malaysia 523 C4
Melanesia *Region* Pacific Ocean 634 E7
Melbourne Australia 95 G7
Melilla *External territory* Spain, N Africa 28 E2
Melitopol' Ukraine 727 I6
Melk Austria 819 J3
Melo Uruguay 65 F5
Melrhir, Chott *Salt lake* Algeria 28 G2
Melville Island *Island* Australia 95 D1
Melville Island *Island* Canada 169 D4
Mende France 356 E7
Mendi Papua New Guinea 636 C5
Mendoza Argentina 65 B5
Menongue Angola 30 C4
Menorca *Island* Spain 798 J4
Mentakap Malaysia 523 C3
Mentawai, Kepulauan *Island group* Indonesia 451 B3
Meppel Netherlands 601 E3
Mercedario *Peak* Argentina 787
Mercedes Argentina 65 C6
Mercedes Uruguay 65 E6
Mergui Archipelago *Island chain* Burma 833 D10
Mergui Burma 833 D10
Mérida Mexico 551 K5
Mérida Spain 798 C6
Mérida Venezuela 791 D3
Meru Kenya 24 E9
Mesopotamia *Ancient region* Iraq 463 H9
Messina Italy 475 F9
Mestia Georgia 186 C1
Mestre Italy 475 D3
Meta *River* Colombia/Venezuela 791 D4
Metković Croatia 105 E6
Metz France 356 G3
Meuse *River* W Europe 308
Mexicali Mexico 551 B1
Mexico City *Capital* Mexico 551 H6
Mexico *Country* North America 551
Mexico, Gulf of *Sea feature* Atlantic Ocean/Caribbean Sea 551 I4
Meymaneh Afghanistan 80 F6
Miami Florida, USA 864 J10
Michigan *State* USA 864 I5
Michigan, Lake *Lake* USA 864 H5
Micronesia *Region* Pacific Ocean 93

Micronesia *Country* Pacific Ocean 636
Micronesia *Region* Pacific Ocean 634 E6
Mid-Atlantic Ridge *Undersea feature* Atlantic Ocean 89 D6
Middelburg South Africa 784 F7
Middelfart Denmark 258 C5
Middle America Trench *Undersea feature* Pacific Ocean 551 F7
Middlesbrough England, UK 858 E6
Mid-Indian-Ridge *Undersea feature* Indian Ocean 449 D6
Mikkeli Finland 333 D7
Míkonos *Island* Greece 403 F8
Mikuni-sammyaku *Mountains* Japan 478 F6
Milagro Ecuador 285 B3
Milan Italy 475 B2
Mildura Australia 95 G6
Milford Haven Wales, UK 858 C10
Milford Sound New Zealand 606 B8
Mílos *Island* Greece 403 E9
Milwaukee Wisconsin, USA 864 H6
Minatitlán Mexico 551 J6
Mindanao *Island* Philippines 650 E8
Mindoro *Island* Philippines 650 C5
Mindoro Strait *Sea feature* South China Sea/Sulu Sea 650 C6
Mingäçevir Azerbaijan 186 I4
Mingäçevir *Reservoir* Reservoir Azerbaijan 186 H4
Mingāora Pakistan 639 F2
Minho *River* Portugal/Spain 682 C2 798 B3
Minneapolis Minnesota, USA 864 G5
Minnesota *State* USA 864 G4
Miño *River* Portugal/Spain 798 B2
Minsk *Capital* Belorussia 112 E4
Minto, Lake *Lake* Canada 169 H7
Mira *River* Portugal 682 C9
Miranda de Ebro Spain 798 E2
Miri Malaysia 523 I3
Mirim Lagoon *Lagoon* Brazil/Uruguay 65 F6 146 F11
Mirtóo Pelagos *Sea feature* Mediterranean Sea 403 D9
Miryang South Korea 497 D7
Miskolc Hungary 312 F8
Miṣrātah Libya 28 I3
Mississippi Delta *Wetlands* USA 864 H9
Mississippi *River* USA 864 G5
Mississippi *State* USA 864 H8
Missouri *River* USA 864 E4
Missouri *State* USA 864 G7
Mitilíni Greece 403 F6
Mito Japan 478 F6
Mittersill Austria 819 G5
Miyazaki Japan 478 C9
Mjøsa, L. *Lake* Norway 617 C7
Mljet *Island* Croatia 105 E7
Mmabatho Botswana 30 E7
Mmabatho South Africa 784 F4
Moçambique Mozambique 30 I4
Mocímboa da Praia Mozambique 30 I3
Mocoa Colombia 791 B6
Mocuba Mozambique 30 H5
Modena Italy 475 C3
Mödling Austria 819 K3
Modriča Bosnia & Herzegovina 105 E4
Mogadishu *Capital* Somalia 24 G9
Mohéli *Island* Comoros 30 J3

Mo i Rana Norway 617 D4
Mokp'o South Korea 497 B8
Moldavia *Country* E Europe *var.*
    Moldova 727
Molde Norway 617 B6
Moldova *see* Moldavia
Mollendo Peru 285 F10
Moluccas *Island group* Indonesia 75
Mombasa Kenya 24 E10
Møn *Island* Denmark 258 F6
Monaco *Country* W Europe
    356 H8
Monastir Tunisia 28 H2
Monclova Mexico 551 G3
Moncton Canada 169 K8
Mongar Bhutan 114 J4
Mongo Chad 20 E4
Mongolia *Country* NE Asia 566
Monrovia *Capital* Liberia 33 C8
Mons Belgium 126 C4
Mont Blanc *Peak* France/Italy 308
Mont-de-Marsan France 356 C7
Montana *State* USA 864 D5
Montauban France 356 D7
Monte Carlo Monaco 356 H8
Monte Cristi Dominican
    Republic 172 G4
Montecristi Ecuador 285 B2
Montego Bay Jamaica 172 D4
Montenegro *Republic* Yugoslavia
    105 G6
Montería Colombia 791 B3
Montero Bolivia 141 D5
Monterrey Mexico 551 G3
Montevideo *Capital* Uruguay
    65 E6
Montgomery Alabama, USA
    864 H8
Montpelier Vermont, USA 864 K5
Montpellier France 356 E8
Montréal Canada 169 J9
Montreux Switzerland 819 B6
Montserrat *External territory* UK,
    West Indies 172 K5
Monument Valley *Valley* SW USA
    864 D7
Monywa Burma 833 B5
Monza Italy 475 B2
Moose Factory Canada 169 H8
Mopti Mali 33 F5
Mora Sweden 816 B6
Morādābād India 444 D3
Morava *River* C Europe 105 H5
    312 D7
Morawhanna Guyana 791 H3
Moray Firth *Inlet* Scotland, UK
    858 C3
Morelia Mexico 551 G6
Morena, Sierra *Mountain range*
    Spain 798 C6
Morghāb *River*
    Afghanistan/Turkmenistan 80 F6
Morioka Japan 478 F4
Morocco *Country* N Africa 28
Morogoro Tanzania 24 E11
Mörön Mongolia 566 D2
Morondava Madagascar 30 J6
Moroni *Capital* Comoros 30 J3
Morotai, Pulau *Island* Indonesia
    451 I2
Mors *Island* Denmark 258 B2
Moscow *Capital* Russian
    Federation 731 B3
Mosel *River* W Europe *Fr.*
    Moselle 379 B7
Moselle *River* W Europe *Ger.*
    Mosel 126 G6 356 G4
Moshi Tanzania 24 E10
Mosquito Coast *Coastal region*
    Nicaragua 193 G6
Moss Norway 617 C8
Mossendjo Congo 20 C9
Mossoró Brazil 146 I4

Most Czech Republic 312 B5
Mostar Bosnia & Herzegovina
    105 E6
Motala Sweden 816 C8
Motril Spain 798 E7
Moulins France 356 E5
Moulmein Burma 833 D7
Moundou Chad 20 D5
Mouscron Belgium 126 B3
Moyale Kenya 24 E8
Moyobamba Peru 285 C5
Mozambique *Country* SE Africa 30
Mozambique Channel *Sea feature*
    Indian Ocean 30 I6
Mpika Zambia 30 G3
Mtwara Tanzania 24 E12
Muang Không Laos 876 E8
Muang Khôngxédôn Laos 876 E7
Muang Sing Laos 876 B3
Mufulira Zambia 30 F3
Mukachevo Ukraine 727 B4
Mulhacen *Peak* Spain 308
Mulhouse France 356 H4
Mull *Island* Scotland, UK 858 B4
Muller, Pegunungan *Mountains*
    Indonesia 451 E3
Multān Pakistan 639 E4
Muna, Pulau *Island* Indonesia
    451 H4
München Germany 379 E9
Munch'ŏn North Korea 497 C4
Mungla Bangladesh 114 I9
Munshiganj Bangladesh 114 J8
Münster Germany 379 B5
Munster *Region* Ireland 465 C6
Muntinglupa Philippines 650 C4
Muonio *River* Finland/Sweden
    333 A2 816 D1
Mur *River* C Europe 819 I5
Murcia Spain 798 G6
Murgab *River* Turkmenistan 80 E5
Murgab Tajikistan 80 J5
Müritz *Lake* Germany 379 F3
Murmansk Russian Federation
    731 D2
Murray River *River* Australia 93
Murrumbidgee River *River*
    Australia 95 G6
Murska Sobota Slovenia 105 D1
Murzuq Libya 28 I4
Muscat *Capital* Oman 406 I4
Mwanza Tanzania 24 D10
Mwene-Ditu Congo (Zaire) 20 F10
Mweru, Lake *Lake* Congo
    (Zaire)/Zambia 20 G11 30 F2
Myanmar *see* Burma
Mykolayiv Ukraine 727 H6
Mymensingh Bangladesh 114 J6
Myŏngch'ŏn North Korea 497 D2
Mysore India 444 C9
Mzuzu Malawi 30 G3

# N

Nablus West Bank 473 C4
Nacala Mozambique 30 I4
Næstved Denmark 258 E6
Naga Philippines 650 D5
Nagano Japan 478 E6
Nagaon Japan 478 E6
Nāgārjuna Reservoir *Reservoir*
    India 444 D8
Nagasaki Japan 478 B9
Nāgercoil India 444 D10
Nagorno Karabakh *Region*
    Azerbaijan 186I6
Nagoya Japan 478 E7
Nāgpur India 444 D6
Nagykanizsa Hungary 312 D9
Naha Japan 478 A12
Nahariyya Israel 473 C2
Nain Canada 169 J6
Nairobi *Capital* Kenya 24 D9
Najd *Region* Saudi Arabia 406 D4

Najin North Korea 497 E2
Najrān Saudi Arabia 406 D7
Nakamura Japan 478 C8
Nakhodka Russian Federation
    731 F3
Nakhon Ratchasima Thailand
    833 F8
Nakhon Sawan Thailand 833 E8
Nakhon Si Thammarat Thailand
    833 E12
Nakina Canada 169 H9
Nakskov Denmark 258 D7
Nakuru Kenya 24 D9
Nalayh Mongolia 566 G2
Nal'chik Russian Federation
    731 A5
Nam *River* North Korea 497 B4
Namangan Uzbekistan 80 I3
Nam Đinh Vietnam 876 E3
Namib Desert *Desert* Namibia
    30 B6
Namibe Angola 30 A4
Namibia *Country* southern Africa
    30
Namp'o North Korea 497 B5
Nampula Mozambique 30 I4
Namur Belgium 126 E4
Nanchang China 206 I7
Nancy France 356 G4
Nānded India 444 D7
Nanjing China 206 I6
Nanning China 206 H8
Nantes France 356 C4
Naogaon Bangladesh 114 I7
Napier New Zealand 606 F4
Naples Italy 475 E7
Napo *River* Ecuador/Peru 285 E2
Narayani *River* Nepal 114 E4
Narbonne France 356 E8
Nares Strait *Sea feature*
    Canada/Greenland 64 C6
Narew *River* Poland 312 G3
Narmada *River* India 444 C6
Narsingdi Bangladesh 114 J7
Narva Estonia 112 G2
Narva *River* Estonia/Russian
    Federation 112 G2
Narva Bay *Sea feature* Gulf of
    Finland 112 G1
Narvik Norway 617 E3
Naryn Kyrgyzstan 80 J3
Naryn *River*
    Kyrgyzstan/Uzbekistan 80 J3
Nashville Tennessee, USA 864 H7
Nāsik India 444 C6
Nāsir, Buheiret *Reservoir* Egypt
    24 C3
Nassau *Capital* Bahamas 172 D1
Natal Brazil 146 I4
Natitingou Benin 33 G7
Nator Bangladesh 114 I7
Natuna, Kepulauan *Island group*
    Indonesia 523 F3
Natuna, Kepulauan *Island group*
    Indonesia 451 D2
Nauru *Country* Pacific Ocean 636
Navapolatsk Belorussia 112 F6
Navassa Island *External territory*
    USA, West Indies 172 E4
Navoi Uzbekistan 80 F4
Nawabganj Bangladesh 114 H7
Nawābshāh Pakistan 639 D6
Naxçivan Azerbaijan 186 G7
Náxos *Island* Greece 403 F9
Nazca Peru 285 E9
Nazrēt Ethiopia 24 E7
Nazerat Israel 473 C3
Nazerat 'Illit Israel 473 C2
N'Dalatando Angola 30 B2
Ndélé Central African Republic
    20 E6
N'Djamena *Capital* Chad 20 D4
Ndola Zambia 30 F3

N'Giva Angola 30 B5
N'Guigmi Niger 33 K6
Nebitdag Turkmenistan 80 B4
Nebraska *State* USA 864 F6
Neckar *River* Germany 379 C9
Necochea Argentina 65 E7
Negēlē Ethiopia 24 E8
Negev *Desert region* Israel 473 C9
Negro *River* N South America 787
Negro *River* N South America 787
Negros *Island* Philippines 650 D7
Neiva Colombia 791 B5
Nellore India 444 E8
Nelson New Zealand 606 D6
Neman *River* NE Europe 112 C7
Nemuro Japan 478 G2
Nepal *Country* S Asia 114
Nepalganj Nepal 114 B4
Neretva *River* Bosnia &
    Herzegovina 105 E6
Neris *River* Belorussia/Lithuania
    112 D5
Ness, Loch *Lake* Scotland, UK
    858 C3
Netanya Israel 473 B4
Netherlands *Country* W Europe
    *var.* Holland 601
Netherlands Antilles *External*
    *territory* Netherlands, West
    Indies *prev.* Dutch West Indies
    172 H7
Netrakona Bangladesh 114 J6
Neubrandenburg Germany 379 F3
Neuchâtel Switzerland 819 B5
Neuchâtel, L. *Lake* Switzerland
    819 B5
Neumünster Germany 379 D2
Neunkirchen Austria 819 K4
Neusiedler, L. *Lake*
    Austria/Hungary 819 L4
Nevada *State* USA 864 C7
Nevada, Sierra *Mountain range*
    Spain 798 E7
Nevers France 356 E5
New Amsterdam Guyana 791 I4
Newbridge Ireland 465 E5
New Britain *Island* Papua New
    Guinea 636 D5
New Brunswick *Province* Canada
    169 K8
New Caledonia *External territory*
    France, Pacific Ocean 636 E7
Newcastle Australia 95 H6
Newcastle upon Tyne England,
    UK 858 E6
New Delhi *Capital* India 444 D3
Newfoundland Basin *Undersea*
    *feature* Atlantic Ocean 89 D5
Newfoundland *Province* Canada
    169 J6
New Georgia *Island* Solomon
    Islands 636 E6
New Guinea *Island* Pacific Ocean
    634 C4
New Hampshire *State* USA
    864 K5
New Ireland *Island* Papua New
    Guinea 636 D5
New Jersey *State* USA 864 K6
New Mexico *State* USA 864 E8
New Orleans Louisiana, USA 864
    H9
New Plymouth New Zealand
    606 E4
New Providence *Island* Bahamas
    172 E1
New Siberian Islands *Islands*
    Russian Federation 64 F3
New South Wales *State* Australia
    95 G6
New York New York, USA 864 K6
New York *State* USA 864 J6

New Zealand *Country* Pacific
    Ocean 606
Newry Northern Ireland, UK
    858 B7
Neyshābūr Iran 463 I3
Ngaoundéré Cameroon 20 C6
Nha Trang Vietnam 876 H9
Niamey *Capital* Niger 33 H6
Niangay, Lac *Lake* Mali 33 F5
Nicaragua *Country* Central
    America 193
Nicaragua, Lake *Lake* Nicaragua
    193 F6
Nice France 356 H8
Nicobar Islands *Island group* India
    449 E3
Nicosia *Capital* Cyprus 821 B4
Nicoya, Golfo de *Sea feature*
    Costa Rica 193 F8
Nicoya, Península de *Peninsula*
    Costa Rica 193 F7
Nieuw Amsterdam Surinam 791
Niger *River* W Africa 89 F6
Niger *Country* W Africa 33
Niger Delta *Wetlands* Nigeria
    33 I9
Niger *River* W Africa 33 I7
Nigeria *Country* W Africa 33
Niigata Japan 478 E6
Nijmegen Netherlands 601 D5
Nikopol' Ukraine 727 I5
Nile *River* N Africa 24 C4
Nile Delta *Wetlands* Egypt 24 C1
Nilphamari Bangladesh 114 H5
Nîmes France 356 F8
Ninety East Ridge *Undersea feature*
    Indian Ocean 449 E5
Ningbo China 206 J7
Nioro Mali 33 D5
Nipigon, Lake *Lake* Canada
    169 G9
Niš Yugoslavia 105 I6
Nissum Bredning *Sea feature*
    Denmark 258 B3
Nitra Slovakia 312 E8
Niue *External territory* New
    Zealand, Pacific Ocean 634 F7
Nizhnevartovsk Russian Federation
    731 E4
Nizhniy Novgorod Russian
    Federation 731 C3
Nizwa Oman 406 I5
Nkhotakota Malawi 30 G4
Nkongsamba Cameroon 20 B6
Noakhali Bangladesh 114 K8
Nogales Mexico 551 C1
Nordfjord *Coastal feature* Norway
    617 B7
Norfolk Island *External territory*
    Australia, Pacific Ocean 93
Nori'lsk Russian Federation 731 F3
Normandy *Region* France 356 C3
Norrköping Sweden 816 C8
Norrtälje Sweden 816 D7
North Albanian Alps *Mountains*
    Albania/Yugoslavia 105 G7
North America 611
North American Basin *Undersea*
    *feature* Atlantic Ocean 89 C5
North Atlantic Ocean 89 D3
North Bay Canada 169 I9
North Cape *Coastal feature* New
    Zealand 606 D1
North Cape *Coastal feature*
    Norway 617 G1
North Carolina *State* USA 864 J8
North Dakota *State* USA 864 F4
Northern Cook Islands *Islands*
    Cook Islands 679 F5
Northern Dvina *River* Russian
    Federation 308
Northern Ireland *Province* UK
    858 A6

169 F9
Winnipegosis, Lake *Lake* Canada 169 F9
Winterthur Switzerland 819 D4
Wisconsin *State* USA 864 H5
Wisła *River* Poland 312 F4
Wismar Germany 379 E3
W.J.van Blommesteinmeer *Reservoir* Surinam 791 J4
Włocławek Poland 312 E3
Wodzisław Śląski Poland 312 E6
Wolfsberg Austria 819 J5
Wolfsburg Germany 379 D4
Wollongong Australia 95 H6
Wŏnju South Korea 497 C6
Wŏnsan North Korea 497 C4
Worcester England, UK 858 D9
Wrangel Island *Island* Russian Federation 64 E2
Wrocław Poland 312 D5
Wuhan China 206 I6
Wuppertal Germany 379 B6
Würzburg Germany 379 D7
Wuxi China 206 J6
Wyndham Australia 95 D2
Wyoming *State* USA 864 D5

# X

Xaignabouri Laos 876 B4
Xi'an China 206 H6
Xiangkhoang Laos 876 C4
Xai-Xai Mozambique 30 G7
Xam Nua Laos 876 D3
Xánthi Greece 403 E4
Xingu *River* Brazil 146 F4

# Y

Yablonovyy Khrebet *Mountains* Russian Federation 731 H5
Yacuiba Bolivia 141 D7
Yafran Libya 28 I3
Yaku-shima *Island* Japan 478 B10
Yakutsk Russian Federation 731 I4
Yala Thailand 833 E13
Yalta Ukraine 727 I8
Yalu *River* China/North Korea 497 B2
Yamaguchi Japan 478 C8
Yamal, Poluostrov *Peninsula* Russian Federation 731 F3
Yambio Sudan 24 B8
Yambol Bulgaria 403 F3
Yamdena, Pulau *Island* Indonesia 451 J5
Yamoussoukro *Capital* Ivory Coast 33 E8
Yamuna *River* India 444 D4
Yanbu' al Baḥr Saudi Arabia 406 B4
Yangdŏk North Korea 497 B4
Yangtze *River* China *var.* Chang Jiang 206 I6
Yaoundé *Capital* Cameroon 20 C7
Yap *Island* Micronesia 636 B3
Yapen, Pulau *Island* Indonesia 451 K3
Yaqui *River* Mexico 551 D2
Yarmouth Canada 169 K8
Yaroslavl' Russian Federation

731 C3
Yazd Iran 463 G5
Yekaterinburg Russian Federation 731 D4
Yellow River *River* China *var.* Huang He 206 I5
Yellow Sea Pacific Ocean 206 J5
Yellowknife Canada 169 D6
Yĕloten Turkmenistan 80 E5
Yemen *Country* SW Asia 406
Yenakiyeve Ukraine 727 K4
Yenisey *River* Russian Federation 731 F4
Yerevan *Capital* Armenia 186 F5
Yevlax Azerbaijan 186 I4
Yevpatoriya Ukraine 727 H7
Yinchuan China 206 G5
Yogyakarta Indonesia 451 D5
Yokohama Japan 478 F7
Yola Nigeria 33 K7
Yŏngju South Korea 497 D6
Yopal Colombia 791 C4
York England, UK 858 E7
York, Cape *Coastal feature* Australia 95 G1
Yorkton Canada 169 E9
Yos Sudarso *Island* Indonesia 451 K5
Yŏsu South Korea 497 C8
Young Uruguay 65 E5
Ystad Sweden 816 B10
Yucatan Channel *Sea feature* Mexico 551 K4
Yucatan Peninsula *Peninsula* Mexico 551 K5
Yugoslavia *Country* SE Europe 105

Yukon *River* Canada/USA 611
Yukon Territory *Territory* Canada 169 A6
Yumen China 206 F4
Yuzhno-Sakhalinsk Russian Federation 731 K5
Yverdon Switzerland 819 A6

# Z

Zabīd Yemen 406 D8
Zacapa Guatemala 193 C4
Zadar Croatia 105 C5
Zagreb *Capital* Croatia 308 C2
Zagros Mountains *Mountain range* Iran/Iraq 463 F5
Zāhedān Iran 463 J6
Zahlé Lebanon 821 D5
Zaire *see* Congo (Zaire)
Zaječar Yugoslavia 105 I5
Zákynthos *Island* Greece 403 B8
Zalaegerszeg Hungary 312 D9
Zambezi *River* southern Africa 30 D4
Zambezi Zambia 30 D4
Zambia *Country* southern Africa 30
Zamboanga Philippines 650 D8
Zamora Spain 798 D3
Zanzibar *Island* Tanzania 24 E11
Zapala Argentina 65 B7
Zaporizhzhya Ukraine 727 I5
Zaqatala Azerbaijan 186 H3
Zarafshan Uzbekistan 80 F3
Zaragoza Spain 798 G3

Zaranj Afghanistan 80 D8
Zaria Nigeria 33 J7
Zeebrugge Belgium 126 B1
Zefat Israel 473 D2
Zell am See Austria 819 H5
Zenica Bosnia & Herzegovina 105 E5
Zeravshan *River* C Asia 80 H4
Zhambyl Kazakhstan 731 D7
Zhengzhou China 206 H5
Zhezkazgan Kazakhstan 731 D6
Zhlobin Belorussia 112 F8
Zhodzina Belorussia 112 F7
Zhytomyr Ukraine 727 F3
Zibo China 206 I5
Zielona Góra Poland 312 C4
Ziguinchor Senegal 33 A6
Žilina Slovakia 312 E7
Zimbabwe *Country* southern Africa 30
Zinder Niger 33 J6
Zoetermeer Netherlands 601 C5
Zomba Malawi 30 H4
Zouérat Mauritania 33 C3
Zrenjanin Yugoslavia 105 G3
Zug Switzerland 819 C5
Zürich Switzerland 819 C5
Zürich, L. *Lake* Switzerland 819 D5
Zuwārah Libya 28 H2
Zvornik Bosnia & Herzegovina 105 F4
Zwedru Liberia 33 D8
Zwickau Germany 379 F6
Zwolle Netherlands 601 E4

# PICTURE SOURCES

The publishers would like to thank the following for permission to use their photographs:

**Abbreviations:**
l:left, r:right, c:centre, a:above, b:below, t:top

## A,B,C

**Wallace & Gromit/Aardman Animations Ltd 1995:** 181bl **Robert Aberman:** 400crb, bla **ABI Caravans/Kenneth Berry Studios:** 168bla **Action-Plus:** S Bardens: 736ca, bcl, cb Chris Barry: 430cra, 818c, bra R Francis: 88c, 736bla Tony Henshaw: 351bc Glyn Kirk: 88crb, br, 411cb, 818tr P Tarry: 736bl **Advertising Archives:** 14tr **AEA Technology:** 618cbr **AIP Emilio Segre Visual Archives/ Dorothy Davis Locanthi:** 130cl **Airphoto Services:** 59tr **AKG London:** 49bc, 55br, 69c, 72cr, cl, 78crb, 79br, 97cbr, 123br, bcl, bca, 127tc, crb, 138bl, 269tr, ca Disney Enterprises Inc., 294tr, bl, 310cbl, 311cl, cr, 326cr, 359cr, 362tr , 373car, 381c, br, 382tr, br, 386br, 424crb, 428cb, bcl, 439cb, 477cr, br, 484cr, bc, 496cra, 498tcr, 507tr, 521bcr, 535c, cr, cb, 548br, 581tc, 573br, 580tr, bl, bc, br, 588bcl, 589cb, 594cl, cr, 638cr, 649cl, 652bl, 656tr, 671cr, cl, 684cra, crb, 704bl, br, crb, 708bc 724tr, 744br, 745bc, 753tr, 781cbl, 795c, 811tr, tlb, cr, cl, 841bra, 856tr, crb, Erich Lessing: 123trb, 191bc, 192cb, 197bc, 209cla, 228bl, 391tc, 401cl, 428bl, 484bla, c, 498bc, 543ca, cb, 580crb, 594tr, 632br, 648cr, 740br, 753br, 776tr, c Wolfe Fund, 1931, Catherine Lorillard Wolfe Collection, New York, Metropolitan Museum of Art: 776bc **Thanks to Alison/Oilily:** 14crb **Allsport:** 110bra, cra, 351crb, 351bca, 411clb, 430cbr, bcl, 628tr, 803ca, 897bc Agence Vandystadt/ S Cazenove: 736bcr/Richard Martin: 411ccl, 736br /A Patrice: 576cb Frank Baron: 251cr S Botterill: 897cal, cbl H Boylan: 577cbr S Bruly: 937tr Clive Brunskill: 803cr David Canon: 109br Chris Cole: 351crb, 430bl Phil Cole: 110bcl, 251trb Mike Cooper: 128cbr, 577car Stephen Dunn: 628cr Tony Duffy: 88clb S Forster: 577cbl J Gichigi: 736bc Bruce Hazellan: 110trb Mike Hewitt: 351cra, 577br, 829cr Hulton: 109bl, 351cr Info/Billy Stickland: 351br I.O.C.; 628clb D Kidd: 577cr JP. Lenfant: 430cb K Levine: 576bc Bob Martin: 577bl R Martin: 897braG Mortimore: 525cra, 628br Adrian Murrell: 109ca D Pensinger: 411cl Mike Powell: 88cr, 251bla Pascal Rondeau: 251crb, 363bl, 576tr, cr, 577tl, tr, 628bl, 897car, bcl, bl Jamie Squire: 818bcra M Stockman: 576bl Mark Thompson: 88bl, 576br Todd Warshaw: 897br **American Museum of Natural History:** 893br, 895br **Ancient Art & Architecture:** 62tc, 71tr, cl, tc, 73cl, 77cb, 103c, 160bra, 197bl, bcl, 198tr, bl, 233c, 247bra, 252ca, bc, 280cl, 288tr, 292bl, bc, 302t, 310cb, 425bl, cr, bra, c, cl, 427clb, bl, 428br, 434bc, 470bra, 477t, 480cr, cb, 498trb, 557cra, cr, bl, 602cla, 627c, 631cr, clb, bra, bl, br, 648bc, 649bla, bcl, bl, bcr, 652car, cbr, bc, 689cra, 691bl, 706bcl, 708cr, 716tr, 735cl, cr, br, cra, 738bl, 743bl, 752br, 762clb, 764tcr, 768bl, 800cr, 809bcr, 813bca L Ellison: 148tr Chris Hellier: 648clb Gianni Tortoli: 140clb **LJ Anderson Collection:** 69tr **Julie & Gillian Andrews:** 636crb **Anglo Australian Observatory:** 370ca, cb, cal **©Apple Corps. Ltd:** 121tr, bla, bca, bc **Aquila:** 260bcl, 779bc Les Baker: 133tr JJ Brooks: 39br Conrad Greaves: 780br Mike Lane:747c Mike Wilkes: 132bra, 345tr, 761bcr **Arcaid:** Esto/Ezra Stoller: 63br Dennis Gilbert: 63bla Ian Lambot: 63bl **Archiv zur Geschichte der Max-Planck-Gesellschaft, Berlin- Dahlem.** Nachlass Otto Hahn, III Abt., Rep. 14B Mappen Nr 15: 548cr **Archive Photos:** 18bc, 632cr **Archives Curie et Joliot-Curie:** 250c **Ardea:** 24ca, 118tl, 136bc, 261tcb, 319cr, 420cr, 492bl, 702tc, 755cl Ian Beames: 58crb, 165cl H&J Beste: 917ca R M Bloomfield: 761br B& S Bottomly: 55clb Coto Donana: 317bc Hans D Dossenbach: 58bl MD England: 512cb Jean Paul Ferrero: 472bc, 488blb, bcb, bcb, 672br, 899c Ferrero-Labat: 512tc Kenneth W Fink: 756tc, 904c R Gibbons: 235bcl Frances Gohier: 83bca, 260bla, 711cb, 912br Nick Gordon: 644bc Clem Haagner: 529crb Don Hadden: 747crb Masahiro Iijima: 472cbAke Lindau: 318c Eric Lindgren: 124clb John Mason: 82bl, 459tl, 687br, 749c B McDairmant: 33tr E Mickleburgh: 917tl P Morris: 58clb, 99c D Parer & E Parer-Cook: 23cla R.F.Porter: 713cl Graham Robertson: 647br Ron & Valerie Taylor: 337crb, 339tr Adrian Warren: 390bl Wardene Weisser: 260clb, 499c **Arxiumas:** 800c **ASAP:** S Uziel: 474tr **Ashmolean Museum, Oxford:** 707bcr **Australian National Maritime Museum, Sydney:** 97bc **Aviation Picture Library:** 225cr Austin J Brown: 278cr, 884bc, bl, c **A-Z Botanical:** A Cooper: 847cla Michael Jones: 585trbLino Pastorelli: 235br **Barnaby's Picture Library:** Brian Gibbs: 904bla Marc Turner: 590bc **BBC Natural History Unit Picture Library:** 257bcra Hans Christoph Kappel: 83cbl EA Kuttapan: 511cb N O'Connor: 154tr Ron O'Connor: 713tr Pete Oxford: 517cb Ian Redwood: 299br **Beethoven Archiv, Bonn:** 123c, bc, 589cl **Bavarian National Museum, Munich:** 653tr **Bibliotheque Nationale, Paris:** 359tc, 562 **Bildarchiv Preussischer Kulturbesitz:** 103bl **Bilderdienst Suddeutscher Verlag:** 224br **Biofotos:** Heather Angel: 74cr, 155cl, 667bc, 672bl Bryn Campbell: 56cr Geoff Moon: 235bcr Jason Venus: 872tr **Biophoto:** Prof GF Leedale: 405bl **Birds Eye/Walls:** 348l, clb, cb **Bodleian Library, Oxford:** 51bl **Thanks to Boots/Mellors:** 14br, bcl, bl **C Bowman (Photoscope):** 601bl **Kelvin Boyes:** 466cr **Bridgeman Art Library:** Albertina Graphic Collection, Vienna: 638cl, cra Alexander Turnbull Library, Wellington, N.Z.: 604cb Alte Pinakothek, Munich: 708br/Giraudon: 874bra Chris Beetles Ltd, London: 238trb Biblioteca Nazionale, Turin: 498bl, 707br Biblioteca Apostolica Vaticana: 546cl Bibliotheque Nationale, Paris: 197bcr, 361cal, 409tr, 447br, 495clb, 566cra Bonhams, London: 746tr British Library, London: 51crb, 138c, 183cla, 242ca, cl, 255cra, 301tr, 329bc, 469br, 495c, 531clb, 532tr, 543bla, 546tr, 566bl, 610crb, 671bcr, 673cr, 707cra, 735bl, 753cr British Museum: 85trb, 301bl, 725tr, 860cbr/Alecto Historical Editions: 238bla, 329bl Burghley House Collection, Lincolnshire: 704c Christie's Images, London: 73cr, 733cl Department of the Environment, London: 860bcl Fitzwilliam Museum, University of Cambridge: 47crb Galleria degli Uffizi, Florence: 477cal Giraudon:/Lauros: Archives Nationales, Paris: 741bla/Musee du Louvre, Paris: 358br/Musee de la Ville de Paris, Musee Carnavalet: 359tl Highgate Cemetry, London: 535br Historisches Museum der Stadt, Vienna: 123tr Imperial War Museum, London: 906bra Index: 768cbl Institute of Mechanical Engineers, London: 842crb Kremlin Museums, Moscow: 391tcr, 732cra Kunsthistorisches Museum: 302tr Lambeth Palace Library, London: 439bcr Maidstone Museum & Art Gallery, Kent: 861cA Meyer Collection, Paris: 811bc Mausoleo do Galla Placidia, Ravenna: 160bl Philip Mould, Historical Portraits Ltd., London: 800bl Mozart Museum, Salzburg/Giraudon: 123bl Musee des Beaux-Arts, Le Havre: 228br Musee Conde Chantilly: 547tr Musee de Picardie, Amiens/Giraudon: 213cr Musee díUnterlinden, Colmar, France: 381cl Musee National DíArt Moderne, paris: 72bc Museo Naval, Madrid/Index, Barcelona: 228tr Museo del Prado, Madrid: 140cra/Index: 334br Museum of Mankind, London: 531cl National Gallery, London: 507c National Library of Australia, Canberra: 238bc National Maritime Museum, London: 78clb, 301c, 631cb National Museum of India, New Dehli: 421bl, 455br, bcr, 493cl Oriental Museum, Durham University: 746tl, 764tcb, Private Collection: 360c, 371br, 498crb, 515bl, 708cra, 811trb, 826cl Rijksmuseum Kroller-Muller, Otterlo: 477cb Royal Asiatic Society, London: 201clb Royal Geographical Society, London: 673cra St Appollonia Museum, Florence: 515crb Santa Maria Novella, Florence: 71c Schloss Charlottenburg, Berlin: 391tr Thyssen Bornemisza Collection: 861tl Tretyakov Gallery, Moscow: 733tr Trinity College Dublin: 466ca Umayyad Mosque, Damascus, Syria: 470cr Vatican Museums & Galleries, Rome: 776cr Victoria and Albert Museum, London: 160cr, 484br, 587cl **Thanks to British Army Recruitment:** 68cl **BFI Stills, Posters & Designs:** 273cla, 331ca, cb, cbl, 332, 373cbl, 491bc, 656br **British Library, London:** 151clb, crb, 381bl, 448crb, 498bcr, 588bl **The British Museum:** 781bl Education Dept/Simon James: 724bc, 725tc **British Nuclear Fuels plc.:** 697bl **British Petroleum Company plc:** 378br, 626tr, 716bc **The Bronte Society:** 149cr, cl, bcl **SG Brown:** 598crb **Brown Brothers:** 658cb, 868cbr **Tony Weller/The Builder Group:** 157cla, cl **Photographie Bulloz:** Bibliotheque de lìInstitut de France: 507cr, 562 **Michael Busselle:** 116cra **Michael Butler Collection:** 382cb **CADW:** 182tr, cl, c **By Permission of the Syndics of Cambridge University Library:** 607trb, bc **Camera Press:** 254clb, 288bl, 344crb, 376br, 438cr, br, 542tl, 575trb, 775cr, 944cr, cl, 948cr William Carter: 821br A Mamedov: 187br Gavin Smith: 941crb The Times/M Ellidge: 742br Camera Press Ltd: cr **Canon:** 163bl **Canterbury Archaelogical Trust:** 765tr **Mark Carwardine:** 894tl, cl **J Allan Cash Ltd.:** 33c, 76car, 85bc, 209c, 242bca, 312tr, cl, 380c, 404cb, 434br, 473c, 476bc, 490cr, 521bl, 523c, 547cr, 601trc, 610trc, 617bl, 650tr, 683tl, ca, bl, 693br, 706br, 798crb, 799tc, 816clb, 859tl, 823bl, bc **Cephas: Stockfood:** 268br **Channel Four Publicity:** 829br **Mark Chapman:** 152cra, 388tr, 706bcr **Jean Loup Charmet:** 18clb, 205t, 361cbr, 490cla, bc, 566br, 594cra, 781cl Musee Carnavelet: 361ca **Lester Cheeseman:** 25t, 152bc, 833bc **By Permission of the Chelsea Physic Garden:** 510bl **Reproduced by Kind Permission of the Trustees of the Chester Beatty Library, Dublin:** 581cb **Thanks to Chisenhale Castle:** 72bcr **Thanks to the Master & Fellows of Churchill College, Cambridge:** 548tr, bc, cl **CIRCA/Icorec:** 138bra R Beeche: 422tc BJ Mistry: 422bl **Civil Aviation Authority:** 598c **John Cleare/Mountain Camera:** 168cr **"Coca-Cola"** Coke and the design of the contour bottle are registered trademarks of the Coca-Cola Company: 262cl **Stephanie Colasanti:** 450crb **Bruce Coleman:** 118ca, 284br, 761clb, 779bca, br, cr, 822cr Stefano Amantini: 20cla Atlantide: 309cbr, 317bca Trevor Barrett: 234bra Jen & Des Bartlett: 99bcl, 245clb, 384cr, 633br Erwin & Peggy Bauer: 299cb, 512tr, cr, 518br, 699bc, 889cbr, 917clb M Berge: 637tr George Bingham: 96bc E Bjurstrom: 406cr Nigel Blake: 747bl M Borchi: 450br Mark N Boulton: 104cr Fred Bruemmer: 16cra, 674bca, 748bc, 821car Thomas Buchholz: 617t Jane Burton: 74cl, bcr, 82bc, 166bc, 184bla, 420c, 500ca, 622bcl, 699clb, 793crb, 872cr B & C Calhoun: 492tcr, 609bc John Cancalosi: 694bcr, 773tr, 793br Robert P Carr: 155crb Mark Carwardine: 23bl, 518tr Brian J Coates: 55tr Alain Compost: 452bcl, 571bcr, 916cb J Cowan: 665crb, 918cl Gerald Cubitt: 94crb, 235ccr, 524bl, 571bcl, 644br P Davey: 556cr Tony Deane: 258ca Stephen J Doyle: 94ca Francisco J Erize: 57c, 748br Dr P Evans: 472br Jeff Foott: 57clb, 300cl, 751bl, 846bc Christer Fredriksson: 350cra, 816br MPL Fogden: 364clb, 395br, 397tc, 773tl917cr Tor Oddvar Hansen: 747bc BS Henderson: 567cl PA Hinchliffe: 600bl Charles & Sandra Hood: 55bcl, 239cb HPH Photography/Philip vd Berg: 55cl Carol Hughes: 772cl Johnny Johnson: 300cbr, 499t, 675c Janos Jurka: 309car, 674bra, 816ca Dr MP Kahl: 50cl, 343c Steven C Kaufman: 675cr, 694cl Stephen S Krasemann: 117crb, 235bc, 694bl H Lange: 399bc Gordon Langsbury: 74cb Wayne Lankinen: 346bl , 612cal, 761cla Werner Layer: 350crr, 579bc Dr. John Mackinnon: 57br, 640cr Luiz Claudio Marigo: 669cra, 788c McAllister: 406bl, 449br George McCarthy: 90brb, 397tl, 517bl, 585tr Hans Peter Merten: 258ca, 819ca Rinie van Meurs: 674bla, 748clb J Murray: 465br Dr Scott Nielson: 133cr Charlie Ott: 714tcr MR Phicton: 241c Dieter & Mary Plage: 154cr, 647c Dr Eckhart Pott: 136tc, 500bc, 674tr Allan G Potts: 319crb Dr S Prato: 346bla, 472crb Fritz Prenzel: 801bl MP Price: 585cla Andy Purcell: 53bcl Hans Reinhard: 154bla, 235bcl, 513cl, 748bcl, 756tr, 761bcl Dr Frieder Sauer: 500bla, 754bl, 801cra Norbert Schwirtz: 258br John Shaw: 120cl, 714tr Kim Taylor: 54bra, 155br, 158tr, 241bl, 327bl, 342bl, 343bc, 459cl, cbr, 665bc, 780tl, tr, car NO Tomalin: 489bra , 612bla, N de Vore: 449t, 472ca Uwe Walz/GDT: 675tc Rod Williams: 571ca Konrad Wothe: 657tr Gunther Zeisler: 118cl, 556tr, 916bca **Colorific!:** Bill Bachman: 11crb, br Steve Benbow: 268cr, 646cr Randa Bishop: 173bl Pierre Boulat/Cosmos: 29br Catherine Cabrol/GLMR: 790cb Robert

E Ferorelli: 194bl Sylvain Grandaden: 11tr A Joyce: 464cl Catherine Karnow: 174bl J Lassila: 862cla Kay Muldoon: 784bl Jim Pickerell: 66bc J Quiggin: 938t Snowden/Hoyer/Focus: 852tc Penny Tweedie: 11tl, 408cra Richard Wilkie/Black Star: 669crb Rod Williams: 423b Konrad Wothe: 283cb Michael Yamashita: 637tl, 877crb G Ziesler: 440tr **Colorsport:** 88bcl, 380tr, 411c, cclb, 430br, 818br, 937tl, cl **Dee Conway:** 108crb, bl, br, 253cr, ccr, br, 254cla **Coo-ee Historical Picture Library:** 604cbr, bl **Steven J Cooling:** 39bc, bcl, 397cbr, 615bra, 616tc, 690br **Donald Cooper, Photostage:** 272bl, 753bc, 939bc **Cooper Hewitt; National Design Museum, Smithsonian Institution, Art Resource, New York, Gift of Gary Loredo:** 382c **Corbis:** 11bra, 131br, 502cr, 531cr, br, 632c, trb, 728bcl, 760br, 845bc Bettmann: 48bc, 255tr, 294bcr, 360cra, 362br, 372tcr, 457bl, 482cbl, 491cr, br, 596cr, 605crb, 760cb, 763cbr, cbl, 768br, 849t, cl, bl 869tr, 886cl, cr, cb, ca/Reuter: 845bl Bettmann/UPI: 244cr, 269bcr, 275bla, 297crb, 368br, 372cr, 438c, 461bcl, bl, 485cra, 491c, bcr, tr, 503cra, 516br, 671bra, 719tcl, 783bl, 818bla, 869cr, cl, 882bca Jan Butchofsky-Houser: 845tr Ecoscene /Sally Morgan: 671br Everett: 373bl R Hamilton Smith: 865br Wolfgang Kaehler: 729cr Library of Congress: 373t Roman Soumar: 210br UPI: 121c Michael Yamashita: 865tc **Sylvia Cordaiy:** Guy Marks: 15crb, 25br **Costas, New York:** 108bc © The George Balanchine Trust **Courtauld Institute Galleries, London:** 161cb **Croation Catholic Mission:** 575tr **Crown Reserved/Historic Scotland:** 861cl **Culver Pictures Inc.:** 373ca **Mr B J Curtis:** 763br **Cycleurope:** 129tcl

# D,E

DACS, 1997: 477cb **Succession Picasso:** 656bl, c, cr, cl **Paul Daigle:** 38cl **Dartington Crystal Ltd:** 387clb **James Davis Travel:** 66cal, 175tr, 195cbl, 845ca Sveti Stefan: 107tr **Defence Picture Library:** 885clb **Department of Defense, Pentagon:** 887bl **Deutsches Museum, Munich:** 548c, ccr **Dickens House Museum:** 263cl **Dinodia:** Milind A Ketkar: 444t **Disney Enterprises, Inc.:** 269bl **CM Dixon:** 388tcr, 401clb, br, 447tr, 610br, 613bcl, 724cr, 878bl/National Archaeological Museum, Rome: 776crb **Christopher Dobrowolski:** 745cl **Dominic Photography:** 629cbl Catherine Ashmore: 272crb, 629cb Zoe Dominic: 629ca, 836tlb, cl, c **Durban Local History Museum, South Africa:** 372tr **Dyson Ltd:** 262tr, ca, car **Ecoscene:** 523tr Andre DR Brown: 309cal, cbl Donachie: 56br Farmar: 89crb Nick Hawkes: 642br W Lawler: 636bc R Wright: 850blb **EDF Production Transport:** 252cb **Edinburgh University:** 560trb, tr, c **EMI:** 121 **Environmental Images:** Steve Morgan/WIT Wildlife: 234bc**Environmental Picture Library:** Martin Bond: 678br Stewart Boyle: 304ccr Jordi Cami: 883cl David Hoffman: 304tr J Hodson: 883crb Jimmy Holmes: 678cl Steve Morgan: 680br John Novis: 304cr Alex Olah: 353br Peter Rowlands: 894tcPeter Solness: 637crb **Robert Estall Photo Library:** 37br, 170bra, cl, tr,cr Thomas Kelly: 115cb **ET Archive:** 71clb, 116br, 213br, 225cr, 381tr, 469tl, 510tr, 515cl, bc, 588cb, 614cra, 630tr, 738ca, 786tlb, 910bc Archaeological Museum, Venice: 161cl Archive of the Indies, Seville: 789cra British Museum: 320bl, 587tr Chiaramonti Museum, Vatican: 402cb Freer Gallery of Art: 73tc London Museum: 786cl National Museum of History, Lima: 140tr, 790tr National Museum of India: 455cb Plymouth City Art Collection: 659bc Trinity College, Dublin: 214bca Uffizi Gallery, Florence: 214cr Vienna Societa Amici dell Musica : 629cbr **European Space Agency:** 720r **Greg Evans International:** 444ca, 504ca, 505tl, 551crb, 728tr, 784br, 823cb **Mary Evans Picture Library:** , 45bla, 47cb, 49bra, trb, cla, crb, 51ca, cr, 78bc, 97cbl. bca, br, 101br, bc, 116clb, 140bl, 144br, 149bca, 161cbl, bc, 163bca, 166bl, 176bc, 190bl, 191br, 192crb, 197tr, 203br, 210c, cr, 212tr, 227bl, 233tr, bl, 236bra, 238bl, bcr, 247bla, 250tr, cr, bca, trb, 255cb, 263bl, 272trb , 295bl, 296bl, 301ccl, 302cla, bl, crb, br, 303bl, 304bc, 310bc, 311tr, 320cr, clb, 321bl, cr, 326cbr, 352cr, 358car, 359bl, 361bcl, 382cl, 388cbl, bl, 392br, 399tr, 402clb, 413bcl, 416tr, 427crb, br, 439bl, cr, 442bcr, tr, 448tr, cra, 467bl, 470c, 480tr, 481t, 484bl, tr, 485tr, 502bl, 504bra, 509tr, 515cr, 522bl, 526bl, 535cl, 536br, 544cl, bl, 560br, bc, 564t, 582bl, 587cb, 588cr, 594bl, 595cl, cb, 602cbl, 608tr, 610bra, 614tr, 630cbr, 641bc, 645tr, 651cl, 659bl, 673cl, 676tr, 690cl, 704cr, 733tc, 734br, 738bc, 743br, 744tr, 745bl, 753bra, trb, 768car, cbr, bcl, 789cl, 812br, 828bl, 844, 845car, 862tr, 868cb, 882bl, 883tr, 887cl, 898cl, cr, bc, 901tr, 906c, 907bl, 933crb, 941tc, bl, br Explorer: 108c, 361car, cr Fawcett Library: 641t, tr, cra, cb, cr, c, br, 901ccl Institution of Civil Engineers: 148bra Alexander Meledin Collection: 734tr Smith College Library: 710tr **Eye Ubiquitous:** 112ca Paul Bennett: 93b David Cumming: 173br, 798cr G Hanly: 531crb John Hulme: 799cr Matthew McKee: 636tr

# F,G,H

**Chris Fairclough Colour Library:** 403blb, 705bcr **Ffotograff:** Patricia Aithie: 138br, 706bca **Martin Foote:** 11bl, 94cr, 95tc, crb, 217bcl, 282cr, 653bc, 698crb, br, 808cl, 845cb **Footprints:** 450bc **Ford Motor Company Ltd:** 178cra, 305c, 363cr **Werner Forman Archive:** 17c, 480cl, 481bl, 593tc, 648c, 649br, 705tcr, 743cr, 786tr British Museum: 127bl Dallas Museum of Art, USA: 198bcl , 627l Courtesy Entwistle Gallery, London: 17trb Philip Goldman Collection: 77clb Museum f¸r Volkerkunde, Berlin: 17br, 442c National Museum, Lagos, Nigeria: 73tl Peabody Museum, Harvard University, Cambridge, MA: 613bl Private Collection: 233cb, crb, 480bcr, crb, 738c, cb Schindler Collection, New York: 442c Statens Historiska Museum, Stockholm: 935tr V & A Museum: 480br **Format:** Jacky Chapman: 274bc, 275tl Sheila Gray: 901cr Brenda Prince: 335tr **Fortean Picture Library:** 898bl Janet & Colin Bord: 593cb, bl, 762c Dr ER Gruber: 898cal **Fotomas Index:** 526ca, car, 841tcr **Fototeca:** Cesar Soares : 684tr **French Railways Ltd:** 357crb **Freud Museum, London:** 362ca, cb, cl, trb **Paul Gallagher:** 28car **Garden Picture Library:** John Bethell: 374cr, crb C Fairweather: 374cl **Genesis:** 86bra, 797tl, tr **Geological Society Library:** 279br **Geoscience Features Picture Library:** 222bl, 304tc, 655crb, 697bla, 715cl, 715cr, 777blc, 880cl **Geoslides Photolibrary:** 35cr **Giraudon:** 123cr, 198cr, 546bla, 627cb Bibliotheque Nationale, Paris: 329cl Index: 789crb Musee Carnavalet: 361cb D Corrige: 835bcl National Museum, Bangkok: 490br **Jane Goodall Institute:** 390cr, c, crb David Greybeard: 390cla **Granger Collection, New York:** 287cra, c, 360bl, cr, br, cl, tr, 491cl, bl, 856cra, bc **Ronald Grant Archive:** 149bc, 204ccl, cr, br, 244cla, 331cla, 373bc, 388c, 402crb, 516crb, 593cal, bc, 629bl, 719tl, 738br, 789bl, 869crb BBC Press Service: 516bcl CBS/Fox Video: 516trb ( Disney Enterprises, Inc.: 269crb, clb, 331cbb First Independent: 181tr **Guy Gravett/ Glyndebourne, Sussex:** 205clb **Sally & Richard Greenhill:** 14cr, 288crb, 433br, 716cbl, 775ca Kaye Mayers: 213c **Denise Grieg:** 99crb, 100bra Pavel German: 99c, bl, 100br, 488cra, ca, cb, 489bc Nature Focus/GB Baker: 99cl Dominic Chaplin: 100cb/John McCann: 488bla/D Crossman: 489bcr/Gunther Schmida: 99bcr/Tony Stanton: 99tc /AD Trounson: 99cra /Dave Watts: 100cl, cr, clb /Babs & Bert Wells: 99br **Sonia Halliday:** 103br, 160c, bla, 214tc, 427cr, 486tr, 560cr, 605tr, 746bl FHC Birch: 214br Bibliotheque Nationale: 160bca FHC Birch: 401crb Laura Lushington: 669bl, 860bl B Searle: 486cr Jane Taylor: 422br **Hamlyn:** 203clb **Robert Harding Picture Library:** 29tr, 31tl, tc, 77cr, bl, 79cr, 81crb, bc, 101bcl, 153crb, 156t, 157tc, tr, tl, 171tr, bc, 187cla, 194cr, 207cr, bra, 217bcr, 228bc, 288cr, 306cra, 308cl, 315cr, 322bc, 329cr, 356tr, 357bcr, 382clb, 388br, 400cr, 404cl, 406cl, 410cl, 433tr, bcr, 435tl, 442ca, 446cl, t, c, 464c, cbl, 478cl, 490t, clb, 520cr, 526c, 539bl, cr, 547c, 567tr, 587br, 589tl, 612cbl, 614clb, 627cr, 646cb, 689crb, 760tr, 785cl, cr, 792tc, 834cr, 836br, 858cr, 860ca, 868br, 869cb Craig Aurness: 237cr, 559cl Bibliotheque Nationale, Paris: 610cl Bildagenteur Schuster: 847cla, 857cl Alexandre: 17bra /Waldkirch: 380cra N Blythe: 435bcr C Briscoe Knight: 758crb C Bryan: 37tc Camerapix: 19cr Jacky Chapman: 40tr M Chillmaid: 433bl M Collier: 391bl, 635br G & P Corrigan: 206l, 207tr Philip Craven: 610tc, c, A L Durand: 312bl Victor Englebert: 21br, 37bl, cb M Leslie Evans: 27tl Alain Everard: 78cr Explore: 26br FPG International: 48clb, c, 614bca/Icon communications: 869bl Nigel Francis: 681bc Robert Francis: 65tr, 157br, 175cl, 237tr, 476tl Robert Frerck: 66cbr, 516tr, 551ca, 799bl Tony Gervis: 307b, 403cbr K Gillham: 176bra, 404tl, 788cra Gottier: 323cr J Green: 406tr I Griffiths: 520cl Susan Griggs: 650cr Dominic Hanouert-Webster: 816cl Simon Harris: 311br Kim Hart: 90ca G Hellier: 28tr, 77br, 80cra, 152br, 478cra, 481cb, 581tr, crb Walter Hodges,Westlight: 544cra David Martyn Hughes: 681br Uzaemon Ichimura: 836bla IPC Magazines/Womans Journal/James Marrell: 368bl Dave Jacobs/All Rights Reserved: 655crbb F. Jackson: 17cl, 424cla Michael Jenner: 374cra, 408br, 681bl, 760bc, 774bc Victor Kennet: 198c Paolo Koch: 822tl Krafft: 634cr Leimbach: 254tl J Lightfoot: 34bl, 174br R Ian Lloyd: 760cl David Lomax: 208cr, 435tlb, 466br M Long: 214cl T Magor: 424bl Buddy Mays/International Stock: 818crb R McLeod: 923bc HP Merten: 840tr MPH: 684ca L Murray: 403cbl, 404bc Gary Norman/ Operation Raleigh: 792cb David Poole: 27bc, 526cbr Madhya Pradesh: 201bc Rainbird Collection: 94bl Roy Rainford: 126bl, 471bra, 865tlb Walter Rawlings: 63bra, 610tr Geoff Renner: 28tr, 66b, 922trr Chris Rennie: 80tr, cr R Richardson: 392cl, 876t Paul van Riel: 637cra, 763c Jan Robinson: 328c Phil Robinson: 106cl, 314 tcb SADA: 448clb Sasoon: 187ca Sybil Sasson: 447cr JWW Shakespeare: 333ca M Short: 310br James Strachan: 80bl, 682cra S Terry: 475trb Tomlinson: 798tr Adine Tory: 803tr W Westwater: 435tcr JHC Wilson: 448cb Adam Woolfitt: 175tl, 182bl, 183crb, 312bc, 333bl, 524cl, 543bl, 689cr, 799cl, 835br, 838tl, 852cl, tl, 853tr, 859ca 922bl Jim Zuckerman/Westlight: 403br **Harper Collins Publishers Ltd:** 204c, 516bla **Graham Harrison:** 153cra **Harvard University Archives:** 808bc **Hauptstaatsarchiv, Stuttgart:** 400bl **Hencomp Enterprises:** 660br **Jim Henson's Creature Shop:** 331c **Hoa-Qui: Kraft/Explorer:** 880br **Reproduced by Permission of Hodder & Stoughton:** 204cl **Michael Holford:** 51clb, 73cb, 85tr, 116bla, bl, bcl, bcr, 160br, 310bl, 320cl, 424c, 425c, 442bc, 470bl, 495cl, 549clb, 587crb, 593cbr, 649c, 671cl, 738tr, 813cr, cl, ccl, bla, 944cb British Museum: 62t, 253clb, bl, 311bl, 619cl, 652ca, clb, cb, 740tr, 882cr Musee de Bayeux: 860crMusee Guimet: 448bl V & A Museum: 581cblWellcome Collection: 544tr **Thelma Holt/Alastair Muir:** 272cr **Holt Studios International:** 683cl Duncan Smith: 326br **Honda UK:** 128crb **Chris Howes:** 689crb **Christopher Howson:** 375bca **Hulton Getty:** 45cr, 59br, 62bl, 79tl, 98clb, 108clb, bcl, 121cr, 176cl, clb, bca, 158bla, 161tr, 194c, crb, bl, 203bl, 225cb, 248cra, 250bc, 254bl, 255bra, 262br, 266tr, Disney Enterprises, Inc.: 269trb, 272cl, 274bl, 294bc, 331tr, 362bra, bl, 372bl, 373crb, cb, 399bra, cl, cla, bl, 409bl, 415bl, 426cr, br, 448br, 481cla, c, 482bla, 542cl, 560bra, 580cra, cr, 607tr, br, cl, 608cra, bc, bl, 619br, 629tr, 632tr, 645c, bcr, 673bl, 718c, 718crb, 734cl, 740bl, 790cbr, bla, 812tr, 814bl, 829tr, 836bl, 861bl, crb, 868cbl, 869clb, 882cr, 901ca, 905c, cl, 907crb, bra, 908cl, cr, 912tr, 938b, 939bla, 940bra MPI: 399trb **Hunterian Museum:** 354c **Hutchison Library:** 19c, 21t, 30ca, 31tcl, 79bl, 308ca, 328cr, 446cra, 463tr, br, 469tcr, 785ccl, 787c, 791l Timothy Beddow: 26clb, 34tc TE Clark: 477car R Constable: 407tr Christine Dodwell: 32bl, 76cl John Downman: 611tr Sarah Errington: 24b, 115tc, 762crb Robert Francis: 65bc, 195tc, cal, c, 859br Melanie Friend: 106cb, 107clb, c, crb B Gerard: 587bl G Goodger: 859bc P Goycolea: 445tr Maurice Harvey: 36cra, 36br, 172bl Nick Haslam: 112br, 727cr J Henderson: 174car Andrew Hill: 32tl Jeremy A Horner: 77bc, 285t, 590c, 790br Eric Lawrie: 792cra Ingrid Hudson: 784tl Crispin Hughes: 105t, 106bl, 526cbl Eric Lawrie: 141c, 286tc, 787t R Ian Lloyd: 208tl, 449cb, 931cl Michael Macintyre: 637cl B Moser: 596br, 877br Trevor Page: 81tr, 187clb, 253ccl, 706bra Edward Parker: 285br, 286c, br, tcb, 552br PE Parker: 21c Christine Pemberton: 649tr S. Pern: 35br, 67cl, 567br Bernard Règent: 22cl,cr, 96cl K Rogers: 669bcr Nigel Sitwell: 78tr A Sole: 497tl, tr A Silvertop: 931c Tony Souter:

193tr, 194tl **Panos Pictures:** 19cb, 29cl, 186bl, 207br, 785bra Martin Adler: 23br, 194bcla Kathie Atkinson: 771cal P Barker: 32br, 106t, 148cra Giuseppe Bizzarri: 252bl Trygue Bolstad: cbl, 785bla JC Callow: 114tr, 115c Ian Cartwright: 36cla Alfredo CedeÒo: 788tr, 851trb David Constantine: 876brNeil Cooper: 115tr, 194trb, cra Rob Cousins: 784cl Jean Leo Dugast: 444b, 524cr, 760bl, 833cra, 834bc, bl N Durrell McKenna: 67t Marc French: 174cal, t CG Gardener: 770tr Ron Giling: 27cr, 33cr, 650bc, bcl Mark Hakansson: 728tc Jeremy Hartley: 34cl, ca, 35bc, 114bc, 323tr, 452tl Jim Holmes:76clb, 449c, 497bl, bc Rhodri Jones: 186c, cr Victoria Keble-Williams: 16cla B Klass: 114bla Pat & Tom Leeson/Photo Researchers: 54cb G Mansfield: 408tc J. Marks: 31bl, 785bl Jon Mitchell: 195bl James Morris: 37cl, c S Murray: 866trb Shanon Nace: 115cbr Zed Nelson: 115tl M O'Brien: 173t Trevor Page: 26cla, 497br Bruce Paton: 323bl N Peachey: 78cla Betty Press: 26t, crb, bl, 35bla, 930bl David Reed: 30cr, 31br Marcus Rose: 77cl, 731cr D Sansoni: 444cb, 446br, 450tl, cl, 524br Marc Schlossman: 20cra, 23ca, cra, 716br J Shanerly 877c Jon Spaull: 731cl,Sean Sprague: 22br, 23bc, 142tl Chris Stowers: 208tc, cl, 451br, 452bc, 525bc, 728tl Tayacon: 523cl Liba Taylor: 23cl, 314tc, 348ca, 727cl, 803bcl, Penny Tweedie: 32tc, 253cl, 408cla Max Whitaker: 218cb, bl, bcl Gregory Wrona: 313cr, 728bcr **Parker Library, Corpus Christie, Cambridge:** 51bra **WR Pashley Ltd:** 129cla **David Paterson:** 473tr, crb **Penguin Children's Books:** 204cb **Ann & Bury Peerless:** 151cr, 214bra, 447cl, 487tcr, 705bl **Performing Arts Library:** Clive Barda: 273cra, crb, 630cra Fritz Curzon: 253tr **Photo Researchers Inc.:** Tom McHugh: 154br **Pictor:** 67cr, 94clb, 126tc, 169l, 175br, 208bl, 379cr, 404bl, 476c, 601cr, 749tr, 822cl **Pictorial Press:** 718bc **Pictures Colour Library:** 314bl, 404cra, 475tr, 617cl, br, 821cal, 822br **Graham Piggott:** 788cr **Ian Pillinger:** 41cra, 45b, 46 **The Planetarium:** 651cra Jill Plank: 283bl **Planet Earth Picture Library:** 217br, bcr, bcl, 241br, 472tr, 810bl, bc, 812cl K & K Ammann: 450tc Kurt Amsler: 194bra Sean T Avery: 38cla Andre Barstchi: 714cr Gary Bell: 635car, 672bcr S Bloom: 440cra Myer S Bornstein: 616tcb John R Bracegirdle: 234br, 317tcr, 353bcr, 533t Philip Chapman: 189cr Mary Clay: 396cb, 756br M Conlin: 556ca Richard Coomber: 616cl, 715c Rob Crandall: 788cl, 794tc Beth Davidson: 616bl, bc Wendy Dennis: 317bra G Douwma: 916ca, cbbr John Downer: 82tr, 299tr, 396br, 609bra J Eastcott: 793bla Ivor Edmonds: 385br, 398cbr John Evans: 162clb Elio Della Ferrera: 39cr Nigel Downer: 316bla Alain Dragesco: 39tl C Farneti: 793ccr D Robert Franz: 616tcr, tr Nick Garbutt: 571bl, bc Roger de la Harpe: 39tr, 785t, bc Steve Hopkin: 750ca K Jayaram: 82cl Adam Jones: 616ca, tc Anthony Joyce: 397bc Brian Kenney: 256br Alex Kerstitch: 770cl David Kjaer: 317cbr Ken Lucas: 39cr, 235bla, 615cbr, 616bcr, 770br D Lyons: 579tr John Lythgoe: 615bcl, 793t David Maitland:802bc Richard Matthews: 57bl, 353bc, 794crb Mark Mattock: 289cal David Jesse McChesney: 777bl Dr Martin Merker: 756bl , cr Jon & Alison Moran: 699br P de Oliveira: 916crb Pete Oxford: 162bl , 640cbr, 794cal David A Panton: 616tl Doug Perrine: 622t, 755bra C Petron: 599cbr Linda Pitkin: 239ccr Rod Planck: 616bca Mike Potts: 615c Mike Read: 316crb Keith Scholey: 794tr, bc Peter Scoones: 38br, 483cr, 534bc Johnathon Scott: 38bcl, 39bl , 165bl, 396bl, 506bc Seaphot/Dick Clarke: 239cr/J & G Lythgoe: 568cl N Sefton: 472cr, 483clb Anup & Manuj Shah: 38c, 82cb M Snyderman: 483bl Peter Stephenson: 83bc Jan Tore Johansson: 317br Mills Tandy: 616br Nigel Tucker: 82cr Peter Velensky: 82bca Tom Walker: 615bcr, cb, 616crb John Waters: 83tc, 787cb JD Watt: 919cr Margaret Welby: 793c Bill Wood: 909bra Andrew Zvoznikov: 729t **Polish Cultural Institute Library:** 313cra **Popperfoto:** 18cr, bl, bc, 19cl, 45ca, cla, cra, 72bl, 79tr, c, 225tr, cbr, br, 251bl, 301cr, 344cb, 359bra, 372c, 530bl, trb, 628cla, 632bc, 646cl, bl, 659br, 684bl, 719tr, 736cr, 742cl, 786bla, 818bl, 829crb, 831cl, 887crb 905bc, 908tr, cla, clb, 944cla, 947cb, 948br Brunskill: 411cr Liaison/Magani: 582br Reuters: 14cb, cl, 618cbr, 675cl, 857bla/Peter Andrews: 786br **Premaphotos Wildlife:** KG Preston Mafham: 100tc, 794bcr **Pressens Bild:** 520bra, 857crb **Public Record Office:** 247bl Crown: 861bc **Quadrant Picture Library:** 179tr, ca, 180bra, 306tl, 842bcl, bcr, 843cb

# R,S,T,

**Racal:** 695c **RAF Museum, Hendon:** 485cbr, br **Railtrack North West:** 842clb **Redferns:** 121bca, 482c, 587bc Michael Ochs Archives: 482bl Pankaj Shah: 587tc **Renault:** 357clb **Reunion des Musees Nationaux:** 151tr, 835cb **Rex Features:** 68bcr, 171cbr, 219cl, 275trb, 331tc, 340br, 391clb, 530br, tr, 581bl, 575bcr, 718clb, 718bl, 719bl, 727t, 790bca, 861crb, 881cl, 884bla, 896tr, 939bcla, bra, 940cra, cr Action Press: 841c Agence DPPI: 897ca, cr ANP Foto: 862trb Jonathon Buckmaster: 40bl Jorgensen: 457tr Clive Dixon: 29bcr, 380bl T Doccon-Gibod: 311cb Fotos International/Frank Edwards: 254br Malcolm Gilson: 311crb Tony Larkin: 219cr Brian Rasic: 719br Sipa Press: 176crb, 210trb, 210crb, 359cb, 411cbr, 530crb, c, 684bc, 834tr, 887bcr, 923bl, 932cr Foulon/Tavernier: 303cl Stills: 254bcl Tom Stockhill: 19bl Greg Williams: 153bl Richard Young: 653br **Roskilde Festival:** 328bc **Rover Group:** 859bca **The Rowland Company/Ariel:** 277trb **The Royal Collection** 1997 Her Majesty Queen Elizabeth II: 507bl, 708cl **Royal College of Music, Junior Department:** 630bl **Royal College of Physicians:** 654br **Royal Geographical Society, London:** 521cl, 810br **Royal Photographic Society, Bath:** 693cra **Charles Russell:** 120bl **The Sainsbury Centre for Visual Arts:** 746bcr, bla **Peter Sanders:** 407tl, cl, cr, 435tr, 468cr, 469c, bl **Hans Sas Fotografie:** 324cl. cr **NJ Saunders:** 73clb **Floyd Sayers:** 282clb, cb, 300t, bcr, 667ca, 916bra **Scala:** 72tr, 215cb, 307cl, 329tc, 401tr, 402ca, 583cr, cl, 708bra, 724c, ccr, 746bc, bra, 813br Accademia, Venice: 707bcl Biblioteca Mariana, Venice: 707cla S Pietra, Vatican: 707bl **Science Photo Library:** 91br, 131cr, 199cl, 226bl, 230c, 278bc, 287tr, 298br, 306bl, 319br, 354br, 363br, 375cra, 376bcr, 378cl, 398cb, 456tr, 501bc, 559cr, 584br, 585bcl, bcr, 598bca, 661bc, 696bl, 743bc, 778bc, 782br, 796bl, 829bc, 838crb Agema Infra Red Systems: 911cr Los Alamos Photo Laboratory: 618br Doug Allan: 56tr Peter Arnold Inc/Volker Steger: 457tc/Szuson J Wong: 542bl Bill Bachman: 230bl Alex Bartel: 296cra A Barrington Brown: 87bra Alex Bartel: 298bcl, 558br, 584br Julian Baum: 814cr Tim Beddow: 542ccl, c Biology Media: 441cl Martin Bond: 12bc, 252car, 387cr, 740bc Dr Tony Brain: 138cl, 916clb Dr Eli Brinks: 744cl BSIP Laurent: 145crb BSIP LECA: 144cl BSIP VEM: 264crb, 769c BSIP Taulin: 441br Dr Jeremy Burgess: 190cl, 231bra, 342cb, 371tr, 584cl, 585bcra, 626cbl, 767c, 815br, 870clb, 871crb Mark Burnett: 45clb CC Studio: 766br 742cr Cern, P.Loiez: 655cbb J Loup Charmet: 697cl, 871cb Pr S Cinti, Universite díAncone: 873clb Mark Clarke: 268clb Clinique Ste Catherine/CNRI: 744bl CNES, 1990 Distribution Spot Image: 259br, 532br CNRI: 376cl, 643tc/RM Tektoff: 555tc Prof C Terlaud: 542ccr Andy Crump, TDR, WHO: 863tr, 933tr W Curtsinger: 912trb Custom Medical Stock Photo: 145tc, 645cr/R Becker: 414bc, 441c Mike Devlin: 376c Luke Dodd: 370clb, 538br Martin Dohrn: 221bl, 268bc, 643br John Durham: 654cra Ralph Eagle: 322bcar Harold Edgerton: 653: lb ESA: 230cl Dr F Espenak: 739ccl Eye of Science: 145cr, 415clb, 555crb, 653bl Sindo Farina: 626bl Dr Gene Feldman, NASA GSFC: 280ca Vaughan Fleming: 717br Sue Ford: 322bla Simon Fraser: 64cl, 199br, 578bra, 625cr/Newcastle University Robotics Group: 717cr A & H Frieder Michler: 554t, 584c D Gifford: 437cra G Gillette: 553bcl Geospace: 471bl Carlos Goldin: 266br Allen Green: 721cbl Alan Greig: 353bl J Greim: 415trb Tony Hallas: 807cr, 870bc Hale Observatories: 370bl, 814tr David Halpern: 378cra Y Hamel, Publiphoto Diffusion: 841cb Adam Hart-Davis: 376blr, 695cr John Heseltine: 710br James Holmes/Hays Chemicals: 13bl/Oxford Centre for Molecular Sciences: 559crb/Rover: 717cb Anthony Howarth: 139br B Iverson: 909blDr WC Keel: 370cbr James King-Holmes: 670br, 697bca Labat/Lanceau, Jerrican: 717cl Gary Ladd: 87tlb Scott Lamazine: 765br Francis Leroy/Biocosmos: 709crb Dr Andrejs Liepins: 190bla Dick Livia: 232cb Bill Longcore: 226cb Dr Kari Lounatmaa: 268cl D Lovegrove: 891tr Dr P Marazzi: 268c Marine Biological Laboratory: 386bl M Marten: 554brW & D McIntyre: 503bcl, 541cr, bc David McLean: 230clb John McMaster: 199cb John Mead: 467br, 828br Peter Menzel: 232crb, 281cla, 306bla, 625br, 810bra, 891cra Dr David Miller: 673br Hank Morgan: 710tc Professor P Motta, Department of Anatomy, University La Sapienza, Rome: 766tl, tcl, tc, 769bl S Nagendra: 931bl Nasa: 86tc, tr, 91bla, 130bc, 236br, 280bra, 471br, 572clb, 660tc, 739cr, 796cr, 797cr, bra, 826bc, 828tcr, 870bcl, cbl, 896bc 922tl /GSFC: 282cbl, 678tl, tcl, tc National Center for Atmospheric Research: 698cr National Institute of Health: 824br National Library of Medicine: 645bc National Snow & Ice Data Centre: 891bra NIBSC: 414bl, 555tlb NOAA: 456bl NOAN: 370bc Novosti Press Agency: 86cl, 698bra, 739bl NRAO/AUI: 370crb NRSC Ltd: 471bc David Nunuk: 13tr Claude Nuridsany & Marie Perennou: 342cra, 346br, 555bcl, 698cl, clb George Olson: 281bl Omikron: 744bc Oxford Molecular Biophysics Laboratory: 744cr Pacific Press Service: 522cr David Parker: 87bl, 232cl, 277bl, 282bl, 416cb, 642bra 716bcl, 796clb /ESA/CNES/Arianespace: 792br P Parvlainen: 572cra Alfred Pasieka: 138cl, 436cl, 553bl, 909br Dr DJ Patterson: 914c Petit Format/Nestle: 709cra Philippe Plailly: 377bc/Eurelios: 298cb, 553br, 850bl Max-Planck Institut fur Extraterrestriche pysik: 870bcr Chris Priest: 697bra J Prince: 413bl Professors PM Motta, T Fujita & M Muto: 190clb Prof. P Motta/Dept of Anatomy, University La Sapienza, Rome: 414br, 582cl Professor Tony Wright, Institute of Laryngology & Otology: 278cl John Radcliffe Hospital: 541ccr J Reader: 506cr, tc Roger Ressmeyer, Starlight: 87tr, bla, 92bc, 812cb, 828bca, 870cla Dr H Rose: 919tc Rosenfeld Images Ltd: 315tr, 456tc, 503bl Royal Greenwich Observatory: 87bca, 663cr, 870br Royal Observatory Edinburgh/AATB: 870cra Rev. Ronald Royer: 230ca, 814bra Peter Ryan: 823br Joe Rychetnik: 739ccr Ph Saada/Eurelios: 695cb J Sanford: 572c, cb, 828tc Tom Van Sant/Geosphere Project, Santa Monica: 279tr, 280tl Francoise Sauze: 716cbr David Scharf: 131bl, 555bra, 643tr, 767cr, cb Dr K Schiller: 544c Secchi-Lecaque/Roussel-Uclaf/CNRI: 144bc, 709cl Blair Seitz: 742bl Dr Seth Shostak: 87tc, 739crb SIU: 873bca D Spears: 909c St Bartholemew's Hospital: 200cb Synaptek: 717bc Andrew Syred: 248tr, 553bra, 584cl Tainturier Jerrican: 200cbr G Tompkinson: 414cb, 744c Alexander Tsiaras: 44cbr US Dept of Energy: 742crb US Library of Congress: 344c USSR Academy of Sciences/Nasa: 797cb Andy Walker/Midland Fertility Services: 710tcl Garry Watson: 541crb X-ray Astronomy Group, Leicester University: 370cr Frank Zullo: 370tr **Science Pictures Ltd:** 554bra **Science & Society Picture Library:** 277br, 287cb, 360bla, 371cr, 485cl, 503crb, 645cl, 695crb, 721c, 825cl, 874bc, 948bcl Bowsfield/BKK: 467crb, ca NMPFT: 695br National Railway Museum: 843bc Science Museum: 178cb, 467cl **Steve Setford:** 352cb **Sewerby Hall Museum/Simon Kench:** 485cr, cb **The Shakespeare Centre Library: Joe Cocks Studio Collection:** 753bl Gill Shaw: 62bcr, 221tc, 605br **Shell UK Ltd:** 262cr **Shiner Ltd:** 129tr **Jamie Simson:** 464cbr **Skoda Auto:** 313bc **Sky Sports:** Kerry Ghais: 875br Sam Teare: 875bcl **Harry Smith Collection:** 393bc **JCD Smith:** 860cbl **Sophia Smith Collection:** 849cr **Smithsonian Institution:** 176tr **Smithsonian Institution Astrophysical Observatory:** 370br **Society for Co--operation in Russian & Soviet Studies:** 424cra, 516tcrb, 732c, 733cra, 795t, cra, bra D Toase: 733cbr **Sony Classical Archives:** 811bl **South American Pictures:** 141bcl, 790cr Nicholas Bright: 792cla Robert Francis: 67ca, 193ca, cb, 521bra Kimball Morrison: 198br Tony Morrison: 65crb, 66cbl, 67cb, 140c, crb, bcr, 142bc, 146c, 147c, br, 194br 198cl, 549cra, 684c, 789cr, br, 791r Chris Sharp: 792c **Southampton Oceanography Centre:** 620trb **The Spanish Tourist Office:** 799tr, tcr **Spectrum:** 94cl, 126br, 148crb, 193bl, 313t, 479cbr, 625c, 650c, 842c, 844tl, 852cr **Frank Spooner:** 466bl, 881tc, 901br, 938c Carlos Angel: 286bl K Bernstein: 887c Keith Butler: 646cbr Gamma: 19ca, 173cb, 201tr, 275tr, 391br, bcr, 392cb, tr, 407br, 433ca, 506trb, bl, 589br, 618cb, 857bl, 862br, 882cbr

646cbr Gamma: 19ca, 173cb, 201tr, 275tr, 391br, bcr, 392cb, tr, 407br, 433ca, 506trb, bl, 589br, 618cb, 857bl, 862br, 882cbr 920tl, 941tr, 948t, cl, bcr, 933c Aventurier: 22cb, 275crb, 541br/Dieter Blum: 781tr Figaro/G de Laubier: 374bc /Gerard Kosicki: 222bla/Don Perdu/Liaison: 181br /Ribeiro Antonio: 173ca /Chiasson-Liaison: 21cbr, 68bla/Edinger: 717bl/Sassaki: 273tc Simon Grosset: 69br Paul Massey: 596crb R Nickelsberg: 735c Paul Nightingale: 128cb Richards/Liaison: 172cr Rigwood: 882clStills/Fotoblitz: 181bc Heinz Stucke: 635tr Sporting Pictures: 109cl, 110bl, bcl, 147tr, 411bc, 803tc, c, bl Doug Barwick Collingwood: 96tr Staatsbibliothek zu Berlin-Preussischer Kulturbesitz, Musikabteilung mit Mendelssohn-Archiv: 580clb Starland Picture Library: ESA: 280cr, 282c State Archives of Michigan: 849clb, br Stiftsbibliothek, St. Gallen: 197cr Still Pictures: 34cr Alain Compost: 451tr, clb Andy Crump: 207tl Mark Edwards: 35bl, 147bc, bl, 525bl Carlos Guarita/Reportage: 32tr, 637bl Dominque Halleux: 35tl Klein/Hubert: 30tr A Maslennikov: 313cb Gerard & Margi Moss: 75bl Jorgan Schytte: 27cb, 36cr H Schwartzbach: 467trb R Seitre: 451c Tony Stone Images: 173c, 216c, cbr, 356tl, 430bcr, 434cl, 435tcl, 476tr, 505tr, 541tl, 683cr, 930tr, 934crb Lori Adamski Peek: 128cl Glen Allison: 304tcr Christopher Ameson: 219bl Doug Armand: 172tr, 944cra Bruce Ayres: 774cl Brett Baunton: 612car Tom Bean: 172cr John Beatty: 28cr Oliver Benn: 474tcl Paul Berger: 679tr Christoph Burki: 16clb Michael Calderwood: 551cl P Chesley: 603bra Philip H Coblentz: 612cb Tony Craddock: 169r, 303cb Ary Diesendruck: 15cr, 146bl S Dietrich: 474cr Chad Ehlers: 357cl R Elliott: 473bc DH Endersbee: 858br Robert Everts: 207cl, 435trb Ken Fisher: 791c John Garrett: 630br Alain le Garsmeur: 206r Hans Gelderblom: 268bl C Gupton: 413br B Hands: 934cra David Hanson: 834cra, 867clb Robert van der Hils: 66t D Hiser: 92bl, 194cla J Hiser: 552tr Jeremy Horner: 286tl Hans Peter Huber: 141bl S Huber: 435cl George Hunter: 174cbr R Iwasaki: 478cr Warren Jacobs: 114ca Jacques Jangoux: 21car Simon Jauncey: 376crb David Job: 612cbr Richard Kaylin: 782bl Alan Kearney: 639cl P Kenward: 853cla H Kurihara: 603ca Robert Kusel: 392trb John Lamb: 16crb, 92tr Franz Lanting: 285c J Lawrence: 589tr Yann Layma: 323c A Levenson: 479bl G Brad Lewis: Mark Lewis: 612bl Philip Long: 834cla Yves Marcoux: 170br Will & Deni McIntyre: 146cr Mike McQueen: 25cra Manfred Mehlig: 819c Hans Peter Merten: 258bl John Morley: 244cb Z Nowak Solins: 313cl R Passmore: 357bcl Nicholas Parfitt: 24cbr, 386tl Jean Pragen: 835clb Colin Prior: 791b Greg Probst: 612tr Donovan Reese: 611bl Martin Rogers: 635cb Michael Rosenfeld: 262cb, 933bl Lorne Resnick: 15cra, 29bl, 835tr RNHRD NHS Trust: 542cr M Rosenfeld: 741cr J Running: 552tl C Saule: 881br Kevin Schafer: 285bl J Selig: 433bra M Segal: 865bl A & L Sinibaldi: 416tc Hugh Sitton: 25clb, 27tc, 934bl Chad Slattery: 90cb David Harry Stewart: 275br Sarah Stone: 195cb Mike Surowiat: 15clb Thatcher/Kaluzny: 313bl Tom Till: 881bc NO Tomalin: 612bla Darryl Torckler: 923br N Turner: 407cMark Wagner: 44tr John Warden: 65tc Randy Wells: 864br, 866crb

S Westmorland: 435bcl, 596cl Ralph Wetmore: 295c Ken Wilson: 115cbl Art Wolfe: 24car, 286bc Rex Ziak: 867c Sygma: R Ellis: 441bl Yves Forestier: 676crb The Tate Gallery, London: 745tr, 746br Techniquest: 583cra Telegraph Colour Library: 11cbl, 44cbl, 322bl, 625t, crb, 655tr, 741bl, 774tr, 841tlb, 859bra, 875bcr Action Plus: 831crb Bavaria-Bildagentur: 840ca Benelux Press: 541tr Bildagentur World: 387cal Colorific/Fred Ward, Black Star: 564br, cra John McGrail: 268tr P Titmuss: 588bcr Topham Picturepoint: 16tr, 19tr, 194cbl, 382crb, 390tr, 424bra, 481cl, 485bl, 506cl, 653clb, 786bl Associated Press: 315bra, 481br, clb, 863cr, 933cr Dinodia/R Shekhar: 445cb Tom Miner/Image Works: 869bla Press Association: 576clb Toyota: 843cbr Tracks: 121cb, crb TRH: 885bl Trinity College Dublin: 192cr Trip: 525cl, 775cla M Barlow: 113tr T Bognar: 479br I.Burgandinov: 731clb CC: 452c, 635bl D Cole:680cr Dinodia: 445bl A Dinola: 76cr M Feeney: 799bc A Gasson: 273cr F Good: 762tr Z Harasym: 561bc Ibrahim: 105bl, 463cl V Kolpakov: 81bla, 112tr, 113bra, trb, 187bl M Lee: 68bl T Lester: 877blD Maybury: 561bl C.Rennie: 727ca Helene Rogers: 408clb, 421br, 445cl, 464cb, 469bla, 561br, 573cb, crb, 696br, 821bl, 822bl S Shapiro: 487cra V Shuba: 112cb Eric Smith: 96c, br, bra, 833ca W Steer: 404cr Streano/Havens: 867ca A.Tjagny: 729c A Tovy: 208tcb, 479cl, 590br B.Turner: 696ca, 762bc R Vargas: 862bcr Y. Varigin: 731c J Wakelin: 524trb, 683tr I Wellbelove: 404br TH Foto Werburg: 105c M Wilson: 106c Tunnels & Tunnelling, Miller Freeman Publishers Ltd: 851tcr Mark Twain House, Hartford, CT: 856c, bl, bla Mark Twain Museum, Hannibal, Missouri: 856br

# U, V, W

United Nations: 863tc J Isaac: 933tc United States Navy, Dept. of Defence, Washington: 812crb, bl

Hans Verkroost: 215cbl, 216cbl, bra, 216bcr Jean Vertut: 809cb Courtesy of the Victoria and Albert Museum, London: 73tr, 242bl, 746bcl Vintage Magazine Company © DC Comics : 606br Roger Viollet: 358c VIREO/ Greenwalt: 817cl Wadsworth Atheneum, Hartford, USA, J Pierpont Morgan Collection: 401cr Wales Tourist Board: 860br Wallace Collection, London: 358bc, 631cl Frederick Warne: 205cr Waterways Photo Library: Derek Pratt: 148bl Wellcome Institute Library, London: 264bl, 414cbr, 544tl, tc, 555cl, 766cr, 873bl, 874tr, bl, bca Elizabeth Whiting Associates: 368cl The Wiener Library: 426t, c, cb Peter Wilson: 314cbl Windrush Photos: Roy Glen: 492cl, cr, trb Women's Transport Service/FANY: 906tl Woodfin Camp & Assoc.: Woolwich Building Society, Jim Wilson, All Rights Reserved: 232cr World Pictures Features-Pix: 89cra, 540ca, 603bc, 636cra, 637br, 693bcr World Trade Organisation, Geneva: Tania Tang: 841bla World Wildlife Fund: J Mayers: 234bl

# Y, Z

Yorkshire Sculpture Park: 745br Zefa: 20br, cr, 22tr, 37ca, 75c, tr, 96trc, 107br, 110bc, 142c, 148cr, 184clb, bl, 208br, 216bl,

222clb, bc, 227cr, 252tr, 296cr, 334cl, 348br, 363crb, 376bcl, 380tc, 385tr, 395bl, 401cra, 402c, 429crb, 450cb, 464bl, 475br, 501bl, 502tr, 522bc, 538tr, 547cla, 601bc, 629cr, 655cb, 670clb, 685bra, 690bl, 714br, 716bl, 729cl, 732crb, 795cl, 810cl, 822cra, 875bl, 911cra, br, 912bc, 842br, 864cr, 865trb, 867bcr, 880bl, 881cr, tr, 883clb, 885c, 933cr, 934cl, t Walther Benser: 680cl Boutin: 733bl Cameraman: 445br Damm: 407cb, 838cb Dr Dyballa: 64bl Geopress: 90bl Ned Gillette: 386tr Hecker: 260tr Heinrich: 186t Honkanen: 36cl, 187tr Hummel: 21cla Kitchin: 698bl Jaemsen: 226cla Lanting: 334cb Maroon: 464cr Mednet: 131bc Schneiders: 106tr Streichan: 379ca, 380br, 626tl Stockmarket: 714bl, 933bc Sunak: 206c A&J Verkaik: 810bla Voigt: 308tr

Additional photography by: D. Agar, Max Alexander, Peter Anderson, Roby Braun, Paul Bricknell, Geoff Brightling, John Bulmer, Jane Burton, Martin Cameron, Tina Chalmers, Gordon Claytone, Jim Coit, Neil Cooper, Joe Cornish, Phil Crabb, Tim Daly, Geoff Dann, Phillip Dowell, John Downs, Peter Downs, Michael Dunning, Andreas Einsiedel, Gerry Ellis, Phillip Enticknap, Neil Fletcher, Lynton Gardiner, David Garner, Bob Gathany, Philip Gatward, Christi Graham, Frank Greenaway, Derek Hall, Alison Harris, Paul Hayman, John Heaver, John Heseltine, Alan Hills, John Holmes, Kit Houghton, Chas Howson, Colin Keates, Luke Kelly, J. Kershaw, Gary Kevin, Barnabas Kindersley, Dave King, Bob Langrish, Cyril Laubscher, Richard Leeney, John Lepine, Bill Ling, Mike Linley, Neil Lukas, Ronald Mackechnie, Liz McAulay, Andrew McRobb, Trevor Melton, Neil Mersh, Simon Miles, Ray Moller, M. Moran, Tracey Morgan, David Murray, Nick Nicholls, Martin Norris, Sue Oldfield, Stephen Oliver, Nick Parfitt, John Parker, Janet Peckham, Liberto Perrugi, Roger Phillips, Jill Plank, Martin Plomer, Susanna Price, Tim Ridley, Dave Rudkin, Guy Ryecart, Kim Sayer, Karl Shone, Steve Shott, David Spence,Chris Stevens, James Stevenson, Jane Stockman, Clive Streeter, Peter Stringer, Harry Taylor, Mathew Ward, Linda Whitwam, Alan Williams, Alex Wilson, Jerry Young: 57, 119, 120, 125, 133, 203, 204, 245, 260, 270, 278, 326, 350, 364, 365, 419, 431, 440, 458, 459, 512, 513, 556, 615, 672, 689, 699, 700, 711, 712, 713, 754, 773, 817, 858, 855, 878, 899, 900 Michael Zabe

Jacket: British Museum: front cl; back cl Robert Harding: spine br David King: front cra; back cra Rex Features: front tl,ccl; back tl,ccl Mary Rose Trust: front bc NJ Saunders: front cr; back cr

Dorling Kindersley would like to thank the following: American Library Association/Newbery Award, American Museum of Natural History/Lynton Gardiner, Board of Trustees of the Royal Armouries, Leeds, Ashmolean Museum, Oxford, Barley Lands Farm Museum and Animal Centre, BBC Team for Visual Effects/Modelmaker, Thurston Watson, Birmingham City Museum, Blue Note Records, Booth Museum, Brighton, Bolton Museum, British Library Assocation,British Museum, London, The Buddha Padipa Temple, Wimbledon, London, Canterbury Cathedral, Classic Car Magazine, Commonwealth Institute, Co-operative Museum, Rochdale, Danish National Museum, Charles Darwin Museum, Downhouse Kent, Design Museum, London, Downe House Natural History Museum, Edinburgh SUSM, ESA, Exeter City Museums & Art Galleries, Royal Albert Memorial Museum, Exeter Maritime Museum, Glasgow Museums, Golders Green United Synagogue, Alison Harris, Horses: Moscow Hippodrome, Mr Conteras, Les Saintes Maries se la Mer, France, Mr & Mrs LE Bigley, Haras National de Saint Lo, France, Lady Fischer, Kentucky Park Horse Park, Patchen Wilkes Farm, Nigel Oliver Singleborough Stud, European Horse Enterprises, Berks, Miss M Houlden, Amaco Park, Spruce Meadows Canada, Mr & Mrs Clive Smith, Nashend Stud, UK, Pat & Joanna Maxwell, Lodge Farm, Arabian Stud, UK, Mrs Hampton, Briar Stud, UK, Miss S Hodgkins, Mrs Carter, Witton, Wilts, Grethe Broholme, Canada, Haras National de Pau, France, Pat Buckler, Canada, Miss Mill, M & P Ramage, Mount Farm, Clydsedale Horses, Tyne & Wear, Mr Brooks, Rare Breeds Farm, Mill Lnae, Hildenborough, Kent, Mrs Rae Turner, Mrs C Bowyer, Sally Chaplin; Kew Gardens, Hunterian Museum, Imperial War Museum, Instituto Nacional de Antropologia, Mexico, Jewish Museum, London Planetarium, London Transport Museum, Manchester Museum of Labour History, Manchester Museums, Hugh McManners, Motorcycle Heritage Museum, Westerville Ohio, Musee du Louvre, Musee Marmatton, Musee díOrsay, Paris, Museo Archeologico di Napoli, Museum of London, Museum of Mankind, Museum of the Moving Image, London, Museum of the Order of St National John, Museum of Scotland, NASA, National Army Museum, London, National Maritime Museum, London, National Motor Museum, Beaulieu, Natural History Museum, London, Norfolk Rural Life Museum, Old Royal Observatory Greewich, Oxford University Museum, Pitt Rivers Museum, Oxford, Powell Cotton Museum, Pratt & Whitney, Royal Armouries,Royal British Columbia Museum, Victoria, Junior Department, Royal College of Music, Royal Geographic Society, Royal Museum of Scotland, Royal Pavillion Museum, St Mungo Museum of Religious Life & Art, Glasgow, Science Museum, London, Scott Polar Institute, Societe D'Economie Mixte D'Argenteuil-Bezons, Tower of London, Tulane University, University of Chicago, University Museum of Archaeology & Anthropology, Cambridge, University Museum of Zoology, Cambridge, Wales Tourist Board, Wallace Collection, London, Frederick Warne for permission to use Beatrix Potter books and merchandizing Warwick Castle, Wilberforce House/Hull City Museums, Woodchester Mansion, Atuell Hampton Manor House and Worthing Art Gallery and Museum

# CREDITS

## ILLUSTRATORS

**David Ashby:** 42tl, tca, 150tl. 216cra, 218tl, 244tl, 291l, 410tl, 455tl, 539tl, 689tl, 693tl, 757c, b, 809tl, 812cr. **Penny Boylan:** 218cl. **Dave Burroughs:** 122tr, 303tl, 395cr, 556bl. **Karen Cochrane:** 71tl, 88tr, 109ca, br, bcl,110tl, 130br, 152cl, 160tl, 184br, 203tl, 210tr, 224tl, 238tl, 250tl, 255tl, 263tl, 272tl, 284br, 287tl, 288tl, 301tl, 323tl, 326tl, 334tl, 348tl, 351acr, c,bl, 371tl, 374tl, 390tl, 399tl, 409tl, 470tl, 480tl, 482tl, 495tl, 530tl, 535tl, 553c, 563acl, 565cr, 587tl, 588tr, ac, c, 608tl, 631tl, 641tl, 646tl, 651tl, 673tl, 685tl, 704tl, 707tl, 718tl, 741tl, 753tl, 760tl, 763tl, 804tl, 808tr, 831acr, bcr, bl, br, 849tl, 874tl, 882tl, 886tl, 887tl, 890r, 911cl, c, bc. **Michael Courtney:** 144l, 415tl, 429r, cr, 441 cr. **Angelika Elsebach:** 57cl, 118br, 132bl, 133tl, bl, 136bl, 154br, 256bl, 337c, 640cl, 702bl, 747cbr. **Simone End:** 52tl, 54tl, 58tl,74tl, 82tl, 99tl, 104tl, 109tl,117tl, bl,120tl,122tl, 124tl,132tl, 135tl,bl,cbr, 154tl, 155tl, 162tl,cr, 165tl, 177tl,184tl, 189tl, 256tl, cl, 265tl, 270tl, 276tl, 283 tl, 289tl, 316tl, 327tl, 336tl, 342tl, 343tl, 345tl, 346tl, 350tl, 351tl, 354tl, 364tl, 366tl, 393tl, 396tl, 411tl, 418tl, ccr, 419 tl, 420tl, 430tl, 431tl, bcl, 458tl, 472tl, 483tl, 488tl, 492tl, 511tl, 517tl, 527tl, 533tl, 556tl, 567tl, 568tl, 573tl, 578tl , 584tl, 599tl, 609tl, 615tl, 624tl, 633tl, 640tl, 643tl, 644tl, 647, 654tl, 657tl, 663tl, 665tl, 667tl, 668tl, 669tl, 672tl, 674tl, 677tl, 687tl, 694tl, 701tl, 711tl, 713tl, 736tl, 737tl, 747tl, 748tl, 751tl, 754tl, 755cl, clb, 756tl, 761tl, 770tl, 772tl, 779tl, cr, 780tr, 801tl, 803tl, 806tl, 817tl, 818tl, 854tl, 872tl, 889tl, 893tl, 894cl, 897tl, 899tl, 902tl, 904tl, cr, 909tl. **Nick Hewetson:** 340 b,752acr, cr, cl, bcl, bcr, bl. **John Houghton/Brighton Illustration:** 85tl, 583 tl, **Chris Lyons:** 757bcl, 828cl. **Pond & Giles:** 57tl,108tl, 144tl, c, bcr, 167tl, 234tl, 245tl, 253tl, 260tl, 264tl, cl, cr, 278tl, cl, 299tl, 322tl, cl, br, 339tl, 362tl, 383tl, 384tl, 386acr, 414tl, 423tl, 429tl, cl, 436tl, b, 437tl, tc, 440tl, 441tl, bcr, cr, 491tl, 498tl, 499tl, 502tl, 506tl, 519tl, tr, 554tl, 555ac, 575tl, 582tl, 596tl, 622tl, 628tl, 643c, 709tl, 715tl, 715b, 749tl, 765tl, 767tl, 769tl, acl, 774tl, 824tl, 873tl, bcr, 909bcr. **Sallie Alane Reason:** 11tc, 17tcr, 18tr, 47tr, 49tc, 51tr, 77tr, 84tr, 101tc, 116tr, 127tr, 138tr, 160tr, 171cl, 176c, 191tr, 196cr, 197cl, 198tc, 209tr, 210bl ,212cl, 213cl, 217tr, 238cra, 247c, 255cl, 259tr, 262tl, 281tr, 291tr, 302c, 307tr, 353cl, 368tl, cr, 386bl, 396tr, 400tr, 401cl, 410acl, 425tr, 426cl, 427tr, 428tr, 439tcl, 442tc, 447c, 455tc, 468tc, tr, 477cl, 480bl, 486c, 490tr, 502c, 526tr, 531tr, 539tr, 540tr, 549tl, 556tl, 557tr, 565tr, 577tr, bc, br, 580tl, 594tr, 596tr, 610tr, 613tr, 614tl, 626cr, 627acr, 631tr, 648tr, 652tr, 658tr, 673acl, tr, 684cl, 687cl, bcr, 688tr, 704tr, 721br, 724tr, 732br, 735tr, 739bc, 740cl, 743tr, 752tr, 781tr, 790tc, 813tr,868cr, 878tc, 905tr, 907cl, cr. **Colin Salmon:** 12tl, 86tl, 87tl, 92tl, cl, br, 101tl, 130tl, bl, 139tl, cr, 196tl, 198tl, 199tl, 226tl, ca, cb, cr, 230tl, 295tl, bcr, 296tl, 298tl, 304bl, 352tl, acl, 363tl, ac, 370tl, 375tl, 398tl, cr, bcl, 416tl, 417tc, 442tl, 508tl, cl, br, 514tl, acr, 520tl, br, 522tl, bcr, 538tl, c, 550tl, 558tl, 571tl, 627tl, tr, 655tl, 660tl, 690tl, 697tl, 717tl, 739tl, 778tl, cl, 782tl, tc, ac, cl, cr, 796 tl, tr, 807tl, 814tl, 815cl, 837tl. **Rodney Shackell:** 182bcl, 183tr, 247tl, 439 tl, 546 tl. **Peter Visscher:** 163tl, cr, 405 tl, 828tl. **John Woodcock:** 11tl, 14tl, 15tr, 16tc, 17tl, 44tl, bl, 47tl, 51tl, 56tl, 59tl, 61tl, 65tl, 66ca, 67ca, 68tl, 69tl, 75tl, 76tc, 77tl, 80tl, br, 81tl, 84tl, 85tl, 89tl, 90tl, 91tl, bl, 93tl, 94tc, 95tl, br, 85r, 89tl, 90tl, 91tl, 93tl, 94tc, 95tl, br, 97tl, 105tl, 114tl, 116tl, 121tl,123tl, 126tl, cr, 127tl, 128tl, 131tl, 138tl, 140tl, 141tl, 143tl, 146tl, 147tl, 148tl, 149tl, 151tl, 152lc, 161tl, 169tl, cra, 170tl, 171tl, 172tl, 178 tl, 181tl, 182tl, 186tl, 188tl, bl, 190tl, ca, cr, 191tl, 193tl,197tl, 206tl, 207tc, cl, 209tl, 212tl, 213tl, 215tl, 216tl, 217tl, 221tl, 222tl, 223tl, 231tl, br, 233tl, 236tl, 242tl, 248tl, 252tl, 259tl, 268tl, 269tl, 274tl, 277tl, 279tl, 280bc, 281bc, 282tl, 285tl, 297tl, 302tl, 305tl, 307tl, 308tl, 309tc, 310tl, 312tl, 315tl, 318tl, 320tl, 328tl, 330tl, 335tl, 340tl, 344tl, 353tl, 356tl, 357acl, 358tl, 360tl, 372tl, 373tl, 376tl, 377cl, 378tl, 379tl, bl, 380tl, 381tl, 387tl, 388tl, 391tl, 392tl, 400tl, 401tl, 406tl, 413tl, 414cl, 415c, cbl, cbr, 421tl, 424tl, 425tl, 426tl, 427tl, 428tl, 429b,cr, 433tl, 434tl, 438tl, 439tl, 441acl, 444tl, 445tc, 447tl, 449tl, 451tl, acr, 452tl, 453tl, 456tl, 461tl, 465tl, bcr, bc, 466tl, 467tl, 468tl, 471tl, 473tl, br, 476tl, 477tl, 479tl, 484tl, 485tl, 486tl, 490tl, 493tl, 497tl, cl, 501tl, 503tl, br, 504tl, 507tl, 510tl, 515tl, 519cl, bc, 521tl, 523tl, 526tl, 531tl, 532tl, 536tl, cl, bl, 540tl, 541tl, 543tl, 548tl, 549tl, 551tl, cr, 552tl, 553tl, 557tl, 560tl, 561tl, 562tl, 565tl, 566tl, c, 572tl, 574tl, 577tl, cl, 579 tl, 580tl, 581tl, 590tl, 593tl, 594tl, 595tl, 598tl, 602tl, tr, 603tl, 606tl, bl, cl, 610tl, 611tl, 612tc, 613tl, 619tl, cr, 620tl, 621tl, c, 625tl, 629tl, 630tl, 638tl, 642tl, 648tl, 650tl, br, 652tl, 653tl, 656tl, 658tl, 670tl, 671tl, 676tl, 679tl, 681c, 683t, 682tl, 683tl, 684tl, 691tl, 695tl, cl, 696tl, 698tl, 699tl, 705tl, 709bl, cl, 710cl, 716tl, 720tl, cl, bl, bc, 722tl, 724tl, 727tl, 729tl, 730t, tl, 731t, tl, 732tl, 734tl, 735tl, 738tl, 739bc, 740tl, 742tl, 743tl, 745tl, 752tl, 757tl, 762tl, 765cr, 766cr, 768tl, 769bcl, 776tl, 781tl, 783tl, bcl, 781tl, 783tl, bcl, 784tl, cl, 785cl, 786tl, 787tl, 788c, 789tl, 791tl, 792c, 793tl, 795tl, 798tl, c, 799tl, 800tl, 808cl, 810tl, 811tl, 812tl, 813tl, 823tl, 824tr, bc, 825tl, bcl, 826tl, c, 829tl, 832tl, 833tl, 835tl, 840tl, 842tl, 843tl, 845tl, 850tl, 851tl, 852tl, acr, 856tl, 857tl,858tl,,bcr, 859tl, 860tl, 862tl, 864tl, bl, bc, 868tl, 875tl, 878tl, 884tl, 885tl, 890tl, 891tl, 896tl, 898tl, 901tl, 905tl, 907tl, 910tl.

**Additional illustration by:** Luciano Corbello, Peter Serjeant, Mike Saunders

## MODEL MAKERS

**Mark Beesley:** 560c, 572c. **David Donkin** Models: 92 cra, c, cl, cr, 289 c, 434 c, 697acr. **Peter Griffiths:** 15bl, 56bl, 75bl, 91r, 93bl, 130c, 259c, 281c, 308bl, 353c, cl, 505b, 513br, 583b, 611bl, 677c, 681c, 691c, cl, 695tr, 716ac, 732bl, 777c, 787bl, 808cr, 814b, 815c, 825cr, 840b, 841cr, 850c, 862c, 871l, acr. **Paul Holzherr:** 171c, 191c, 400 c, 453 cr, 557 c, 613 bcr, 752c. **Melanie Williams:** 354 ac.

## PHOTOGRAPHERS

**David Agar:** 540 c, cr, cl. **Geoff Brightling:** 122l, 241cra, 567 tc, cr, 806c, cr. **Andy Crawford:** 130c,215c, 247tr, 295 c, cl, cr, 296 tr, cr, 303 cr, 304 bl, 352 cb, 353 c, cl, 363 c, 368 c, 416 tr, br, acr, 417 tl, tr, c, cr, 461 br, 468 bc, b, 504 bl, 508 cl, 509 t, 520 tr, bl, 531 b,c, 598 acl, 603 bl, cc, 655c, 677c, 690cl, cr, 717c, 758cr, 759, 796c, 808cr, 809cr, c, 814b, 815c. **Michael Dunning:** 226tr. **Steve Gorton:** 15bl, 56bl, 75bl, 85cl, br, 93bl,226bc, 227cl, cr, 256c, 296 br, 308 bl, 344 cb, 354 ac, 417 bcr, 434 c, 440acl, 503b, 522tr, c, br, cr, 560c, 583b, 593acr, 603acr, 611bl, 690bc, bcl, 697cr, 748tcr, 756acr, bcr, 767br, 787bl. **Christi Graham:** 443. **Frank Greenaway:** 104c, 117c, 118c, 119, 138c, 177crb, clb, blb, 234cra, 246c, ca, 256tr, 257c, 260 bl, 276t, cra, cr, 283c, 299 cra, cr, 327c, 346tc, tr, 363bcl, 366bl, 393c, cl, cr, 394, 395cl, c, cr, 440c, 513bcl, 573tr, c, cl, bl, 644tr, cl, 647tr, c, 654c, 657c, 663bl, 665c, cr, 667c, 668c, br, 678tr, 701c, 713c, bcb, 770ac, 801c, 847tr, c. **Mark Hamilton:** 41c, 171c, 191c, 203tc, 400 c, 453 cr, 454 c, cr, 515 tr, 557c, 613 bcl, 752c, 836tr, bc. **John Heaver:** 291, 292. **Alan Hills:** 686 **J. Kershaw:** 439, 441, 455 cl, bcl, bcr, 539 r, cra, cl, cr, br. **Simon Miles:** 304 cl, cla. **Gary Ombler:** 163cla, 341 t. **Sam Peckham:** 540 bcl. **Tim Ridley:** 121cl, cr, 362 c, cl, cb, ca. **Janet Pearson:** 293, 410 acr, cr, cbr, b. **Jim Seagar:** 42b. **Clive Streeter:** 164, 199c, bl, cr, 200tl, 226, 296 bl, 375 tc, 398 c, 417 acl, 553 cr, 558 tc, bl, cr. **Mathew Ward:** 91r, 98br, 143c, 202, 218cr, cl, 219tr ,bl, 220cl, c, cr. 221br, 231c, 232tcl, bcr,242tr, 243t, 244cbl, 252cl, 259 c, 277 cl, cr, 281 c, 297 c, 328 tr, bl, 340 tl, 341 b, 348 cb, 438 bcr, 456 c, cr, 457 tc, 502 b, br, 503 c, 536 br, 537 bl, 542 cl, 562 cl, 564, 589 cr, 603 cl, 604 c, cl, 619 cr, 642bl, 646c, 651cl, tr, br, 670cl, 681c, 685c, cl, acr, 691c, cl, br, 695tr, 716ac, 732bl, 742ca, c 760c, 777c, 783cl, c, br, 804c, cl, bcr, 805t, c, 825cr, bc, 826bl, 827, 829acl, 840b, 841cr, 850c.

# ACKNOWLEDGEMENTS

**Dorling Kindersley would like to thank the following people and organizations for their assistance in the production of this book:**

**Additional design, editorial, and research assistance:** Rachel Foster, Rebecca Johns, Maggie Tingle, Francesca Stich, Sue Copsey, John Mapps, Keith Lye, Nancy Jones
**Additional picture research assistance:** Ingrid Nilsson, Helen Stallion, Andy Sansom, Joanne Beardwell, Sarah Pownall and Andrea Sadler
**Additional DTP design:** Tamsin Pender, Tanya Mukajee
**Additional cartographic assistance:** David Roberts, Roger Bullen, Steve Flanagan, Jane Voss, Sarah Baker-Ede, Jan Clark, Tony Chambers. Michael Martin
**Indexers:** Hilary Bird, Ruth Duxbury
**Proofreader:** Marion Dent
**Jacket design:** Chris Bramfield

All embassies, consulates and high commissions for supplying information; Aga Khan Foundation; American Express; Amnesty International; Angel Sound Recording Studio; Anti-Slavery International; Argyle Diamonds; Arjo Wiggins; Army and Navy Stores; AT&T; Austrian Tourist Board; Barclays Bank; BBC TV, Susie Staples and the Newsround team; Beaties of London Ltd; BECTU; BIFU; Booths Museum; Boots the Chemist; BP; Braemar Antiquea; Birdland; Brighton Sea-Life Centre; British Equity; Cat Survival Trust, Terry Moore; Centre for Information on Language Teaching; Chubb Safe Equipment Company; CILT; City and Guilds of London Arts School; Civil Aviation Authority; Clubb-Chipperfield Ltd; Copec S.A.; Corporation of London; CPSA; Cusden Architects, Wharmsby; Divya Pande; Dudley and West Midlands Zoo, Peter Suddock; Dyson Appliances; Electrox; Gerald Eddy; European Union Information Centre; Finnish Church, Rotherhithe; Food and Agriculture Organization; Food Marketing Institute; Micheal Foreman; Sir Norman Foster and partners; Friends of the Earth; GEC-Marconi Limited; Geffrye Museum; German National Tourist Office; Goethe Institute; Joanna Gough; Greenpeace; HM Prison Service; Sam Hill; Honeywell School, Dick Cooper and Divya Pande; Howard League for Penal Reform; Howletts and Port Lympne Zoo, Jeremy Watson; Imperial War Museum; Institute of Civil Engineering; Italian Cultural Institute; Japan Festival Education Trust; Japan Foundation; Japan Society; Japanese National Tourist Organisation; Jordan Information Bureau; Kew Gardens; Kings College, London; Kit Alsopp Architects; Korea Trade Centre; Lebanon Tourist and Information Office; Lloyds Bank; Hugh Lockhart-Ball; London Patent Office; Gerald Lovell; Makaton Vocabulary Development Programme; Malaysian Tourist Board; Maria Montessori Training Organisation; Mellors Reay and Partners Ltd; Metropolitan Police Force; Middlesex County Court; Midland Bank plc; Museum of Mankind; National Museum of Labour History; National Trust, Clandon Park; Nature Magazine; Daphne Neville; New Forest Nature Quest, Derek Gow; Norwegian Tourist Board; Emma O'Brien; OPEC; OXFAM; Park Beekeeping Supplies, Godfrey Munro; Michael Parsons; Patent Office; Model magazine, Peace Pledge Union; Philippine Tourist Board; Pirelli/Young & Rubicam; Powell/Cotton Museum; Prison Reform Trust; Proctor and Gamble Limited; Professor Cloudesley Thompson; RMT, Laurie Harris; Recline & Sprawl; Renault; Roehampton Golf Course; Royal Institution of Naval Architects; RSPB; Sainsbury's; Genevieve St. Julian-Brown; Scout Association; Sesmarine (International) Ltd; SNCF; Stanley Gibbons Ltd, Mark Peg; Phoebe Fraser Thoms; TUC; Twycross Zoo; UNISON; Viking Society; Frederick Warne for Beatrix Potter; Volkswagen UK; Paul Walsh; Watts, Capt. O M; Whitakers, Malcolm Dyer; Arjo Wiggins; Sarah Wilson; World Wide Fund for Nature; Zanussi; Woolwich Building Society.